# Constitutionalism and Dictatorship

It is widely believed that autocratic regimes cannot limit their powers through institutions of their own making. This book presents a surprising challenge to this view. It demonstrates that the Chilean armed forces were constrained by institutions of their own design. Based on extensive documentation of military decision making, much of it long classified and previously unavailable, this book reconstructs the politics of institutions within the recent Chilean dictatorship (1973–1990). It examines the structuring of institutions at the apex of the military Junta, the relationship of military rule with the prior constitution, the intra-military conflicts that led to the promulgation of the 1980 constitution, the logic of institutions contained in the new constitution, and how the constitution constrained the military Junta after it went into force in 1981. This provocative account reveals the standard account of the dictatorship as a personalist regime with power concentrated in Pinochet to be grossly inaccurate.

Robert Barros teaches Political Science at the Universidad de San Andrés in Argentina.

CAMBRIDGE STUDIES IN THE THEORY OF
DEMOCRACY

General Editor
ADAM PRZEWORSKI New York University

OTHER BOOKS IN THE SERIES
Jon Elster, ed., *Deliberative Democracy*
Adam Przeworski, Susan Stokes, and Bernard Manin,
eds., *Democracy, Accountability, and Representation*
Adam Przeworski et al., *Democracy and Development:
Political Institutions and Well-Being in the World,
1950–1990*

*Dedicated to the memory of my father,*
*Vincent Joseph Barros*

# Constitutionalism and Dictatorship

## Pinochet, the Junta, and the 1980 Constitution

**Robert Barros**

*Universidad de San Andrés*

CAMBRIDGE
UNIVERSITY PRESS

PUBLISHED BY THE PRESS SYNDICATE OF THE UNIVERSITY OF CAMBRIDGE
The Pitt Building, Trumpington Street, Cambridge, United Kingdom

CAMBRIDGE UNIVERSITY PRESS
The Edinburgh Building, Cambridge CB2 2RU, UK
40 West 20th Street, New York, NY 10011-4211, USA
477 Williamstown Road, Port Melbourne, VIC 3207, Australia
Ruiz de Alarcón 13, 28014 Madrid, Spain
Dock House, The Waterfront, Cape Town 8001, South Africa

http://www.cambridge.org

First published 2002

Printed in the United Kingdom at the University Press, Cambridge

*Typeface* Centennial Light 9.5/12.5 pt.     *System* QuarkXPress [BTS]

*A catalog record for this book is available from the British Library.*

*Library of Congress Cataloging in Publication data*

Barros, Robert, 1957–
    Constitutionalism and dictatorship: Pinochet, the Junta, and the 1980
constitution / Robert John Barros.
        p.   cm. – (Cambridge studies in the theory of democracy)
    Includes bibliographical references and index.
    ISBN 0-521-79218-5 – ISBN 0-521-79658-X (pbk.)
    1. Constitutional history – Chile.   2. Chile – Politics and government –
1973–1988.   3. Civil-military relations – Chile – History.   I. Title.   II. Series.

KHF2919 .B37 2002
320.983′09′045–dc21

                                                                            2001037758

ISBN   0 521 79218 5   hardback
ISBN   0 521 79658 X   paperback

# Contents

Contents

# Foreword

Why a book about a dictatorship in a series on theories of democracy?

*Constitutionalism and Dictatorship: Pinochet, the Junta, and the 1980 Constitution* describes the process of legalization of a dictatorship. Since the story is full of drama, I will not reveal the plot. But the ending is known. A brutal military dictatorship, unadorned by any civilian institutions, handling opponents with arbitrary repression, departed from power according to the rules it set nine years earlier. Why dictators set these rules and why they obeyed them is the subject of Robert Barros's story. The puzzle this story raises, however, has deep consequences for understanding the rule of law under democracy.

In the classical liberal view, only a divided government can be a limited one. As Hampton (1994) and Kavka (1986) argued against Hobbes, this is the foundation of the rule of law. Moreover, a mere separation of powers is not enough, since separation of powers leaves unlimited latitude to the legislature, decisions of which must be implemented by all other branches of government. What is needed is a system of checks and balances that makes it impossible for any particular authority to undertake actions unilaterally, without the cooperation or consent of some other authorities.

The Madisonian view asserts that a government divided in this manner will be constrained to act according to rules. To quote Manin (1994, 57), "Each department, being authorized to exercise a part of the function primarily assigned to another, could inflict a partial loss of power to another if the latter did not remain in its proper place . . . each would be discouraged from encroaching upon the jurisdiction of another by the fear of retaliation . . . the initial distribution of power would hold: no relevant actor would want to deviate from it." As one agency counters another, actions of the government as a whole become limited and predictable.

Institutional design obviously matters. The particular agencies must have the means and the incentives to check one another. In particular, if the government as a whole is to be limited, there must be no agencies that can check others without being subject to checks by them, no "unchecked checkers." If the legislature can pass laws without the consent of the executive or a review by courts, "parliamentary supremacy" results. If the courts can dictate to other branches of the government and these branches cannot control the courts, the power of the judiciary is unchecked. If the executive is not supervised by the legislature, the outcome is policy without law. Moderation emerges in this conception only if every action of any branch requires cooperation of some other branch to be effective.

But what is the source of power of government agencies? Why would the legislature accept decisions of the courts? Why would the executive implement instructions of the legislature? It is sufficient to look at communist constitutions to see that a formal division of institutional powers is not sufficient to limit the government. Although some of these constitutions would satisfy any liberal, communist rulers used the single party to control all the institutional powers. Divided powers were just a façade.

The difference between democracies and dictatorships lies not simply in their respective institutions but in the relations of real powers supporting these institutions. The Italian judiciary became an effective check only when it was backed by big business and the media. In turn, the Venezuelan Congress and the Supreme Court found themselves powerless against the president when Hugo Chávez could muster overwhelming popular, as well as military, support.

The experience of the Chilean dictatorship is particularly eye-opening. It shows that a government may follow rules even if the divided powers that check one another are not institutional. It is sufficient that each has real power. In Chile, the four branches of the armed forces, which together formed the *Junta de Gobierno*, had a long tradition of autonomy and strong corporatist interests. None of the four military branches wanted another to dominate the government. Hence, from the beginning of the dictatorship, Junta decisions had to be taken by unanimity, so that each branch checked the others. The result was that even though the Junta as a whole had the capacity to act at will, internal differences led it to conform to the constitutional document it originated and even to decisions of the Constitutional Tribunal it created. Hence, Barros argues, any division of power is sufficient to generate limited government as long as these powers are separate and real. Note that even though the Constitutional Tribunal was appointed by the military, it soon assumed autonomy and on various occasions ruled against the Junta. The opposition to the military regime thus found in the Tribunal an institution to constrain the Junta.

As Holmes (forthcoming, 42) observes, "Societies may approximate the rule of law if they consist of a large number of power-wielding groups, comprising a majority of the population, and if none of them is so strong as to be able thoroughly to dominate the others." By this criterion, law did not rule in Chile: The power of the Junta as a whole was unchecked and unconstrained. Its supporters were a distinct minority. Yet because the military was internally divided, the rules it promulgated ended up binding its actions.

Institutions are effective only if there is some distinct external power behind them. This is not to say that institutions are purely epiphenomenal, that they merely implement underlying relations of brute power. The fact that under democracy political institutions separate governments, legislatures, and courts has autonomous consequences. Democratic institutions do not simply express – they tame – powers that stand behind them. But institutions do not function in a social, economic, or military vacuum. In this way, Barros's exemplary study of dictatorship provides a magnifying glass for inspecting democracies.

Adam Przeworski

# Acknowledgments

Writing about a much-criticized dictatorship is not a good way to make friends. I was fortunate to have a few friends before I embarked on this project, I learned to suffer their ribbing about passing over to the other side, I and still managed to incur numerous intellectual and personal debts in the course of researching and writing this book. My interest in the relationship between law and dictatorship grew out of field research in Chile for a dissertation at the University of Chicago. As I advanced with the original project, I became increasingly taken by the legalism of the Chilean dictatorship and the manner in which every step in the 1988–1990 transition had a constitutional foundation. I must thank Adam Przeworski for spurring me to switch topics and to take on the question that really fascinated me – the peculiar relationship between constitutionalism and dictatorship in Chile.

This proved to be a wise decision. For although I never expected that I would enter so deeply into a regime whose operations were often secret, perseverance, determination, and a good bit of detective work opened doors and led me to unexpected sources. Persistent requests for interviews eventually allowed me to meet many of the key players in this drama. I owe many debts to the officers of the Chilean armed forces, legal advisors to the military government, and members of the Constituent Commission who generously gave of their time, endured my questioning, and took my research seriously. In particular, I must thank Guillermo Bruna, Senator Julio Canessa Robert, Juan de Dios Carmona, Gen. Sergio Covarrubias, Adm. Mario Duvauchelle Rodríguez, Enrique Evans de la Cuadra, Senator Sergio Fernández Fernández, Pablo Kangiser, Gen. Fernando Lyon, Mónica Madariaga, Alejandro Silva Bascuñán, Col. Julio Tapia Falk, Sergio Rillón Romani, Justice Eugenio Valenzuela Somarriva, Col. Arturo Varela, and Rear Adm. Rodolfo Vío Valdivieso.

Without their cooperation and leads I would have only scratched the surface of this history.

Early stages of the research and writing of this book were supported by an International Doctoral Research Fellowship from the Joint Committee on Latin American Studies of the Social Science Research Council and the American Council of Learned Societies, a Fulbright-Hays Training Grant from the U.S. Department of Education, and a William Rainey Harper Fellowship from the University of Chicago.

I also owe innumerable debts to the many libraries and institutions that gave me free reign in their holdings and archives. My days of poring over documents and taking notes were made all the more enjoyable thanks to the cordial assistance and friendly conversation of the librarians and staff at these institutions. I thank the staff at the *Biblioteca de Derecho*, *Pontificia Universidad Católica*, Mariela Miranda and Ruby Trobok at the *Colegio de Abogados de Chile*, Marcela Achura at the *Fundación Jaime Guzmán*, Rafael Larraín and the staff of the *Tribunal Constitucional de Chile*, the staff of the *Sección de Referencias Legislativas* at the *Biblioteca del Congreso Nacional*, and María Inés Bravo at the library of the *Facultad Latinoamericano de Ciencias Sociales*.

At different stages of work on this book I incurred numerous debts with colleagues and friends. Early on, Phillipe C. Schmitter encouraged me to jettison an overly ambitious comparative project and work on Chile. In Chile, Carl Bauer, Manuel Antonio Garretón, Angel Flisfisch, Hérnan Gutierrez, Enrique Hermosilla, Norbert Lechner, Fernando Leiva, Tómas Moulian, Manuel Ogando, and Ken Roberts provided consistent encouragement, insights, and friendship. Later, on my return to Chicago, Jon Elster, Bernard Manin, and Adam Przeworski were sources of invaluable support and stimulation. Subsequent revisions have benefited from comments from Claudio Fuentes, Marcelo Leiras, Fernando Leiva, Carlos Maldonado, Norbert Lechner, and Ken Roberts. As always, errors in the text are my sole responsibility.

Friends in Chicago and Buenos Aires also played an important role in seeing this project through. I thank, in particular, Carlos H. Acuña, José Cheibub, Ingrid Creppel, Leopoldo Estol, Roberto Gargarella, Gary Herrigel, Jack Knight, Rodrigo Lara Serrano, Susana Poblet, Kimberly Stanton, and Eduardo Zimmermann. My sister, Patricia, also deserves my thanks. She early on recognized that this was more than a little paper.

# Abbreviations

| | |
|---|---|
| AdCdE | *Actas del Consejo de Estado* |
| AdCP | *Anteproyecto de Constitución Política* |
| AHJG | *Actas de Sesiones de la Honorable Junta de Gobierno* (Minutes of the Sessions of the Honorable Government Junta) |
| AOCC | *Actas Oficiales de la Comisión Constituyente* (Official Minutes of the Constituent Commission) |
| CdJM | *Código de Justicia Militar* (Code of Military Justice) |
| C.L. | *Comisión Legislativa* (Legislative Commission) |
| COAJ | *Comité Asesor de la Junta* |
| DINA | *Dirección de Inteligencia Nacional* (National Directorate of Intelligence) |
| D.L. | *Decreto Ley* (Decree-Law) |
| D.O. | *Diario Oficial* (Official Daily) |
| D.T. | *Disposición Transitoria* (Transitory Disposition) |
| MIR | *Movimiento de Izquierda Revolucionario* (Movement of the Revolutionary Left) |
| PC | *Partido Communista de Chile* (Communist Party of Chile) |
| PdNCP | *Proyecto de Nueva Constitución Política* |
| PDC | *Partido Democrata Christiano* (Christian Democratic Party) |
| PPD | *Partido por la Democracia* (Party for Democracy) |
| RN | *Renovación Nacional* (National Renovation) |
| SGdG | *Secretaría General de Gobierno* |
| Trans. y Antec. – D.L. | *Secretaría de Legislación, Decretos Leyes Dictados por la Honorable Junta de Gobierno, Transcripciones y Antecedentes* (Secretary of Legislation, Decree-Laws Decreed by the Honorable Government Junta, Transcripts and Records) |

| | |
|---|---|
| Trans. y Antec.<br>– Leyes | *Secretaría de Legislación, Leyes Dictados por la Honorable Junta de Gobierno, Transcripciones y Antecedentes* (Secretary of Legislation, Laws Decreed by the Honorable Government Junta, Transcripts and Records) |
| TRICEL | *Tribunal Calificador de Elecciones* |

# Introduction

This book is about the military dictatorship that governed Chile for sixteen and a half years from September 11, 1973 through March 11, 1990. It is widely accepted that this was a dictatorship dominated by a single man, General Augusto Pinochet Ugarte, and that the centralization of power in his person explains the exceptional duration of military rule in Chile. This book is also about a central problem within modern political theory: the nature of absolute power and whether rulers who hold such power can effectively constrain themselves with institutions of their own making. Generally, it is believed that such autocratic self-binding is impossible. The reasoning is simple and long-standing: Dictators cannot subject themselves to rules because dictators can always change rules that restrict their power or else violate them without facing sanction. For this reason, effective constitutional limitation of authoritarian power is generally held to be impossible.

This book calls into question both of these established wisdoms. Contrary to the "personalization of power" view, it demonstrates that the course of the dictatorship in Chile was shaped by a collegial military junta. Shortly after the coup, this junta demanded rules to regulate power among the armed forces and later introduced and sustained a constitution which set into operation institutions that limited the dictatorship's power and prevented it from unilaterally determining the outcome of the October 5, 1988 plebiscite which triggered the transition to democracy in 1990. Contrary to the established view that dictatorships stand above law and are structurally incapable of being subject to institutional constraints, the dictatorship in Chile is a case of an autocratic regime being bound by a constitution of its own making. This case suggests that when power is founded upon a plural body, institutional limits upon nondemocratic power can be viable, forcing us to rethink a long tradition in the analysis of political power.

These findings are surprising and striking. The force of the standing view cannot be underestimated: The opposition between dictatorship and constitutionalism is perennial and undisputed. Dictatorships do not use constitutions to limit their own powers, nor do they allow themselves to be bound by the provisions of any constitution. Regardless of the many controversies – past and present – over the characterization, explanation, and comparability of various historical authoritarianisms, virtually all parties to these debates agree that rule free from legal or constitutional restraint is a hallmark of dictatorial power. Nondemocratic regimes are differentiated and classified along a number of dimensions, such as the character of their ruling apparatuses, the scope of their attempts to penetrate and administer social and economic activity, their mobilizational or exclusionary nature, as well as whether they emphasize ideology and/or racial politics.[1] Nevertheless, despite the plethora of denominations that follow – fascism, totalitarianism, nazism, authoritarianism, post-totalitarianism, bureaucratic authoritarianism, dictatorship, to name only some – and the recurrent disputes over the uniqueness of particular cases,[2] all of these regimes, as autocratic forms of state, are unified by their exercise of power beyond any limits of law or institutions.

Even beyond the comparative analysis of authoritarian regimes, the irreconcilability of authoritarianism and legal-constitutional constraints is a truism within the theoretical literature. As the following chapter shows, the origins of this perspective can be traced to the theories of sovereignty developed by Thomas Hobbes and Jean Bodin in the seventeenth century, and their views are echoed, though within a different conceptual apparatus, in much of the contemporary literature on institutions, particularly that focusing on credible commitments, self-binding, and constitutionalism. Autocrats cannot be subject to

[1] Many of the distinctions drawn with these dimensions are owed to Juan Linz's (1970, 1975) reconsideration of the totalitarian model in light of Franquist Spain.
[2] The "integration" of Nazi Germany into a comparative framework has been extremely troublesome, as the acrimonious *Historikersteit* demonstrated during the late 1980s in West Germany. In dispute was whether the crimes of the Third Reich could be compared to the atrocities committed by other brutal dictatorships, in particular Stalin's terror, and whether such comparisons amounted to apologia by way of relativization. Maier (1988) reviews the ethical, political, and historiographical backdrop to this debate. For a recent entreaty calling for comparative analysis of Nazi Germany with other cases, particularly Fascist Italy, from a perspective distinct from that which sparked the Historian's Dispute, see Mason (1993). Stalin and Hitler have been set side by side in a recent comparative collection (Kershaw and Lewin 1997).

rules because autocrats can always free themselves from rules that subject them. This book suggests otherwise.

Similarly, my characterization of the Chilean dictatorship is equally unconventional. Much more so than any other recent case of military rule in Latin America, dictatorship in Chile is identified with a single personage – General Pinochet – an association that has only been heightened by the October 1998 detention of Pinochet in London and the successive efforts to try the dictator. In the now standard and widely influential scholarly analyses of the "Pinochet regime," the course of military rule in Chile reduces to a story of how Pinochet concentrates and wields power unchallenged. From this perspective, relatively shortly after deposing Allende and assuming state power alongside the commanders of the other branches of the armed forces and the national police in 1973, Pinochet gains control of the executive, relegates the other commanders to a subordinate position in a weak, rubber stamp legislative junta, and at the same time deftly manipulates promotions and retirements in the armed forces, thereby curtailing the careers of any potential rivals and consolidating power unlimited.[3] Pinochet's personalization of power then explains both the longevity of military rule in Chile and the constitution enacted in 1980, which from this angle is read solely as an instrument for perpetuating Pinochet in power and later imposing constraints upon democracy in the postmilitary period.[4] In this manner, Pinochet emerges as the archetype of personalized, "one-man" dictatorial rule.

This characterization of the dictatorship has also figured in comparative theories that seek to explain how different subtypes of authoritarian rule affect the longevity of nondemocratic regimes. With different emphases, scholars have argued that regimes that concentrate power in a single person or party are likely to be more enduring than military regimes, as the latter are often beset by corrosive factionalism, intermilitary divisions, and subsequent military-institutional pressures to return to the barracks (Remmer 1989a; Geddes 1995; 1999). This book demonstrates that the Chilean

---

[3] The initial impetus for the "personalization of power" approach was Arriagada's (1985, 1986) analysis of Pinochet's manipulation of legal norms regulating promotions and retirements in the army. Further extensions are found in Remmer 1989a; 1989b; and Valenzuela 1995.

[4] Interpretations of the constitution from this perspective can be found in Linz 1992, 454; González Encinar et al. 1992; and Ensalaco 1994, 411–12. As a result of the continued force of the 1980 constitution, Linz and Stepan (1996, 205–19) view Chile as an "incomplete transition," and Loveman (1991) characterizes it as a "tutelary democracy."

dictatorship should not be included among the cases claimed to support this argument.

The military dictatorship in Chile was not personalist. Regime cohesion and longevity did not rest upon the concentration of power in a single person or party, but upon a collegial organization of power that was institutionalized through rules and procedures which protected and reinforced the original plural foundation of military rule. This plural organization of the Chilean armed forces – the fact that historically the military had been structured as three separate, independent services – gave rise to an immediate need for rules and eventually provided a foundation for securing the constitution even when it constrained the dictatorship. In Chile, autocratic institutional self-limitation was possible because the collective organization of the dictatorship denied any single actor of the authority to shape rules at their discretion.

The development of this argument necessarily involves an extensive empirical reconstruction of the legal and constitutional practices of the Chilean military once in power. In the course of this book I present a wealth of new material documenting deliberations and decision making within the military junta. As a number of scholars have noted, despite all the attention focused on the last wave of military rule in Latin America, our knowledge of the political institutional structure of authoritarian regimes and their decision-making processes is relatively slim (Fontana 1987, 11, 19; Remmer 1989a; Huneeus 1998, 72).[5] Though on the basis of the apparent force of the personalization of power argument, some have claimed that Chile is an exception to this pattern (Pion-Berlin 1995, 149), as I progressed in my research I became increasingly aware of how little we actually knew about the internal workings of the dictatorship.

Leaving aside the many factors that may motivate scholars to avoid the study of autocratic regimes, the gaps in our knowledge result largely from the information constraints that autocratic regimes deliberately set to shroud their internal processes from public view. The dictatorship in Chile was no exception. From the first days of military rule, the regime shrouded its internal practices behind a veil of secrecy and mystery. The meetings of the Junta were secret, and within the government, tasks and access to information were often compartmentalized

[5] As Remmer (1989a, 24) correctly notes, "Scholars moved from the study of democratic breakdowns to the study of democratic institutions without pausing to analyze the authoritarian phase that came in between."

4

to prevent all but a handful of top officers from attaining a sense of the overall situation, intentions, and stratagems at play within the government. These deliberate information constraints provided obvious strategic advantages to the military government, as they increased the regime's capacity for surprise and unpredictability and forced domestic and international actors to elaborate their responses on the basis of only minimal information about positions and evolving correlations within the government. Similarly, this nonpublic style of rule forced analysts to impute decision-making processes from the artifacts of results and the public by-products of decisions – events and crises, public declarations, policies, decree-laws and administrative decrees, journalistic accounts, and, often, rumors – rather than actual documentation of how the military structured its rule and made decisions.

Unlike most earlier studies, this account of the dictatorship relies primarily on documents generated by the everyday operation of the junta and its advisory bodies. Diligent detective work during field research in 1992 and 1993 led me to discover archive after archive of untapped primary material pertinent to reconstructing the legal and constitutional organization and practices of the military regime. Many of these sources had been classified long ago and were becoming available as part of the transition; some had been neglected by social scientists, others were shown to me by retired officers who took an interest in my research, and still another set of documents became available after the 1991 assassination of an important civilian advisor to the regime. These documents provide a fascinating entrée into some of the most restricted chambers of the dictatorship and led me to gradually rethink my conception of power relations within the regime, which initially followed the personalization approach. These materials include: the massive legislative archive organized by the *Secretaría de Legislación* of the Junta; the long mythical *Actas de Sesiones de la Honorable Junta de Gobierno*, actual verbatim transcriptions of the Junta's sessions from 1973–1990; the voluminous minutes of the Constituent Commission, the civilian advisory committee that provided the Junta counsel on constitutional problems during the first years after the coup and penned the first draft of the 1980 constitution; the more concise minutes of the Council of State, a second advisory body that reviewed the Commission's draft; and the personal archive of Jaime Guzmán, a central figure in the story that follows and the chief constitutional advisor and public ideologue of the military regime through the early 1980s. Guzmán was gunned down by an assassin's bullet on

April 1, 1991 as he made his way out of the Catholic University, where he taught constitutional law.

I should say something about the Junta's legislative archive and minutes, as these are key sources for my narrative. The legislative archive consists of over three hundred bound volumes that compile individual legislative histories for most, though not all, of the decree-laws and laws enacted by the dictatorship. These histories gather together the paperwork generated as bills circulated through the Junta's legislative system. As these documents consist of legal analyses, amendments proposed by the different commanders in chief, and reports on the range of agreement and disagreement on a bill at a given moment, this archive makes it possible to reconstruct the evolution of positions within the military junta on a range of matters, including many issues not studied in this volume. Although by the military's own decree-law the public was to be allowed access to the legislative histories (with the exception of laws pertaining to national defense or designated as secret), prior to 1990 use of these materials was apparently limited to law students preparing theses on narrowly defined legal issues.[6] As part of the 1990 transition, this archive was transferred to the *Biblioteca del Congreso Nacional de Chile* in Santiago, where it is housed today.

The official minutes of the Junta's sessions, the *Actas de Sesiones de la Honorable Junta de Gobierno* (hereafter AHJG), complement the legislative histories by providing transcripts of the Junta's regular meetings, thereby making it possible to fill the verbal gaps in the documentary record. As the minutes reveal, the sessions were recorded, thereby preserving an exceptional source of access to deliberations within the regime.[7]

During my research, I never expected to view these papers. Still, I always ended my interviews by asking for the whereabouts of these minutes, which in the lore of the dictatorship had attained mythical status. Usually I received elusive answers, doubts about their existence, or claims that if they existed only Pinochet had them. One day, however, I was told that just before the transfer of power the members of the Junta agreed to transfer a copy of the minutes to the *Biblioteca del Congreso Nacional de Chile*. Throughout 1992 and early 1993, I repeat-

---

[6] The Junta's minutes contain evidence that opposition politicians and lawyers faced obstacles when they sought access to these antecedents.

[7] Occasionally, one comes across parenthetical notes in the minutes stating that a few words were lost because of a change in tapes.

edly asked at the library for the minutes and consistently an otherwise extremely helpful librarian denied any knowledge of them. At the end of a second interview late in my research, a retired official invited me to his home to have lunch and take a look at his papers. Upon entering his study, he asked me, "What do you think?" I turned, looked at the wall, and to my shock saw a bookshelf covering a wall from floor to ceiling with black, leather-bound volumes marked *Actas de la HJG* (HJG being an abbreviation for *Honorable Junta de Gobierno*). At the time, I had figured out that I could have access to important snippets of the minutes at the *Tribunal Constitucional de Chile* and was working with these extracts. I immediately checked the minutes that I was familiar with and they were identical. Negotiations ensued, and after agreeing that I would never reveal this person's identity, I left that afternoon with four volumes containing the minutes for the first year of military rule in my bag. For the following three months, once every few days I met this person at the entrance to a parking lot in downtown Santiago. Each time we went to his car, he opened the trunk, and I emptied my bag and refilled it with the volumes for the following year. Without this retired officer's cooperation, on the basis of my prior research I probably would have made the same argument that I present here, but certainly my support for it would have been considerably weaker. Despite my immense gratitude, I must respect our agreement not to reveal his identity.

As I was concluding my work with these minutes, I discovered that the Library of Congress was actually in possession of the minutes. In early March 1993, one of the employees insisted that she show me a new acquisition being held in the director's office. Though I already was familiar with the specific item, I went along as it was easier than objecting. Upon turning to leave the office, I faced a wall full of bound volumes whose markings I by then recognized and whose contents I was already familiar with. Subsequently, scholars have been given access to these materials at the library.

My account of institutional politics within the Chilean dictatorship proceeds as follows. Chapter 1 examines the theoretical dimensions of the problem of autocratic self-limitation and suggests conditions under which nondemocratic regimes might subject themselves to limiting rules. The rest of the book, which essentially consists of two parts, analyzes the institutional practices and evolution of the military junta. Chapters 2–4 study the preconstitutional organization of the dictatorship, while Chapters 5–7 detail the making, content, and effects of the 1980 constitution.

Chapter 2 reconstructs the conflictive process whereby the Junta in 1974 and 1975 instituted rules to regulate the exercise of executive and legislative powers within the regime. Although General Pinochet gained control of the presidency at this point, this chapter demonstrates that Pinochet never attained the absolute dominance commonly attributed to him. Rather, a partial separation of powers and the adoption of decision by unanimity set fundamental constraints preventing any Junta member from dominating the legal system. The distinctiveness of this collegial foundation for military rule is highlighted in a comparative section at the end of the chapter.

Although this initial organization set limits within the Junta, as a body the Junta was unchecked during the period prior to the constitution. Chapters 3 and 4 demonstrate that despite the continued operation of institutions empowered to uphold the law and the constitution, when the Junta was in agreement its authority was free from any institutional constraint. This point is developed in Chapter 3 in reference to the status of the 1925 constitution and the Supreme Court's power of judicial review. The chapter also the examines the *Contraloría General de la República*'s (Comptroller General of the Republic) power to review the legality and constitutionality of executive decrees. Chapter 4 further demonstrates the absence of legal constraints upon the regime by focusing on the inability of the judiciary to protect individual rights before the massive repression that followed the coup. Two dimensions are studied: the relationship between the Supreme Court and the military tribunals in time of war, and the limitations of the *recurso de amparo*, a legal writ similar to *habeas corpus*, before extralegal methods of repression. This chapter also examines how the Junta deliberately manipulated the law in an attempt to deflect international pressure concerning human rights abuses. These moves provide the backdrop to some of the internal conflicts that led to the decision to enact a new constitution.

Chapter 5 reconstructs the internal political dynamics that culminated in the enactment of the 1980 constitution. Contrary to the personalization of power approach, I show the constitution to be a compromise that brought to a close renewed conflicts over the institutional structure of the Junta. Before attempts by Pinochet to concentrate executive and legislative powers, the commanders of the navy and the air force successfully defended the original collegial character of the dictatorship. This defense of the junta as an institution explains why the constitution effected no changes to the organization of the dictatorship and, consequently, appeared only to prolong Pinochet's personal power.

Chapter 6 examines the institutional logic contained in the main text of the 1980 constitution. It reveals that the constitution was designed to contain future civilian political actors within a strongly constitutional framework, not assure continued political power for General Pinochet. This point is developed by examining the conception of institutions that informs the constitution's more controversial innovations, such as the National Security Council, nonelected senators, and limits upon the president's authority to remove military commanders.

Chapter 7 studies how the constitution effected military rule during the last nine years of the dictatorship. I show that the constitution restricted the Junta's prior authority to unilaterally modify the constitution and activated a constitutional court with full powers to uphold the constitution, even against the dictatorship. This analysis reveals how the constitution immediately constrained the Junta and how the Junta's capacity to freely define the further implementation of the constitution was checked by the constitutional court's mandatory review of the organic constitutional laws that filled out the constitution. In this manner, the 1980 constitution began to grow apart from its makers and limited them, with fundamental consequences for the 1988 plebiscite on the Junta's candidate for the second presidential term under the constitution. This chapter shows that during the final years of military rule the Junta was subject to institutional limits of its own creation.

Chapter 8 returns to the theoretical implications of institutional limitation in the context of dictatorship. Drawing from the Chilean case, it speculates about the conditions under which actors bearing discretionary authority may seek to restrict their unlimited power, the motivations that may drive such practices, the sources of stability for institutional limits once in place, and the effects of constraints. I conclude by insisting that pluralism within a ruling bloc is the fundamental condition under which government may be limited by institutions, even in a nondemocratic context.

## Chapter One

# Dictatorship, Legality, and Institutional Constraints

The opposition between constitutionalism and dictatorship pervades the contemporary social sciences and reflects a long-standing theoretical conception of absolute power. This chapter explores the theoretical dimensions of the relationship between institutional constraints and dictatorship. After noting the prevalence of conceptions that view authoritarian power as unlimited, I explore at length the many aspects of the standard argument against autocratic self-limitation. To do this, I set out a conception of institutional limits, discuss the theory of sovereignty as an explanation of why rulers bearing absolute power cannot limit themselves, caution against conceptual confusions that might suggest facile – though inadequate – responses to the traditional theory, and conclude by presenting an account of the conditions under which institutional constraints might be effectively introduced under an authoritarian regime.

## Dictatorship and Unbound Power

Since the beginning of the twentieth century the opposition of democracy and dictatorship has increasingly dominated political discourse on forms of government. In contrast to earlier classifications which elaborated variations on the classical trichotomy of monarchy, aristocracy, and democracy, the contemporary discussion of political regimes is largely exhausted in the dualism of dictatorship and democracy. Although scholars use a range of terms to refer to authoritarian regimes and have elaborated a number of subtypes, the principal criterion for differentiating dictatorship and democracy is the manner whereby laws binding upon a territory's inhabitants are created: In dictatorships laws are imposed from above, whereas through the mediation of elections and representation, laws emerge in democracies from among the very citizens who are subject to them. This distinction between heteronomous and autonomous modes of creating and modifying legal systems, whose clearest formulation is Kelsen's (1945) general theory of the state as a legal system, dominates comparative political approaches to regimes: In most cases authoritarian regimes are defined negatively in terms of their nondemocratic character.[1]

Yet notwithstanding the prevalence of this dichotomous classification based on how individuals attain public office and the authority to govern and make law, analyses and definitions of dictatorship tend to stress how power is wielded. In practice, the initial distinction is displaced toward a classification organized around whether power holders are constrained by legal-institutional restraints. This shift is clearly seen in the numerous and varied definitions of dictatorship which characterize autocratic rule as the exercise of state power without restraint. Franz Neumann (1957, 233), for example, defines dictatorship as "the rule of a person or a group of persons who arrogate to themselves and monopolize power in the state, exercising it without restraint." Similarly, in the *International Encyclopedia of Social Science*, dictatorship appears as "the unrestricted domination of the state by an individual, a clique, or a small group" (Stammer 1968, 161). Ernst Fraenkel (1969, xiii), in turn, writing during World War II about Nazi Germany, refers to the "prerogative state," which he describes as a "governmental system which exercises unlimited arbitrariness and violence unchecked by any legal guarantees."

The notion that dictatorial power is absolute and unconstrained by institutions is not specific to presumably dated theories tied to the heyday of the totalitarian framework. The subsequent reappraisal among historians of Hitler and Stalin's omnipotence, the development

---

[1] These are the criteria used by Linz (1975) in his typology of nondemocratic regimes, as well as in the guidelines for classifying regimes recently elaborated in Przeworski et al. 2000. I am aware that by interchangeably using such terms as authoritarianism, autocracy, and dictatorship, I obscure important conceptual distinctions. For example, in Linz's typology, authoritarianism is not the genus but a subtype developed in contrast to totalitarianism and also distinguished from other subtypes of nondemocratic rule, such as "post-totalitarianism" and "sultanism" (Linz and Stepan 1996). Similarly, Kelsen's opposition is with autocracy, not dictatorship. The former is broader and technically more accurate than the everyday language of dictatorship, which from a historical perspective is a misuse of the term. On this point, see Bobbio 1989, 158–60. On the classical Roman dictatorship which gives rise to this problem, see Rossiter 1948, chap. 2; Friedrich 1950, chap. 13.

of more elaborate typologies of nondemocratic rule, and the invention of the category of bureaucratic authoritarianism in Latin America during the 1970s left untouched this conception of authoritarian power as legally unlimited.

The shift away from analyzing the course of Nazi Germany and the Soviet Union under Stalin in terms of the intentions of a single personage has not affected how scholars view power in the two regimes. The question of whether the policy of these dictatorships should be viewed as the implementation of the deliberate dictatorial will of a single individual or as the cumulative product of ad hoc, chaotic rivalries and antagonisms among individual power blocs has sparked considerable controversy among historians, particularly those studying Nazi Germany.[2] Hans Mommsen, the chief advocate of qualifying Hitler's alleged omnipotence, explicitly links pluralism within the dictatorial power bloc with unlimited power. He argues that Hitler's aversion to institutional restrictions on his power gave rise to increasingly informal modes of decision making, progressive fragmentation of the political system, and ongoing internal rivalries that ultimately prevented any political rationality and led to the self-destruction of the state. These plural power bases within the Nazi state did not alter the unconstrained character of power, but allowed for the "unbridled arbitrary rule of each man for himself among the Nazi elite (Mommsen 1976, 195)."[3] Though not necessarily monolithic, even for so-called "revisionist" historians dictatorial power remains absolute.

A similar point can be made with regard to the influential distinction between authoritarian and totalitarian regimes that Juan Linz developed as a way of understanding Franquist Spain (1970; 1975). This distinction emphasizes differences in the forms that nondemocratic rule assumes, not a difference in the character of power in authoritarian and totalitarian regimes. The essential difference Linz noted was the absence in authoritarian regimes of attempts to wholly dominate society by mobilizing social actors through proregime organizations and by suppressing all independent forms of association. The absence of the totalitarian combination of strong ideology, a single party, and mass mobilization through the party's auxiliary organizations made possible the "limited social pluralism" that Linz identified as constitutive of authoritarianism and the key to the dynamics of this

---

[2] For an initial formulation of the terms of the German discussion, see Mason 1981. More recent contributions can be found in Childers and Caplan 1993, and Mommsen 1997.

[3] For a similar perspective, see Kershaw 1997.

regime type. Notwithstanding these differences, power in both regime types remains formally unlimited. Referring generally to nondemocratic regimes, Linz (1975, 183) notes that they tend to impose their domination through law but leave "the interpretation of those laws to the rulers themselves, rather than to independent objective bodies, and apply[ing] them with a wide range of discretion." Whether totalitarian or authoritarian, authoritarian power is institutionally unlimited.

This same conception is found in writings on the "new" or "bureaucratic" authoritarianism and transitions to democracy in Latin America. Although some scholars insisted that labeling military regimes "fascist" was incorrect, beyond stressing the exclusionary character of military rule, the research on authoritarianism in Latin America during the 1960s and 1970s did not repose the nature of autocratic power. Rather, scholars were concerned primarily with a critique of modernization theory (O'Donnell 1973) and the economic determinants of authoritarianism (Collier 1979). When political features were touched upon (Cardoso 1979), it was to underscore the distinctiveness of both the military forces in power – the armed forces ruling as "an institution" instead of a single *caudillo* (dictator) – and their project – to retain power and rule directly rather than intervene to oust and replace an unacceptable president, as in the "moderator model" analyzed by Stepan (1971). Once attention shifted toward the conditions for transition to democracy, the legally unconstrained character of authoritarian military power came to the fore as scholars stressed the uncertainty inherent in moments of regime liberalization and transition (O'Donnell and Schmitter 1986). Without institutions capable of holding them to their promises, authoritarian power holders, as long as they retained political capability, could at any moment reverse prior commitments to respect rights or proceed to elections, a specter which rendered uncertain the course of all such situations. This uncertainty discovered in transitions is constitutive of autocratic power. In Przeworski's (1988, 60) words, "a particular regime would be authoritarian if there existed some power apparatus capable of overturning the outcomes of the institutionalized political process." Authoritarian power, regardless of its specific form, stands above the law.[4]

---

[4] In his recent work on the rule of law, Guillermo O'Donnell (1999, 334) restates this traditional view: "The distinctive mark of all kinds of authoritarian rule, even those that are highly institutionalized and legally formalized (a Rechtsstaat, in the original sense of the term), have somebody (a king, a junta, a party committee, or what not) that is sovereign in the classic sense: if and when they deem it necessary, they can decide without legal constraint."

We find further evidence of this conception of authoritarian power as discretionary and subject only to the will of those who bear power in the self-conception of authoritarian power holders themselves. Whether they attain absolute power through a violent rupture with the standing constitutional order or through a legally continuous transmutation of democracy into dictatorship by suppressing party competition or representative institutions, dictators typically justify their discretionary hold on power as an imperative imposed by the immediate concrete situation – subversion, insurrection, severe unrest, economic crisis, natural disaster, or any other extreme crisis. Before such states of affairs, they argue, absolute power is justified because normal rules and institutions are too cumbersome or have broken down and inaction threatens to undermine state and national security. This type of argument was prominent among the commanders of Latin American military regimes who portrayed Left-inspired popular mobilization as subversion and a form of irregular war (Perelli 1990). In these cases, action, the concrete goal, the measure, as unilaterally defined by those in command of the state, takes precedence over any and all legal, institutional, or procedural norms in force, even those enacted by the authoritarian regime itself.[5]

From this perspective, dictatorial power is essentially extranormative and instrumentally rational. The authority to decide what action to take derives not from a prior legal order but from the present fact of the actual possession of state power. In Carl Schmitt's (1985b, 13) words, "authority proves that to produce the law it need not be based on law." Or, as the popular formulation contends, authoritarianism is the rule of men, not law.

This understanding of dictatorship explains why scholars focus scant attention upon legal and constitutional institutions under authoritarian regimes. When they are discussed, these phenomena are portrayed as instruments of rule or as rituals that are enacted to place a veneer of legitimacy upon regimes which also operate arbitrarily by secretly committing egregious acts beyond the law.[6] In neither case

---

[5] The most acute presentation of this view is given by the controversial German legal theorist Carl Schmitt (1985a, 1985b). As he notes (1985b, 13), "The exception appears in its absolute form when a situation in which legal prescriptions can be valid must first be brought about. . . . There exists no norm applicable to chaos. For a legal order to make sense, a normal situation must exist, and he is sovereign who definitely decides whether this normal situation actually exists."

[6] See, for example, Loewenstein 1951; Sartori 1962; Bonime-Blanc 1987; Shain and Linz 1995, 11–14; and Smith 1996.

do these practices limit the machinery of the state and contain its activity within preestablished legal and constitutional bounds. We can classify these types of authoritarian constitutionalism using categories drawn from Karl Loewenstein's typology of constitutions (1951, 203–6).[7] In contrast to "normative" constitutions which guarantee rights and structure a frame for democratic competition and government, Loewenstein distinguishes "nominal" and "semantic" constitutions. A nominal constitution on paper upholds the values of democracy and limited government, but despite its legal validity is not effective and is a constitution in name only. A semantic constitution, on the other hand, is fully activated and holds, but merely formalizes the existing locus and exercise of power which presumably neither guarantees rights nor is democratic. By these terms, authoritarian constitutions are either nominal or semantic: They are ineffectual facades or else only codify authoritarian power arrangements. In both cases these constitutions are of dubious force. Thus, in the standard view autocratic constitutions are such in name only: They are not a source of institutional arrangements that effectively bind authoritarian power holders to act within the confines of preestablished procedural and substantive rules. In Loewenstein's words, the absence of effective constitutions in authoritarian contexts is structural: "Autocracy cannot operate under a constitution and, therefore, as a rule dispenses with one. It cannot countenance, and would not endure restriction in the exercise of power, because the formalization of authority is inconsistent with its dynamism (1946, 114)." As a consequence, nominal or semantic constitutions stand or fall with the regimes that enact them.[8] Constitutionalism and the rule of law represent practices to be instituted or restored upon the demise of nondemocratic regimes, but not phenomena that warrant close attention in authoritarian contexts.[9]

---

[7] These categories are further discussed in Sartori 1962.

[8] With the exception of the Chilean constitution of 1980, this has been the norm in Latin America. According to one study (Complak 1989, 69) of "de facto governments" in Latin America during the period 1930–1980, in eight cases the de facto government derogated the prior constitution and instituted a constitution of its own making. In all of these cases these constitutions were in force only as long as the authoritarian government remained in power. The wave of constitution making that followed the collapse of state socialism also appears to confirm this point. On these processes, see Elster, Offe, and Preuss 1998.

[9] This perspective is extremely common. For examples, see Sartori 1962 and Bonime-Blanc 1987, as well as most writings on law in the Soviet Union or Nazi Germany, such as Berman 1966; Fraenkel 1969; Linz 1975; or Beirne 1990.

## Sovereignty, Self-Binding, and Limits

Despite the ubiquity of the view that autocratic power is absolute and unlimited in practice, does the fact of absolute power imply that autocrats cannot under any circumstances bind their own power with institutions? Is a form of constitutionalism other than the merely nominal or semantic wholly incompatible with concentrated power, or can autocrats institute limits that restrict their discretion and in some sense subject them to rules and institutions?

A long tradition, whose origins can be traced to Jean Bodin and Thomas Hobbes's theories of sovereignty, denies that institutional restraints are compatible with absolute power. Recently, following a substantively identical argument, the same conclusion is reached in new institutionalist and rational choice analyses of self-binding, precommitment, and credible commitment. As part of a larger concern with institutions and economic development, these studies ask whether autocrats – be they the kings of France and England during the seventeenth century or reform-oriented leaders of centrally planned economies – can credibly promise to not interfere with property rights, and by so acting sustain incentives for private investment.[10] Like Bodin and Hobbes on the feasibility of subjecting political sovereigns to law, these theorists answer in the negative: Autocrats cannot self-limit their powers because they cannot free themselves of the very discretion that defines their power as absolute and allows them to overrule institutional constraints as expedient.[11] Not only then do autocrats in practice stand above law and institutions; it cannot be otherwise: Absolute power is constitutive of autocracy and, paradoxically, omnipotence reaches its limit at that point where autocrats might attempt to limit this power.

Although I accept the structure of the problem as posed by Bodin, Hobbes, and, more recently, new institutionalist writers, there are alternative solutions under which institutions that limit power at the

---

[10] See, in particular, North and Weingast 1989 and North 1990, 1991, 1993. Litwack (1991) addresses the problem in reference to market reform in Soviet-type economies. Root (1994) presents a historical comparison of France and England.

[11] Thus, Olson (1993, 571) writes that dictators cannot credibly promise not to confiscate wealth "because autocratic power by definition implies that there cannot be any judges or other sources of power in the society that the autocrat cannot overrule." Similarly, Elster (1989, 199), argues that the Chinese Communist Party cannot assure legal certainty to economic agents because "It has many sorts of power, *but not the power to make itself powerless*" (italics in original).

apex of an authoritarian regime can be sustained while the regime remains nondemocratic. Under specific conditions, which I will argue concern the composition of the authoritarian power bloc, autocratic regimes can effectively self-limit their powers. Though we will have to ask what such limits protect, effective constraints can be compatible with nondemocratic rule. Before I can suggest how self-binding is possible in an authoritarian context, some conceptual groundwork must be laid. This is necessary to specify the problem of autocratic institutional self-limitation and to avoid theoretical confusions that lead some scholars to dissolve the problem or accept false solutions. To this end, I will seek to detach the idea of institutional constraint or limit from its association with constitutionalism and some versions of the rule of law; introduce the concept of sovereignty; and distinguish between institutional limits and other forms of constraint, as well as between the rule of law and rule by law. Autocratic self-binding through institutions is independent of other types of constraints and rule by law, and this independence must be acknowledged to clarify the structure of the tension between institutional limits and autocracy. Once these contours are in relief, we can examine conditions under which autocratic self-binding may occur.

## The Nature of Institutional Limits

To avoid short-circuiting from the outset the study of authoritarian self-limitation, it is important to detach the notion of institutional limit or constraint from broader understandings of constitutionalism. As criteria for limits on power, both rights-based and republican conceptions of constitutionalism are stringent enough to foreclose consideration of legal constraints outside of liberal or democratic contexts. If "constitutional" is meaningful only in reference to a fundamental law and a corresponding institutional framework that effectively guarantees and protects individual rights (Sartori 1962), its use as a standard of limit would disqualify most autocracies from study and obscure the possibility that institutional limits may protect the rights and interests of only a subset of actors without ceasing to be effective. Similarly, if we associate limits with a republican understanding of constitutions in which the constitution stands as a higher law created by a people to structure and protect a democratic framework of government, we also reach a stalemate. The criteria of popular origin would exclude authoritarian constitutions for having been made and imposed unilaterally from above, as would the requirement that they structure a government framework that allows the governed to be the ultimate source of all political authority.[12] Either approach to constitutionalism ends up reiterating by definition the original antinomy between limits and authoritarianism.

This impasse can be avoided by detaching the concept of institutional limit from the ends associated with constitutionalism. Such limits, according to Charles Howard McIlwain (1947, 21), are the "one essential quality" that traverses the history of constitutionalism. Regardless of differences in emphasis, all variants of constitutionalism conceive of constitutions as a higher law that establishes and makes effective legal limits on state actors. Written constitutions structure and arrange the powers of the state, specify restrictively the functions that correspond to each authority, and create negative powers that enable incumbents to block attempts by other state authorities to exceed the authority conferred upon them by the constitution. As a set of higher order enabling rules, the constitution sets limits upon the procedures and scope of power and sets in operation institutions that uphold these limits.

For present purposes the variety of specific mechanisms that constitutions establish to divide and limit power is of less interest than the general structure and effects of institutional or legal limits.[13] First, institutional limits are contingent upon the existence of rules that provide standards with which to qualify the validity of acts committed by different state authorities. That is, they depend upon rules that stipulate how and in what areas specific officials or powers may properly act. Examples are rules that guarantee rights that cannot be contravened by ordinary legislation or executive acts, as well as rules that restrictively confer specific powers. These rules thus provide legal criteria with which to identify and criticize departures from legitimate authority as positively set by these same rules.

Second, these limits are upheld by state authorities who among their powers hold authority to actively control authorities regulated by law. In these instances, whether it be a higher court exercising judicial review, a body reviewing the legality of executive orders, or a legislature sitting in judgment of a state official in an impeachment proceeding, the controlling power exercises a negative power. It does not take

---

[12] For a typology of how constitutions are made, see Elster 1997. Arato (1995) evaluates the legitimacy of these different forms.

[13] On the variety of constitutional forms and mechanisms, see Vile 1967; Casper 1989; van Caenegem 1995; Elster 2000, chap. 2.

positive action; instead, by exercising its control power it blocks an action of another body, holding it to its powers authorized by standing legal/constitutional law.[14]

Third, the exercise of negative powers implies that state powers are divided: For one branch to check another, powers must be distinct. In fact, institutional limits, in the form of checks and balances, were incorporated to pure theories of the separation of powers to provide mechanisms to effectively uphold a division of powers and enjoy the virtues associated with a separation of powers. In this context, institutional limits complement broader institutional arrangements that limit power by diffusing authority and preventing any single actor or branch of government from controlling all of the machinery of the state and wielding it at its whim. Thus, for example, a separation of legislative and executive powers may constrain an executive from acting arbitrarily by restricting it to the execution of laws made by another body. Such a separation of powers, though, may not imply limited government, as the legislature may remain free from any rules that constrain the areas in which it can legislate. Furthermore, a pure separation of powers in which each branch, staffed by different persons, exclusively exercises a separate function of government, though it may divide powers, lacks institutional mechanisms with which to restrain an agency or actor that exercises its power improperly and encroaches upon the function of another branch (Vile 1967, 18–19). Nevertheless, although a separation of powers does not necessarily involve institutional limits as I am discussing them here, the operation of institutional constraints does require that powers be divided so that one authority may check another.[15]

Fourth, by blocking improper exercises of authority or encroachments upon the powers of others, institutional limits defend antecedent decisions (Sejersted 1988, 142). In these instances the controlling body upholds the previously enacted rules which delimit the form and range of powers held by each authority. Institutional limits thus produce a subordination of present power to rules, that is, to prior decisions. Under most constitutions, this prior decision – the constitution itself – and the web of limits that it defines not only trumps legislation through mechanisms of constitutional review but also includes rules that make

---

[14] The distinction between positive and negative power is developed by Sejersted (1988). Hart (1961, 64–69) presents a similar conception of legal limits.

[15] This division, though, will not involve a pure separation of powers. On this point, see Vile 1967, 18–19; and Manin 1994.

it difficult to subsequently modify the constitution. These barriers to facile change include stipulation that the constitution either be amended by a body other than the ordinary legislature or by the latter following a special, more demanding procedure. In very abstract terms, this logic of holding present action to a past decision is the essence of what we may call constitutionalist rule of law: Laws rule instead of men because state officials can exercise no authority other than that conferred by the law/constitution and regular legislative majorities cannot mold past decisions to suit present purposes.

In general terms, then, an institutional limit implies a legal standard, a mechanism of enforcement, a division among the authorities subject to the standard and those who uphold it, with the result that actors are constrained by prior decisions in the form of rules. It is precisely in this general sense that institutional limits have traditionally been held to be incompatible with autocratic power. Although they were not formulated with regard to dictatorships, Thomas Hobbes's and Jean Bodin's accounts of the logic of sovereignty explain why absolute power cannot be subject to rules, and insofar as the structure of power in dictatorships resembles absolutism their theories set the terms of the puzzle that we must address. Furthermore, as already mentioned, these formulations anticipate the arguments of contemporary analyses of credible commitment.

### Sovereignty and Absolute Power

Sovereignty is the power that comprises the attributes of an ultimate deciding agent – be it a person or a body of persons – entitled to make rules and settle controversies with some degree of finality at the apex of a legal hierarchy (King 1987, 492). Though for both Hobbes (1991, chap. 18) and Bodin (1992, bk. 1, chap. 10) this supreme power encompasses the authority to: establish rules that are generally binding; declare war and make peace; settle controversies and enforce the rules; and choose the principal officers of the state, the key faculty is the power to make and repeal law, and the sovereign is that person or group of persons who holds this power.[16] The two principal charac-

---

[16] Bodin (1992, 58) states that the power to legislate comprehends all of the other marks of sovereignty. The same general argument appears throughout Hobbes's *Leviathan*. Both, however, maintain that legislative power may be held indirectly if an actor other than the agent who directly legislates can freely select the legislator. In these instances, the actor exercising full powers of selection is sovereign, as it can replace the legislator at will and thereby indirectly mold the law.

teristics of sovereignty which lead these theorists to maintain that sovereignty cannot be limited by legal institutions concern the location of this power and its finality.

With regard to location, sovereignty refers to the highest power in a legal system and should not be conflated with an entire legal order. The concept of sovereignty involves a principle of hierarchy whereby the validity of any law or authority derives from a superior law or authority. In other words, a legal system may contain multiple levels at which state officials make decisions and enact rules, but their acts are valid only because a higher rule or authority has granted such powers to these officials. In this regard, sovereignty is wholly compatible with limits that hold lower officials to rules at subordinate levels of a legal-political system. However, for both Hobbes and Bodin, the finality inherent to sovereignty makes any legal limitation of the apex of the legal hierarchy structurally impossible: If we trace powers and authorities up the legal hierarchy, we reach a point where the decision-making system closes in a final authority beyond which there can be no appeal. Whereas some legal scholars (Kelsen 1945; Hart 1961) contend that this final decider may consist of a set of rules, Hobbes rejects this possibility and insists that final authority can only reside in some person or group of persons. For Hobbes contends that to be effective rules must be interpreted, and if a purported sovereign is bound by a law, then a higher authority must stand who interprets and enforces the binding rule; should even this authority be in turn bound, the same requirement reiterates, until ultimately, by regress, we arrive at a final interpreter who stands above rules and is sovereign (Hampton 1986, 98–105; Hobbes 1991, 224). As Hobbes and Bodin repeatedly insist, if a purported sovereign authority is limited we have misidentified the sovereign; elsewhere an unbound power must stand. The decisions of this supreme authority, the sovereign, are final in the sense that no subordinate authority can (or is authorized to) override it. Sovereign power is therefore supreme because, although it may repeal or overrule any other rule or authority within the hierarchy, it cannot be reversed by any of them (Hart 1961, 102–4; King 1987, 493; Goldsmith 1996, 278).

Consequently, freedom from any subjection to limiting institutions is not essentially a matter of the will of a particular power holder but a structural characteristic of any supreme body or person that stands as the highest power in a particular legal hierarchy. If this agent is truly supreme and not subordinate, no higher mechanism of enforcement can exist to hold it to a prior limit; and even if the sovereign authority attempts to circumscribe its power through the creation of an institutional limit, any self-imposed legal restriction cannot be effectively binding. Its efficacy can only be contingent, conditioned by the acquiescence of the sovereign who at all points retains the power to decide and make law at will and consequently to reverse a prior decision and suppress any legal checks if deemed expedient.[17] As Hobbes (1991, 184) explicitly states, "For having the power to make, and repeal Law, he [the bearer of sovereignty] may when he please, free himself from that subjection, by repealing those laws that trouble him."[18] Institutional limits may be effective at subordinate levels of government; however, should the organs exercising these controls rule in ways considered inappropriate by the highest legislative authority, this sovereign can override them by modifying the relevant legislation to preclude the irritating interpretation or, at the extreme, suppress the controlling body. Thus, sovereign power is absolute and by its very nature free from the constraint of institutional limits. The sovereign cannot be held to a prior decision because the sovereign always remains free to decide and to reverse her prior decisions.

Hobbes's argument about absolute sovereignty is not intended to refer to only one among many forms of government. Hobbes contends that effective government always requires a final human decision maker because he discounts that a system of divided powers is viable in practice, viewing it as a formula for conflicts among powers and an eventual dissolution of the state. Contemporary political theorists, such as Gregory Kavka (1986, 165–68, 225–36) and Jean Hampton (1994, 38–42), have challenged this claim by arguing that systems in which the "final decider" is a set of rules that structure a division of limited powers can and have proven to be feasible. The details of these arguments are not pertinent here. Still, we should note that both theorists leave standing Hobbes's argument as an account of autocratic regimes; both Kavka and Hampton premise constitutional systems of divided and limited government upon periodic democratic elections, and neither suggests that autocracies may be limited. Although modern dictatorships differ in important respects from the absolute monarchies

[17] As mentioned, the contemporary literature on credible commitments restates this argument from a different theoretical perspective to argue that autocracies cannot effectively bind themselves.

[18] The principle that a single party cannot bind itself is discussed at length by Holmes (1988, 210–12), who also considers the democratic variants developed by Pufendorf and Rousseau to deny that popular sovereignty may be limited.

that Hobbes describes,[19] the concept of sovereignty appears to describe the structure of power in authoritarian regimes and to explain why such regimes cannot subject themselves to institutional limits.

Before suggesting conditions under which institutional limits can be compatible with dictatorship, it is necessary to distinguish institutional limits from other forms of constraint, as well as from rule by law. If we conflate the second term of either of these distinctions with institutional limits, authoritarian self-limitation might not appear to be problematic. However, such conceptual confusions only apparently undermine the force of the problem of sovereign reversibility.

Limits and Rule by Law. It is important not to confuse certain forms of rule of law with institutional limits because autocracies can be highly legalistic without being limited. In Hobbes's theory the irreconcilability of sovereignty and legal limits is a tension internal to the operation of a legal system; it persists even when authoritarian rulers do not rule arbitrarily in the sense of constantly ignoring or violating their own norms. Absolutism is not a function of the use of extralegal resources to hold onto power but a characteristic of unconstrained legislative power. Law is its currency, and the detection of highly institutionalized legal practices or of subordinate agencies and actors subject to institutional constraints and operating according to rules is not sufficient grounds to conclude that an authoritarian regime is limited. As we have seen, lower level constraints are allowed for in Hobbes's theory and other legal practices that might appear to imply limits are also compatible with unlimited power.

The legal theorist Joseph Raz (1979), for example, has argued that the properties associated with the rule of law are independent of whether the law-making body is limited or not. These properties include that: (1) laws be prospective, publicly promulgated, and clear; (2) laws be relatively stable; (3) the making of particular legal orders, such as administrative regulations, be subject to open, stable, clear, general rules; (4) laws be consistently applied by an independent judiciary; and (5) law enforcement agencies not pervert the law by applying it discretionarily. When a legal system satisfies these requirements,

---

[19] In Hobbes's account the sovereign is a legitimate authority because her power has been authorized by a social contract. More generally, Neumann (1957, 234) notes that kings are held to possess a legitimate title to office – be it hereditary, elective, or arising of a social contract, whereas dictators do not.

actors subject to its terms can know what types of behavior are required of them, develop expectations, and act accordingly since they face a clear, predictable framework of rules. Rule of law, in this sense, "is designed to minimize the danger created by the law itself" (Raz 1979, 224); it seeks to avoid the types of uncertainty and unpredictability that subjects face when norms are ambiguous or unknown, inconsistently applied, or retroactively applicable. The doctrine does not specify any requirements regarding how laws are made or the purposes that they serve and is wholly compatible with systems in which lawmakers themselves are not subject to law. In the *Leviathan*, Hobbes himself expends considerable energy describing the nature of law in terms that conform with this sense of the rule of law.[20] This type of rule of law, which we may refer to as rule by law to avoid confusion with constitutionalist rule of law, can be in the interest of autocratic rulers insofar as it provides mechanisms to assure that central dictates are being correctly enforced. For example, a formally independent judiciary not only can allow a ruler to deflect resentment and avoid responsibility for imposing punishments, if accompanied by a system of appeals reaching the highest levels, it can also provide central authorities with an independent flow of information about how lower-level authorities are implementing the law, while also allowing it to use appellate decisions to impose desired interpretations of the law (Shapiro 1981, 53–56).

My insistence that unlimited power is compatible with rule by law is not meant to suggest that authoritarian regimes regularly rule in this manner but to underscore that the problem of institutional limits is independent of the rule of law understood in this sense. Autocracies are notorious for deviating from the requirements of rule of law. These deviations may concern characteristics of a regime's legal and judicial system or involve practices that altogether disavow or violate even the regime's own legal requirements.[21] Generally capricious, arbitrary rule

---

[20] Hobbes 1991, chap. 26–28. In this legal organization of the state, law is publicly promulgated, prospective, general, applied by a public authority, and punishments not founded in such law or applied by agents without legal authority are described as "act[s] of hostility" (1991, 215). For an interpretation of Hobbes as a theorist of the rule of law, see Oakeshott 1983.

[21] Examples of the former include: the doctrine of analogy, by which an individual may be punished for committing an act not expressly prohibited by law but "analogous" to one prohibited; the retroactive application of law; the trial of political opponents by special administrative boards or military courts that are not required to follow standard trial procedures; and the administrative detention of individuals, without any requirement that they have committed a criminal offense, as may be authorized by standing emer-

of this type nevertheless tends to be restricted to a relatively minor subclass of nondemocratic regimes (Chehabi and Linz 1998). As Fraenkel (1969) suggests in his study of Nazi legal practices, even highly repressive dictatorships are likely to take the form of a "dual state": In specifically political realms, power holders may directly apply administrative sanctions or extrajudicial force upon political adversaries, while they allow the rule of law to operate in less conflictive areas, such as the market or the repression of moderate opponents. The tendency of dictatorships to operate legalistically has been emphasized by a number of studies of authoritarian and post-totalitarian regimes (Linz 1970, 268–69; Linz 1975, 287; Shain and Linz 1995, 10–16; Martínez-Lara 1996, chap. 1). Whether these practices conform with accepted standards of rule of law in each case needs to be assessed. Yet even when they do, rule by law should not be confused with institutionally limited power.[22]

*Noninstitutional Constraints and Sovereignty.* Similarly, it is important not to conflate the argument that autocratic power is legally unbound with a claim that authoritarian power holders are free from all forms of constraint. The theory of sovereignty concerns freedom from rules, not the manner by which any number of material and political factors may frustrate the realization of regime objectives, restrict the range of feasible ends authoritarian rulers may pursue, lead autocrats to prudentially temper the exercise of their power, or even force upon them outcomes they never desired or anticipated. These constraints may include the finitude of resources and administrative capabilities; the presence of powerful external actors; the political dynamics of rivalries, factions, and power plays within a regime; the perceived

gency powers. Though the dividing line is hazy and permeable, examples of practices that are often arbitrary even in regard to a dictatorship's own law include: the seizure of property without legal justification; detentions effected without following judicial or administrative formalities that are unrecognized or denied by the state; extrajudicial executions; the assassination of political opponents; and the kidnapping and murder of persons, followed by the illegal interment or destruction of their remains.

[22] Stable rule of law, though, is highly dependent upon limited government. As Fraenkel noted (1969, 56–57), the jurisdiction governed by law under the Nazi dictatorship always remained secondary to the "prerogative state," as the ruling clique could at its discretion decide whether a case be adjudicated in accordance with law or be handled "politically." Since these actors themselves are not subject to law, "the jurisdiction over jurisdiction rests with the Prerogative State." This point suggests that, although compatible in principle with autocracy, stable rule by law in nondemocratic regimes is contingent upon a broader subjection of state actors to rules, such that jurisdictions are not permeable to discretionary, political manipulation.

need to hold together a diverse coalition of supporters; or the need to gain the cooperation of key economic actors. In all contexts, such extra-institutional constraints narrow a decision maker's feasible choice set and influence their actual political capacities. Theorists of sovereignty were not claiming that absolute rulers could act free from these types of constraints.[23]

Any dictator, or for that matter, any ruler, who is strategic and concerned with effectively exercising and retaining power will be constrained in this sense by the need to pragmatically assess objectives and anticipate how decisions are likely to affect other officials, powers, and agents that may be capable of frustrating regime policy objectives, disrupting the government, or displacing the ruler from power (Tullock 1987, 115–16).

Such material and political constraints upon authoritarian power have been noted in studies of particular military regimes, and this type of constraint figures prominently in Linz's analyses of authoritarian as opposed to totalitarian regimes.[24] In Linz's works, the political as opposed to legal-institutional character of these constraints is indisputable. In his usage, "limits" generally refer to how the properties of authoritarian coalitions or originating contexts constrain regime elites from mobilizing or pursuing regime institutionalization along totalitarian lines. Thus, rulers are constrained from asserting forceful ideological commitments because an exclusive ideology would break the equilibrium among the diverse support groups which Linz associates with limited pluralism in authoritarian regimes; in turn, this lack of a strong ideology limits the capacity of the regime to mobilize mass support which, if effective and channeled through a single party, would also threaten components within the ruling coalition (Linz 1975, 268–70). In a similar manner, Linz (1973) emphasizes how the post-World War II disavowal of nondemocratic legitimacy formulas has constrained authoritarian regimes from attempting to institutionalize along the lines of single-party or corporatist forms of representation.

---

[23] On this point, see Hart 1961, 65. Perhaps in no instance was the gap between claims to state power and effective capacity greater than during the absolutist period. On the historical weaknesses of the absolutist state in Europe, see van Caenegem 1995, 78–88. On limits more generally during the early modern period, see the essays in Dunn 1990. Also see Bobbio 1989, 89–90.

[24] The manner whereby military presidents in Brazil were constrained by the interplay between hard-line and soft-line factions is stressed by a number of scholars (Stepan 1971, 248–66; Cardoso 1973, 168–72; Stepan 1988; and Skidmore 1989). Neuhouser (1996) examines political constraints upon economic policy implementation under successive military regimes in Ecuador.

These types of constraints, as well as those given by factionalism within the military, may be central to explaining the dynamics of particular authoritarian regimes, but they do not constitute institutional limits upon authoritarian power holders.

Most scholars who note these types of "limits" in authoritarian contexts usually are not addressing the problem of sovereignty. Still, it is important to draw out the difference between material and political constraints and institutional limits because references to the former may lead readers to erroneously think that limited authoritarianism is relatively unproblematic. The distinction is even more significant because some writers have confused the two types of constraints to argue that autocrats can in fact effectively bind themselves.

In an important essay, whose central thrust is to stress how relatively fixed rules enable democratic practices and thereby challenge the view that constitutions are constraints upon democracy, Stephen Holmes (1988), for example, fails to adequately distinguish these two forms of constraint and allows an autocrat who prudentially restrains the use of her powers before factual constraints to stand as refutation of the Bodin/Hobbes thesis that "a will can not be bound to itself." At one point, he noticeably confuses institutional limits and political and material constraints to minimize the theoretical problem posed by Hobbes. He writes, "A constitution-maker can never be an unbound binder, any more than a sovereign can be an uncommanded commander." Why is this so? Because, "To influence a situation, an actual power-wielder must adapt himself to preexistent patterns of force and unevenly distributed possibilities for change. The influencer must be influenced: that is a central axiom of any realistic theory of power" (1988, 222). In other words, sovereigns are limited by what I have called political and material constraints. In the same essay and elsewhere, Holmes discusses Bodin's recommendation to sovereigns to desist from arbitrary rule, emphasizing how such restraint actually increases a king's power because it permits him to mobilize cooperation and avoid antagonizing subjects who might destabilize his authority (1995, 109–20). In particular, he stresses Bodin's exhortation that a commonwealth "should by laws, and not by the prince's will and pleasure, be governed" (1962, 490, as cited in Holmes 1995, 114). However, as just discussed, rule by law does not dissolve absolute power, and all of the restrictions that Holmes discusses similarly leave the sovereign position of the ruler intact. Holmes seems to be aware of this problem, as he often notes that these limits are prudential and informal. Nevertheless, he (1995, 109, 111, 112, 118) repeatedly presents them in terms of an opposition between "limited" and "unlimited" power or rule, suggesting that such constraint resolves the incompatibility posed by Hobbes, when in fact the forms of prudential self-restraint he refers to are limited only in reference to the sovereign's freedom to rule capriciously, not her position as supreme authority within the legal system. Hence, although Holmes calls this self-binding, it is not clear why such "precommitment" should be construed as tying the hands of the ruler, as nothing constrains her from reversing prudential practices and commitments when expedient.

Neither to confuse institutional limits with the rule of law, nor to conflate them with constraints given by the strategic context of action, is to refute Hobbes's claim that autocratic power cannot be bound by rules. An autocrat may have much to benefit from disabling her capacity to freely reverse herself and modify rules and laws at her discretion, but the benefits that may accrue from controlling discretion are no guarantee that an authoritarian regime can avail itself of a technology with which to both effectively free itself of the discretion that is intrinsic to sovereignty and remain in command. Without such an institutional mechanism capable of holding rulers to prior commitments and laws, the facility with which any autocracy can legislate always leaves open a potential for disjuncture between present decisions and earlier ones. These three dimensions – the insufficiency of perceived benefits, the problem of intertemporality, and the need for institutions – are central themes in the literature on commitment.

## Precommitment and Credible Commitment

The literature on credible commitment is directly relevant to the problem of sovereignty and limits as it seeks to explain why and how an actor possessed of discretionary authority might seek to constrain her own future freedom of action.[25] This literature provides an extended discussion on why absolute power may not be in an actor's interests over time and why institutional constraints may be beneficial. In its general form, the problem of credible commitment applies to both single individuals and interactions among multiple actors, including collective actors, such as the state: When an agent possesses discretion and may reverse herself at will, that actor may only be capable of

---

[25] The seminal formulation of the commitment problem with regard to political institutions is found in North and Weingast 1989. Other discussions are Weingast 1990; Shepsle 1991; North 1993.

inducing desired behaviors in herself or others if she can provide credible assurances that she will not depart from the course of behavior or policies foreseen as beneficial; to do so often involves the use of some device to disable the discretion that would allow a failure to follow through on a commitment.

In this manner, the literature on credible commitments points to the shortcomings of anticipated benefits as a foundation for behavior, the frailty of voluntary self-restraint, and the need for institutions to overcome the suboptimal consequences that free discretion may produce over time.[26] Though North and Weingast (1989) have suggested that seventeenth-century institutional change in Britain is an example of a ruler using institutions to credibly commit herself, a close reading of their argument suggests that the Glorious Revolution does not involve a sovereign bound by institutions of her own making. Before developing this point, two aspects of the credible commitment approach should be stressed.

First, benefits expected to accrue from a course of action are insufficient to make a commitment credible. Regardless of the gains anticipated from fulfilling promises or pledges, whenever the *ex ante* motivations for striking a bargain and the *ex post* reasons for executing it may differ, there is a commitment problem.[27] In such instances,

---

[26] The prisoner's dilemma that arises when two parties commit to an exchange yet institutions for enforcing contracts are not available is the classic example that has focused the attention of new institutionalist economists. In this case, both parties may recognize that they each would gain from trade and agree to a trade, but when the time comes to actually exchange goods neither party has an incentive to follow through, since neither can be assured that the other will not cheat him. In this situation the commitments involved in promising to exchange are not credible. Under certain conditions parties in such a context will find it worthwhile to cooperate: play is repeated indefinitely, parties possess information about other players' past behavior, and there are a limited number of players. Nevertheless, these conditions are too restrictive and unrealistic to explain impersonal exchange on a large scale, and much of the literature explores how institutions can provide assurances of cooperation that make possible gains from trade, producer specialization, and economies of scale. This is a major theme in North's work on institutions and economic development (1990, 1991, 1993). Milgrom, North, and Weingast (1990) and Greif, Milgrom, and Weingast (1994) explore different nonstate institutions which facilitated the development of impersonal trade over time and distance in early modern Europe.

[27] The possible sources for such changes in incentives over time are many. Among others, these include the effects of weakness of will, passions, and time inconsistency resulting from strategic interaction or hyperbolic discounting, among others – and have been studied extensively (Loewenstein and Elster 1992; Elster 2000). Any of these factors can cause an imperfectly rational actor to forgo actions which they had initially chosen as optimal in favor of alternatives that are best in an immediate time period but inconsistent with the actor's original preferred course of behavior over time.

as Shepsle (1991) has argued, commitments are only credible when they are imperative; that is, when the players involved have no alternative but to perform their antecedent commitments because their discretion to do otherwise has been disabled or a third party coerces performance. Thus, credible commitments imply limits upon the capacity to reverse an earlier decision.

Second, making commitments credible through self-binding is an intentional strategy. Actors deliberately restrict their freedom of action in anticipation of expected benefits (Elster 1984; 2000). The classic example is Ulysses abdicating control of his vessel and having himself bound to the mast so he could pass the island of the Sirens and hear their enchanting song without crashing upon the rocks. Elster and others have discussed various devices for political precommitment, such as central banks, procedural delays, legislative committee structures, federalism, and constitutions, though recently Elster has questioned whether these institutions are put in place to bind their creators or actually to bind others (Elster 2000, chap. 2). In any event, the imposition of constraints is understood to be an enabling device, as scholars who reassess the argument that constitutions constrain democracy have stressed.[28]

If examined on both these counts, North and Weingast's (1989) account of English institutional change during the seventeenth century does not appear to constitute a case of autocratic self-limitation. These scholars ably document both the fiscal problems of the Stuart kings during the early 1600s and how the crown's shortsightedness and arbitrary exercise of its absolute power antagonized property holders who could have potentially eased the crown's finance problems. They also present considerable evidence of the substantial increase in government expenditures and debt, the emergence of regular public and private capital markets, and the decline in interest rates on public borrowing that followed once the 1688 revolution ushered in institutional changes that limited the king's ability to legislate unilaterally, alter

---

[28] See, in particular, Holmes 1988 and Sejersted 1988, 143–46. Sejersted makes the extremely suggestive point that the unwillingness to be subject to former decisions implies a constraint upon the ability to bind others because at some point these other actors may also enjoy the same unlimited power to change laws and policies. Thus, to anchor one's deeds, "Some sort of negative power is necessary not only to check, but paradoxically also to protect positive power" (Sejersted 1988, 145). This desire to secure substantive deeds might be one motivation for a dictatorship to impose and accept limits upon its sovereignty. This, though, would require that authoritarian power holders not highly discount the future and that they have objectives other than merely maintaining themselves in power.

jurisdictions, and mold the judiciary at will by establishing parliamentary supremacy. Yet, although North and Weingast stress the deliberate nature of credible commitment when they assert that their account addresses one of two ways whereby "a ruler can establish such commitment," they provide evidence that undermines any claim that this case might represent an instance of autocratic self-limitation. These points concern the intentional character of institutional change and the effects of these changes upon the sovereignty of the monarchy.

First, these scholars themselves admit that the institutional changes to which they attribute enhanced government credibility were not instituted by the king, but "were forced, often violently, upon the Crown" (1989, 804, 828). The Crown did not seek institutional reform to secure its financial position; rather, it was bound because property holders in Parliament gained control of the law after decades of ongoing conflict over royal prerogative and arbitrary rule.

Second, the revolution fundamentally constrained the powers of the king. As, North and Weingast recognize, the revolution established parliamentary supremacy (1989, 816). Rather than the king tying his hands and remaining sovereign, he was bound by Parliament. In the process sovereignty shifted to Parliament, which they acknowledge was not subject to institutional limits, despite the incentives that led Parliament to behave responsibly. Indeed, the English case seems only to ratify a point made by the theorists of absolutism: A king subject to limits is no longer sovereign. No monocratic ruler can effectively be bound except by ceasing to exercise supreme power.

It would appear that it is impossible for an authoritarian regime to establish institutional devices that effectively constrain autocratic discretion. The theory of sovereignty indicates that a ruler cannot be bound by her own promises, a point confirmed by research on credible commitment in early modern Europe. Nevertheless, as I will argue in the following section, this dead end follows only if we hold steadfast to two assumptions that are not necessarily warranted. One is the tendency to equate authoritarianism with monocratic rule. The other is the assumption that sovereignty is absolute and cannot be divided. If the first assumption is relaxed and we concede the possibility that an authoritarian regime may be structured upon an internal pluralism of actors, then it becomes conceivable that power can be subject to institutional limits without necessarily transforming the nondemocratic character of the regime. To what extent such a scenario should be understood as a process of self-binding, though, is a separate question which we also need to address.

## Nonmonocratic Dictatorship and Collective Foundations for Ongoing Institutional Limits

As both the theory of sovereignty and the literature on credible commitments contend, supreme actors can effectively be bound by institutions only if they can be freed of the discretionary authority that otherwise allows them to modify any rules or institutions that constrain them. Given this condition, if the power to make rules is held by a single actor, there is no solution to the problem of sovereignty: A unitary actor *qua* individual cannot effectively obligate herself. As Hobbes (1991, chap. 26, 138) aptly noted: "For he is free, that can be free when he will: Nor is it possible for any person to be bound to himselfe; because he that can bind, can release; and therefore he that is bound to himselfe onely, is not bound." If sovereignty resides in a unitary actor, that actor can at her discretion free herself from any limiting past decisions by currently enacting new rules that remove or modify restrictions. Thus, institutional limits may operate and constrain the sovereign, but as long as this actor retains the authority to modify the rules that emplace and authorize the controlling institution, the operation of such constraints remains contingent. They are effective at the sovereign's will and can be suppressed at any point.

How this capacity to change any norm may be disabled is the central problem that any theory of autocratic self-binding must resolve. Still, the barriers to institutional limits on power in the context of a unitary authoritarian power bloc are broader. As I discussed previously, ongoing, effective institutional limits require: positive legal standards specifying the range of valid powers held by different authorities; a separation of powers to prevent any one person or authority from unilaterally imposing her will and to allow different powers to hold each other to the prior rules; and, above all, rules that remove this framework of powers and rules from facile modification by the rule-making power. Independent of the problem of sovereign reversibility, if all powers in an authoritarian regime are invariably fused in a single actor or body, the types of separation of powers that are required to enable controlling powers will be unavailable. For example, even when they leave legislative sovereignty unchecked, controls upon an authoritarian executive require a plurality of actors within the authoritarian power bloc.[29]

---

[29] Such an executive will be subject to the laws made by a separate legislature only if the executive does not hold powers to select the members of the legislative body or supplant

The dual requirement that ongoing institutional limits involve a separation of powers and an inability of the supreme legislator to discretionarily modify the legal framework suggests that effective institutional constraints – whether in an authoritarian or democratic regime – may only be possible in the context of a collective sovereign. In addition to allowing a separation of powers, a collective ruling bloc – such that a plurality of actors must coordinate to act as one – will require procedural rules and may also permit the institution of more demanding procedures for modifying "constitutional" rules than those used to legislate. If so instituted, authoritarian legislators can be constrained by a higher constitution not subject to facile modification at their hands.

The insight that, in contrast to monocratic forms, collective forms of rule require procedural rules can be traced to Machiavelli (Bobbio 1987, 65). Wherever a plurality of actors composes the rule-making body, procedural rules will be required to define what types of acts by members of the collectivity are sufficient to qualify as a valid decision of the body – such as how many members must concur and what steps they must follow to enact law. In those instances in which rule making requires other rules to define the procedural steps that must be followed for decisions to be made, the rule-making authority does not stand wholly above rules. However, the procedural rules that enable unique decisions to emerge from a collectivity do not impose a legal limit upon the legislative power since, if the required forms are followed, the body can legislate on any matter it wishes (Hart 1961, 69–76).

Still, it should be emphasized that these constitutive rules constrain individual members of the collective decision-making body. By defining the standard forms of coordination, they exclude other procedures for decision and, even when they are not enforced by another power, they provide members with legitimate grounds to criticize attempts to deviate from procedures previously established as rules.

The interdependence between such rules and institutional positions within a dictatorship can be one possible reason for some members within an authoritarian power bloc to seek to elevate constitutional rules beyond facile modification. Insofar as rules that delimit powers and define procedures protect the positions of individual members within the collective ruling body, some members may develop an

the body by enacting laws by decree. For in these cases the executive indirectly or directly legislates. The frailty of nominally independent legislatures in Spain and Brazil before authoritarian executives that hold such powers is examined in Chapter 2.

interest in the stability of these rules. Furthermore, should the absence of an organ empowered to enforce these rules give rise to repeated attempts to transgress agreed-upon procedures, actors threatened by such attempts may demand the institution of a third body to uphold constitutional rules, as well as the introduction of further procedures that limit the lawmaking authority's capacity to modify the resulting institutional framework. Under such a scenario, institutional and individual self-interest within a collective body can give rise to institutional limits.

I should stress that two extra-institutional conditions are likely to be needed for plurality within a collective ruling body to be a foundation for institutional constraints. First, the members of the collective body, despite a common interest in assuring their dominance, must possess and sustain substantively heterogenous interests. Otherwise, if all members of the ruling body are steadfastly unified by an invariant common purpose, the situation is no different than under a monocratic dictatorship; even if such a regime introduces a division of functions, when the ruling apparatus is unified it may reverse its own measures at its discretion. Ongoing heterogeneity, then, is necessary to motivate differences and an interest in rules, as well as to make unlikely the levels of coordination that would allow the suppression of any limits introduced. Second, some additional factor is probably required to prevent the suppression of the plural foundations of rule, that is, to prevent any single actor from concentrating all authority and establishing a personalist regime. This factor may be a balance of coercive capabilities among the component members of the ruling body that renders any violent attempts to centralize power uncertain, or perhaps aspects of the larger political environment that create incentives for cooperation within the regime by elevating the anticipated costs to authoritarian incumbents of any regime breakdown.

This insinuation of authoritarian actors possessing coercive capabilities suggests that divided authoritarian power can arise in situations in which military force itself is divided and separate forces possessing independent military resources form the authoritarian power bloc. Therefore, we may expect to find conditions for collective rule and possibly institutional limits under military dictatorships in which the armed forces are organized as separate services and rule jointly in a junta. As I have already suggested, a stable collegial equilibrium will require that no branch of the armed forces predominate over the others and that military capabilities among the branches are sufficiently symmetrical as to deter the use of force within the power bloc.

Although these conditions can be specified analytically, in most cases we do not know enough about the internal workings of military dictatorships or particular armed forces to validate these hypotheses with data on actual cases. In part, the insufficiency of our knowledge reflects the many restrictions that researchers face when they attempt to study dictatorships and military institutions, since both typically close themselves off before outsiders. However, just as constricting are influential conceptual approaches that either aggregate armed forces into "the military" without acknowledging the often plural structure of many national armed forces or else unify armed forces on the basis of a purported shared ideological orientation, such as adherence to the so-called "national security doctrine" in the Latin American cases.[30] Similarly, by viewing military regimes only in their dimension as dictatorships over society, many accounts of military rule discount potential sources of internal difference or view them as disequilibria that erode regime cohesion and trigger demands for a return to the barracks, not elements of joint rule that may be organized and channeled through institutions. As a result of these approaches, the study of military juntas as collegial forms of rule that are capable of sustaining a division of authoritarian power is largely an undeveloped field of study.[31]

As we will now see, the collegial organization of the Chilean armed forces immediately created a need for rules and procedures within the military Junta. These were adopted in 1974 and 1975 and though this initial framework did not limit the sovereignty of the Junta, it provided the foundation for instituting the constitution and later sustaining institutional limits even when they blocked the Junta's original preferences.

[30] For examples of this approach to Latin American armed forces, see Child 1985; Perelli 1993; Pion-Berlin 1989; and Zagorski 1992. Each of these authors posits a tight connection between military doctrine and behavior.

[31] Frederick Nunn (1975) has also pointed to the conceptual imprecision with which the term "junta" is regularly used.

# Chapter Two

# The Constitution of the Exception:
# Defining the Rules of Military Rule

When on September 11, 1973, the Chilean armed forces and *carabineros*, the national police, ousted the properly elected government of Salvador Allende, seized power, and unleashed a violent repression against the Left, they unambiguously broke with standing constitutional norms regarding the obedient and nondeliberative character of the armed forces, valid methods of accession to and abdication of office, the separation of powers, and the rule of law.[1] By these acts the Chilean armed forces put an end to democracy and opened the door to dictatorship. Though the exclusionary and repressive character of the military's rule was blatant from the outset, what type of dictatorship would follow was not immediately evident. Within a day of the coup, the armed forces arrogated to themselves the "Supreme Command of the Nation," formed a four-man *Junta de Gobierno* composed of the commanders in chief of the army, navy, and air force and the director general of the national police force, *carabineros*, and pledged to respect the law and the constitution insofar as the situation permitted.[2]

---

[1] In addition to the articles specifying the qualifications and procedures for selecting the president, the relevant articles of the 1925 constitution are ART. 3, 4, and 22:

    ART. 3. No person or assembly of persons has authority to arrogate the title or representation of the people, to usurp its rights, or to make demands in its name. Violation of this Article is sedition.

    ART. 4. No magistracy, or person, or assembly of persons, not even under the pretext of extraordinary circumstances, is empowered to assume any other authority or rights than those that have been expressly conferred upon them by the laws. Every act in contravention of this Article is void.

    ART. 22. The public force is constituted solely and exclusively by the armed forces and the carabinero guards, which entities are essentially professional, organized by rank, disciplined, obedient and non-deliberating. Only by virtue of a law may the manning of these institutions be determined. . . .

[2] The respective members of the Junta de Gobierno were: Gen. Augusto Pinochet Ugarte, Adm. José Toribio Merino Castro, Gen. Gustavo Leigh Guzmán, and Gen. César Mendoza Durán.

However, these initial measures were ambiguous and raised a number of questions. First, what would be the scope of the new regime's powers? The concept Supreme Command of the Nation was without referent within the Chilean constitutional tradition and provided few clues as to the range of powers assumed by the military. Second, once the scope of these powers was settled, how would their exercise be organized among the armed forces? Would one force dominate the executive or would mechanisms for power sharing be instituted? Similarly, how would law be made? Would procedures be designed to involve each armed force or would a strong man emerge and concentrate executive and legislative powers? Third, what concrete institutional forms, if any, would the military's pledge to respect the law and the constitution assume? Would existing organs of legal and constitutional control, such as the Supreme Court and the *Contraloría General de la República*, be allowed to challenge the military regime's executive and legislative acts, or would the fulfillment of this pledge be merely subject to regime discretion?

All of these questions loomed large with the military's coercive imposition on September 11, 1973. However, the Chilean armed forces themselves did not have clear answers to these questions, as was revealed by the legal and institutional vacuum that followed the coup. In September 1973, the armed forces shared a negative consensus regarding the need to bring to a halt the extreme crisis precipitated by the Left in power, but otherwise the Chilean military did not come to power with a grand design or regime prototype. The institutional organization of military rule would have to be settled once in power. Nevertheless, within the space of two years the officers in the Junta had agreed upon and put in place institutional arrangements which settled most of the questions outlined above. In late 1973 the Junta clarified that the Supreme Command of the Nation implied the exercise of executive, legislative, and constituent powers. In the course of 1974, the manner of exercise of constituent powers and the relationship between the Junta and the judiciary were worked out after encounters with the Supreme Court over judicial review of decree-laws and Court supervision of military justice. In 1974 and 1975, the scope and procedural organization of executive and legislative powers were settled in two steps. The first definition, arrived at in mid-1974, concerned the tenancy and scope of executive powers, and was followed a year later by an agreement creating institutions and procedures to structure the legislative process.

These two agreements, inscribed in decree-laws, instituted a partial separation of powers within the dictatorship, which operated as a first set of limits internal to the regime. Executive powers were clearly delimited from legislative powers and legislative procedures were instituted that precluded executive dominance of lawmaking. Although the opposite is widely believed, under this system Pinochet could not unilaterally legislate nor mold the Junta at his whim. Pinochet retained a vote in the Junta,[3] but the legislative system was structured around the principle of unanimity and had been intentionally designed to provide each commander with an institutionally protected channel for voice and veto in lawmaking. As a result, even though the Junta as a body was not subject to effective external institutional constraints – a point that is the subject of the following two chapters – internally, among the military commanders, power was limited: No single actor could unilaterally impose binding norms upon the other actors within the power bloc.

This chapter traces this process of dictatorial institutional design and evaluates the significance of these institutions as limits on absolute power within the dictatorship. It reconstructs the steps by which the commanders of the Chilean armed forces gave legal and institutional structure to their rule. In particular, the chapter focuses on the definition of executive and legislative powers and procedures.[4] I proceed through the following sections: The first establishes the absence of any initial institutional plan among the armed forces and describes the first period of military rule during which executive and legislative powers were indiscriminately fused; most of the rest of the chapter reconstructs the deliberations and decision making within the Junta regarding the need for an internal separation of powers; and the final section evaluates the significance of internal institutional constraints in light of the personalist interpretation of military rule in Chile and the comparative experience of other cases of authoritarian rule.

This reconstruction seeks to show that in the course of 1974 and early 1975, the military commanders devised and instituted organizational rules and procedures with the deliberate objective of securing

---

[3] Pinochet would retain a personal vote within the Junta until the 1980 constitution went into effect in March 1981. The 1980 constitution affected only minor changes to the institutional arrangements analyzed here. These changes are discussed in Chapter 7.

[4] The manner of exercise of constituent powers and the Supreme Court's power of judicial review are addressed in Chapter 3, which is the first of two chapters examining whether the constitution, the judiciary, and the *Contraloría General de la República* – the three traditional, institutional ramparts against arbitrary acts of authority – set limits upon the prerogative power of the military junta. Chapter 4 analyzes the efficacy of the judiciary as a constraint upon extralegal repression.

the original collegial character of the military junta and of preventing any single armed force from centralizing executive and legislative power and dominating the other branches of the military. The motivation for making rules structuring competencies and procedures did not derive from the military's purported commitment to re-establish the rule of law, as one civilian advisor contended (Cuevas 1974). Rather, the process of rule making was impelled by the fact of intermilitary conflicts at the apex of the dictatorship. In Chile, dictatorial institutional design was the outcome of a conflictive process in which the commanders of the navy and the air force repeatedly asserted themselves to block attempts by Pinochet to centralize executive and legislative power. In this context, rules structuring powers and procedures codified the terms of resolution of these confrontations. They specified in law mutual expectations regarding participation of the services in the dictatorship and, in this case, instituted mechanisms which assured each commander the opportunity and legal right to articulate, represent, and hold steadfast to individual opinions in the legislative decision-making process.

The significance of the legislative junta as an institutional constraint internal to the dictatorship has generally been dismissed by analysts of military rule in Chile. In part, this underestimation of the Junta can be attributed to the Junta's nonpublic modes of deliberation and decision making. Sessions of the Junta were secret and what transpired in them was known at best in distorted form through rumor or the manipulated disclosures of the Junta itself.[5] In this context, scholars have built their characterizations of the military regime upon the more public dimensions of military institutional definition, particularly Pinochet's simultaneous position as commander in chief of the army and president, as well as the longevity of his tenure in both offices. From a comparative perspective, Pinochet's position within the dictatorship is without parallel within recent authoritarian regimes in Latin America. However, these public dimensions are only half of the story

---

[5] This secrecy and insulation of debate from public scrutiny was highly functional for the rule of the armed forces, as it allowed the commanders in chief to articulate differences internally without eroding the Junta's capacity to publicly present its power as undivided and monolithic. Furthermore, secrecy shielded any policy divergences from being manipulated by interested political or corporate actors and helped prevent spillover into the ranks of the military institutions. By allowing the Junta to articulate differences without publicity, the insulation of decision making was decisive in preventing the emergence of debilitating cleavages within or among the armed forces, a politicization that the highest ranking officers understood would undermine their domination.

and do not warrant casting the dictatorship as a monistic, personalized regime with power concentrated in Pinochet.

## Initial Unknowns

Aside from the agreement on the urgency of putting an end to the Allende government, the Chilean armed forces came to power in September 1973 with at best rudimentary conceptions of how to structure a military government. This limited military preparation for governing was largely the flip side of Chile's exceptional tradition of institutional stability, constitutionalism, and legalism. Aside from implying inexperience in power, this legacy was also reflected in the formally constitutionalist stance of top military officials, particularly army commander in chief, Gen. Carlos Prats González. During the months leading up to the coup, this professional orientation made plotting and planning against the Allende government difficult and precluded extensive agreements regarding the postcoup organization of military power.

The solidity and resiliency of Chilean liberal and democratic institutions and political society prior to the 1973 coup were unparalleled in South America and noteworthy even by European standards. Following independence in 1810, Republican institutions and constitutional government were rapidly established and consolidated. After a brief period of post-independence instability, which included seven constitutions in less than two decades, political order was restored and exceptional constitutional stability ensued, such that prior to 1973 only two constitutions were ever in force, those of 1833 and 1925. A combination of factors has been cited as contributing to this capacity to contain political and social conflicts within liberal and democratic institutions: the relatively rapid articulation with the global economy after independence and the emergence of mining-based sources of fiscal rents; the growing independence of Congress from the executive after the mid-1800s; the early appearance of political contestation among sectors of the dominant classes prior to both the extension of the suffrage – which was gradual in Chile – and the creation of a strong state bureaucracy; the incentives to enter the political system given by proportional representation and the pragmatism of the Radical Party, which sought alliances successively with parties of the Right and the Left; the resulting competitiveness of the party system and the fragmentation of political forces which encouraged and necessitated compromise and accommodation; and the enduring political strength of the traditional parties which was boosted by the overrepresentation of rural areas and the survival of mechanisms of oligarchic control over elections in the countryside through the late 1950s.[6]

Within the resulting multiparty matrix, Congress provided the central arena of political negotiation and functioned continuously for stretches that can be matched by few other legislatures in the world. Following its foundation in 1831, the Chilean Congress functioned normally and was renewed by regular elections for ninety-three years without interruption, and the two occasions prior to 1973 during which Congress was closed (1924 and 1932) were relatively brief.[7] The solidity of other state institutions prior to the coup was equally striking. One legal historian has traced the origins of the presidency and the judiciary to the sixteenth and seventeenth centuries (Bravo Lira 1990, 31), and the Chilean Supreme Court, founded in 1823, is the second oldest in the Americas after the U.S. Supreme Court (Verdugo Marinkovic 1989, 54).

This stability of representative government had a major impact on the Chilean military. Unlike the militaries of many other South American countries, the Chilean armed forces were disciplined, hierarchical, and professional organizations, narrowly centered on defense matters. The armed forces faced the political crises of 1972–1973 without any recent experience of intervention or of administering the state. Their last incursion into politics had been during the 1930s and had been traumatic: The military bore most of the political costs of the depression, and the politicization of officers set the army, navy, and air force against one another, resulting in a severe erosion of military discipline, organization, and prestige before the civilian population. This negative experience of military politicization gave rise to self-consciously nonpolitical, constitutional, and professional armed forces during the 1930s.[8] The doctrine and practice of military professional-

---

[6] On these various components of democratic stability in Chile, see Gil 1966; Zeitlin 1968; Pinto 1970; Valenzuela 1977; Moulian 1982; Valenzuela 1985; and Scully 1992.

[7] On the first occasion, Congress was interrupted from September 1924 through March 1926; the second time Congress was suspended between June and December 1932 (Bravo Lira 1977, 39).

[8] As Nunn (1976, 195–96), a historian of the Chilean military, has noted, "Earlier than other Latin American countries, Chile endured the disastrous effects of a professional military organization fallen prey to frenetic, individualistic ambitions, rivalries, and jealousies, and the outcome convinced civilians and military men alike that the armed forces should indeed remain 'essentially obedient,' as the constitution dictated." Arriagada (1985, 107–9) cites contemporary accounts of officers, including one by Admiral Merino's father, then director general of the navy. On the emergence of military subordination to the constitution in the aftermath of intervention, see Nunn 1976, 223–32; Varas, Agüero, and Bustamante 1980, 71–79; and Maldonado 1988.

ism, reinforced by the solidity of civilian rule after 1932, meant that, unlike their Argentine or Brazilian counterparts, the Chilean armed forces did not have extensive past experience of coup making or military rule to draw upon – these had to be worked out along the way.[9]

From what is known about the planning of the coup, it is reasonable to conjecture that the officers plotting Allende's overthrow were in no position to arrive at extensive agreements regarding the institutional contours of military rule nor the content of specific policies. Though General Pinochet (1982, 75) claims that active preparations for a coup began in the army in late June 1972, the accounts of other officers suggest otherwise. Particularly within the army, the constitutional stance of Gen. Carlos Prats, the commander in chief, made any deliberation by officers extremely risky and tenuous;[10] planning appears to have begun considerably later than Pinochet claims; the coup was primarily the initiative of the navy and the air force; and coordination among the different services began only after the failed June 29, 1973 coup attempt by a Santiago tank battalion.[11] The principal concerns of

[9] The contrast with Argentina is striking. The process of decision making that I am about to describe – which took almost two years in Chile – in Argentina took place prior to the March 24, 1976 coup, allowing the junta to issue the day that it took power its statute and regulations specifying how executive and legislative powers would be exercised. According to Fontana (1987, 42–48) inter-service deliberations regarding the structure of the military regime began in mid-1975.

[10] In his memoirs, General Prats (1985, 225–50 passim, 289–94 passim) recounts a number of incidents involving detected breaches of discipline prior to the June 1973 Tancazo; in two separate cases these resulted in officer resignations, one involving a colonel, the other a general. Prats (1985, 401, 403) claims that by June 1973 it was clear that he could no longer rely upon military intelligence, the Servicio de Inteligencia Militar (SIM), to investigate plotting and contacts between officers and the extreme right. These sources provided no intelligence anticipating the June 29, 1973 uprising of the 2nd Armored Battalion (Prats 1985, 434).

General Prats was appointed commander in chief of the army in October 1970, days after the assassination of Gen. René Schneider, and held the post until his resignation on August 24, 1973. Prats and his wife, Sofia, were assassinated in Buenos Aires, Argentina, on September 29, 1974, when a bomb blew apart their car. In November 2000, Enrique Arancibia Clavel was sentenced to life imprisonment by an Argentine Court for being an accessory to the assassination, which the court concluded had been an act of the DINA.

[11] Beginning the day after the Tancazo, at the initiative of the commanders in chief of the navy and air force, Adm. Raúl Montero Cornejo and Gen. César Ruiz Danyau, regular, joint meetings of top officers drawn from each service were held to discuss internal security (Prats 1985, 423). Though the specific officers attending varied from session to session, these meetings were informally known as the "Group of Fifteen," as each service was represented by five generals or admirals (carabineros did not take part in these deliberations). These joint deliberations took place with full knowledge of the Ministry of Defense and the commanders in chief, including the constitutionalist head of the army, General Prats. Therefore, it is doubtful that they were the site of explicit coup

the conspirators were internal security, controlling telecommunications, and assuring that all officers in command of troops adhered to the movement (Varas 1979, 127–28), as the officers involved feared that any vertical or horizontal division of the armed forces would lead directly to civil war. Until just days before the coup, navy and air force plotters were unsure of General Pinochet's intentions.[12] In this context, the first priority was to assure the success of the coup, not anticipate the practical organization of military power.

Thus, at the time of the coup there had been preparation for taking action against the Allende government, but little coordination among the armed forces as to how to govern or how long to remain in power.[13] At most there appears to have been a "gentlemen's agreement" that the presidency of the Junta would rotate among its members (Huidobro 1989, 265). In any case, even if the officers plotting the coup had arrived at agreements regarding the structure of a military government, such accords almost certainly would have had to be renegotiated *ex post*, since positions of authority within each service were likely to be affected by the outcome of the movement and the solidity

---

planning. However, the sessions did allow high-level officers to gauge the disposition of officers in other branches and establish working contacts. Other officers (Díaz Estrada 1988, 105; Huidobro 1989, 131, 135–39, 154–59) concur that at this point interservice contacts to organize a coup began. Air Force General Gustavo Leigh (1988, 129) claims that the first contacts with the navy occurred somewhat later, in late July 1973, following the funeral of Allende's assassinated naval aide-de-camp.

[12] According to Air Force General Nicanor Díaz Estrada (1988, 105), then the second-ranking officer in the General Staff of National Defense, Pinochet refused to discuss politics at "Group of Fifteen" meetings. Even after becoming commander in chief on August 23, 1973, Pinochet was thought to be loyal to Prats's constitutionalist position (Arellano Iturriaga 1985, 37; Prats 1985, 436, 510). By all accounts, the chief instigators within the army were Gen. Sergio Arellano Stark and Gen. Oscar Bonilla Bradanovic. Díaz Estrada (1988, 108) indicates that Arellano had been the navy's contact in the army and that as late as September 8, 1973, the navy and the air force were unsure of Pinochet's stance. According to Rear Adm. Sergio Huidobro (1989, 228–29), who was Admiral Merino's liaison on September 9 when Pinochet was finally pressed to define himself, Pinochet until that day had only committed to Adm. Patricio Carvajal to keep the army in its barracks in the event of a coup attempt and not move to suppress it. It was not until two days before the coup that Pinochet agreed to joint action (Pinochet 1982, 114–15; Arellano Iturriaga 1985, 47–48; Huidobro 1989, 230–35). At the time, Admiral Carvajal was chief of the General Staff of National Defense. He appears to have been the linchpin in coordinating the coup among the different services. On deliberations within the armed forces prior to the coup, also consult Arriagada 1985, 50–70.

[13] Interview with retired Gen. Julio Canessa Robert, Santiago, Chile, July 17, 1992, and interview with Gen. (J) Fernando Lyon, Santiago, Chile, November 23, 1992. At the time of the coup, then a Colonel, Canessa was the director of the *Escuela de Suboficiales* in Santiago. He would serve as the army's representative in the Junta from December 1985 through December 1986.

of each chain of command during the coup attempt itself. Hence, any credible agreements probably could only have been made once the officer corps in each service had settled. Such shake-ups did occur on September 11, 1973, at the apex of both the navy and *carabineros* – Rear Adm. José Toribio Merino displaced Adm. Raúl Montero Cornejo as commander in chief of the navy, while Gen. César Mendoza Durán, the eighth ranking general in the national police force, usurped the position of director general from Gen. José María Sepúlveda.[14]

This lack of prior agreement on the institutional and legal structuring of military rule was evident during the first days after the coup in the form of a situation of total legal exception and absolute de facto rule. With much of the constitution in tatters, military commands took the place of ordinary civil and penal laws. The armed forces issued *bandos* to convey commands to the civilian population. *Bandos* were exceptional penal and administrative edicts which had no constitutional foundation and, in accordance with the *Código de Justicia Militar* (Code of Military Justice, hereafter *CdJM*), were to be used during time of war to regulate troops and the inhabitants of occupied territories.[15] The first *bando* on September 11, 1973 notified the population that acts of sabotage would be sanctioned "in the most drastic manner possible, at the very site of the act, and with no limit beyond the assessment/decision of the authorities there." On the 11th and following days, the Junta issued further *bandos* to impart commands to civilians and notify the population of measures being taken to establish order. *Bandos* were used to institute a curfew, summon prominent political figures to turn themselves in at the Ministry of Defense, prohibit public assembly, authorize the summary execution of individuals engaged in armed resistance, institute prior press censorship and suspend radio broadcasts, dissolve Congress, and justify the armed forces' intervention.[16]

---

[14] Montero's position within the navy had been greatly weakened by his participation in Allende's cabinet, whereas Merino, who had been serving as acting commander in chief in his place, enjoyed broad support among naval officers.

[15] For commentary on the legal status of *bandos*, see Astrosa 1985, 133–34 and Garretón, Garretón, and Garretón 1998, 21–30. ART. 77 and 78 of the CdJM provided the statutory foundation for *bandos*. ART. 34 of the Law of Internal State Security also granted the military heads of "emergency zones" authority to publish *bandos* affecting civilians. These emergency zones and their corresponding heads had been designated in D.L. No. 4 (*Diario Oficial*, hereafter *D.O.*, September 18, 1973), which declared a State of Emergency throughout the country.

[16] The quote is from *Bando* No. 1. Congress was dissolved by *Bando* No. 29 on September 13, 1973. The ideological justification for the coup was presented in *Bando* No. 5, dated September 11, 1973. A mandatory text in compilations commemorating military

The Junta itself was formally constituted only on the morning of September 12, following the hasty drafting of the *Acta de Constitución de la Junta de Gobierno* (D.L. No. 1, D.O., September 18, 1973) by naval legal counsel and its approval by the three commanders in chief and the director general of *carabineros* (Fontaine 1988, 13; Huidobro 1989, 262–65).[17] The precedents drawn upon for this decree-law, as well as the ambiguities in its content, further suggest that the armed forces did not share a common plan defining how to structure the military government. According to Sergio Rillón Romani, the naval legal advisor who sketched the first draft of D.L. No. 1, the decree-law was modeled after the founding document of Chile's preceding junta, the Socialist Republic of 1932, and this claim is borne out by the considerable similarity between the first two decree-laws of 1973 and the first two decrees of the 1932 Junta.[18]

Similarly, this first institutional proclamation did little to define the scope and powers of the new military government. It stated that the officers had constituted a government junta and assumed the *Mando Supremo de la Nación* (Supreme Command of the Nation). However, the nature of the authority thereby assumed was ambiguous because *Mando Supremo de la Nación* had no meaning within the Chilean constitutional tradition.[19] As a result, whether and how the Junta would

intervention, *Bando* No. 5 stated that, despite its initial legitimacy, the Allende government had become "flagrantly illegitimate" because it had repeatedly violated the constitution and the law, destroyed the economy, and fostered a crisis and breakdown of national unity which threatened Chile's internal and external security. These antecedents, the document continued, were sufficient to justify the deposition of Allende in order to "avoid the greater evils that the present vacuum of power might produce, inasmuch as there are no other reasonably successful means to achieve this, our purpose being to reestablish the economic and social normalcy, peace, tranquility, and security of the country which have been lost" (Soto Kloss 1980, 139).

[17] Though drafted and signed on the 12th, D.L. No. 1 was dated retroactively to the 11th and published in the first edition of the official gazette to appear after the coup. It is said that publication was delayed by continued sniping in downtown Santiago which prevented access to the newspaper's headquarters. The first edition of the Diario Oficial after the coup was published on 19, September 1973, but was dated retroactively to September 18, 1973, in a symbolic gesture to Chile's independence day.

[18] For the similarity in inaugural decrees, compare the 1973 decree-laws with *Decreto No. 1,728, de 4 de Junio de 1932*, and *Decreto No. 1,752, de 6 de Junio de 1932*, both in *Contraloría General de la República* 1933. Interview with Sergio Rillón, Santiago, Chile, September 28, 1992. Rillón was legal advisor to the Under Secretary of the Navy from 1961 until the coup. In September 1973 he held the rank of *capitán de navío* – the naval equivalent to the army rank of colonel – in the justice service of the navy. Rillón later went on to hold various legal advisory positions to the military government and was one of Pinochet's closest civilian advisors during the 1990s.

[19] The closest referent in the 1925 constitution (ART. 60) is the description of the President of the Republic as the *Jefe Supremo de la Nación* (Supreme Head of the Nation).

exercise executive, legislative, and constituent functions was left open. The decree-law designated General Pinochet president of the Junta and committed the Junta to respect the independence of the judiciary and to uphold the constitution and the law, but this last pledge was subject to the typical dictatorial proviso that it would be fulfilled "to the extent that the present situation of the country permits" in light of the goals set by the Junta. Regarding the presidency of the Junta, no specific powers were conferred with the title.[20] Rather than an organizational constitution of the structure of military rule, D.L. No. 1 was merely a first instrument to legalize the Junta. It did little to settle uncertainty regarding the scope and bounds of the powers that were to be assumed by the new military regime.

During these first days after the coup, the perceived imperatives of the "present situation" displaced ordinary legal procedures and guarantees. To confront the "emergency" the Junta immediately broadened for itself and subordinate officers the scope of legally permitted discretionary authority. At its first official session on September 13, 1973, the Junta agreed that before emergency situations each commander should resolve situations independently and inform the Junta afterward (*AHJG*, 1, September 13, 1973, 1).[21] Decree-laws were also enacted that delegated broad authority to division commanders and the commanders of emergency zones. This delegation included authority to command, prohibit, and sanction acts that were punishable only because they had been defined as crimes in *bandos* issued by these same officers.[22] During the first few months of military rule, the

In this capacity, the president is responsible for maintaining internal public order and external security within the framework of the law and the constitution (Silva Bascuñán 1963, 223). Rillón claims the expression was mistakenly used due to haste. Interview with Sergio Rillón, Santiago, Chile, September 28, 1992.

[20] ART. 3, D.L. No. 1, D.O., September 18, 1973.

[21] The *Actas de la Honorable Junta de Gobierno (AHJG)*, the minutes of the Junta sessions are not paginated continuously but by session. These documents are cited as follows: (AHJG, session number, date, page number).

[22] These faculties were legal insofar as ART. 75 of the CdJM authorized the partial delegation of exceptional faculties during time of war. D.L. No. 8 (D.O., September 19, 1973) delegated the exercise of military jurisdiction and the dictation of *bandos* to division commanders, while D.L. No. 51 (D.O., October 2, 1973) modified the CdJM to allow the delegation of all faculties and removed a restrictive clause that prohibited the delegation of the faculty of approving sentences imposing the death penalty.

Despite their foundation in law, the definition of crimes by *bandos* was an exception to the principle "*nullum crimen, nulla poena, sine lege*." As Astrosa, the foremost scholar of Chilean military penal law notes, the only limit on the authority to specify crimes by *bando* was that the purpose of the sanctions be to protect the security and discipline of the troops (1985, 133).

**46**

supremacy of law was further undermined by the Junta's decision to temporarily suspend the *Contraloría General de la República*'s review of the legality of administrative decrees and resolutions (*toma de razón*) prior to their going into effect (AHJG, 1, September 13, 1973, 4).[23] In the short run this decision greatly amplified the regulatory prerogative of the military government.

Although the first days after the coup were marked by an implosion of legal norms and an explosion of military prerogative, the armed forces quickly took first steps to centralize and coordinate lawmaking and administrative capacities and to give proper legal form to the regime's first measures and arrogation of government authority. Immediately, a legal advisory and coordinating committee, the *Comité de Asesoría y Coordinación Jurídica de la Junta de Gobierno* (Juridical Advisory and Coordinating Committee of the Government Junta) was created[24] and – virtually within days of the coup – a commission of prominent professors of constitutional law and former politicians, the Constituent Commission, was appointed to begin work on drafting a new constitution. Steps were also taken to halt the initial dispersion and duplication of authority by centralizing the transmission of orders to departmental and provincial commanders through the Ministries of the Interior and National Defense (AHJG, 3, September 16, 1973) and by having the legal advisory committee review all *bandos* before publication (AHJG, 11, September 28, 1973). Toward the same ends, matters that had been regulated by *bandos* were legalized as decree-laws. Thus, for example, Congress, though dissolved by *Bando* No. 29 on September 13, 1973, ten days later was dissolved again by decree-law (D.L. No. 27, D.O., September 24, 1973). This conversion of *bandos* sometimes involved modifying legislation enacted by democratic governments. In this manner, changes decreed by the Junta were incorporated into the formal corpus of the prior legal framework.[25] A series

---

[23] The *Contraloría* and the *toma de razón* are discussed in the next chapter.

[24] The committee was legally established on September 12, 1973 in *Decreto Supremo* (hereafter, *D.S.) No. 668, (Guerra)*, D.O., September 21, 1973. The official staff of the committee consisted of one officer from the justice service of each of the armed forces and *carabineros*. As was customary, it was presided over by the highest ranking officer appointed. This was Capitán de Navío (J) Sergio Rillón, the naval justice officer, and it subsequently became a convention that the navy would appoint the superior officer to legal advisory organs and, thereby, preside over them.

[25] D.L. No. 5 (D.O., September 22, 1973), the first decree-law to modify precoup legislation, is a good example. In addition to clarifying that the state of siege was to be understood juridically as in "state or time-of-war," D.L. No. 5 enacted a number of modifications to the CdJM. These included the addition of a clause authorizing military

of decree-laws was also enacted which built a bridge to prior public law. By this means, prior legal authority and offices were conferred to the Junta or other new de facto officials. This legal link facilitated and validated procedures and appointments within the public administration and decentralized state agencies.

Though this first series of legalistic measures might be imputed to a normative preoccupation with restoring legality among top military officers, nothing in the nature of these first measures warrants such an interpretation. Rather, military concern with legal forms can easily be explained in instrumentally rational terms. First, there is the bureaucratic, hierarchical character of the armed forces and the military's concomitant tradition of operating via formal rules and commands. Yet, the imperatives of administering the state were probably more pressing. As in any modern state (Poggi 1978), law in Chile provided the language through which to address subjects, as well as the means with which to organize, coordinate, and move the multiple offices and bureaucracies that comprise the state apparatus. Insofar as the Chilean state was structured in terms of impersonal, legally rational norms, the Chilean armed forces had no alternative but to make use of legal forms if they were going to effectively take control of the state and assure administrative continuity beyond the first days during which state activities could be suspended and public order handled with purely military commands and coercion.

Although the Junta immediately turned to law as one "language" of rule (and clearly not the only one, given the intensity of the repression), it is striking that during their first months in power the members of the Junta were little concerned with making rules that would specify who would exercise specific powers and regulate how decisions would be made among themselves. We can speculate that a demand for such rules may be likely to arise only when conflicts are anticipated among the members of the decision-making body. Here, differences in experience might explain the sharp contrast between the absence of any initial dictatorial public law in Chile and the immediate promulgation of such a body of law by the Argentine armed forces upon taking power

personnel to use deadly force against anyone attacking the armed forces. D.L. No. 5 also modified the *Ley Sobre Control de Armas* (Arms Control Law, Law 17,798) and the *Ley de Seguridad Interior del Estado* (Law of Internal State Security). The decree-law drastically increased penalties for a variety of offenses and introduced the death penalty for certain violations in time of war. Prior to D.L. No. 5, neither law provided distinct penalties for acts committed during time of war.

in March 1976.[26] The Argentine military's concern with regulating interservice power relations in 1976 and the subsequent dispersion of power within the dictatorship have been attributed to a desire among the different service commanders to prevent any personalization of power as occurred during the de facto presidency of retired Gen. Juan Carlos Onganía, who ruled after 1966 without any military counterbalance once the original military junta was dissolved (Perina 1983, 173; Remmer 1989a, 39). In Chile, such proximate precedents were absent, and a concern with the need for procedural rules emerged only as the dangers and inconveniences of unregulated decision making became apparent. Thus, in the course of 1974 and 1975, the dictatorship's public law was enacted as a by-product of internal conflicts over the nature of the presidency of the Junta, legislative procedures, and the fusion of legislative and executive functions in the Junta.

## 1974–1975: The Separation of Powers

The military overthrow of Allende and the dissolution of Congress immediately translated into a concentration of power within the Junta. At first extreme powers were concentrated in the persons of the four commanders who made up the Junta. In mid-November 1973, the Junta enacted a decree-law to clarify that the term *Mando Supremo de la Nación* implied the full exercise of constituent, legislative, and executive powers;[27] these three powers were indistinguishably embedded within the Junta as a body. The original designation of General Pinochet as president of the Junta was purely nominal and had no juridical or practical import, as the powers and prerogatives of this office were not specified and all members of the Junta were simultaneously engaged in executive and legislative functions. Similarly, active-duty officers from all branches and *carabineros* were fulfilling ministerial responsibilities within the "executive." Though nomenclatural distinctions were utilized to differentiate legislative acts (decree-laws) from executive acts (supreme decrees and resolutions), both functions were indiscriminately fused within the Junta.[28]

---

[26] This formal organization of powers and regulation of executive and legislative procedures set in place on March 24, 1976 in Argentina is analyzed in Groisman 1983 and Fontana 1987.

[27] ART. 1 of D.L. No. 128, D.O., November 16, 1973. The context and reasons for this decree-law are discussed in Chapter 3.

[28] The maintenance of the distinction between law – albeit decree-law – and executive orders was specified and regulated immediately in D.L. No. 2 and D.L. No. 9 (D.O., September 18 and 24, 1973, respectively).

**49**

During the first months of military rule, the Junta met as a body almost daily, usually in marathon secret sessions which ran from mid-morning until late into the evening. In these meetings the Junta resolved upon every type of situation – internal security, appointments, the handling of "prisoners of war," the investigation of crimes allegedly committed by the leaders of the Unidad Popular (UP) government, foreign affairs, economic policy, relations with the judiciary, administrative reorganization – regardless of whether the matter under consideration was properly a competence of government or legislation (AHJG, 1–56, September 12, December 28, 1973).

At first the only differentiation among the members of the Junta was one of functional responsibilities. At its third session (AHJG, 3, September 16, 1973, 1), the Junta members distributed the coordination of the "most important fronts" among themselves: Generals Leigh and Mendoza were given the "internal front," Admiral Merino the "economic front," and all four the "external-military front." This division of labor became the basis for ministerial councils which grouped cabinet members by policy areas. Each was headed by a junta member: Admiral Merino presided over the Economic Council, General Leigh oversaw the Social Council, and General Mendoza was in charge of the Agricultural Council.

In the absence of any external legislative body, at least initially, it appears the members of the Junta saw no need to locate executive and legislative decision making in distinct bodies. This indifference to any separation of powers was evident in the changing institutional dependence of the *Comité de Asesoría y Coordinación Jurídica*, the legal advisory and coordinating committee. At its origins, during the first days of military rule, the committee answered to the Under Secretary of War in the Ministry of Defense, but in late September it became part of a newly created Under Secretary of Juridical Coordination in the *Secretaría General de Gobierno*. The latter was traditionally a non-ministerial office, dependent on the presidency and responsible for advising and coordinating affairs with the cabinet (Silva Bascuñán 1963, 3:253).[29] In early 1974 the committee became part of the *Comité Asesor de la Junta* (Advisory Committee of the Junta, hereafter *COAJ*) which, despite the reference to the Junta in its name, within the regime at least was clearly identified with General Pinochet.

---

[29] The *Subsecretaria de Coordinación Jurídica* was created by D.L. No. 36, D.O., October 2, 1973.

However, in the course of the first half of 1974, this intermingling of legislative and executive functions began to be questioned by top officers in the Junta. The impetus to clarify the legal institutional structure of the military government came from two directions. On one hand, the continued operation of the Supreme Court and the *Contraloría* required that the constitutional structure and powers of the regime be clarified if each of these institutions was to exercise their respective faculties of judicial review and prior legal control of administrative acts (*AOCC*, 13, November 7, 1973, 3–4).[30] On the other, informal decision making proved extremely inefficient and prompted demands to rationalize and clarify the legislative process: Irregular legislative procedures were time consuming, the Junta was promulgating an excessive number of decree-laws, and their hasty dictation often resulted in sloppy legislative technique, which subsequently necessitated additional decree-laws to rectify mistakes.[31] Furthermore, the absence of defined competencies resulted in an overlapping and, at times, contradictory informal division of labor among officers and advisory bodies, and, perhaps most significantly, the absence of known rules and faculties meant that, beyond informal mutual expectations, the roles and powers of the commanders in the Junta were unclear. This void provided fertile ground for the play of personal ambitions and machinations to monopolize power. Eventually such attempts led Admiral Merino and Air Force General Leigh to demand a formal clarification of the Junta's institutional structure and the introduction of a partial separation of legislative and executive functions.

[30] Through session 246 the *Actas Oficiales de la Comisión Constituyente* (hereafter, *AOCC*), the official minutes of the Constituent Commission, were published serially and paginated by session. Thereafter, consecutive pagination was adopted. Henceforth, through session 246, these minutes are cited as follows: (*AOCC*, session number, date, page numbers). The subsequent sessions, which are paginated continuously, are cited simply as: (*AOCC*, page number); when pertinent, the date of the session is mentioned in the text.

[31] The excessive volume of legislation was stressed in an undated memorandum to the Junta urging an overhaul of legislative procedures. Written around April 1974, this document noted that in just six months the Junta had enacted 350 decree-laws, whereas 220 laws per year was the average per year during the five years prior to the coup. Junta de Gobierno, "*Memorandum Sobre Asesoría Jurídica y Trabajo Legislativo de La Junta*," N.D., TD, Guzmán Papers, Fundación Jaime Guzmán, Santiago, Chile.

One of the many examples of poor legislative technique was D.L. No. 77, D.O., October 13, 1973. This decree-law outlawed and dissolved the Left and Marxist political parties, but had to be modified because it omitted one party and referred to another by its colloquial rather than legal name (D.L. No. 145, D.O., November 27, 1973). Similarly, D.L. No. 5, pertaining to the state of siege, was corrected because of deficiencies in legislative technique.

**51**

## Defining the Presidency: The Demise of Rotation

The nondefinition of the powers and term of the presidency of the Junta created a major vacuum during the first months of military rule. D.L. No. 1 designated Pinochet as president of the Junta, but did not define any attributes, term, nor procedures for subrogation or succession. It has been argued (Arriagada 1985, 60–61) that Pinochet was given the title as recompense for his role as "swing-man" in the coup: Although he played a negligible role in planning the coup, Pinochet's acquiescence tipped the balance in its favor.[32] By virtue of seniority in rank, which was the standing rule for determining precedence among officers of equal rank, Gen. Gustavo Leigh, the commander in chief of the air force, ought to have been named president of the Junta.[33] Regardless of why Pinochet was appointed, his designation was probably understood to be temporary since the members of the Junta had informally agreed that the office rotate among them, with one-year terms. This informal commitment, however, was never codified in any legal instrument, and within one year of the coup the rotating presidency had ceased to be an alternative.[34]

The demise of the rotating presidency was part of an operation to strengthen the position of General Pinochet. Unlike Admiral Merino and General Leigh, each of whom had garnered solid support within their respective institutions during the precoup struggle against Allende, General Pinochet's standing in the army was weaker. The prominent army players in preparing the coup were generals and colonels who ranked below General Pinochet, many of whom held important cabinet and administrative positions during the first months after the military takeover. Thus, to consolidate his authority in the army and thereby stabilize his position in the Junta, Pinochet had to achieve ascendancy over these influential army officers. One way to do

[32] The concept of "swing-man" and its importance in military interventions is developed in Needler 1966.

[33] Leigh became commander in chief of the air force on August 18, 1973, Pinochet assumed the rank on August 23, 1973. Pinochet (1982, 114) notes that on September 9, 1973, Leigh reminded him that according to the rule of seniority Leigh should have been president of the Junta.

[34] According to Rear Admiral Huidobro, during the review of the draft of D.L. No. 1, Pinochet objected to the inclusion of any article stipulating a rotating presidency on the ground that this had been the object of a gentlemen's agreement and should remain as such (1989, 265). General Leigh claims that on September 11, he proposed a rotating presidency (Varas 1979, 56). In an early press conference, Pinochet stated that the presidency would rotate (*New York Times*, September 29, 1973). For other accounts, see Arellano Iturriaga 1985, 66; and Arriagada 1985, 150–51.

this was to step out of the coequality of the collegial Junta and attain preeminence.[35]

This strengthening of General Pinochet's position was one of the principal tasks of the COAJ. The COAJ was formed during the last days of September 1973 at the initiative of the army. Its putative purpose was to provide the Junta with ongoing expert, technical advice, by centralizing legislative and policy analysis in one organ. However, the driving objective behind the formation of the COAJ was to strengthen General Pinochet's position and provide him with the counsel that Merino and Leigh both enjoyed but Pinochet lacked.[36] Structured along the lines of a general staff, with a military system of organization and analysis, the staff of the COAJ was dominated by army officers.[37] Since it was involved in the preparation of legal projects, the COAJ also became the umbrella for the judicial advisory and coordinating committee, which was headed by a naval justice officer. According to one account (Cavallo, Salazar, and Sepúlveda 1989, 27), the COAJ's first task was to bury any prospect of a rotating presidency.

The sequence of events between the last months of 1973 and the promulgation of the *Estatuto de la Junta de Gobierno* (D.L. No. 527, D.O., June 26, 1974), which settled the issue of the presidency, is sketchy at best. Still, the available documentation reveals that in the course of defining the legal structure of the Junta, the functions of the

---

[35] An uncontested position within the Junta also would allow Pinochet to further consolidate his position in the army by modifying legal procedures regulating promotions and retirements in the army. This process has been extensively analyzed in Arriagada 1985. As I stress below, despite the common belief to the contrary, Pinochet's authority over the chain of command in his service never extended to the other branches.

[36] Interview with Army General (R) Julio Canessa, Santiago, Chile, July 17, 1992. Canessa was the first head of the COAJ. According to Canessa, General Pinochet had tried to convince the rest of the Junta to accept the COAJ as an organ of the Junta in October 1973. *Carabineros* accepted immediately, Admiral Merino reluctantly accepted, and General Leigh allegedly resisted. Six months later, just before the COAJ was given legal form, General Pinochet acknowledged these earlier "vacillations" (AHJG, 109, April 2, 1974, 2).

[37] According to Col. (R) Arturo Varela, the highest ranking air force representative in the COAJ through January 1975, the number of officers assigned to the COAJ of rank of major or higher by each service was: eight from the army, four each from the navy and *carabineros*, and one from the air force. Colonel Varela later served as Secretary in General Leigh's cabinet and as Gen. Fernando Matthei's sole head of cabinet after General Leigh's ouster from the Junta in 1978. Interview with Col. (R) Arturo Varela, Santiago, Chile, June 6, 1992. Another account maintains that General Leigh had proposed that three of his closest civilian legal counselors enter the COAJ as advisors. Pinochet supposedly accepted, but the appointments were never made (Cavallo et al. 1989, 27).

COAJ itself became a focus of conflicts, drawing attention to the importance of separating executive and legislative functions.

Early on, at the prompting of the Supreme Court, the Junta instructed the chief legal counsel (*auditores*) of the armed forces to collectively work out an organic statute for the Junta (AHJG, 7, September 21, 1973). Although the *auditores* requested the opinion of the Constituent Commission, the commission played a negligible role in defining the legal structure of the Junta. The commission quickly divided over whether the 1925 constitution remained in force, whether it was possible to juridically limit the military's exceptional powers, and whether these included the use of constituent powers, a discussion to which I return in the following chapter. Once the Junta decided to submit the legal regulation of the Junta to the General Staff of National Defense, the highest interservice body, the commission's participation came to an end (AOCC, 16, November 13, 1973, 4).[38]

The stratagems that eventually precipitated a resolution on the presidency were worked out in the COAJ and the *Secretaría General de Gobierno* (*SGdG*). The documents that survive clearly indicate that the opposition "collegial-versus-presidential rule" was superimposed upon different perceptions of the purpose and duration of military power. Arguments against a rotating presidency took a number of forms. One memo, for example, stressed that collegial rule was impractical and would have divisive consequences at a mass level if the junta members remained on equal standing.[39] Another document, drafted by the *Comité Creativo* (Creative Committee) of the SGdG, examined the presidency in light of the historical options before the Junta. These alternatives were posed as a choice of becoming either a mere "historical parenthesis," understood as a transitory regime which would eventually return power to the previous political class and face the prospect of retributive justice, or a regime that lays the foundations for an enduring "new stage" in Chile's history, which upon a return to democracy would be sustained by a "new civic movement." This second option, it

---

[38] The only legal by-product of the commission's review was a draft of D.L. No. 128, which, as already noted, clarified the term *Mando Supremo*. When the Statute of the Junta was ready for promulgation, Enrique Ortúzar, the president of the Constituent Commission, refused to attend the public ceremony held to mark the promulgation of the statute because the commission had not reviewed the decree-law (AOCC, 48, June 25, 1974, 2).

[39] As the memorandum noted, despite his title, General Pinochet remained one among equals; only the title differentiated him from the other Junta members, and in official acts no differentiations were made. *Memorandum*, December 4, 1973, Guzmán Papers, Fundación Jaime Guzmán, Santiago, Chile, p. 5.

was argued, required an extended period of military rule that would be facilitated by a prompt renunciation of a collegial executive, and was held to be far more attractive than facing the judgment of civilians in the short run.[40]

The prospect of extended military rule, however, was not embraced by all junta members, nor was it accepted by all army generals, and these associations charged the institutional question since its association with a foundational strategy greatly altered the stakes in any institutional definition. The payoffs no longer were limited to the relative power positions of the respective commanders in chief, but now included the perceived costs and benefits of opting for extended military dictatorship. In 1974, any such commitment represented a profound break with Chile's constitutional and military traditions, as well as an open rupture with widespread civilian expectations that the armed forces were engaged for a relatively brief period of emergency military rule which would be followed shortly by a return to democratic and constitutional normalcy.[41]

---

[40] Comité Creativo, "*Memorandum: La Junta y su opción como destino histórico. Implicancias proximas*" [1973], TD, Guzmán Papers, Fundación Jaime Guzmán, Santiago, Chile. This document includes a prescient analysis of how "success" can affect later appraisal of the past (pp. 2–3). It argued that if the Junta stood only as a historical parenthesis, it would soon be judged by democratic criteria for a number of acts. The document explicitly mentioned the bombing of the Moneda, the suicide of Allende, the many executions handed down by war councils, the detention of political prisoners on islands and in jails, the dissolution of Congress, the legal proscription of Marxist parties and publications, press censorship, the indefinite recess of the democratic parties, the cancellation of the mandate of municipal councilmen, the intervention of the universities, and the total suspension of all forms of university autonomy. The document claimed that such conflictive measures could only be justified if the military succeeded in creating a new order. Only new creation could give these acts meaning and modify the criteria by which they are judged. As an example, the document pointed to the differing fates of the leader of a failed military coup who goes to jail for sedition and the head of a successful coup who assumes power and is recognized as chief of state. The document insisted that an identical moral act could receive a radically different historical judgment if it opened up a new destiny for a society. From the perspective of opening up a new historical period, the document concluded that the Junta should not fear being ruthless, but rather consider such force the key to success.

[41] During the first months of military rule many sectors, both civilian and military, appear to have expected the military interregnum to last only three to four years, with November 1976, the date Allende's term was to have expired, standing as a symbolically charged limit. Shortly after the coup, for example, Patricio Aylwin, then PDC president and head of the hard-line, right-wing faction of the party, stated, "Two or three years will suffice to have the country return to democratic legality" (*Ercilla*, October 24, 1973). However, some civilian media, particularly *El Mercurio* and *Qué Pasa*, quickly developed a foundational discourse to justify prolonged military rule. The ideological trajectory of this argument and its imbrication with neoliberal restructuring are carefully reconstructed in Vergara 1985.

Settling the nature of the presidency therefore assumed proportions far broader than merely defining an office and its faculties. General Pinochet's machinations to be named President of the Republic were part and parcel of a scheme to institute an absolute dictatorship. The discovery of this operation triggered crises in December 1973 and April 1974,[42] and precipitated a resolution in June 1974 after a nonarmy officer became aware of the contents of a draft statute for the Junta being elaborated in the COAJ.[43] A sense of the intent of these maneuvers and the opposition they elicited can be gleaned from a preliminary draft of the Statute of the Junta, which has been preserved in the legislative archive of the Junta and is marked with penciled-in corrections.[44]

The draft of a statute for the Junta, which differs markedly from the decree-law enacted, was not merely a proposal or outline of intentions, but a fully articulated statute, structured by title, paragraph, and article. Its most significant and controversial provisions concerned the presidency and decision rules for legislation. ART. 3 proposed to bestow upon the president of the Junta the title President of the Republic and foreclosed any rotating presidency by confining the office to the officer heading an order of institutional precedence and by not mentioning any term of office.[45] With regard to legislative powers, ART. 10 of the draft entailed the elimination of the the informal convention that Junta decisions be taken unanimously, as the draft proposed that decree-laws

---

Until the promulgation of the 1980 constitution, the Junta never legally codified a *plazo* (term) for the duration of military rule. D.L. No. 1 referred only to the Junta's mission, its "patriotic commitment to restore *Chilenidad*, justice, and the institutionality" which had been systematically broken (*quebrantados*) and destroyed by the foreign ideology of Marxism. With regard to specifying a term limit, as with so many other potentially divisive resolutions, the guiding principle within the Junta appears to have been to postpone any debate and resolution until absolutely necessary. An additional strategic dimension argued against setting any term: within the regime it was understood that the mere announcement of a *plazo* would precipitate immediate political reactivation.

[42] Air Force General Nicanor Díaz (1988, 112), then second-ranking officer in the General Staff of National Defense, as well as coordinator (through April 1974) of all military intelligence services, recounts being informed by a member of naval intelligence that General Pinochet was plotting to do away with the Junta and have himself named President of the Republic. The British news weekly *Latin America* reported (January 18, 1974) rumors of tensions between Admiral Merino and General Pinochet over the presidency. Díaz also mentions sharp encounters between General Leigh and General Pinochet over this issue in April 1974.

[43] Off-the-record interview. Santiago, Chile, December 14, 1992.

[44] "*Anteproyecto Estatuto de la Junta de Gobierno*," in D.L. No. 527, in *Trans. y Antec.* – D.L., vol. 19, 279–81.

[45] The order was: army, navy, air force, *carabineros*.

be approved by absolute majority and that the president hold a deciding fifth vote to settle any ties. Unanimity was to be retained only to
enact modifications to the constitution.[46]

Had these two provisions been accepted, relations of power within
the Junta would have been radically altered. Of the two modifications,
adoption of the title President of the Republic had fewer immediate
ramifications. Though largely symbolic, the move nonetheless con-
noted an open break with Chile's deeply legalistic, constitutional tradition in which titles were meaningful and not merely symbolic. In
Chile, President of the Republic implied a popularly elected head of
state, whereas the Junta was unabashedly a de facto government: To
attach the title of the former to the head of the latter was to blatantly
belie the Junta's initial claim to be a regime of exception intent on
restoring the supremacy of law and the constitution.[47] Far more consequential would have been any departure from the convention of
unanimous decision. Legislating by absolute majority, with General
Pinochet holding a swing vote, in practice implied a dictatorship of the
commander in chief of the army, free from any limitation by the other
commanders. Regardless of any semblance of a separation of executive and legislative functions, under such an arrangement Pinochet
would have been free to legislate at will since General Mendoza, the
head of *carabineros*, was in an extremely weak and dependent position after the coup and rarely, if ever, adopted stances at odds with the
commander in chief of the army. With Mendoza's vote largely assured,
General Pinochet would have been in a position to force a tie and use
his second vote to dominate as he deemed expedient. The suppression
of unanimous decision making was a formula for a dictatorship of the
army president.

## D.L. No. 527: The *Estatuto de la Junta de Gobierno*

There is no documentation of the deliberations and decision-making
process that led up to the promulgation of D.L. No. 527, the Statute of

---

[46] As a positive rule, unanimity was inscribed in decree-law for the first time only in June
1974 in D.L. No. 527. Prior to this decree-law, D.L. No. 128 had only mentioned that
valid decree-laws required the signature of all four Junta members. The unanimity decision rule later was also inscribed in Transitory Disposition 18 of the 1980 Constitution.

[47] After his destitution, General Leigh (Varas 1979, 59) claimed that he opposed the adoption of the title along similar grounds and that Admiral Merino shared his position.
This is likely, as Admiral Merino was consistently a constitutional conservative and an
opponent of toying with the 1925 constitution.

the Junta (*Estatuto de la Junta de Gobierno*).[48] Nevertheless, the eventual text of statute reveals that the momentous proposals contained in the earlier proposal did not prosper – neither the title President of the Republic nor the adoption of majority rule were accepted.[49] Nor did the statute grant Pinochet powers to manipulate promotions and retirements in the other forces. The statute put an end to any doubts about whether the presidency would rotate by adopting the formula proposed in the preliminary draft: The presidency would correspond to the incumbent in the first slot of precedence (D.L. No. 527, ART. 7), General Pinochet, rather than be designated by the Junta as in D.L. No. 1. Pinochet did win his battle to use the title President of the Republic, at the end of 1974.[50]

Aside from the glaring fact that D.L. No. 527 regulated a de facto government whose supremacy ultimately rested on force, the Statute of the Junta was noteworthy in two respects: It consisted exclusively of constituent provisions and its enumeration of powers did not significantly depart from the 1925 constitution. D.L. No. 527 contained no declarations of principles, nor provisions regulating substantive policy areas, and in large measure merely adapted constitutional powers to the context of exceptional military rule. The concordance with the 1925 constitution is striking. The articles that enumerate powers (ART. 5, 9–10), particularly executive powers, are verbatim reproductions from the 1925 constitution (ART. 45, 71–72, respectively)

---

[48] The Statute of the Junta was promulgated as D.L. No. 527, D.O., June 26, 1974. Soto Kloss's (1980) compilation of the Junta's "constitutional" law up to the 1980 constitution reprints this decree-law. The absence of any record in the minutes of the Junta sessions may be read as evidence of the controversial nature of this proposal. During the first years of military rule, "difficult" legislation was often debated in private sessions with only the four Junta members in attendance. In these situations the absence of legal counsel, the alleged urgency of resolution, and the imperative of maintaining the unity of the Junta apparently were often deployed to pressure for acquiescence to controversial legislation. Such experiences may have also contributed to Admiral Merino and General Leigh's insistence that standard legislative procedures be agreed upon and formally instituted. In interviews, military officials who had worked in the COAJ and civilian legal advisors to the Junta were consistently evasive when I asked about the circumstances leading up to D.L. No. 527. At most, they acknowledged that my interpretation that the statute was promulgated to regulate internal differences "might be correct."

[49] ART. 2 inscribed for the first time the all-important unanimity decision rule, "The Government Junta will adopt its decisions by the unanimity of its members."

[50] This decision was made in a private session and promulgated in D.L. No. 806, D.O., December 17, 1974. General Leigh presents his account in Varas 1979, 59–60. The introductory paragraphs of the decree-law invoked the separation of powers instituted by D.L. No. 527 and the need to "maintain the nation's historic tradition" as reasons for using this title.

with only occasional modifications to remove references to Congress or, in some subsections, to require consultation with or agreement from the Junta.

The regulation of the president's powers clearly reveals this borrowing from precedent. The president of the Junta, like the president of the Republic in the 1925 constitution (ART. 71), was responsible for the administration and government of the state, and held broad authority to maintain public order and external security. At least nominally, the Statute of the Junta (ART. 9) committed the president to ruling according to law – his authority could be exercised only in "accordance with the present Statute, the Constitution, and the laws." The "special attributes" of the president were identical to those found in the 1925 constitution, with the Junta's agreement required whenever approval by the Senate had previously been stipulated.[51] The Junta did, however, depart from the 1925 constitution when it limited the president's traditional power to freely appoint his cabinet, undersecretaries, intendents, and governors by requiring Junta confirmation for each of these appointments (ART. 10, no. 3) and when it required the president to consult the Junta whenever he appointed higher court magistrates, granted private pardons, or deployed the armed forces (ART. 9, no. 4, 10, 11, respectively).[52]

Notwithstanding the many appropriations from the 1925 constitution, the Junta did not follow precedent when it defined executive-military relations. One of the more controversial provisions of the military's 1980 constitution is the restriction of the president's traditional prerogative of naming and retiring at will the commanders in chief of the armed forces. Yet strikingly the commanders of the armed forces in 1974 were not willing to grant such authority to a president drawn from their own ranks. This is significant, as D.L. No. 527 is usually seen as a first step in the consolidation of Pinochet's personal

---

[51] Senate agreement had been required under the 1925 constitution when the president appointed ambassadors; conferred the ranks of colonel (or the equivalent naval rank, *Capitán de Navío*) or higher; or commanded the armed forces in person (ART. 72, no. 5, 7, 14, respectively). ART. 14 of D.L. No. 527 also required Junta agreement in all other instances where Senate agreement was required – whether in the constitution or by statute – to appoint or dismiss an official.

[52] Compare ART. 72, no. 5, 6, 12, 13, respectively, of the 1925 constitution. The requirement of Junta confirmation of ministerial appointments was later indirectly modified by D.L. No. 966, D.O., April 12, 1975. D.L. No. 527 also required the signature of Junta members to order unauthorized expenditures during exceptional situations (ART. 9, no. 8). Under the 1925 constitution this had traditionally been a presidential power, the exercise of which required the concurrence of all cabinet members (ART. 72, no. 10).

power over the armed forces as a whole. However, the statute did not extend to the president of the Junta; in some instances, it actually restricted traditional presidential powers regarding military promotions.

Following the principle of Junta agreement as a substitute for Senate confirmation, the statute followed the 1925 constitution in having the president confer the highest ranks subject to Junta agreement. In the statute, the ranks conferred were restricted to general and admiral (D.L. No. 527, ART. 13).[53] This decision limited the range of officers subject to designation by the president, which in all cases was limited by the requirement of Junta unanimity. Pinochet held no authority to unilaterally interfere with the chain of command in the different services of the armed forces. The most significant restriction upon the president of the Junta's authority concerned the position of commander in chief. In contrast to constitutional presidents, the military president retained no authority to appoint or retire the commanders in chief of the armed forces. The only provision for replacement of junta members was in the event of "death, resignation, or any type of absolute impediment" (ART. 18). In these cases, the succeeding commander in chief would be designated by the remaining members of the Junta. Thus, contrary to what is widely believed, Pinochet's discretionary powers over the army did not extend into the other services.

These modifications to the traditional powers of the president suggest that the commanders of the navy and the air force defended the autonomy of their respective services. As they had done when they defended the unanimity decision rule, these commanders reasserted their original positions of power by limiting external interference within their respective services, thereby securing their authority as commanders in chief. This personal authority of all junta members was further consolidated a year and a half later when the Junta enacted a decree-law which released the commanders in chief from standing legal regulations stipulating obligatory retirement upon reaching maximum service limits (D.L. No. 1,640, D.O., December 30, 1976).[54]

---

[53] By ART. 72, no. 7 of the 1925 constitution, subject to Senate confirmation, the president conferred the ranks of colonel, captain of the navy, and the various ranks of general and admiral. On the process of evaluation, retirement, and promotion in the armed forces prior to 1973, see Arriagada 1985, 167–73.

[54] The standing legal norms required retirement upon completing thirty-eight years as an officer and forty years of service. This decree-law accompanied D.L. No. 1,639 (D.O., December 30, 1976), which allowed the president to maintain higher ranking officers (generals in the army, air force, and *carabineros*, and vice admirals and rear admirals in the navy) in active service beyond these same service limits if they were performing

As a result, in contrast to military practices during the 1976–1983 dictatorship in Argentina, the Chilean commanders freed themselves from norms which would have required retirements and changes in the composition of the Junta. The members of the Junta thus transformed their existing positions into posts without any temporal limit.

With respect to constituent and legislative powers, the Statute of the Junta had little to say (ART. 4–6), further suggesting that the principal purpose of the decree-law was to settle the issue of the presidency. For obvious reasons, the statute was silent about the generation of the legislative power, and provided no mechanisms for impeaching public authorities or for scrutinizing (*fiscalización*) acts of government. However, the organic statute did differ from the constitution by limiting the colegislative faculties of the president: The Junta was granted legislative initiative in areas of government spending and taxation which previously had been the exclusive initiative of the president.[55] Otherwise, the statute left the enactment of procedures and organs for exercising legislative and constituent faculties to future regulation in a complementary decree-law (ART. 6).

## Defining Legislative Procedures

The Junta began to work on the regulation of legislative procedures immediately following the promulgation of the Statute of the Junta. It is telling that these deliberations rapidly gave rise to explicit demands for a separation of functions and in early 1975 culminated in the decision to create the *Secretaría de Legislación* and the *Comisiones Legislativas*. Once again, a COAJ move to arrogate control over the formation of decree-laws fueled controversy, prompting Admiral Merino and General Leigh to insist upon the need to separate executive and legislative functions and to enact legislative procedures which would institutionalize this separation.

After the promulgation of D.L. No. 527, legislative procedures were first discussed toward the end of July 1974 (AHJG, 141, July 30, 1974, 3–9). During the first discussion, General Canessa, the head of the COAJ, presented a general overview of the deficiencies of the existing

government functions. These extensions at all times were subject to Pinochet's discretion. On these two decree-laws, see Arriagada 1985, 138–42.

[55] These restrictions on the legislative initiative of Congress had been introduced by a 1943 constitutional reform and further extended by the 1970 reform (Silva Bascuñán 1963, 3:168–72; Evans 1970, 91–93; and Evans 1973, 39–45).

system and suggested an alternative procedure along with justificatory documents and a draft decree-law regulating legislative procedures. Canessa's criticism stressed that existing informal procedures lacked steps which would assure that the decree-laws enacted concurred with the overall policies of the Junta. He noted that bills arrived directly from an interested Ministry, were given a legal, though not political, review in the Juridical Advisory and Coordinating Committee (sometimes this step was omitted), and only in the final stages, once it was ready to be signed, was the bill presented to the Junta. Often, the number of projects or their urgency prevented each member from studying each project in detail, and decree-laws were often signed independently by each junta member. Furthermore, he argued, given the ease with which the Junta could legislate, ministries were seeking legislation to resolve relatively minor difficulties. As Canessa noted, an excessive number of decree-laws were being promulgated, and these were often exceedingly regulatory, difficult to apply, and in need of frequent modification. The greatest drawback that he perceived was that contradictory decree-laws were being enacted, which he attributed to the lack of a common policy (AHJG, 141, July 30, 1974, 4–6).[56] This morass of legislation he concluded could only produce legal uncertainty.

Canessa proposed that a mechanism be instituted to limit ministerial legislative ambitions and to assure full participation of the Junta in legislating. He advocated that the COAJ itself stand as the filter between the ministries and the Junta, giving it responsibility for preparing and coordinating all legislative projects. In this proposal, regardless of their origin in the executive or the Junta, the COAJ would play a major role in the review of legislative initiatives: After receiving ministerial initiatives and background materials, the COAJ would inform the Junta of the project's content and present "a judgement concerning the conformity of the project with the legislative policies of the Government Junta and the government's action" (AHJG, 141, July 30, 1974, Annex 1c, ART. 9). If the Junta approved the idea of legislating (*idea de legislar*), the project would return to the COAJ with broad guidelines and observations. There, in coordination with the ministries and the legal advisory and coordinating committee, a definitive draft and alterna-

---

[56] Canessa presented to the Junta the example of wage policies: A number of decree-laws had enacted wage increases, but it wasn't clear whether the increases specified were minimum or maximum increases, a question unresolved by the contradictory positions sustained by the Ministry of Labor and the Ministry of Economics (AHJG, 141, July 30, 1974, 5).

tives would be prepared (Junta initiatives would begin at this step). This final draft would then be presented to the Junta, which would approve, reject, or amend the bill. Additionally, Canessa advocated allowing the president, upon COAJ recommendation, to skip all steps prior to the verbal presentation to the Junta, if it was deemed that a bill did not directly relate to or affect the legislative policies of the Junta or the government (ART. 13).

The COAJ's presumption to intervene in the legislative process as the standard bearer of a unique, known "legislative policy" of the Junta and the government implied a tremendous source of – and claim to – power and influence in the everyday workings of the military government. These implications must not have escaped the other commanders in chief. After Canessa's presentation, General Leigh insisted that, despite his support for regulating legislative procedures, the legislative committee had to be directly dependent upon the Junta and wholly separate and independent from the COAJ. Only in this manner, he argued, could legislative powers be adequately separated from the executive. Admiral Merino backed this position, and despite General Canessa's rejoinder that a separation of executive and legislative powers would be detrimental, the Junta returned the proposal to the COAJ with instructions to prepare a new project incorporating General Leigh and Admiral Merino's positions (AHJG, 141, July 30, 1974, 9).

The regulation of legislative procedures did not appear on the agenda again until March 1975, when it was the sole topic of a day-long session, followed by a series of sessions which were exclusively dedicated to the legislative process until agreement was reached in mid-April 1975. At the first of these sessions the new head of the COAJ, Army General Aníbal Labarca, presented a proposal only slightly different from Canessa's original formula. In response, General Leigh immediately voiced disagreement. The project, he argued, "interferes in connection with the substance of the separation that should exist between the executive area and the legislative area. . . . the Advisory Committee continues to be the central nucleus of the system" (AHJG, 184, March 12, 1975, 3). Leigh proceeded to present an alternative decree-law that separated legislative procedures by creating a Legislative Council, composed of two representatives for each member of the Junta, which would handle all steps in the study of legislative projects: elaboration, commentary, drafting, and exposition before the Junta. Admiral Carvajal, who sat in for Admiral Merino at this session, supported Leigh's position immediately, and an extended discussion ensued on the shortcomings of unregulated decree-law making, the

COAJ's role, and the need for a separation of powers (AHJG, 184, March 12, 1975, 4, 5–17).

It should be stressed that the need to specify legislative procedures was explicitly posed as a problem of separation of powers. As Leigh noted, the foundation for his project was the "independence of government legislation from the other Powers of the State" (AHJG, 184, March 12, 1975, 6). Once Labarca insisted upon granting a central role to the COAJ, Leigh underscored the need for a separation of powers: "The Advisory Committee is reviewing absolutely everything. The Advisory Committee is using its legislative organ for every matter, of any order, whether executive, legislative, or general. The spirit of what we want is to separate the legislative function, not leave it located in the Advisory Committee" (AHJG, 184, March 12, 1975, 8).

There were a variety of concerns behind the navy and the air force's demand for a separation of powers. The most general motivation was efficiency: The confusion of powers and lack of clear procedures had resulted in a practical disaster. As General Leigh remarked, so many decree-laws were being promulgated that the Junta was "creating a veritable juridical jungle."[57] Another impetus was to prevent officers from other services from making inroads into areas of authority held by Admiral Merino and General Leigh. For example, after the formation of the Juridical Advisory and Coordinating Committee, this organ – as well as its subsequent institutional permutations – was always presided over by a navy justice officer, even after it became a subsection within the COAJ. The committee was the butt of COAJ analysts, who disparaged its narrowly juridical and technical focus. This legalism, they claimed, left the Junta without the political counsel needed to coordinate and consolidate the Junta's policy, a void which the COAJ was eager to fill. For the navy to retain its institutional position within the legislative process, it had to block these pretensions of the army-dominated COAJ.

These conflicts with the COAJ also reflected substantive policy differences. After the coup, the navy had been in charge of economic policy and had brought into the government the civilian, neoliberal economists who came to dominate economic policy and planning. The economic section of the COAJ, on the other hand, was staffed by pro-statist,

---

[57] Leigh attributed this situation to the lack of a clear set of procedures: "The system must be trimmed; it depresses me to see how up until now projects arrive to each member of the Junta, individually, without any antecedents and without any exposition" (AHJG, 184, March 12, 1975, 4, 6).

nationalist, army economists, who were viewed with apprehension by the economists in ODEPLAN, the planning office which was the seedbed for neoliberal economic restructuring. Therefore, limiting the COAJ's influence in the legislative process was also key for the navy's project of economic restructuring.[58] Finally, a separation of the executive and legislative functions was also of interest to General Pinochet since it might contribute to the consolidation of the presidency.

The separation of legislative and executive functions was also understood to involve a separation of persons. Thus, at first it was agreed that the preliminary decision on initiating legislation would be the exclusive competence of Admiral Merino, General Leigh, and General Mendoza, who together would also direct the study and elaboration of all projects. General Pinochet would return only at the final stage of exposition and resolution on a project, though he would be allowed to submit observations at any stage (AHJG, 184, March 12, 1975, 6–9, 13–16). Similarly, the possibility of organizing the system with extensive involvement of the ministerial councils, which General Leigh had initially suggested, was eventually abandoned since it would have detracted personnel from the executive. Cabinet ministers, consequently, were restricted to informing on projects of their competency (AHJG, 184, March 12, 1975, 10–12, 14; 185, March 12, 1975, 4–5).

However, the division of labor by policy area in the ministerial councils became the basis for three legislative commissions which were to process and prepare all projects within their respective areas of expertise. Each commission was presided over by a Junta member. On the principle that General Pinochet should be excluded from the elaboration of decree-laws, no legislative commission was created for him.[59] A special fourth legislative commission was also created to handle matters of national defense. This commission differed from the others in that its structure reproduced the collegial composition of the Junta. At one point it was agreed that Admiral Merino would also preside over

---

[58] On the symbiosis of the navy and the free market economists, see Fontaine 1988. Tensions with the COAJ are discussed on pp. 73–74.

[59] These areas of competence, which had been decided on earlier, were formally specified in the supreme decree regulating legislative procedures (ART. 2, D.S. No. 220, D.O., April 21, 1976). The division was as follows:

Commission I (Navy): Finance; Economics; Development and Reconstruction; Mining; and Foreign Relations.

Commission II (Air Force): Interior; Labor and Social Welfare; Education; Public Health and Justice.

Commission III (*Carabineros*): Agriculture; Land and Settlement; Public Works; Housing and Urbanization; and Transportation.

this commission (AHJG, 189, April 9, 1975, 5), but this was never specified in any regulation or decree-law.

Once the basic scheme was agreed on, the text was refined in subsequent sessions as organizational details were worked out.[60] One important innovation was the creation of the *Secretaría de Legislación*, which was to stand as the heart of the legislative system. As the locus of formal juridical analysis and coordination, the Secretary of Legislation was to coordinate the flow of projects and documentation through the system. The Junta reached agreement and signed the text of the decree-law organizing the legislative system on April 17, 1975, but delayed publication to allow a dry run and to draft regulations governing the legislative commissions and the Secretary of Legislation. Shortly afterward, a preliminary version of the regulation was agreed to and the appointment of commission members began (AHJG, 196, May 15, 1975, 5). Judging from the minutes of the Junta, it appears that the Junta began to work under the new rules in Session 208: This is the first session identified as a "Secret Legislative Session," previous sessions had been identified only as "Secret Session" (AHJG, 208, June 24, 1975, 1). D.L. No. 991 itself was only published on January 3, 1976, once the legislative system was already up and running.

### D.L. No. 991

The legislative procedures established in D.L. No. 991 and its complementary regulations (D.S. (J) 220, D.O., April 21, 1976) unquestionably rationalized the process of legislation. In contrast to the preceding informal system, the new procedure specified a precise sequence of steps – with deadlines along the way – for the presentation, juridical analysis, elaboration, amendment, and approval of legislative initiatives.

Bills entered the system through the Secretary of Legislation, where the secretary confirmed that the bill entered with the required supplementary documentation, assigned it to the corresponding superintending commission, distributed the bill to the other commissions, and prepared a purely juridical review of the bill's substantive legal implications, formal articulation, effect on existent legislation, and concordance with the overall legal system. The Secretary of Legislation did not review the merit or expediency of the projects reviewed. These

---

[60] Legislative procedures were refined in Junta sessions 188, 189, and 191, held on April 8, 9, 16, 1975, respectively.

political and technical matters were the prerogative of the legislative commissions.

Notwithstanding the division of labor by policy areas, each commission drafted and presented observations on all bills to the corresponding commission overseeing each particular bill. This commission then further studied the initiative, incorporated any observations and objections, and attempted to produce as harmonious a draft as possible. Articles still subject to disagreement were presented with the alternative redactions in dispute. The revised bill, accompanied by a brief explaining modifications and the positions of each commission, then returned to the Secretary of Legislation for elevation to the Junta. D.L. No. 991 also provided restricted procedures for handling classified projects.[61] Yet, except under duly qualified circumstances, no other procedures could be used to process decree-laws (ART. 29).

In this manner, in conjunction with the Secretary of Legislation, the legislative commissions provided an organization for simultaneously processing multiple legal initiatives. The provision for careful, independent study and the articulation of contending positions lessened the burden on the Junta as a body since the ongoing working of the system delimited areas of consensus and disagreement prior to final consideration of the bill within the full Junta.

With only slight modification in 1981 to bring it into line with the constitution, the system of legislative commissions functioned until the termination of military rule in 1990. Despite the common characterization of the Junta as a rubber stamp legislature, this system provided an institutional foundation for each commander to deliberately elaborate independent positions. At all stages these procedural rules granted opportunities for voice and, notwithstanding the immersion of the overall system in secrecy, the legislative process was structured internally according to principles of publicity and transparency. By law, the Secretary of Legislation had to distribute to each legislative commission copies of all documents entering or moving within the system – all bills, reports, commission observations, and amendments had to be distributed regardless of origin. In this manner, procedural mechanisms were constructed that permitted each junta member to articulate and represent opinions and disagreements from the outset on all

---

[61] Pursuant to ART. 27 of D.L. No. 991, classified projects were subject to an alternate set of procedures which excluded the regular members of the commission from participating, restricted study and review of bills to the commander and his immediate military legal counsel, and required verbal rather than written reporting.

legislative proposals, as well as to individually initiate legislation on any matter.[62]

Although the power of final decision remained an exclusive competence of the Junta, it is misleading to minimize the importance of the legislative commissions because they "enjoyed no decision-making autonomy" (Huneeus 1997, 76). The legislative commissions were not ancillary groupings of civilian advisors whose counsel could be heeded or ignored by the Junta. Rather, the legislative commissions were the central working organs through which each commander elaborated a concrete position on the myriad of legislative proposals before the Junta. As will be seen repeatedly in subsequent chapters, this system assured each commander in chief the legal counsel and institutional time that is essential for developing informed positions on matters of legislation. In this sense, regular legislative procedures were an important safeguard against the artifice of imposing decree-laws on grounds of urgency or the need to maintain the unity of the Junta, a ruse that had been repeatedly used prior to the enactment of D.L. No. 991 and the creation of the Legislative Commissions. In conjunction with the unanimity decision rule, the newly created legislative system gave each commander channels to effectively influence the content of decree-laws or, when irredeemably subject to objections, block them from becoming law.

## Personalization and Authoritarian Institutional Constraints

By mid-1975, after a period of unregulated power, the Junta had completed the codification of its internal procedures and organization. Whereas executive and legislative powers initially were fused and the only decision rule was unanimity, by mid-1975 a legal system which clearly differentiated powers – in function, competencies, and personnel – and specified positive procedural rules for making rules had been instituted. As I have documented, these arrangements introduced a separation of powers at the apex of a highly concentrated system of power. Pinochet emerged with the presidency in his hands, but the other commanders in chief defended and institutionalized their role in the legislative process, thereby setting in place a first institutional

---

[62] ART. 13 of D.L. No. 991 tacitly modified D.L. No. 527 by allowing Junta members to individually initiate legislation (Guzmán Dinator 1978, 51). Under the Statute of the Junta, legislative initiative was an exclusive power of the Junta de Gobierno as a body (ART. 5), thereby requiring unanimity at the outset to review a project. Under D.L. No. 991, bills could be introduced without having to first gain support of the Junta.

**68**

check. We will see that this check was decisive in all subsequent institutional developments, particularly the decision to enact the 1980 constitution and in allowing the constitution to operate as a limit upon both the military executive and the legislative junta during 1981 through 1990.

Despite the key role it played throughout the years of military rule, the legislative junta and any possibility of institutional constraints internal to the regime have generally been dismissed in scholarly accounts of military rule in Chile. In part, the distortions in these interpretations may be attributed to the Junta's nonpublic operation and the unavailability until recently of any documentation of its operation. Yet, these accounts also stand on fallacious inferences drawn from Pinochet's simultaneous retention of the post of commander in chief of the army and president, as well as the unanimity decision rule. Typically, Pinochet's position as commander in chief of the army and president emerges as the cornerstone for characterizing the dictatorship as "personalist": as commander in chief, Pinochet molds and manipulates the army, checking any internal challenges to his dominance; as president, he attains policy control and subordinates the commanders of the other forces to mere legislative activities, which purportedly he dominated as well.[63] From this perspective, "one-man rule," uncontested control of the "executive-army high command," and a "sultanistic" institutional structure allowed Pinochet to avoid the corrosive factionalism, inter-military divisions, and subsequent institutional pressures for military withdrawal which scholars have identified as factors that explain the lesser longevity of military as against personalist or single-party regimes.[64] Command of the army and control of the executive are thus extended to imply absolute dominance and freedom from any limits arising out of the original collegial structure of the Junta and its institutionalization during 1974–1975.

[63] Variants of this interpretation can be found in Huneeus and Olave 1987; Huneeus 1988; Remmer 1989a, 1989b; Constable and Valenzuela 1991; Spooner 1994; and Valenzuela 1995. This characterization is also widely accepted in broader comparative works. See, for example, Geddes 1995.

[64] Geddes (1995; 1999) provides a game theoretical explanation of differences in regime durability among military, personalistic, and one-party regimes in terms of the structure of incentives characteristic of each regime type as well as time-series data confirming the greater longevity of personalistic and one-party regimes. Remmer (1989a, 40), on a set of Latin American cases, also presents evidence of the greater durability of what she calls "sultanistic military regimes." For an argument that personalization does not necessarily produce military regime cohesion, see Isaacs 1993, 105–13. The characterizations cited respectively correspond to Valenzuela (1995), Varas (1995), and Remmer (1989a).

This section highlights the comparative distinctiveness of institutional limits in Chile by way of a critical examination of the position of the presidency and unanimity in the personalization of power argument. Note that the personalist characterization of military rule in Chile is built upon two aspects of Pinochet's tenure during the military regime: (a) the simultaneous concentration of the powers of the presidency and those of commander in chief of the army, and (b) the absence of any replacement of the president in the course of the sixteen and a half years of military rule. Both are undeniable and comparatively atypical facts. However, the issue is whether they imply absolute dominance and an absence of limits within the Junta. Must a unipersonal presidency be incompatible with constraints set by another body? I don't think so and I insist that proponents of personalization fail to demonstrate Pinochet's dominance over the other members of the Junta. I will proceed to develop these points and highlight the comparative significance of the Chilean case in three steps. First, I will acknowledge the largely exceptional character of Pinochet's dual status as commander in chief and president. Subsequently, I will highlight the weakness of claims made about Pinochet's dominance of lawmaking, and I will conclude by emphasizing how Pinochet's inability to mold the composition of the Junta allowed it to operate as a limit, a point whose significance becomes apparent once the Chilean Junta is compared with legislatures in other authoritarian regimes, particularly the Franquist Cortes and the Brazilian congress during 1964–1985.

### The Military as Institution and as Government

Advocates of the personalization approach underscore Pinochet's extraordinary position within the dictatorship by comparison with the attributes of other heads of authoritarian regimes. These comparisons tend to be organized around the relationship between the "military as government" and the "military as institution," that is, between the military figures who constitute the core leadership directing the government and the bulk of the military organization as a defense organization (Stepan 1986, 72–78; 1988, 30). Here, the relevant dimension is whether one pole dominates. It has been argued that the fear that an overly powerful "military as government" may politicize promotions and retirements and thereby disrupt the normal functioning of the "military as institution" is cause for militaries to adopt measures to prevent a personal dictatorship by a military commander. These mechanisms have included requiring top-level officers to retire from active service before assuming the presidency, as well as procedures to assure turnover at the apex of the executive. Variants on both these formulae were used in Argentina and Brazil during the most recent military governments.

Argentina in 1976 is the case in which elaborate institutional plans and procedures were devised by the armed forces prior to taking power. According to Fontana, the March 1976 coup was preceded by extensive negotiations among the three armed forces which culminated in agreement that the presidency after the coup would be held by a retired officer selected by the military junta (1987, 46–48). But this agreement was not initially implemented; Gen. Jorge Videla became president while remaining commander in chief of the army. This *situación de excepcionalidad* caused severe tensions within the Argentine junta during 1977 and 1978, as the navy pressed for a "fourth man" to assume the presidency; that is, a retired officer outside the junta of the three active commanders in chief. In August 1978, after extensive interservice negotiations, this formula was finally implemented and Videla retired from the army in order to retain the presidency. As part of these agreements, Videla's retirement was coupled with the retirement of the other commanders in chief, as well as periodic selection of a new president by the junta.[65] Yet, the succession of military presidents during the *Proceso* did not consistently follow junta selection nor involve a "fourth man." In December 1981, Gen. Leopoldo F. Galtieri deposed Videla's successor, Gen. Roberto Viola, and held the presidency while remaining in command of the army. Shortly after Argentina's defeat in the Malvinas/Falklands War, in June 1982 Galtieri was ousted by the army high command. The latter's unilateral designation of a successor, General Bignone, led the navy and the air force to withdraw from the government, resulting in the temporary dissolution of the junta.[66] Although the separation of president and

---

[65] The retirement of the commanders in chief after a "maximum of three years" had been stipulated in ART. 1.3.2 of Law 21.256, the law passed the day of the coup to regulate the functioning of the Argentine junta and executive. However, Fontana's account of the renewal of commanders and the presidential successions of 1978 and 1981 makes it clear that these processes were not the result of norm-bound procedures but of intense intra- and interservice negotiations at each juncture involving the high commands of each service and not only the members of the junta (1987, 63–72, 119–25). Videla was succeeded as president in March 1981 by his successor as commander in chief of the army, Gen. Roberto Viola.

[66] After the designation of new commanders in the navy and the air force, the junta was reconstituted in September 1982 and remained in operation until five days prior to the inauguration of elected President Raul Alfonsín in December 1983.

commander in chief was not consistently followed in Argentina during 1976–1983, the number of presidents – four – sets the Argentine dictatorship apart from the Chilean, as does the periodic renewal of commanders in chief and therefore junta members.

This combination of retirement and multiple presidencies also became a pattern in Brazil during the 1964–1985 period of military rule. As in Chile, the Brazilian armed forces came to power in 1964 without a detailed institutional blueprint for organizing military power (Stepan 1971, 216; Martínez-Lara 1996, 15).[67] However, in contrast to both Argentina and Chile, military rule in Brazil did not involve the formation of an interservice military junta. In this context, the relationship between the "military as an institution" and the military executive evolved out of dynamics associated with the military's initial decision to seize only executive power, leave Congress in operation, and allow for future elections at the different levels of federal and state government.

The acceptance of Congress and the extant electoral timetable appear to have shaped military executive relations in Brazil in two ways. On the one hand, the fear of adverse electoral outcomes early on fueled army hard-liners to successfully pressure for expanded authoritarian powers and a regime horizon extending beyond a single presidential term. This intramilitary dynamic turned succession into a practical matter. On the other hand, given the limited scope of the military's intervention and its commitment to regular elections and a semblance of constitutionalism, the presidential term at least initially appeared as the natural measure for the military government, as did the prohibition of a second term which was proscribed by the 1946 constitution. This perspective was reinforced by the moderate position of the first military president, Gen. Castelo Branco, and the faction around him. Here, Castelo's personal opposition to holding the presidency beyond his initial mandate meant that any extension of military rule after March 1967 would require the selection of a new president. By refusing to cling to power, Castelo Branco set the precedent, consistently followed, of using the presidential term as the span for each military president.[68]

---

[67] On the institutional evolution of the Brazilian military regime, see Alves 1985; Skidmore 1988; and Martínez-Lara 1996, chap. 1.

[68] Castelo's term did not end on January 31, 1966 (the final day of ousted President Joâo Goulart's term) but ran until March 1967. This extension was mandated by a July 1964 constitutional amendment. Castelo initially opposed this extension, and in October 1965, at a juncture of hard-line imposition, he insisted that a clause be included in Institutional Act No. 2 making himself ineligible for another presidential term (Skidmore 1988, 40, 64).

Why and how did this mechanism work in Brazil? Many scholars explain the succession of five military presidents in terms of a "military consensus" that a caudillo or military strongman would not emerge from the military government (Stepan 1971, 218; Skidmore 1988, 159, 64; Hunter 1997, 29). There is little concrete evidence of this consensus other than that presidential successions occurred regularly. Once the military in 1965 decreed that presidential elections would henceforth be indirect, the selection of the official candidate became the critical moment in each succession. This nomination process was not formally regulated, but by most accounts the official candidate was selected by senior officers after different slates had been sounded out among junior officers. Here an important difference emerges with Argentina and Chile, as I interpret it. In Brazil, the army was purportedly the dominant force (Skidmore 1988, 97; Stepan 1988, 24–25). It was always assumed that the president would be a general drawn from the army. Thus, although other branches were involved in the selection process, the key was the decision of the army high command.[69]

If this view is correct, Brazil was an "oligarchic" military regime not because military rule involved the joint governance of three arms but because the president was selected by a plural body, the army high command.[70] In this context, the capacity of an outgoing president to select a successor largely depended on the level of factionalism within the army, as this would determine the strength of rival candidacies and pressures for compromise. It should be stressed that military presidents in Brazil did not possess direct military resources that could be used to extort continued power. As a rule, once elected, presidents retired from active duty (Hunter 1997, 29). Like civilian presidents during 1946–1964 and now, Brazilian presidents held the title of commander in chief of the armed forces, but this command was mediated through the individual service chiefs. Thus, more consistently than in Argentina and in contrast to Chile, the presidency in authoritarian Brazil was separated from the rank of commander in chief of the army.

[69] Consultations among the three branches during the succession crisis that followed Costa e Silva's 1969 stroke are described in Skidmore 1988, 93–94. According to Alves, this process was clearly slanted in favor of the army: of the 104 generals who made up an unofficial electoral college which operated as a first filter, eighty-five were army generals (1985, 105, 317 n.6).

[70] Remmer classifies Brazil and Uruguay as "oligarchic" military regimes (1989a, 36–37). In her model these are regimes with a low concentration of authority (rotation of presidents) and a low fusion of military and government roles.

However, despite this separation, the military executive did hold institutional resources that could influence positions within the army,[71] and as hard-liner positions were weakened under Geisel nominations largely followed executive preferences, though not without conflicts and miscalculations; in fact, the latter led to the defeat of the official candidate in the 1985 election and the end of military rule.[72]

In cases where mechanisms of retirement and turnover function, military heads of state might be said to be subordinate to the military as an institution. In this sense, such authoritarian power holders are apparently constrained by military institutions. However, we should note that these mechanisms are usually informal and do not necessarily involve regular, ongoing constraints upon the exercise of power once in office, which are found in the Chilean case in realms regulated by law (I will return to this point when I discuss the weakness of the Brazilian congress). Perhaps, if these types of interactions between armed forces and military governments are thought to be the principal or only mechanisms whereby military presidents may be controlled, their absence in Chile might be thought sufficient to establish Pinochet's dominance. Yet such a position can only be adopted by casting a blind eye to the significance of the legislative junta as a first institutional limit internal to the military dictatorship.

## Unanimity and Legislative Vetoes

Notwithstanding the influence of the personalist interpretation, the fact that Pinochet was commander in chief of the army and president is equally compatible with an alternative characterization of the dictatorship and a recognition of institutional constraints after 1975, however circumscribed. For the personalist interpretation to hold, scholars must demonstrate that Pinochet's dominance extended to the legislative process or that lawmaking under the dictatorship did not matter. The usual strategy has been to infer the former on the basis of claims about the implications of decision making by unanimity. However,

[71] Castelo Branco introduced strict rules about promotion and retirement, which for the first time placed limits on how long generals could remain on active duty (Skidmore 1988, 48; Hunter 1997, 28–30). Turnover at the highest levels meant that generals could not build enduring independent bases within the army. Institutional Act No. 17, decreed amidst the difficult succession of 1969, also gave the president the power to transfer to the reserve any officer "who commits or plans to commit a crime against the unity of the Armed Forces" (Skidmore 1988, 151). This is said to have been an effective deterrent against military insubordination and factionalism (Hunter 1997, 31).

[72] On these successions, see Skidmore 1988, 151, 199–200.

this strategy fails because it is founded upon erroneous inferences about purported theoretical properties of unanimous decision making. Without a convincing demonstration of Pinochet's simultaneous control of lawmaking, the personalization of power characterization of military rule in Chile collapses.

Before discussing the significance of unanimous decision making in legislation, we should recall that Admiral Merino and General Leigh knowingly opted for naval and air force marginalization from the executive as a step in the implementation of what they understood to be a separation of powers explicitly conceived as a safeguard against army dominance. Both accepted Pinochet's personal control of the presidency in exchange for agreement upon an institutionally protected role and veto in the legislative process. In this light, the well-documented (Huneeus 1988, 110–24) greater participation of army officers in government positions is not surprising. Rather than control of the presidency, the critical issue is whether the legislative junta operated as an effective counterbalance and check upon Pinochet.

In this regard it is commonly argued that Pinochet's retention of a vote in lawmaking allowed him to dominate the legislative process. In all cases this claim takes the form of an assertion unencumbered by empirical evidence. Variously it is asserted that "By 1975 General Pinochet had the power to legislate and to determine the application of the state of siege" (De Brito 1997, 43), or that the Junta was a "weak legislature beholden to executive initiatives" (Valenzuela 1995, 38), or that no legislation could pass without the approval of General Pinochet (Arriagada 1985, 162). If carefully qualified a partial truth may be squeezed out of each of these claims, yet none of them establish that Pinochet could unilaterally enact decree-laws over the will of the other Junta members. Given the unanimity decision rule and Pinochet's continued presence in the Junta through March 1981, the general's assent obviously was required to enact decree-laws. In this context, the Junta was a weak legislature in that it could not impose legislation without executive concurrence. But this fact provides no basis for inferring omnipotence. Similarly, the exercise of state of siege powers was an executive prerogative, but their use was contingent upon Junta concurrence in the form of a decree-law declaring a state of siege.

It is here that the peculiar properties of unanimity must be stressed. Historically, unanimous decision making has been used in situations in which actors could not conceive of a general corporate unity apart from the individuals or units forming a given association; in these situations, no collective will could exist if any member dissented. In such contexts where the strong sense of individuality among the constituent units precludes any use of majority rule, unanimity provides a mechanism that assures that outcomes do not violate the component individual interests (Simmell [1908], 243; Heinberg 1926, 63–64). By granting each participant an absolute veto, unanimity guarantees to each member "the right to preserve his own interests against those of the other members" (Mueller 1989, 102). As a device typical to collegial organs, unanimity debars dominance among equal parts (Wolff 1951, 30). Unanimity thus corresponds to a specific structure of prior group relations which is preserved and protected by the mutual vetoes that are constitutive of this specific decision rule. Both these effects of unanimity and the circumstances that give rise to its use were prevalent in Chile during the military period.

Given the unanimity decision rule, Pinochet's vote did not emasculate the other members of the Junta as proponents of personalization suggest. Rather, it was the ever-present possibility of a veto which constrained Pinochet and prevented him from legislating at will. The records of the Junta's operation as a legislative body demonstrate that there is no empirical basis for characterizing the Junta as a rubber stamp legislature subservient to the whims of General Pinochet. After mid-1975, as we will see repeatedly in subsequent chapters, Admiral Merino and General Leigh did not become pawns of General Pinochet. Although the majority of legislative initiatives emanated from the executive, for a bill to become a decree-law it had to attain the approval of all four junta members. Projects that gave rise to impassable disagreements rarely proceeded to a vote: Either the wrinkles in a project were ironed out to everyone's satisfaction or the project died in the system. Typically, projects that failed to garner unanimous support after repeated circuits through the legislative system were withdrawn from consideration by the executive and returned to their ministry of origin for further study: Such cases were not uncommon. As a result actual vetoes were rare – though they did occur. In this manner the unanimity decision rule gave each commander a legitimate procedural means with which to block averse legislative outcomes.

The adoption of the unanimity decision rule by the Chilean armed forces was also concordant with the underlying structure of prior group relations among the armed forces. Although the Chilean armed forces and *carabineros* came to power as an institution, "as the organization that the State provides for the safeguard and defense of its physical and moral integrity, and of its historical cultural identity,"[73] no such organization existed apart from the individual services. The Chilean army, navy, and air force were independent institutions, each with distinctive traditions, identities, and organizational styles. There was no tradition of institutional subordination to a single branch, as occurs when an active service general holds the post of Minister of Defense. In Chile, since the 1930s, defense ministers were always civilians, with each service coupled to the ministry via its respective undersecretary. In this context of service autonomy, the concept of the "military as institution" as a given, prior organizational substrate is misleading. Both "the military as institution" and the "military as government" could only emerge out of coordination among the commanders of the different services. As I have shown throughout this chapter, Admiral Merino and General Leigh consistently defended the autonomy of their services, by clinging steadfastly to the unanimity decision rule and by restricting the president's traditional powers over military appointments to prevent any army intromission into the career paths within their respective forces.

## Legislative Independence in Comparative Perspective

In addition to being an ongoing end mediated through the Junta, this defense of service autonomy also provided the ballast which anchored the legislative junta as an organ separate from the executive. Any separation of powers requires not only that organs exercising different powers be distinct, but also that none of the powers separated be capable of selecting the personnel who staff the other organs. If this condition does not hold, any formal separation of powers is merely illusory. In 1974 with the enactment of D.L. No. 527, Admiral Merino and General Leigh safeguarded the separation between the legislative junta and the executive when they denied the military president any formal authority to name and remove the commanders of the other services. Without the authority to name commanders, General Pinochet could not use such appointments to conform a legislative organ subservient to his preferences. This independence of the Junta, founded on the security of its members, was further consolidated in 1976 when the commanders freed themselves of standing norms requiring retirement upon reaching the maximum years of service. Here the irregular ouster

---

[73] D.L. No. 1, D.O., September 18, 1973.

of General Leigh from the Junta in June 1978 arises as a difficult exception which will be discussed in more detail in Chapter 5. However, for now it is sufficient to note that this crisis did not result in any modification to the unanimity decision rule, nor any attribution of powers of selection to Pinochet, nor did it prevent Admiral Merino and General Leigh's successor, Gen. Fernando Matthei, from henceforth developing and defending positions at variance with General Pinochet. General Pinochet could not mold the Junta at his will.

The critical importance of service autonomy as a foundation for the separation of powers within the Chilean dictatorship emerges forcefully when legislatures under other authoritarian regimes are considered. The character of this work and the absence of comparative studies of authoritarian legislatures precludes any broad examination of these cases. However, the experiences of the Franquist *Cortes* and the federal Congress in Brazil during 1964–1985 are sufficient to underscore the comparative significance of the legislative junta in Chile as an institutional constraint. Spain is a natural case for comparison because the "Pinochet regime" has been presented as akin to Gen. Francisco Franco's personalized dictatorship (Huneeus 1998). However, against the backdrop of the legislative military junta in Chile, the weakness of the Spanish *Cortes* reveals how inappropriate is this placement of Pinochet alongside Franco. Brazil, on the other hand, is relevant because the retention of Congress would appear to imply the presence of an institutional check independent of the military executive. Here too, however, we find that the military executive held and exercised considerable authority to directly and indirectly alter the composition of Congress and thereby undermine Congress as an independent legislative organ.

Though both have been characterized as personalized regimes, the dictatorships of Franco and Pinochet differed considerably.[74] Unlike Pinochet, Franco did not rule subject to any collective military power nor any independent body with legislative powers, even after the creation of the *Cortes* in 1942. Franco was named head of state and *generalissimo* of the armed forces in September 1936 by a junta of rebellious generals. However, by this act the *Junta de Defensa Nacional* abdicated its powers to Franco, who had conditioned his acceptance upon a grant of full state powers free from limits (Fusi 1985, 46). As successive laws clarified and reiterated, Franco's powers included the

---

[74] For interpretations of Franquist Spain as a personalized dictatorship, see Fusi 1985 and Tusell 1988.

authority to decree general legal norms.[75] These powers were not restricted after the Civil War ended in 1939, nor were they diminished by the creation of a corporative legislative assembly, the *Cortes*, in 1942.

According to one historian, "Franco created the Cortes as an instrument of collaboration with his functions, not as a legislative Chamber that would limit his powers" (Fusi 1985, 79). This claim is borne out by the limited powers held by the *Cortes* and the mode of designation of its members. Franco held direct powers of appointment which allowed him to guarantee a supportive majority in the *Cortes* (Gunther 1980, 38, 312). Even so, the role of the *Cortes* in the legislative process was carefully circumscribed: The *Cortes*'s chief function was to deliberate and advise the government, not bear independent decision-making authority which it lacked; the government could enact large numbers of bills without consulting the *Cortes*; and even for those matters for which the *Cortes*'s approval was required, Franco held an escape clause allowing him to sidestep the *Cortes* and enact legislation by decree (Gunther 1980, 38–39). By most accounts, the *Cortes* was at best a sound box that could be used to amplify decisions taken elsewhere, or an arena for the expression of divergences internal to the "families" composing the Franquist elite (Tusell 1988, 217–19), but not a body that could shape the content of legislation, even when this was at variance with the preferences of the government.

This last conclusion equally holds for the Brazilian Congress during the years of military rule spanning 1964 to 1985. There is no denying that the whole course of military rule in Brazil was shaped by the military's initial decision to govern alongside an elected Congress. Elections and Congress became the focal points for the intramilitary dynamics that defined the first years of military rule and were a constant concern of military strategists throughout the post-1974 liberalization period. Though a political referent and problem for the military, Congress could not stand as an effective institutional constraint upon the military government. In the 1985 indirect presidential election, a divided official party did allow the opposition candidate Tancredo Neves to carry the vote in Congress, but the military executive always held the upper hand in defining the rules of the game that culminated in this outcome.

Military presidents asserted their dominance over Congress throughout the long period of military government. Within a week of overthrowing President João Goulart, the military set the tone for its

---

[75] The relevant norms are: ART. 17, Law of 30 January 1938; and ART. 7, Law of 8 August 1939. These laws are reproduced in De Esteban 1982.

relations with Congress, declaring in the preamble to Institutional Act No. 1, ". . . it should be clear that the revolution does not intend to legitimate itself through Congress. On the contrary, it is Congress that is made legitimate by this institutional act, which could only result from the inherent and revolutionary exercise of constituent power."[76] In addition to measures affecting the judiciary, this first act severely limited the powers of Congress, and in subsequent years military governments never hesitated to unilaterally grant themselves expanded powers as expedient. The litany of measures enacted during the military period to confront immediate crises, mold the composition of Congress, and recast the party system is dizzying and cannot be reconstructed here.[77] The general pattern was for military presidents, often under pressure from hard-line sectors of the army, to assert their dominance whenever the government feared that it was about to lose a compliant majority in Congress or this majority balked at implementing the executive's preferences. At such critical junctures, the president would decree, without congressional approval, institutional acts or decree-laws conferring expanded powers upon the executive. These acts usually conferred a range of powers. Those affecting the legislature variously included authority: to cancel at all levels of government the mandates of elected officials and representatives;[78] to leg-

[76] Institutional Act No. 1 was decreed on April 9, 1964. The preamble is reproduced in Alves 1985, 32.

[77] For the political backdrop to these executive interventions, as well as the measures enacted, see Fleischer 1983, Alves 1985, and Skidmore 1988. A summary of executive/legislative relations is provided in Martínez-Lara 1996, chap. 1.

[78] Authority to cancel electoral mandates was given by Institutional Acts Nos. 1, 2, and 5, of April 9, 1964, October 27, 1965, and December 13, 1968, respectively. Both Institutional Acts No. 1 and No. 2 included expiration dates (June 15, 1964 and March 15, 1967) after which the executive ceased to enjoy the powers conferred by them. Thus, without authority to purge Congress, President Costa e Silva in December 1968 had to work through Congress when he attempted to lift the parliamentary immunity of Márcio Moreira Alves, an outspoken critic of the government, whose speeches condemning torture had incited military hard-liners. Though the proregime party, ARENA held a majority, the Chamber of Deputies voted against the government, and the president responded with Institutional Act No. 5. In addition to granting a range of discretionary repressive powers, the act reinstated the power to cancel electoral mandates and allowed the president to close Congress, which was done the same day through Supplementary Act No. 38. Unlike the other two acts, Institutional Act No. 5 did not include an expiration date and remained in force until its repeal by a constitutional amendment in June 1978. By Alves's count, 189 members of the federal Congress were purged under Institutional Act Nos. 1, 2, and 5, eight of them during Ernesto Geisel's *apertura* (1985, 98). It should be noted that purges allowed the government to determine the size of the majorities necessary to legislate and modify the constitution: Seats vacated by purges were not filled and quorums were determined by the number of effectively occupied seats (Alves 1985, 64).

islate by decree and to issue institutional or complementary acts;[79] to close the federal Congress and state and municipal assemblies;[80] and to amend the constitution at will.[81]

The institutional weakness of the Brazilian Congress in this context of broad executive discretionary powers was epitomized by the events of April 1977. Although the November 1974 congressional elections, which saw a surge in voting for the opposition MDB, resulted in the government's loss of the two-thirds majority necessary to amend the constitution, the new balance within Congress did not limit the executive's capacity to modify the constitution. Two days after a joint session of Congress defeated a proposed constitutional amendment to reform the judiciary, Geisel closed the Congress and proceeded in following days to enact by decree a number of amendments to the constitution, including a provision lowering the quorum required to modify the constitution to an absolute majority.[82] Before presidents bearing authority to unilaterally override its decisions or suppress it altogether, the Brazilian Congress could not stand as an institutional limit constraining the desires of successive military presidents.[83]

These brief comparative glances at Brazil and Spain underscore the distinctiveness of the Chilean military junta and the institutional

---

[79] Authority to grant decree-laws and complementary acts was conferred by Institutional Act Nos. 2 and 5.

[80] This power, as already noted, was given by Institutional Act No. 5 and was also held under Institutional Act No. 2. By this authority, Congress was closed for one month in late October 1966 and from December 1968 through October 30, 1969. President Figueiredo also closed Congress for two weeks in April 1977. During these periods the president legislated by decree.

[81] This power was granted by Institutional Act No. 5 (Martínez-Lara 1996, 18), and in October 1969 the military used this power while Congress was closed to substantially modify its own 1967 constitution. In April 1977, two other amendments to the constitution were unilaterally decreed under authority of Institutional Act No. 5 (Alves 1985, 148–51).

[82] These amendments, which became known as the "April package," included changes in the manner of apportionment in the lower house, the composition of the Senate, and the size of the electoral college used to choose the president, as well as the judicial reforms defeated by Congress (Alves 1985, 148–51, Skidmore 1988, 190–91).

[83] Even after the June 1978 repeal of Institutional Act No. 5, which had been the source of many of its discretionary powers, the executive retained mechanisms that enabled it to legislate despite congressional opposition. The principal of these was the *decurso de prazo*, by which "urgent" bills introduced by the executive were automatically approved if not considered by Congress within a certain limited time (initially thirty, later changed to forty and then sixty days). Thus, a government filibuster for the required period would guarantee approval of "urgent" executive initiatives. The *decurso de prazo* originated with Institutional Act No. 1, was reinstated by Institutional Act No. 2, and incorporated in 1967 into the military's constitution.

definitions agreed upon in 1974 and 1975. Unlike his Spanish and Brazilian counterparts, General Pinochet never enjoyed authority to legislate by decree nor to mold the composition of the legislative body at his discretion. Contrary to accepted characterizations of the dictatorship, what was unique about Chile was not the fact of a unipersonal president, but the separation of a collegial legislative, possessing multiple vetoes, from the executive. This division of powers introduced a first institutional limit internal to the dictatorship: The executive could not simultaneously act and legislate without the concurrence of another body. If sovereignty is understood as the power to create and apply binding norms upon a territory and a people, then sovereignty in Chile under the military regime was divided.

I should stress that I make no claim that this partial separation of powers implied limited government, understood as an arrangement in which governmental powers are circumscribed by institutions that effectively uphold and protect individual rights. The point is rather that institutionally defined limits were operative within the dictatorship, albeit among an extremely narrow group of persons – the three military commanders and the head of *carabineros*. These limits should be understood solely in reference to these officers. The separation of powers operated to protect their respective interests and rights and to assure that legislation enacted was expressive of agreements among all four members of the Junta. Limits, therefore, were a mechanism whereby regime cohesion could be generated.

Yet beyond the Junta, at least until the new constitution went into effect in March 1981, there existed no organ capable of holding the dictatorship to constitutional and legal limits. This absence of external institutional limits is examined at length in the following two chapters. As will be seen, the Junta, when in agreement, could easily override the Supreme Court and the *Contraloría General de la República* and thereby render largely formal their powers of legal and constitutional control. However, the Junta was not always in agreement, and the fact that power was organized on the basis of a plurality of actors, however narrow, gave rise to dynamics which would have been impossible if a single actor concentrated executive and legislative powers. The collegial organization of the Junta, anchored in the unanimity decision rule, and recurrent substantive differences within the Junta will explain why the regime enacted a constitution in 1980, its content, and why the Junta tolerated the operation of external institutional constraints during the 1981–1990 period, even when these institutions ruled against the military and ultimately contributed to the dissolution of military rule. Before society, the existence of internal limits did nothing to alter the regime's character as a dictatorship, particularly since the operation of the Junta was carefully shrouded from public view. Nevertheless, the separation of powers enacted in 1974–1975 would decisively shape the subsequent course of military rule in Chile.

# Chapter Three

# The Constitution and the Dictatorship: The Supreme Court and the Constitutionality of Decree-Laws

The relationship between the constitution and the exception was posed immediately with the Chilean armed forces' irregular assumption of power on September 11, 1973. In its first legal act, the Junta did not openly suppress the 1925 constitution. Rather, in ART. 3 of D.L. No. 1 (D.O., September 18, 1973), the Junta vowed to "guarantee the full effectiveness of the attributions of the judiciary and respect the constitution and laws of the Republic, in the measure that the present situation in the country allows for the better fulfillment of the postulates it [the Junta] has set itself." In other words, the constitution was to remain nominally in force but its supremacy would be subordinate to the imperatives of the state of exception as defined by the Junta.

However, as was generally the case during the first period of military rule, the initial implications of this vow were vague and ambiguous. A number of questions arose immediately regarding the implications of this dualism of nominal constitutionalism and emergency rule. First, would institutions empowered to exercise constitutional and legal control, such as the Supreme Court and the *Contraloría General de la República*, in any way limit de facto power? Second, how would the exception affect the constitution? Would the Junta proceed arbitrarily without regard for constitutional forms or would it modify the constitution as necessary to have it conform to its will, or eclectically employ one procedure or the other as it deemed expedient?

From an external perspective these questions appear gratuitous: The 1925 constitution had been trampled and could in no real sense limit military power after September 11, 1973. As has already been noted, the *pronunciamiento militar* involved a breach of all constitutional norms regarding the nonpolitical character of the armed forces, methods of access to office, the separation of powers, and the rule of law. Similarly, the Junta's enactment of laws by decree was an incontrovertible violation of constitutional procedure for valid lawmaking. Both in its origins and in its exercise of power the military government had quashed the cornerstone of the 1925 constitution, the principles of separation of powers and rule of law, which were embodied in ART. 4: "No magistracy, or person, or assembly of persons, not even under the pretext of extraordinary circumstances is empowered to assume any other authority or rights than those that have been expressly conferred upon them by the laws. Every act in contravention of this Article is void." This article expresses the essence of constitutionalism as a practice of limited government: State powers and authorities exercise only faculties expressly conferred upon them by the existent constitutional and legal framework, which itself is protected by multiple checks and balances, as well as demanding amendment procedures. On September 11, 1973, the corresponding matrix of institutions and procedures in Chile had been so badly sundered that the Junta's commitment to uphold the independence of the judiciary and to respect, to the extent possible, the constitution and standing laws appeared purely declamatory. Since the military had been willing to trample the constitution to come to power, what would prevent it from interpreting broadly its own escape clause – "insofar as the present situation in the country allows it" – to justify departures from its commitment. Given that the military could at its discretion decide when the constitution held and when it didn't, the 1925 constitution hardly retained any force to limit military prerogative.

However, such an external perspective is insufficient for understanding the tension between controlling institutions and military discretion that ensued with the Junta's vow to maintain the independence of the judiciary and to respect, insofar as conditions permitted, the constitution and standing laws. As one Chilean legal scholar (Verdugo Marinkovic 1977, 22) has insisted, the coup displaced the foundations of the 1925 constitution: With the constitution's violation in September 1973, the ultimate foundation for any continuity of the constitution ceased to reside, however indirectly, in the original constituent power, the people, and shifted to the Junta, whose decision alone maintained the constitution nominally in force. Yet the pledge to uphold the constitution and respect the independent functioning of the judiciary posed the practical question of the formal relationship among military rule, the remnents of the constitution, and those organs formally empowered to review executive and legislative acts. Notwithstanding the Supreme Court and the *Contraloría General de la República's* sympathy toward the new regime, the relationship between the military junta and these organs was, in principle at least, conflictive. The court was empowered to adjudicate conflicts on the basis of law, uphold the supremacy of the constitution, and protect individuals from arbitrary infringements of their rights. The Junta, on the other hand, was formed to confront a situation which was perceived to be without solution within the existing constitutional and legal framework and which demanded action beyond the bounds of the legally permitted. For these two organs to coexist amicably, somehow the boundaries separating acts subject to law and susceptible to judicial control had to be delimited from those subject only to the discretion of the military government.

This chapter and the next examine how these boundaries between law and prerogative were defined during the first period of military rule. Immediately after the coup the key issues that had to be resolved were whether and if so how the Junta would exercise constituent powers, as well as whether the Supreme Court would oversee the system of military justice. This chapter focuses on the first aspect, the resolution of constitutional issues surrounding the Supreme Court's power of judicial review. After reviewing the debates within the constitutional commission regarding the status of the 1925 constitution and the Junta's amendment powers, I reconstruct and evaluate the exchanges between the Supreme Court and the Junta over how constituent powers would be exercised. The third section examines the impact of preventive legal review of administrative decrees by the *Contraloría General de la República*.[1]

This analysis will demonstrate that although the Supreme Court and the *Contraloría* set formal limits upon the military regime's legislative and administrative prerogative, these constraints were relative given the Junta's capacity to override either institution when its members were in agreement. Still, within those realms regulated by law, the Supreme Court and the *Contraloría* did present a formal limit upon the prerogative powers of the military regime. Each one's respective fac-

---

[1] The following chapter analyzes how the judiciary exercised its constitutional mandate to guarantee individual rights of due process and liberty. It examines at length the two potentially most explosive points of contact between the judiciary and the armed forces after the coup: the Supreme Court's mandate to supervise the administration and operation of all courts of justice and its constitutional mandate to protect personal liberty from extralegal infringement. As we will see when we consider the Supreme Court's abdication of its disciplinary faculties over the military tribunals in time of war, as well as its jurisprudence regarding the *recurso de amparo* (a variant of *habeas corpus*), the Supreme Court proved incapable of effectively upholding constitutional guarantees designed to protect the procedural and human rights of individuals persecuted by the security forces or arrested under the state of siege.

ulties of constitutional and legal review compelled the military to formally adhere to the principle of legality by requiring it to consistently employ proper legal forms. That is, in the face of a possible legal or constitutional challenge, the Junta could exceed a given constitutional or legal parameter in a decree-law or administrative order without risk only if it first modified the pertinent constitutional or legal precept. Although this formal limit did not substantively constrain the dictatorship's constituent and legislative powers, the operation of both institutions had significant consequences for power relations within the Junta. More specifically, the particular manner whereby the Junta resolved the question of the Supreme Court's constitutional review powers left the 1925 constitution in tatters, and would be one justification for enacting a new charter.

## The Status of the Constitution of 1925

The constitution of 1925, like all written constitutions, in itself was a mere piece of paper. Its supremacy and efficacy depended on the actual functioning of the institutions and checks and balances that it defined. Of these, the Supreme Court, through its power to declare inapplicable any law found contrary to constitutional precepts, was the foremost institution empowered to uphold the supremacy of the constitution. Immediately after the coup, the Supreme Court petitioned the Junta to specify the scope of its powers and define its juridical structure so that the Court could properly exercise its jurisdiction and faculties. One outcome of this process was the definition of executive and legislative powers in D.L. No. 527 and 991, discussed in the preceding chapter. However, the Supreme Court's chief concern was the status of the constitution and constituent powers, in particular that the Junta clarify whether its powers included amending the constitution, as how this issue was settled would determine whether or not the Court would continue to exercise its power of judicial review. If the Junta claimed that its decree-laws overrode the constitution whenever the two conflicted, the Supreme Court would have no role in assuring the constitutionality of decree-laws. If the Junta didn't assert this supremacy, the Court would still need some rule to allow it to distinguish decree-laws that modified the constitution from simple decree-laws subject to constitutional review. Such a rule of recognition was also imperative for the constitution to retain a clear identity: If the "constitution" were to be recognizable, norms of constitutional rank needed to be easily identifiable.

Upon consultation by the Court, military legal counsel in November 1973 first posed before the Junta the question of whether the Junta's arrogation of the *Mando Supremo de la Nación* encompassed the power to modify the constitution. By this date, the Junta had only once expressly modified the constitution to dissolve the short-lived constitutional court, the *Tribunal Constitucional*. Aside from this precedent, the military had not explicitly specified that it would wield constituent powers. After queries from the Supreme Court, Adm. Vío Valdivieso, the chief counsel to the navy, convoked a special session of the newly formed Constituent Commission to prepare a draft decree-law clarifying the status of constituent powers. As Admiral Vío told the commission, "It is necessary . . . to solve these types of procedural problems to avoid that the Supreme Court might declare inapplicable a decree-law tomorrow" (AOCC, 13, November 7, 1973, 3). In other words, the status of constituent powers had to be clarified to assure the legal-constitutional supremacy of the military.

## The Constituent Commission

In its origins and mandate the commission reflected the initial indeterminateness of the constitutional question. At the first session of the Junta mention was made that Jaime Guzmán was heading a group studying the promulgation of a new constitution (AHJG, 1, September 13, 1973), and a week later the Junta decided to form a commission to prepare a draft constitution from among this group of civilian lawyers advising General Leigh (AHJG, 7, September 21, 1973, 1–2). Three days later – less than two weeks after the coup – the Constituent Commission officially met for the first time.[2] Its initial members were constitutionalists and politicians on the Right: Enrique Ortúzar Escobar, Sergio Díez Urzúa, Jaime Guzmán Errázuriz, and Jorge Ovalle Quiroz. In early October, after pressure from the Christian Democratic Party (PDC), the first Minister of Justice Gonzalo Prieto Gandara requested that the group be broadened, leading to the incorporation of Gustavo

---

[2] The Constituent Commission was given legal form on October 25, 1973 by D.S. No. 1,064 (*Justicia*), D.O., November 12, 1973. Within the regime there was later some controversy over the group's name because some feared that it suggested that the commission held constituent powers. To remove any doubts about the group's purely advisory character, its name was changed in 1977 to *Comisión de Estudios de la Nueva Constitución* (Commission to Study the New Constitution). Nevertheless, to avoid confusion I refer to the group by its original name. The commission was also familiarly known as the "Comisión Ortúzar," after Enrique Ortúzar, its president.

Lorca Rojas and two prominent members of the PDC, Enrique Evans de la Cuadra and Alejandro Silva Bascuñán.[3] All of these figures were prominent lawyers, linked to Center or Right parties, and a number of them had been members of Congress or Ministers in previous administrations.[4]

Although some commission members had connections to specific junta members, unlike members of other commissions established by the Junta, these lawyers were not delegates of individual junta members nor were they civilian spokesmen for some form of military ideology. In this regard, the Constituent Commission was an exception to the convention of collegial staffing, which was the norm for inter-service committees. This exceptional format probably reflects the group's civilian composition, its advisory character, and the secondary status of its mission at the time of its formation. Guzmán, as we will see, would become the single most influential advisor to the government on institutional issues, at least up until 1983. Ovalle was tied to Leigh, and would serve in different capacities as a close legal advisor.

---

[3] According to Evans, Patricio Aylwin, then PDC party president, had insisted before Minister of Justice Prieto that members of the PDC be incorporated into the commission since the PDC represented a third of the electorate. Evans told me that the PDC then asked him to join the commission. Alejandro Silva Bascuñán received a written request to join the commission and did not request party approval before joining. At the time, Silva was a partner in the same law firm as Sergio Diez, a point which in Silva's view may have been a factor in his inclusion. Both Evans and Silva were prominent constitutional scholars and members of the Christian Democratic Party (PDC). Interviews with Enrique Evans and Alejandro Silva Bascuñán, Santiago, Chile, August 6, 1992 and July 24, 1992, respectively.

[4] Enrique Ortúzar, designated by the group to be President of the Constituent Commission, had been Minister of Justice to Jorge Alessandri Rodríguez and had authored the constitutional reform package presented to Congress in 1964. Sergio Díez, a member of the National Party, after serving three terms in Congress had been elected to the Senate in the January 1972 by-election in Linares. Another National Party member, Gustavo Lorca was teaching constitutional law at the University of Chile, Valparaíso at the time of the coup, and had also served three terms in Congress. Jorge Ovalle, a lawyer and professor of constitutional law at the University of Chile, was a member of *Democracia Rádical*, a right-wing splinter from the Radical Party. Enrique Evans had been undersecretary of justice to President Eduardo Frei Montalva and was professor of constitutional law at the Catholic University. At the same university, where he eventually would also teach constitutional law, Jaime Guzmán emerged in 1967 at the head of the *gremialista* opposition to the *Reforma Universitaria*. By September 1973, Guzmán, a regular commentator on the television roundtable "*A esta hora se improvisa*," was a well-known critic of the Allende government. Alejandro Silva Bascuñán, a Christian Democrat, also taught constitutional law at the Catholic University and in September 1973 was serving his third term as president of the *Colegio de Abogados*, the national lawyers guild. Evans and Silva were each authors of important treatises on the 1925 constitution (Silva Bascuñán 1963; Evans 1970; 1973).

Guzmán and Ortúzar during the life of the commission would often be privy to controversial government decisions before other commission members. Despite these ties, the internal dynamics of the group did not permit arguments from authority to justify these turns. Rather, the commission met as a body of civilians deeply committed to constitutionalism and Chile's legal tradition, and the extensive records of their deliberations document that the group only countenanced arguments from reason.

The commission was formally subordinate to the Ministry of Justice and held a broad mandate to "study, elaborate, and propose a draft of a new Political Constitution of the State and its complementary laws."[5] The group worked with considerable autonomy from the military government. The Constituent Commission was not subject to any time limit, nor did it receive any preliminary substantive or procedural guidelines from the Junta. The Constituent Commission enacted its own bylaws and internal procedures,[6] established five subcommissions to draw up preparatory studies,[7] and set its own agenda without intrusion, aside from occasional requests from the Junta for counsel on contingent constitutional problems. Nor is there any evidence that the members were following party orders.[8] From the outset the group met

[5] This mandate was specified in the supreme decree that instituted the commission, D.S. (Justicia) No. 1,064, D.O., November 12, 1973.

[6] Among other provisions, the bylaws stipulated a quorum of four, procedural rules for discussion and cloture, majority decision making, the admissibility of written minority opinions, and the keeping of official minutes, including a record of votes. These regulations are reproduced in AOCC, 10, October 25, 1973, 14–16. The bylaws were faithfully followed throughout the group's nearly five years of activity. In March 1974, when Alicia Romo Roman was designated, the quorum was increased to five. It was reduced back to four in July 1975 after it became clear that other commitments prevented Romo from regular participation.

[7] Subcommissions were immediately formed to study judicial powers, party and electoral laws (including the formation of new electoral registries), regulation of mass media, property rights, and internal administration and regional decentralization. The work of the subcommissions was to be preparatory to drafting complementary laws for the constitution. Almost without exception, these subcommissions were staffed by civilian lawyers, many of whom were affiliated with the PDC or one of the traditional Right parties, and a number of their members had held ministerial responsibilities in the Alessandri or Frei administrations. For the initial membership of these subcommissions, see AOCC, 9, October 23, 1973, 2–3. Another government commission, formed to draft a national security code, is often incorrectly referred to as a subcommission of the Constituent Commission. Ortúzar's presidency of this group as well may have given rise to this confusion. On the *Comisión Redactora del Código de Seguridad Nacional*, see note 31, page 188.

[8] According to Enrique Evans, the PDC never gave him any instructions on how to act within the Constituent Commission. Interview with Enrique Evans, Santiago, Chile, August 6, 1992.

in closed sessions, and the voluminous record of their deliberations clearly establishes that the commission members spoke in their capacity as jurists and professors of constitutional law.[9] This shared orientation, however, did not preclude recurrent procedural and substantive arguments over how best to reconcile democracy and the rule of law in the aftermath of the constitutional and social crisis engendered by Allende's presidency.

Contrary to common misconceptions, the group from the very beginning understood its task to consist of drafting a constitution for a democratic, representative regime. The resulting constitution was expected to embody conventional principles of constitutionalism – albeit with some modifications to take account of the 1972–1973 crisis. The members of the Constituent Commission did not conceive of their work as laying the basis for an alternative regime nor for prolonged military rule, and it was generally assumed that the commission's constitution would be implemented as part of a return to civilian rule, following popular ratification by referendum. The commission expressed this democratic orientation in the November 1973 memorandum prepared for the Junta, "*Metas u objetivos fundamentales para la Nueva Constitución Política de la República.*" This statement of principles and anticipated institutional correctives did not contain any significant departures from Chile's constitutional tradition, an absence quickly seized upon by the nationalist far Right.[10]

Notwithstanding this shared democratic and constitutionalist orientation, the commission members differed sharply on procedural matters, particularly before the question of whether advising the Junta

---

[9] The *Actas Oficiales de la Comisión Constituyente* (AOCC), some approximately nine thousand pages, are the official minutes of the commission's deliberations. The complete official minutes became available in 1983, two years after the 1980 constitution went into effect. The minutes do not employ direct quotes, but as one of the commission secretaries noted, the debates are reproduced virtually verbatim (interview with Rafael Larrain, Santiago, Chile, November 3, 1992). Through session 245, minutes for individual sessions were published serially, but only after a considerable delay. Beginning with session 246 the name of the group changes to *Comisión de Estudio de la Nueva Constitución Política de la República* and the publication adopts continuous pagination across sessions. This change in format suggests that the minutes of the later sessions were printed only after the Commission had completed its work. Session 417, on October 5, 1978, was the final meeting of the commission.

[10] See the December 1973 letter and article Carlos Cruz-Coke sent to Pinochet, reproduced in AOCC, 20, January 15, 1974, 10–13. Cruz-Coke advocated a functional, corporative second chamber, as well as presidential authority to dissolve Congress once each term. For further elaboration of the nationalist critique of the commission, see Cruz-Coke 1975. The *Constitutional Commission*'s memo is reprinted in Soto Kloss 1980, 11–31.

on immediate constitutional matters detracted from the drafting of a new constitution. The November 1973 consultation regarding the status of constituent powers set off the first of these debates.

## The Constituent Commission and the 1925 Constitution

The crux of the debate in November 1973 turned on whether the constitution remained in force after the coup and whether the Junta should declare that it possessed constituent powers. Two broad positions emerged, each of which expressed a divergent conception of the commission's role and its relationship with the Junta. These opposing positions proved enduring, and variants of each later would be voiced at every significant juncture, virtually until the commission completed its work. At the heart of this controversy were sharp differences over whether advising the regime on contingent constitutional problems could in any way contribute to an eventual return to constitutional democracy. The November 1973 controversy is important because for the first time it brought to the fore a central tension which up until the promulgation of the 1980 constitution repeatedly stymied the Junta and its advisors: the very real possibility that putting a constitutional veneer upon military rule and attempting to dictate the terms of a post-military constitutional order might be divergent, antithetical goals. Until the constitution was enacted, civilian and military officials could not reconcile the two alternative orientations to constitutional politics and each was perceived as proceeding along a separate and, usually, contradictory track. The two poles in this debate were epitomized in the arguments of Alejandro Silva Bascuñán and Jaime Guzmán. Silva, a distinguished Christian Democratic professor of constitutional law, obstinately insisted on the autonomy of democratic constitution making from military rule and denied that the dictatorship could be limited by law. Guzmán, on the other hand, consistently argued for combining work on the future constitution with an open, pragmatic relationship with the Junta.

Somewhat counterintuitively, Silva's opposition to advising the Junta rested upon on a democratic conception of constitutionalism, which he consistently sustained until he resigned from the commission in March 1977 once the PDC was outlawed. Silva insisted that the coup had sundered the 1925 constitution, leaving it ineffective and, consequently, the Junta could not exercise constituent powers. In this democratic conception the original constituent power resides in the people, and regardless of popular support for the coup, Silva argued, the military's intervention could not be construed as an act of the constituent people. Although in the "situation of emergency" the Junta held absolute powers and was enacting norms that "rationally" could be construed as concerning constitutional matters, the key point for Silva was that these exceptional measures were not expressive of "a juridical intent of the Chilean people, but rather a purpose tantamount to little more than a survival instinct on the part of our people" (AOCC, 14, November 8, 1973, 5). Furthermore, since the military had assumed plenary de facto powers, Silva maintained, the Junta's acts, not the constitutional framework, established the "fundamental law." Decree-laws had become the highest ranking legal norms; no higher law stood above the Junta's decrees. In this sense, the coup had "de-constitutionalized" the constitution and reduced its articles to having the same force as ordinary legislation (AOCC, 14, November 8, 1973, 8). Some months later, Silva further clarified this point; "formal de-constitutionalization" marked a profound break within the legal system, as the single constitution had given way to an informal, "customary" constitutional system, something he referred to as "a juridical path which continuously evolves and transforms in response to changes in determinate circumstances." In this situation, Silva concluded, the constitution could not be effective precisely because it is "impossible to constrain an authority that holds full powers" (AOCC, 28, April 2, 1974, 19). Thus, as in the original theory of sovereign reversibility, the military regime could be limited neither by the 1925 constitution nor by its own acts.

Silva drew significant practical implications from this theoretical position: Insofar as military rule turned on exceptional plenary powers beyond constitutional restraint, any efforts at "constitutionalizing" the exception were only a diversion from the commission's primary task of drafting a democratic constitution for an eventual return to civilian rule. Like other commission members, Silva assumed that this constitution would be promulgated only after ratification by the "original" constituent power, the Chilean people, in a nonfraudulent plebiscite that would take place with electoral registries and full electoral oversight.[11] Although Enrique Ortúzar, the commission's president, initially held that the Junta was obliged to consult the commission before any

---

[11] See Enrique Evans's comment to this effect (AOCC, 14, November 8, 1973, 7). Also indicative of this commitment to free ratification of the eventual constitution was the group's ongoing – and amply documented – concern over government delays in establishing the *Rol Unico Nacional*, the national identification system which was to provide the basis for a noncorruptible system of voter registration.

modification to the constitution,[12] Silva unfailingly protested on the many occasions that the Junta sought the commission's advice on constitutional and legal matters and, finally, during the drafting of the *Actas Constitucionales* in 1976 and 1977 refused to collaborate when the commission worked on such queries.

In opposition to Silva's position, Jaime Guzmán insisted that regardless of the status of the 1925 constitution, the Junta possessed constituent powers, even if these were only derivative. For Guzmán, this conclusion followed from the fact that Chile had a written constitution on September 11, 1973, the day of the coup. Given this starting point, either the constitution had ceased to be effective – and decree-laws had become the highest norms within an ongoing customary constitutional framework – or the constitution continued in force except for those articles expressly repealed by the Junta. Even in the first case, which corresponded to Silva's evaluation of the constitutional situation, Guzman argued, it would have been necessary for the military to exercise constituent powers to repeal the constitution.[13] Nevertheless, Guzmán advocated the second interpretation, which he noted corresponded to the Junta's understanding of the status of the constitution as expressly set forth in D.L. No. 1. From this perspective, the Junta possessed constituent powers by default since the organs competent to enact amendments to the constitution had been dissolved (AOCC, 14, November 8, 1973, 7).

In the debate that followed, Guzmán eventually predominated, and over Silva's sole dissident vote the group eventually decided to formally proclaim in the decree-law being drafted that the Junta possessed con-

---

[12] As Ortúzar stated in March 1974, "the Commission cannot conceive of the constitution being modified without its knowledge or intervention. The Fundamental Charter may be amended expressly or by means of the dictation of a decree-law that in fact implies the modification of its dispositions – but, obviously, in both cases this must be done with this Commission's participation, as has been understood by the *Junta de Gobierno* and its Advisory Committee" (AOCC, 25, March 25, 1974, 17). Although the Junta did consult the commission on many occasions, it soon belied Ortúzar's understanding that consultation was obligatory in all cases. As was mentioned in note 38, page 54, in June 1974 Ortúzar refused to attend the public ceremony marking the promulgation of the Statute of the Junta (D.L. No. 527) because the commission had not been consulted prior to the enactment of this important decree-law.

[13] Only one commission member, Jorge Ovalle, maintained that the constitution was no longer in force but that the Junta possessed constituent powers (AOCC, 14, November 8, 1973, 7). This position was politically untenable. When Ovalle suggested that the suspension of the constitution be inscribed in law, Admiral Vío countered that such a declaration was politically inadvisable and likely to have a negative international impact (AOCC, 13, November 7, 1973, 4).

stituent powers. This resolution left open whether the Junta would employ any special procedure to modify the constitution. For the Supreme Court this was the decisive issue, since whether or not the court would continue to exercise its powers of judicial review, particularly in regard to the Junta's decree-laws, depended on whether a category of constituent decree-laws was created alongside simple decree-laws. However, the commission saw no need to create a category of norms of higher rank and the discussion concerning the *recurso de inaplicabilidad* reveals that no one within the commission viewed the Supreme Court as a potential check upon the Junta's legislative power.

On this point, Silva and Guzmán were in agreement. Since he held that the constitution was not in force, for Silva there could be no contradiction between the content of a decree-law and a constitutional norm (AOCC, 14, November 8, 1973, 8).[14] Guzmán, on the other hand, assumed the supremacy of the military's decree-laws and was concerned that the court retain its review powers but only pertaining to laws passed prior to the coup (AOCC, 14, November 8, 1973, 7). Given this consensus, the commission's draft decree-law did not recommend any criteria to distinguish constituent from regular legislation – both were to assume the indiscriminate form of decree-laws – and thus the commission condoned tacit modifications to the constitution. In order to circumvent any challenge to the constitutionality of these tacit modifications, the commission approved a clause stipulating, "When the content of a decree-law is contrary to a constitutional precept, it will be understood that it has been dictated in exercise of the Constituent Power. Therefore, in its regard, the appeal for inapplicability will not be admissible" (AOCC, 14, November 8, 1973, 11).

This clause would have provided an automatic brake on any judicial challenge to the military's enactments, yet it was not included in D.L. 128, apparently because the president of the Supreme Court advised that it was superfluous because it was obvious.[15] D.L. No. 128 "clarified and interpreted ART. 1 of D.L. No. 1," and declared that since September 11, 1973, the Junta had assumed constituent, legislative, and executive powers (D.O., November 16, 1973). It reiterated that the judiciary would function independently in accordance with the consti-

---

[14] Ovalle shared this position, but insisted that the only way to block the Supreme Court from challenging the constitutionality of decree-laws was by inscribing in law the fact of the constitution's suspension (AOCC, 14, November 8, 1973, 7).

[15] According to Sergio Díez in the Constituent Commission (AOCC, 68, September 5, 1974, 25). Guzmán repeated this explanation in the Junta the same day (AHJG, 153, September 5, 1974, 8).

tution. According to ART. 2, which apparently committed the Junta to the principle of legality, the constitutional and legal order would remain in force insofar as not modified in the form specified in ART. 3. This article, in turn, merely stated that both constituent and legislative acts would be issued as decree-laws. No formal means of distinction were provided for, but ART. 3 also stipulated, "The dispositions of the decree-laws that modify the Political Constitution of the State, will form part of its text and will be taken as incorporated into it."

## The Supreme Court and Decree-Laws

Some eight months after the Junta enacted D.L. No. 128, the Supreme Court responded. On July 24, 1974, in *"Federico Dunker Briggs,"* the full court ruled on the applicability of D.L. No. 449, which set maximum rents on urban real estate. Although the court found that the decree-law did not contravene the constitutional guarantee of property rights (ART. 10, no. 10), the Supreme Court asserted its constitutional authority to decide issues of constitutionality when posed in live cases before the judiciary. This power was given by ART. 86, paragraph two, of the constitution: "The Supreme Court, in individual cases under its cognizance, or which have been submitted to it on action interposed in a case pending before another court, may declare inapplicable for that case any legal provision as contrary to the constitution. This appeal may be taken at any stage without suspending the proceedings." The declaration of inapplicability of a legal precept, therefore, had restricted effects. It did not derogate the unconstitutional norm, but only prevented its application in the specific case at hand.[16]

In its July 1974 decision, the Supreme Court ruled that tacit modifications of the constitution were unacceptable: Unless a decree-law expressly stated that it amended the constitution or enacted constitutional norms, the decree-law was a "mere body of legal precepts," and, as such, would be subject to the Supreme Court's constitutional review.[17] In other words, the Supreme Court did not interpret D.L. No. 128 as granting a constitutional carte blanche to the Junta: Decree-laws that contravened the constitution, if enacted without any indication that they were constitutional amendments, would be struck down by the court when challenged in live cases.

---

[16] On the Chilean Supreme Court's faculty of reviewing the constitutionality of legislation, see Silva Bascuñán 1963, 3:432–45; Bertelsen 1969, 1985; and Precht 1987.

[17] The sentence is reproduced in *Fallos del Mes*, July 1974 (188):118–21.

In this manner, in July 1974 the Supreme Court not only defended its power of judicial review but also implicitly defended the principle of legal certainty, by refusing to allow the identity of the constitution to become unrecognizable, amidst an ever-growing profusion of decree-laws. Prior to this ruling, the issue of legal certainty, or better, constitutional certainty, had already been raised by some military advisors and officials. Their principal concern was not to assure the identity of norms of higher rank that would stand over and limit the Junta, but to assure the identity of those decree-laws which because of their constitutional rank would be binding upon future majorities after the period of military rule ended. In order to bind civilian actors in the future to the terms of the dictatorship's impositions, the identity of the constitution had to remain intelligible. Motivated by this concern, Guzmán in April 1974 began to argue against tacit modifications to the constitution and for discriminating "constitutional decrees" or "*actas constitucionales*" from simple decree-laws to allow certainty as to the rank of each norm. To this end, he also advocated a complete review of already enacted decree-laws to sort out which were of constitutional rank (AOCC, 28, April 2, 1974, 10, 18–23).[18] This advocacy of constitutional decrees was also shared by the Minister of Justice, Gonzalo Prieto, but, as Prieto told the commission, his opinion on this matter was not valued within the government, as advisory bodies to the Junta, including the Under Secretary of Juridical Coordination, supported the use of tacit modifications (AOCC, 28, April 2, 1974, 10). Thus, although some civilian advisors to the military were sensitive to the importance of constitutional certainty and the need to formally distinguish constituent acts, the issue remained latent until the Supreme Court through its jurisprudence forced the Junta to begin to expressly amend the constitution. However, as we will see, the Junta's response to the Supreme Court's challenge only exacerbated the problem of identifying which norms were constitutional after the coup.

A few months after its warning in "*Federico Dunker Briggs*," the Supreme Court made good on its threat to declare unconstitutional decree-laws that contravened the constitution. On October 4 and 9, 1974, in cases brought by employees who had been fired from semifiscal agencies after the coup, the Supreme Court ruled that ART. 6, paragraph 1, of D.L. No. 472 (D.O., May 20, 1974) was inapplicable because

---

[18] In Guzmán's words, it was necessary "to differentiate that which should translate into the permanent intention of the [future] governments, from that which should serve to implement or carry out a government's policies" (AOCC, 30, April 9, 1974).

it violated property rights guaranteed by Art. 10, no. 10 of the 1925 constitution. Although their dismissals were sanctioned by decree-laws that granted authority to reshuffle and purge positions in the state administration,[19] the plaintiffs were suing for extraordinary indemnity due them for having been fired for reasons other than those stipulated in the *Código de Trabajo* (Labor Code). The military had sought to bar such claims with D.L. No. 472, which expressly excluded extraordinary indemnity for individuals fired under such circumstances. Still, the Supreme Court ruled that such compensation was an acquired right and, as such, a form of property which could be denied only by encroaching upon the plaintiffs' property rights. Thus, as the Court ruled, the constitution would supersede the Junta's decree-laws.[20]

### The Junta's Counterjurisprudence: D.L. No. 788

Although the *"Federico Dunker Briggs"* ruling of July 1974 prompted legal advisors to begin considering how to block the Supreme Court from declaring decree-laws inapplicable and the October rulings immediately came to the Junta's attention, the Junta did not enact its own "counterjurisprudence" until December 1974 when it promulgated D.L. No. 788 to again regulate the use of constituent powers (D.O., December 4, 1974).[21] There are no official records documenting the preparation or discussion surrounding this decree-law in the Junta's legislative archive or the *Actas*. Nonetheless, ancillary materials contained among Guzman's personal papers indicate that D.L. No. 788 was a compromise away from initial proposals that would have emaciated the Supreme Court's powers of judicial review. These materials include a preliminary draft proposal which differs markedly from the decree-law enacted. The extent of these differences suggests that the first proposals were controversial, which may explain the Junta's delay in responding, as well as the absence of documentation. This draft indicates that D.L. No. 788 marked a key juncture in defining the institutional contours of military rule, not only because of the unintended consequences the decree-law eventually did have, but also because of the significance of the path not taken.

---

[19] D.L. No. 6 and 22, D.O., September 19 and October 2, 1973, respectively.

[20] For these decisions, see *"Rojas, Oscar y otros con Empresa de Comercio Agrícola,"* in *Revista de Derecho y Jurisprudencia*, second part, third section, 1974, 71:180–83, and *"Graciela Matamala Walker y otros,"* in *Fallos del Mes*, October 1974 (191):208–16.

[21] The term "counterjurisprudence" is borrowed from Precht 1987, 97.

At first, the Junta's legal and constitutional advisors worked on a legal response aimed at assuring the absolute supremacy of the Junta over the Supreme Court. On September 5, 1974, the *"Federico Dunker Briggs"* ruling came up in the Constituent Commission in the course of a discussion concerning whether the constitution prevented the Junta from allowing foreign investment in untapped mineral and gas reserves. In this context, Guzmán pushed the commission to assert the supremacy of the Junta. He adamantly stressed that the Junta wielded unlimited powers and could not be constrained by the constitution. Institutional limits had thwarted earlier governments, but do not constrain the Junta. In Guzmán's words, "For reasons whose analysis is not germane, a Government has come to direct the destinies of the country that does not face these limits; it has assumed total power. Thus, it is responsible only before God and History for its actions." With regard to the substantive issue in question – constitutional constraints upon allowing foreign investment in mining – Guzmán maintained, "if this government self-limits itself in this area, where nothing and no one is limiting it, and where nothing nor anyone stands before it who can justify, nor could ever justify, not doing what should be done because a juridical limit prevents it – apart from natural law, the government faces no such limit –, then we are reaching very grave levels of confusion" (AOCC, 68, September 5, 1974, 23, 24).[22] Guzmán reminded the commission of the article that it had originally recommended to the Junta to circumvent Supreme Court challenges to decree-laws, and concluded "there cannot be an unconstitutional decree-law" (AOCC, 68, September 5, 1974, 25).

Later the same day the matter was reviewed within the Junta. Toward the end of a session on emergency powers (discussed in the next chapter), Guzmán brought the Supreme Court's shifting jurisprudence to the Junta's attention and a discussion ensued over the reasons for the change in the Supreme Court's position (AHJG, 153, September 5, 1974, 8–9). Mónica Madariaga, General Pinochet's niece and legal advisor, attributed the shift to the influence of the *Contraloría* which was against tacit modifications to the constitution. Merino held the *Contraloría*'s position to be reasonable since the Junta had established a precedent of expressly modifying the constitution when it added a transitory article to the constitution to allow Chile to indemnify the

---

[22] Despite Guzmán's certitude, the issue of constitutional limits on foreign investment did greatly preoccupy the Junta. For a discussion of the political constraints associated with constitutional amendments to privatize copper mining, see pages 105–107.

Anaconda Company and thereby settle ongoing controversies and law-suits initiated after the firm's 1971 nationalization without compensa-tion.[23] Guzmán and General Pinochet, however, thought the superiority of all decree-laws over the constitution could be easily resolved with a very brief decree-law. In Guzmán's words, it was a matter "of four lines" (AHJG, 153, September 5, 1974, 9). Despite the simplicity of the solution, no action was taken at the time.

Legal advisors to Pinochet continued to search for ways to assert the Junta's preeminence over the Supreme Court in October 1974 when the Supreme Court overruled ART. 6 of D.L. No. 472. As soon as the press reported the Supreme Court's decision, Mónica Madariaga sent a memorandum to Pinochet, accompanied by a draft decree-law con-structed to stave off any further questioning of the constitutionality of the Junta's decree-laws.[24] Madariaga's draft consisted of a preamble and only two articles. The preamble forcefully reasserted the Junta's prerogative to modify the constitution as it wished and without review. First, it cited earlier references to the constituent power in D.L. Nos. 1, 128, and 527 to underscore that the Junta had never established a distinct procedure for enacting constitutional norms – the rank of a norm depended solely on its "juridical content or substance." Further-more, it was argued, the Junta had used express modifications only in specific instances when it wanted to ensure legal certainty. Otherwise,

---

[23] The decree-law referred to, D.L. No. 601 (D.O., July 24, 1974), was promulgated on the same day that the Supreme Court presented its position rejecting tacit modifica-tions in the *"Federico Dunker Briggs"* ruling. Given the complexity of the legal and con-stitutional issues raised by the Anaconda settlement, it is almost certain that the Junta consulted both the Supreme Court and the *Contraloría* prior to the promulgation of D.L. No. 601. Despite the proximity of these two events, Madariaga's explanation is, therefore, credible. A decree-law virtually identical to D.L. No. 601 was later promul-gated to indemnify the Braden Copper Company, the Kennecott Copper Corporation, and the Kennecott Sales Corporation (D.L. No. 710, D.O., October 24, 1974).

D.L. No. 601 was not the first decree-law to expressly modify the constitution. On three prior occasions the constitution had been expressly modified: As already men-tioned, D.L. No. 119 (D.O., November 10, 1973) modified Transitory ART. 17 to dissolve the *Tribunal Constitucional*; D.L. No. 170 (D.O., December 6, 1973) modified ART. 85, concerning the annual review process for judges; and D.L. No. 175 (D.O., December 10, 1973) modified ART. 6, to add an additional cause for depriving individuals of their nationality as Chileans – to have engaged from abroad, during a state of exception, in attacks on the essential interests of the State.

[24] In Jaime Guzmán's personal archive, the memo and the draft decree-law are attached to a clipping from *El Mercurio* on the Supreme Court's ruling. See *"Aclara Sentido y Alcance de los Decretos Leyes Nos. 1 y 128, De 1973, y 527, De 1974,"* N.D., T.D., Guzmán Papers, Fundación Jaime Guzmán, Santiago, Chile. Although the memo carries no date, the clipping bears a stamp transferring the material for study to the COAJ, signed by Pinochet and dated October 8, 1974.

nothing obliged the Junta to indicate that it was employing constituent powers each time it amended the constitution. As the preamble concluded, it was the "interpreter's" (i.e., the court's) responsibility to determine which norms were of constitutional character when these had been enacted without any indication that the Junta was employing its constituent powers. The bill's two articles reasserted the status quo: ART. 1 declared that the enactment of constitutional dispositions had not required nor would require any special formalities, while ART. 2 expressly stated that articles of the constitution that regulate the *recurso de inaplicabilidad* "had not applied and would not apply to those decree-laws that modify or have modified constitutional precepts without formally mentioning this circumstance."[25] In effect, the Supreme Court would have to accept tacit modifications and its review powers would pertain only to laws enacted prior to the coup, not the legislative acts of the military government.

Had this decree-law gone into effect, it would have made a shambles of the Supreme Court's claim to uphold the supremacy of the constitution and undermined the military's relatively cordial relations with the court. A sharp break with the Supreme Court likely would also have had immediate political impact on the military's civilian base of support. The court had played a key role in the legal struggle against the Allende government and any move against the judiciary could have turned important sectors of the centrist and conservative political class away from the regime.[26] What considerations led to the shift are unclear. The available archival materials contain no documentation of what transpired between the initial presentation of this draft decree-law and the eventual promulgation of D.L. No. 788. However, the text of law enacted reveals that a significantly different tack was taken.

These differences are not immediately apparent in the preamble to D.L. No. 788, which restated many of the principles contained in Madariaga's earlier proposal, largely to assert the sovereignty of the Junta. The preamble acknowledged that the Junta had not distinguished legislative and constituent acts, defended its authority to do so, and forcefully asserted the Junta's supremacy over the Supreme Court. Echoing Hobbes's argument concerning the reversibility of sovereign

---

[25] "*Aclara Sentido y Alcance de los Decretos Leyes Nos. 1 y 128, De 1973, y 527, De 1974*," N.D., T.D., Guzmán Papers, Fundación Jaime Guzmán, Santiago, Chile.

[26] The opposition elicited in April 1974 within the Constituent Commission by an earlier proposal that would have undermined the judiciary supports this conjecture and was expressed in these terms. On the controversy over this reform, which sought to facilitate the investigation and trial of former *Unidad Popular* officials, see pages 154–156.

acts, the preamble insisted that any act of self-limitation by the Junta was reversible: To admit the interpretation that tacit modifications were unacceptable, paragraph g) of the preamble stated, would be "admissible only if one accepted that the Junta itself has restricted the exercise of the Constituent Power that it has assumed, without any power of derogating this purported self-restriction, these suppositions are inadmissible for the reestablishment of the normal institutional evolution of the country" (*Considerando g*), D.L. No. 788, D.O., December 4, 1974). Notwithstanding these assertions of the Junta's superiority, toward the end of the preamble the Junta acquiesced to the Supreme Court's position. It acknowledged the advisability of expressly indicating the constitutional rank of any modifications and recognized the force of the court's review powers over ordinary decree-laws.

The articles of D.L. No. 788 reconciled this dual position by validating all prior unconstitutional decree-laws and by committing the Junta to express modifications in the future. Thus, by ART. 1, all prior decree-laws that are "contrary to, or are opposed to, or are different, from some precept" of the constitution were given the status of norms modifying the constitution, whether they expressly or tacitly, partially or totally, modified a norm. ARTICLES. 2 and 3 stipulated that henceforth any norms contrary to the constitution would stand as amendments only if the Junta expressly stated that they were being dictated in use of constituent power.[27] By clarifying rules for recognizing instances of constitutional amendment, D.L. No. 788 resolved the status of the Supreme Court's faculty of constitutional review and allowed the court to exercise its powers in their entirety. However, this clarification occurred at the cost of blurring the boundaries between the constitution and the law.

In part, this continued blurring was the Supreme Court's responsibility. For even though the preamble of D.L. No. 788 stipulated that the rank of a decree-law could be determined from its "juridical substance or content,"[28] when faced with appeals challenging the constitutional-

---

[27] For unknown reasons, Valenzuela only heeds ART. 1 and as a result misconstrues D.L. No. 788. He writes, "With the stroke of a pen, the four-member junta abandoned the principle of a written constitution anchored on popular sovereignty by making it clear that any of its laws took precedence over the constitution and automatically amended it" (1995, 29). Rosenn (1984, 124, n.2) and De Brito (1997, 44) also commit the same blunder.

[28] This criterion of identification was indicated in paragraph c) of the preamble. Paragraph e) also suggested another criterion, that of noncoincidence with the constitution. The significance of this distinction is developed by Soto Kloss (1976, 137–42) and discussed briefly in the following paragraph.

ity of decree-laws dictated prior to December 4, 1974 (the date of promulgation of D.L. No. 788), the Supreme Court consistently applied a mechanical interpretation of D.L. No. 788. The court, typically, first established whether a decree-law contravened the constitution, and, if it did, proceeded to note whether it had been dictated prior to December 4, 1974. If these two conditions were met, the Supreme Court would rule that the seemingly unconstitutional precept was actually a "tacit and partial modifying norm," which meant that the appeal for inapplicability at hand would be rejected: For instead of a contradiction between a statute and a norm of higher constitutional norm, the case would involve an opposition between "equally fundamental provisions both of the same constitutional rank." Following this procedure, on January 24, 1975, in "*Salvat M. Alfonso*," the Supreme Court rejected an appeal for the inapplicability of ART. 6 of D.L. No. 472 on the grounds that this very precept – whose unconstitutionality had led to the dictation of D.L. No. 788 – now possessed the character of a tacit amendment to the constitution.[29]

## D.L. No. 788 and the Loss of Constitutional Certainty

D.L. No. 788 allowed the Junta to settle its relationship with the Supreme Court but at the cost of rendering indeterminate the identity of the constitution. This particular resolution weakened the distinction between constitutional and legal precepts. As pro-Junta jurists argued (Soto Kloss 1976; Fiamma 1977b), D.L. No. 788 only exacerbated the problem of constitutional certainty and was totally at odds with the Junta's stated commitment to restore the rule of law. The crux of this argument was that noncoincidence with constitutional norms was not a sufficient criterion for establishing that a precept was constituent. Decree-laws that did not coincide with the constitution could either be distinct from constitutional norms – for example, those that created a new institutional order – or contrary to them in that they contradicted existing constitutional norms (Soto Kloss 1976, 148). To raise the latter to constitutional rank, as the Supreme Court's jurisprudence did, undermined the character of constitutional norms as constituent, as precepts structuring institutions and rights

---

[29] Between January 24 and 30, 1975, the Supreme Court restated this jurisprudence regarding D.L. No. 472 on sixteen occasions. For the first ruling and a list of the other cases, see *Fallos del Mes*, December 1974 (193):300–3. The quote is at page 302.

capable of providing procedures and limits for ordinary lawmaking and governance.[30]

The point can be illustrated by considering the decree-law which sparked the controversy with the Supreme Court over its review of decree-laws. D.L. No. 472 denied state employees fired under D.L. Nos. 6 and 22 their legal entitlement to extraordinary indemnification for irregular termination of employment. The decree-law, which the Supreme Court had at first ruled contrary to the right to private property, merely declared that certain categories of individuals were not entitled to indemnification. By virtue of D.L. No. 788, however, this precept became a "tacit and partial modification" of ART. 10, no. 10 of the constitution. Yet, the manner whereby this decree-law modified ART. 10, no. 10 was unclear. For example, did D.L. No. 472 imply that the right of property no longer held generally? As Soto Kloss and Fiamma argued, decree-laws that contradicted the constitution in this manner lacked the substantial content of constitutional norms, and granting them constitutional status only increased uncertainty as to the constitutional precepts in effect.

Thus, although the clarification of rules of recognition for the exercise of constituent powers committed the Junta to consistently differentiate constitutional amendments from ordinary legislation after D.L. No. 788, this settling of tensions with the Supreme Court came at the cost of the identity of the constitution. With D.L. No. 788 the preceding 787 decree-laws suddenly were raised to constitutional rank. Even though not all of these decree-laws necessarily contradicted the substance of the constitution, many of them contradicted its terms in a manner similar to D.L. No. 472, leaving open many questions as to how the constitution had been modified. The consequent indeterminacy of the constitution would in the following years lead to the collapse of the constitution as an identifiable framework of higher law.

Notwithstanding this unintended consequence, the Supreme Court's limited power of judicial review did set a formal limit on the Junta's legislative power: After December 1974 any decree-law "contrary to," "opposed to," or "different from" an existing constitutional norm would be interpreted by the Supreme Court to be a modification to the constitution only if its text explicitly stated that the decree-law was being

---

[30] This can be expressed in the language of Hart's (1961) categories: The elevation to constitutional status of primary rules that contradict secondary (constitutional) rules blurs the distinction between rules that impose obligations and those that confer powers, with the result that the identity of the secondary rules which are the foundation of the legal order is lost.

enacted in exercise of the constituent power. Given that statutory and constituent acts both required unanimity, the requirement of express modification was merely adjectival: All the four commanders had to do to modify the constitution was lead off a decree-law with the phrase "The Junta of Government, in exercise of the Constituent Power, decrees the following." Nevertheless, this merely formal requirement was not insignificant. Express modifications forced upon the members of the Junta considerations of political prudence which were absent from acts of simple legislation since express modifications to the constitution tended to focus national and international attention. This consideration often led junta members to divide over the expediency of toying with the constitution, particularly when the modifications involved earlier amendments that had received strong congressional support. The tortured debate within the Junta over modifying Transitory ART. 17 of the constitution, which nationalized large copper mining, illustrates the contradictory trade-offs involved in expressly amending the constitution.

## *Extrajudicial Constraints: The Example of Copper*

In mid-1975 the military government had offers from foreign capital for large investments to exploit two untapped copper deposits, *El Abra* and *Quebrada Blanca*. However, the particular form of the 1971 nationalization prevented their exploitation: In addition to the large copper mines then under exploitation, the nationalization included mining rights registered to the firms nationalized; these rights became inalienable patrimony of the state. The rights to *El Abra* and *Quebrada Blanca* had both been registered by Anaconda and, therefore, after 1971 belonged absolutely to the state. The dilemma before the Junta was how to provide foreign investors with credible assurances that mining rights would be secure without modifying the nationalization clause which Congress had unanimously approved in July 1971. The Junta, along with top legal advisors and other counsel, spent hours and hours trying to resolve this bind. The intricacies of property rights, mining property, and the wording of Transitory ART. 17 were examined over and over again until finally, after six extended sessions, a satisfactory solution was reached.[31]

---

[31] See AHJG 214, July 15, 1975, 1–20; 216, July 22, 1975, 1–26; 217, July 24, 1975, 1–22; 218, July 29, 1975, 2–18; 223, August 12, 1975, 1–30; 224, August 12, 1975, 1–22.

These discussions reveal the political and not economic character of the junta members' opposition to privatizing copper mining. From the outset, General Leigh and Admiral Merino voiced concern over the political implications of playing with constitutional precepts enacted to nationalize copper. Noting that he was fully aware that in the future large investments would be required to continue to exploit copper, Admiral Merino was adamant: "later another government will do it. But we will not. We will maintain the present situation. And if in the future, to increase production, etc., it is necessary to contribute capital that the State does not possess and it is necessary to privatize or sell to third parties, it will be done, but we will not do it ourselves" (AHJG, 214, July 15 , 1975, 17).

Similarly, General Leigh stated,

> I am absolutely against modifying the constitution in regards to copper. If in the course of the discussion I see another possibility, I may change my opinion. I reserve the right. But a priori I am not an advocate of modifying constitutions, and I am fully in agreement with the Admiral that after the Full Congress, by unanimity, established the nationalization of copper we cannot and should not begin to change the rules of the game. This is of far-reaching significance. (AHJG, 214, July 15, 1975, 18)

These were clear expressions of concern over the political ramifications of any privatization, not an opposition that arose out of statist or nationalist economic conceptions nor apprehensions before institutional mechanisms impeding privatization. Admiral Merino was a strong advocate of free market economics. His latter contributions confirm his willingness to allow foreign investment in copper mining (AHJG, 218, July 29, 1975, 10–11); similarly, General Leigh was not against foreign investment to exploit untapped copper deposits.

Still, the desire to avoid modifying the constitution forced the commanders and their advisors to endure interminable and inconclusive analyses regarding the feasibility of providing juridical security without amending the constitution. Any number of alternatives were discussed, top experts in mining law contributed their knowledge, but no matter the angle of attack the conclusion was always the same: Unless the government was willing to forgo the investments, the only solution was to expressly modify the constitution. General Leigh eventually provided a way of presenting the reform to make it politically acceptable. The constitution would be expressly amended by adding two interpretive transitory articles: one would consolidate the nationalization by rectifying difficulties arising from the original clause's wording, while the other would point to the future, by permitting the sale of, or negotiation of, concessions to mine unexploited copper deposits (AHJG, 218, July 29, 1975, 15).[32]

The Junta was fully aware of the costs of this solution. To stave off political attacks, the Junta closed the door to any privatization of the large copper mines already in operation. Furthermore, the opening to foreign investment was codified restrictively to encompass only those deposits not under exploitation at the time of the decree-law's promulgation, and any concessions or sale of such deposits could be effected only by law. According to Julio Philippi, one of Chile's foremost lawyers, an expert in mining law, and the military government's chief negotiator in the talks that led to a resolution of the conflicts with the copper firms expropriated in 1971, these were draconian restrictions not found in any constitution: "What is being done out of prudence appears to me to be so exaggerated that it is difficult for one to put such a norm in the constitution. Now, from the political point of view, sure, it embellishes the thing much more, but it is a monstrosity" (AHJG, 223, August 12, 1975, 29–30).

Despite the formal facility with which the Junta could modify the constitution, political considerations often advised against expressly modifying the text. Further examples of this reticence are discussed in Chapter 4 when the self-limitation of emergency powers is examined. Before commenting more generally on the reasons why the judiciary could not effect more substantive limits on the prerogative powers of the Junta – most of which equally apply to judiciaries in constitutional regimes with civil law systems – the constitutional and legal control faculties of the *Contraloría General de la República* should be examined. Though these powers were preventive and not judicial, this organ's functions were mechanisms that partially compelled the executive and the state administration to operate within the confines of law, albeit, often, the military's decree-law.

## The *Contraloría* and the Legality of Administrative Acts

The *Contraloría General de la Republica* was (and is) the principal agency controlling the state administration in Chile. Created in 1927

---

[32] The result was D.L. No. 1,167 (D.O., February 27, 1976), which was decreed in express use of the Junta's constituent power. Note that the decree-law was promulgated long after it was approved by the Junta on September 3, 1975.

and raised to constitutional status in 1943 (ART. 21), the *Contraloría* is an independent, autonomous agency which effects fiscal and juridical oversight over the state administration, including supervision and control of revenues and expenditures of all state offices, national general accounting, and review of administrative acts to assure that they conform to the constitution and the law before going into effect (*toma de razón*).

Like the Supreme Court, the *Contraloría* had been embroiled in the interinstitutional conflicts that erupted over the legality of the UP's economic program. Immediately after the coup, top officials from the agency met with the Junta, communicated their support to the new government, and offered their assistance (AHJG, 2, September 13, 1973, 3–4). Except for a brief initial period during which the agency's preventive review of administrative acts was suspended,[33] this cooperation did not involve limiting the *Contraloría*'s extensive faculties to oversee state operations. These, in fact, were actually broadened shortly after the coup.[34] Once the *Contraloría* resumed its fiscal and legal oversight, it exercised these powers without subsequent interruption during the whole period of military rule.

In terms of institutional constraints on the legislative and regulatory capacity of the military regime, the *toma de razón* is the most interesting of the *Contraloría*'s faculties. This power, which was given by statute and not the constitution, involved preventive juridical control of administrative decrees and resolutions. Before going into effect, the *Contraloría* reviewed executive acts to assure that they were authorized by law, affected by the appropriate authority, and used for a legally prescribed purpose.[35] If the *Contraloría* challenged the legality or constitutionality of an administrative act, it returned (*representar*) the decree with an indication of the legal deficiencies needing correction. Represented decrees could be rectified and resubmitted by the respective ministry or else withdrawn. Only upon the *Contraloría*'s approval (*toma de razón*) could a decree go into effect. By law, the president of the republic, with the signature of the complete cabinet, could override the *Contraloría* and insist that a legally deficient decree be

---

[33] According to Horacio Brandy, at the time of the interview the second-ranking lawyer in the Juridical Department of the *Contraloría*, the *toma de razón* was resumed on December 1, 1973. Interview with Horacio Brandy, Santiago, Chile, November 6, 1992.

[34] D.L. No. 38 (D.O., September 24, 1973) extended the *Contraloría*'s oversight and accounting powers to the decentralized state sector.

[35] The *Contraloría*'s authority to exercise preventive legal and constitutional review of presidential decrees was given by Law 10,336 of May 29, 1952.

put into effect, but use of the *decreto de insistencia* was highly controversial and under democratic governments exposed ministers to possible constitutional accusation in Congress and removal from office.[36] It should be noted that the scope of this control was only partial and did not extend to all executive decrees and resolutions. By law, the *Contralor*, the head of the agency, was authorized to dictate resolutions exempting broad categories of executive acts from review. Faced with a growing volume of decrees subject to review, after 1970 it became the norm to review only those administrative acts pertaining to matters specifically excluded from an otherwise blanket exemption (Soto Kloss 1977, 172). Notwithstanding these exemptions, within two months of the coup the *Contralor* issued a resolution (*Contraloría de la República, Resolución No. 1,100*, D.O., November 10, 1973) stipulating that all decrees and resolutions emanating from the Junta or its President – including all modifications to them – had to be submitted for review. Another resolution, issued in 1977, also subjected to review decrees that pertained to such politically sensitive matters as measures related to D.L. No. 77 (the decree-law which outlawed the Left parties), the cancellation of Chilean nationality, detentions ordered during states of emergency, and orders to expel individuals from the country or prohibit their entry, although some of these matters were subsequently exempted from review.[37]

During the sixteen and a half years of military rule, hundreds of thousands of administrative acts were submitted to the *Contraloría*'s legal department for legal and constitutional review. Each year, thousands of decrees were returned to ministries and agencies because of legal defects, as can be seen in Table 1 and in Table 6 (in Chapter 7), and on many occasions anticipation of the *Contraloría*'s tremendous power caused legal advisors considerable anxiety. In general, the *Contraloría* functioned normally under the military government. On no occasion did Pinochet make use of the *decreto de insistencia* to force the implementation of unconstitutional and/or illegal administrative acts.[38]

---

[36] Upon receipt of a *decreto de insistencia*, the *Contraloría* would transmit all pertinent information to the Chamber of Deputies so that this body could decide whether to initiate an accusation against the executive (Gil 1966, 98).

[37] See *Contraloría General de la República, Resolución 600*, D.O., July 18, 1977. Orders of detention, exile, and prohibition of entry into the country were exempted from review by *Contraloría General de la República, Resolución 113*, D.O., January 28, 1978. The reasons for this modification are unknown to me.

[38] This assertion is based on the annual reports for the period. See *Contraloría General de la República, Subdepartamento de Coordinación e Información Jurídica, Memoria de la Contraloría General de la República*, 1975–1991.

**Table 1.** Review of Executive Acts by the Contraloría General de la República (toma de razón) (1974–1980)

| Year | Dispatched[a] | Withdrawn | Exempt | Returned |
|------|------|------|------|------|
| 1974 | 198,269 | n.a. | 66,962 | n.a. |
| 1975 | 183,100 | n.a. | 55,761 | n.a. |
| 1976 | 198,327 | n.a. | 43,881 | n.a. |
| 1977 | 203,025 | n.a. | 49,021 | 14,682 |
| 1978 | 208,633 | 628 | 55,729 | 18,633 |
| 1979 | 137,057 | 742 | 8,955 | 13,127 |
| 1980 | 146,983 | 1,111 | 8,242 | 11,484 |

[a] Includes decree-laws received for registration, supreme decrees, and resolutions.
*Source*: Data compiled from Contraloría General de la República, Subdepartamento de Coordinación e Información Jurídica, *Memoria de la Contraloría General de la República*, 1975–1981.

What type of limit did the *Contraloría* represent? In some ways, the effect of the *Contraloría*'s review of administrative acts was similar to the Supreme Court's control of the constitutionality of decree-laws in that it too compelled the military to uphold formal legal consistency and rule by law. Neither institution set substantive constraints upon the content of executive or legislative acts since their constitutionality or legality was always upheld if the appropriate procedural forms had been respected: Decree-laws could transgress the constitution if they had been promulgated as modifications; likewise, executive acts could exceed statutory limitations if the pertinent statute had first been modified.

Yet this similarity conceals an important difference in the effects of each institution's review powers. The Supreme Court's powers bore upon a single body that possessed both legislative and constituent powers (the Junta), and which consequently could by itself override or circumvent the court if unanimity existed. The subject of the *Contraloría*'s review, the executive, did not possess a similar combination of powers with which to unilaterally override a negative ruling by the *Contraloría*. Since statutory law could not be modified by executive decree, the executive could only act beyond standing legal boundaries by first working new legislation through the Junta. In this manner, by assuring the superiority of statutory law over acts of administration, the *Contraloría* indirectly safeguarded the Junta's powers before

Pinochet within the domain of issues subject to preventive legal review.

However, this safeguard was not foolproof, as was demonstrated in late December 1977 when Pinochet proceeded to impose the January 4, 1978 *Consulta Nacional* despite the *Contralor's* legal and constitutional objections and the unyielding opposition of Admiral Merino and General Leigh. The official pretext for this pseudo-plebiscite was the December 16, 1977 UN General Assembly Resolution condemning human rights violations in Chile, yet the broader political context involved ongoing internal confrontations pitting the navy and the air force against Pinochet over the course of military rule and Pinochet's position within the regime (analyzed in Chapter 5). As they often did, Merino and Leigh attempted to check Pinochet's attempt to seek plebiscitary ratification of his person by arguing that Pinochet had neither legal nor constitutional authority to proceed without a prior constitutional reform and, therefore, the Junta's approval.[39] This position was upheld on December 28, 1977 when Héctor Humeres, the *Contralor*, challenged the constitutionality of the supreme decree that was to regulate the plebiscite. Fortuitous circumstances, however, enabled Pinochet to proceed. By law, the *Contralor* is appointed for life and is irremovable except under exceptional circumstances after impeachment by the Senate. Yet, at the time of this controversy, Humeres was in the process of retiring, and on the afternoon of the ruling, the handling of his retirement papers suddenly was accelerated.[40] Once a new *Contralor* was appointed and the decree was modified to differentiate a now juridically inconsequential *Consulta Nacional* from an actual plebiscite, the *toma de razón* for the authorizing decree proceeded and Pinochet went ahead with the controversial poll.

Note also that the preventive character of the *Contraloría's* review of administrative acts placed a more significant constraint upon the

[39] The wording of the text presented for ratification reveals the personalistic character of this move. The eventual authorizing decree (ART. 2, D.S. (I) 1,308, D.O., January 3, 1978) stated, "In the face of the international aggression unleashed against the Government of our Fatherland (Patria), I support President Pinochet in his defense of the dignity of Chile, and I reaffirm the legitimacy of the Government of the Republic to sovereignly head the process of institutionalization of the country."

[40] On the appointment and removal of the *Contralor*, see Evans 1970, 52. According to Evans, the *Contralor General de la República* is a presidential appointment, requiring Senate approval. By virtue of ART. 14, D.L. No. 527, the Junta therefore had to approve the president's designee. However, I have no evidence as to whether or not the Junta ratified the appointment of then Minister of Labor Sergio Fernández Fernández, as a replacement for Humeres.

prerogative powers of the military government since a legal challenge by the *Contraloría* blocked the impugned decree going into effect. The Supreme Court's judicial review, on the other hand, was applicable only with regard to decree-laws that could pertain to suits and, thereby, come to be impugned in court. This suggests another reason why the judiciary could not stand as a significant limit on the military regime.

## Civil Law and the Limits of Judicial Review

The rupture of the constitutional order did not lead the Supreme Court to significantly alter its jurisprudence on inapplicability from the period 1925 to 1973. Even with regard to the 787 decree-laws dictated prior to D.L. No. 788, the Supreme Court's procedures were continuous with earlier review practices. Both before and after the coup, the Supreme Court limited itself to a comparison of the contested legal text and the constitution in effect at the moment when the appeal was lodged. Only specific legal and constitutional precepts were compared. The Supreme Court's review did not uphold the spirit, values, nor principles of the constitution. The review was confined to the examination of particular legal norms as they regarded specific constitutional norms, and this review was in order only when the legal norm challenged – in its substantive, and not formal, content – was applicable to the case at hand (Precht 1987, 88).

The Supreme Court's limited faculty of constitutional review reflected a broader conception of the judiciary, grounded in nineteenth-century liberal constitutionalism, which set the boundaries within which the Supreme Court could check the Junta. As in other civil law systems, the jurisdiction of the Chilean judiciary was restricted to civil and criminal cases.[41] The courts applied the law to specific cases, and their decisions were binding only on parties to a live case before it; the courts under no circumstance were to be a source of law.[42]

---

[41] On the civil law tradition in Western Europe and Latin America, see Merryman 1969.
[42] This principle was expressed in ART. 3 of the Chilean Civil Code (1855):

Sólo toca al legislador explicar o interpretar la ley en un modo generalmente obligatorio.

Las sentencias judiciales no tienen fuerza obligatoria sino respecto de las causas en que actualmente se pronunciaren.

Only the legislator may explain or interpret the law in a generally obligatory manner. Judical decisions have no obligatory force except in regard to the cases in which they are pronounced.

Limited competency of the judiciary reflected the doctrines of separation of powers and legislative supremacy which were so influential on Chilean constitutionalism and legal thought: Law was to be enacted exclusively by representative assemblies separate from government. Legislative supremacy was understood as the chief counterbalance against government absolutism since representative government limited the government to executing laws not of its own making. Constraints in the liberal constitutional framework are, therefore, essentially political, not judicial. They turn on the institutionalization of legality through legislative assemblies which also exercise oversight aimed at containing the government within the bounds of the law. With the separation of legislation, administration, and adjudication, the judiciary was excluded from any intervention in matters of government and its competency was strictly limited to matters of justice.[43] Conversely, the other public powers – the legislative and the executive – were expressly prohibited from exercising judicial functions. Although this sharp separation of politics and law provided the foundation for an independent judiciary, the constitutional and legal prohibitions on judicial lawmaking and judicial interference in administration inhibited the judiciary from serving as an effective constraint on government, whether constitutional or de facto.

These restrictions, a reflection of the long-standing mistrust of the judiciary within civil law systems, also explain the slow emergence of constitutional review within the Chilean legal system. Until the 1925 constitution, on the grounds that judicial review would give the judiciary preeminence over the legislature by allowing it to annul congressional resolutions, the Supreme Court was denied any explicit authority to review the constitutionality of legislation (Silva Bascuñán 1963, 3:432; Frühling 1978, 18, 39), and in 1925 the principle of legislative supremacy was invoked to justify the adoption of a system of constitutional review with limited rather than general effects, a tradition which the 1980 constitution would respect.[44]

---

[43] Bravo Lira (1976) reconstructs the historical process whereby these powers came to be embodied in separate organs in Chile.

[44] The adoption of judicial review with general effects was considered during the drafting of the 1925 constitution, but rejected (Silva Bascuñán 1963, 3:432–34). It was also considered within the Constituent Commission in 1977 and recommended by both the Constituent Commission and the Council of State (AOCC, 285, 287, April 14 and 26, 1977; *Actas del Consejo de Estado*, hereafter AdCdE, 85, 86, August 14 and 21, 1979). The Junta, however, retained the Supreme Court's traditional narrow faculty in the 1980 constitution (Art. 80).

By the same token, the restriction of this faculty to a review of the substantive content of laws to the exclusion of any review of the constitutionality of the legislative process also derived from a strict adherence to the separation of powers, as evaluation of the process of legislation was seen as an intromission into another organ's powers (Silva Bascuñán 1963, 3:439–40; Silva Cimma 1977, 14; Verdugo Marinkovic 1989, 59). On this principle, the Supreme Court disavowed competency to adjudicate procedural conflicts that arose in the course of legislation or to rule on the validity of decree-laws enacted during periods of de facto rule, and thus until the creation of the Constitutional Tribunal in 1970 no organ was competent to settle executive-legislative conflicts over the form of legislation.[45]

The doctrine of separation of powers as inscribed in Chilean constitutionalism and law also inhibited the judiciary from controlling the legality of administrative acts and the conduct of government officials. Oversight of the latter was an attribute of Congress, which could impeach a range of higher officials – including higher court justices and top military officers – for breaches of legality. Though legislative supremacy implied that the executive should be bound by law, as in other civil law systems, the review of the constitutionality and legality of administrative acts in Chile was granted to a nonjudicial organ, the *Contraloría General de la República*.[46] This tradition of separation of powers and judicial noninterference also greatly undermined judicial mechanisms designed to protect individual rights. As we will see in the next chapter, on the basis of the same principle of nonintromission into other powers, the judiciary repeatedly abdicated any authority to review the executive's use of state of siege powers during the worst years of repression.

In these ways, the principle of separation of powers, which had been formulated to prevent arbitrary rule, set the boundaries in which the judiciary could constrain the military: With the resolution of the issue of constituent powers, the Supreme Court could stand as a formal limit on the legislative acts of the Junta. Insofar as the Supreme Court could rule that decree-laws contrary to constitutional precepts in force were

---

[45] The Supreme Court's jurisprudence on decree-laws enacted by de facto governments between 1924 and 1932 is examined in Cumplido and Frühling 1979.

[46] Similarly, the 1925 constitution provided for the creation of separate administrative courts (ART. 87) to handle cases filed against the administration; however, these courts were never created and the Supreme Court prior to 1973 repeatedly ruled that the lower courts were competent to handle such cases (Silva Bascuñán 1963, 3:429–31).

inapplicable in cases before it, the Court forced the Junta to employ consistent legal forms. Yet, given the facility with which the Junta, when in agreement, could modify the constitution, "the constitution" became a potentially extremely flexible document and the court's limiting powers became equally relative. The same point applies at the level of statute law regarding the *Contraloría*'s review of administrative acts, though with the caveat that modifications to executive regulatory authority required coordination with the Junta.

Both institutions upheld the principle of legality and rule *by* law. Nevertheless, as we have seen, the delay in resolving the constitutional question and the manner of its settlement eventually spared 787 decree-laws from challenge in court. As a result, this resolution allowed the Junta to legislate unchecked during its first year in power. But at the same time, legal certainty, one of the very values that legal consistency is intended to assure, was greatly undermined. Thus, the military's resolution of the status of constituent powers weakened the identity of the constitution. Jaime Guzmán stressed this point in September 1975 when the Constituent Commission debated General Pinochet's announcement that provisional *Actas Constitucionales* (Constitutional Acts) would soon be promulgated. Guzmán noted that the armed forces had used a number of different legal instruments to modify the 1925 constitution: *bandos* in the first days after the coup, then decree-laws that transformed some – but not all – of these *bandos* into statutes, later decree-laws of constitutional rank, some as a result of D.L. No. 788, others because they had been expressly dictated as constitutional decrees. The result was well stated by Guzmán:

> Although it is true that there exists a constitutional system, it is no less true . . . that this is neither clear nor precise. The text of the constitution has been reduced to very few dispositions that maintain their force. The truth is that whoever reads the constitution and observes what is happening in Chile cannot be truly convinced that the constitution is in force. Furthermore, if you tell someone that . . . the Fundamental Charter, except for some modifications, governs the country, such a statement will sound almost ironic, since there have been so many amendments that the constitutional text has lost force. The situation of the Chilean constitutional system is, therefore, precarious and confused. (AOCC, 153, September 23, 1975, 12)

Thus, through the unintended consequences of their own actions, the armed forces contributed to the need for a new constitutional system. Before turning to how the *Actas Constitucionales* revived the question of temporal limits to military rule, the inability of the judiciary to effectively exercise its constitutional mandate to oversee all courts and to protect personal liberty must be examined, as the military's use of repressive force, unhindered by any effective judicial oversight, stimulated intense international pressure for a return to constitutional normalcy.

# Chapter Four

# The Shadowy Boundary between Force and Law: The Judiciary, Repression, and the Cosmetic Limitation of Emergency Powers

With the massive repression unleashed by the military coup, the definition of the boundaries between law and extralegal force immediately emerged as potentially the most explosive point of contact between the judiciary and the military regime. As in any legal system conforming to the rule of law, Chilean constitutional and statutory law stipulated that all arrests had to comply with strict guarantees protecting individual freedoms, incarceration could only follow conviction by trial, and, even under constitutional states of emergency, such as the state of siege, due process remained in force and the scope of emergency powers was delimited. In the days following the coup, before the onslaught of repressive military power, these norms faded from the horizon. Mass detentions, summary executions, bodies in the Mapocho River, and the first military tribunals were clear signals that the precise argument of lawyers had given way to time of war, as the military itself characterized the period for legal purposes.

Nevertheless, despite this abrupt displacement, under the constitution the judiciary held the authority, if not the power, to see that these transgressions were corrected. The judiciary's relevant authority in this new context was twofold. First, on petition, the judiciary was empowered to uphold constitutional guarantees of due process and protect persons from arbitrary arrest. The instrument was the *recurso de amparo*, a writ similar to *habeas corpus*, which on appeal could proceed to the Supreme Court. Second, although the declaration of a state of siege gave military courts jurisdiction over most political offenses, the constitution authorized the Supreme Court to supervise all courts, which implied that the Court held the authority to review and correct the administration of military justice. In principle these powers represented the basis for significant conflict with the military regarding its use of force to repress political adversaries.

This chapter reconstructs how these potential points of conflict were managed during the first years of military rule and evaluates the judiciary's efficacy as an institution empowered to hold the government to legal and constitutional standards regarding the arrest and punishment of individuals purported to have committed political offenses. The main conclusion that emerges from this reconstruction is that the judiciary in Chile did not stand as an effective institutional limit capable of compelling the dictatorship to contain its repressive activity within the confines of the law, even the law set by the regime. This situation left the security services free to pursue and punish "enemies" of the military government without hindrance from effective procedural or juridical restraints. In this context, any limitations upon the military government's use of repressive force could only arise not from the institutions constitutionally empowered to check such abuses but from within the Junta itself. This failure of the judiciary to effectively protect individual rights to personal security and due process can in part be ascribed to volitional failures. In 1974 and 1975, the Supreme Court repeatedly abdicated its constitutional faculties to oversee the military courts. Yet, perhaps far more pernicious was the total inefficacy of the *recurso de amparo* before absolutely illegal forms of detention and torment which wholly disregarded the regular forms and procedures of arrest and confinement that the *recurso* is designed to regulate and uphold.

I precede this reconstruction with a brief account of the stages and characteristics of the repression during the first years of military rule. The subsequent section examines the relationship between the Supreme Court and the military tribunals, and is followed by an account of how the courts and the government processed the many thousands of *recursos de amparo* which were filed on behalf of the disappeared and the detained. The final section discusses how in this context measures to moderate the repression could only emerge from within the military government itself. It examines the first steps taken by the Junta in response to international pressure to "self-limit" its repressive powers. But, as the examples discussed show, acknowledgment of international standards did not constrain the Junta and initially had the perverse consequence of impelling increasingly clandestine and extralegal forms of repression.

## Combating the Enemy in Time of War

Political repression in Chile had profound national and international repercussions and became one the most difficult and enduring legacies of the coup. Its expressions under the dictatorship were multiple: the anguish and enmity of the survivors and the families of the victims, profound divisions within society over the reality and justification of these acts, persistent international pressure to halt human rights violations, and fears of retribution within sectors of the armed forces linked with the security apparatuses. Within the dictatorship, the legacy of repression became a prism through which all major institutional and constitutional options were refracted, as well as a spur to take decisions in these areas.

Defenders of the military regime typically justify the intensity and scope of the repression that followed the coup by claiming that Chile was in the midst of an "internal war" by September 1973. The Junta immediately underscored this bellicose characterization of the situation when it enacted D.L. No. 5 to clarify that the state of siege should be understood as having the rank of "time of war" (D.O., September 22, 1973). Yet, for a number of Chilean legal analysts, the internal war in Chile was nothing more than a "legal fiction" for two reasons. First, although the Chilean Code of Military Justice (*CdJM*) did regulate and define a category of "state of war" in the absence of war with a foreign state, this category did not refer to war in the material sense but to forms of armed rebellion and insurrection which, unlike civil war, under international usage do not qualify as "war."[1] Second, regardless of this first objection, the particular circumstances that legally warranted activation of this "state of war" were absent in Chile in 1973. This peculiar state of exception corresponded only under particular circumstances and only for the pursuit of specific ends: The "state of war" was the juridical complement of naming a general in chief to operate militarily against illicit uses of force by armed rebels or an insurrection during a state of siege.[2]

---

[1] For this reason Montealegre (1979, 418–22) argued that it was a misnomer to designate this peculiar state of exception in the CdJM a "state of war." War involves the licit use of force by recognized belligerents and puts international laws regarding belligerency and neutrality into effect. Accordingly, Montealegre distinguishes between a "belligerent state of war" and a "penal state of war." Montealegre's work (1979, 25–42, 141–71, 416–30) provides the most systematic analysis of the usage of "war," "state of war," and "enemy" in Chilean positive law.

[2] The relevant legal citations are Art. 73, 265, 418, and 419 of the CdJM.

These forms of armed activity were absent in Chile at the time of the coup. Irrespective of an increasingly virulent revolutionary discourse among some parties within and outside the government coalition, the strength of the *Unidad Popular* – and the Chilean Left in general – was social and political, not military. By mid-1973, political conflict had resulted in a severe political and economic crisis but not acts of armed rebellion or insurrection by supporters of the Allende government. The manifestations of the crisis were essentially nonmilitary: general economic chaos, illegal factory occupations and takeovers of farms, political stalemate and polarization, recurrent disturbances of public order, an insurmountable constitutional crisis, the formation of left- and right-wing paramilitary organizations, virulent public debate, calls for the infiltration of the armed forces and a revolutionary resolution of the crisis, as well as isolated acts of violence which resulted in a relatively small number of deaths. Still, despite the depth of the crisis, by the standards of Chilean law there was no material justification for an internal "state of war" nor for military operations of anywhere near the magnitude and fury that ensued. In this sense, the postcoup repression was driven more by perceptions of what was necessary to successfully overthrow the Allende government and disorganize potential loci of opposition to de facto military power than by any demonstrable need for military action against organized, illicit armed associations engaging in acts against internal state security.

This is a point of capital importance, for the absence of significant organized armed activity prior to the coup clearly set Chile apart from other contemporary Latin American political crises that terminated in military dictatorship, particularly in Argentina and Uruguay, where guerrilla forces were active. It may well be true that the verbal violence of the months preceding the coup, with calls for a revolutionary resolution to the crisis, or, at minimum, the armed defense of the government in the event of a coup, distorted military estimations of expected armed resistance. Regarding this point, the quality of the armed force's intelligence on the internal paramilitary threat, as well as the extent of its dissemination among officers, is unknown. In the months and days preceding the coup the armed forces carried out massive searches for arms, as authorized by the *Ley de Control de Armas* which had been passed by Congress in October 1972. However, these searches may not have affected military hypotheses regarding the scope of the Left military threat: The failure to discover large arms caches may have been interpreted as proof that many arms were still in circulation. Furthermore, distorted perceptions of the Left's military strength were shaped not only by the verbal excesses of the Left's more "revolutionary" leaders. Prior to and after the coup, extreme right publicists – often in publications directed at specific branches of the armed forces – launched intense campaigns aimed at unmasking what were argued to be the intrinsically bellicose designs of the Left parties, particularly the Communist Party, which during the Allende years had been conspicuous for its moderation.[3] Whatever its influence may have been on the armed forces, the fraudulence and irresponsibility of the Left's revolutionary grandstanding was exposed on September 11, 1973 as the armed forces rapidly controlled the internal security situation and revealed the military preparedness of the Left to be negligible.[4]

With the exception of fighting in and around the presidential palace, *La Moneda*, which was dramatically bombed and set ablaze by air force fighter planes, an intense gun battle at one factory, and clashes in the shantytown *La Legua*, the armed forces encountered virtually no resistance in Santiago on September 11, 1973. Outside of the capital, the armed forces took control largely without incident,[5] and in the country as a whole the armed forces and *carabineros* suffered very few casualties.[6] To a large degree the ferocity of the coup was driven by symbolic and disciplinary objects, not martial strategy: A massive display of force would set an example and demonstrate the futility of resisting the new authorities – a message equally directed at military officers

---

[3] For examples, see Domic K. 1973a, 1973b, as well as the publications *Tizona* and *Tacna*.

[4] Nothing more pathetically exemplifies the gap between word and deed than Carlos Altamirano's account of his desperate search for a place to hide on September 11, 1973 (Politzer 1990). Amazingly, the *enfant terrible* of Chilean politics – the Secretary General of the Socialist Party, the head of the party's revolutionary left wing, and the most wanted man in Chile – was without protection and without a safe house in which to take refuge!

[5] The sole exceptions were: an isolated skirmish in the Province of Talca that resulted in the death of one *carabinero* after a clash with a group of regional officials attempting to flee toward the Argentine border; an attack on a remote police post in the forestry zone of Neltume, a conflictive stronghold of the MIR's rural organization in the southern Province of Valdivia, that did not result in *carabinero* casualties; and an incident in Antofagasta, where a *carabinero* opposed to the coup took two superior officers prisoner and killed them. These events are narrated in *Comisión Nacional de Verdad y Reconciliación* 1991, 309–11, 396–98, 437–38.

[6] Aside from the deaths of the three *carabineros* mentioned in the preceding note, the only other fatalities suffered by the public forces on September 11, 1973 occurred in Santiago: Four members of the army were killed during the siege of *La Moneda*, three *carabineros* died of gunshot wounds while quelling the resistance at the *Indumet* factory, three more *carabineros* were killed during skirmishes in *La Legua*, and two other *carabineros* died as a result of sniping downtown. By the end of the year, the total number of fatalities had risen to thirty. For a case-by-case account of the circumstances of these deaths, three of which were due to accidents, see *Comisión Nacional de Verdad y Reconciliación* 1991, 432–41.

and conscripts as to Chilean society at large. This symbolic purpose of the repression was admitted by Vice Admirals Patricio Carvajal and Ismael Huerta on the tenth anniversary of the coup. As they noted (1983, 122), "From a strictly military point of view ... to take *La Moneda* a company of special troops would have been sufficient and a half-hour would have been needed. But setting an example was desired."[7]

Still, when reviewing the repression that followed the military coup, one should bear in mind that events on the ground were never as transparent as they may now be cast retrospectively. The following account is a snapshot which until very recently was always blurred by disputes over the very reality of these events and of how and why they occurred.[8] As these events unfolded, and in their aftermath, the coherence and transparency of this account were absent: Acts of repression were shrouded in a myriad of subterfuges, inaccurate official accounts, and denials repeated by a compliant press. Acts were distorted in

[7] As noted in Chapter 2, Carvajal played a pivotal role in planning the coup and was the first Minister of Defense in the military government. Huerta had been a member of Allende's emergency cabinet in October 1972 and was appointed Minister of Foreign Relations immediately following the coup. In July 1974, Carvajal was shifted to Foreign Relations and Huerta became Ambassador to the United Nations.

[8] Only in April 1990, shortly after the inauguration of President Patricio Aylwin, was an official commission created to evaluate and document the most severe human rights violations committed between September 11, 1973 and March 10, 1990 by the military government *and* by private individuals. This commission, the *Comisión Nacional de Verdad y Reconciliación*, presented its report in February 1991. Though criticized for including acts committed by private individuals and for being partial in its restriction to human rights violations and to acts of political violence resulting in death, the *Informe Rettig* – as the report is referred to after the group's president, former Senator Raúl Rettig – is the single most comprehensive and incontrovertible case-by-case account of repression and political violence in Chile during the military government. It is the source for the summary that follows. In February 1992, the *Corporación Nacional de Reparación y Reconciliación* was created to decide upon new reports of human rights violations and those cases for which the Rettig Commission did not form a clear conviction, as well as to effect reparations to the families of the victims. The *Corporación* ruled that 899 of the cases that it reviewed were deaths that resulted from human rights violations (644) or political violence (255); the earlier report had identified 2,298 victims of human rights violations (2,130) and of political violence (168) (*Corporación Nacional de Reparación y Reconciliación* 1996, 565, 576). These reports certainly are not the first descriptions of human rights violations in Chile. However, with the exception of recent works by investigative reporters, most earlier accounts tend to be testimonial or denunciatory, and all have lacked the scope, rigor, and authority of the *Informe Rettig* and the report of the *Corporación*. Among the better works which tend to be substantially confirmed by the official reports, see Frühling 1983; Ahumada et al. 1989; Cavallo et al. 1989; Verdugo 1989; Gómez Araneda 1990; González and Contreras 1991.

epochal narratives fashioned and embraced by victors and vanquished, as well as by wildly disparate estimates of the number of victims on both sides, and experienced in manners far more fragmentary than this summary may suggest. This point must be remembered when reading the later analysis of the Junta's attempts to stave off international criticism by self-limiting its use of extralegal force: For these acts too were embedded within this larger contest over the reality of human rights violations and the manipulation of knowledge of their occurrence. It should also be stressed that the official source upon which the following reconstruction is based, the report of the *Comisión Nacional de Verdad and Reconciliation*, is only a partial account of the repression that followed the coup. The executive order that created the commission in 1990 limited the group's task to clarifying only the most severe human rights violations: disappearances, execution, and torture that resulted in death at the hands of state agents, as well as deaths that resulted from political violence affected by private individuals. Thus, the following overview leaves aside the many individuals who were detained under the state of siege, arrested for purported infractions to the state security law, the arms control law, or the law prohibiting Marxist parties, and, in many cases, subject to torture while under custody.

Thus, in the days immediately following September 11, 1973, the most severe repression was directed against the leaders of the Left political parties, high officials of the Allende government, the members of the president's personal security apparatus (GAP), and former Ministers of State. Within days repression extended to regional and local government authorities, administrators of state firms, members of social organizations and agencies associated with the deposed *Unidad Popular* government, lower- and middle-level militants of the outlawed Left parties, union and community leaders, and innumerable workers, students, agricultural workers, and peasants without any political party affiliation (see Table 2). During the first months of military rule, *carabineros* and military personnel detained thousands of people in raids and mass sweeps in search of arms. Other individuals were detained upon presenting themselves to the authorities on their own accord or after being summoned by *bando*. Of the thousands detained, hundreds subsequently disappeared following detention; in hundreds of other cases, the executed victim's corpse appeared days later, with multiple gunshot wounds the most common cause of death; in other cases, families were notified that a relative had been executed, but often were not given the body for burial.

123

**Table 2.** Fatalities Attributed by the Rettig Commission to Acts of State Repression, by Region, and Party Affiliation (September 11–December 31, 1973)

| Region | Party Militancy | | | | None | Total |
|---|---|---|---|---|---|---|
| | MIR | PC | PS | Other | | |
| Tarapacá | 1 | 2 | 13 | 1 (MAPU) | 8 | 25 |
| Antofagasta | 5 | 10 | 46 | 2 (MAPU,CAR) | 8 | 71 |
| Atacama | 5 | 2 | 11 | — | 1 | 19 |
| Coquimbo | 1 | 7 | 4 | 3 (MAPU) | 7 | 22 |
| Valparaíso | 4 | 10 | 12 | 5 (2MAPU,2CAR, 1PDC) | 10 | 41 |
| R.M. Metrop. (Santiago) | 19 | 54 | 87 | 14 (1IC,3MAPU,3PR, 2PN,4EJ,FACH) | 318 | 492 |
| B. O'Higgins | — | 4 | 2 | — | 2 | 8 |
| Maule | 9 | 3 | 19 | 2 (IC,PDC) | 29 | 62 |
| Bío Bío | 16 | 35 | 34 | 9 (3MAPU,4PR, 1PN,1EJ) | 114 | 208 |
| Araucanía | 6 | 21 | 26 | 6 (1MAPU,4PR,1EJ) | 55 | 114 |
| Los Lagos | 27 | 16 | 31 | 5 (2MAPU,2PR,1EJ) | 49 | 128 |
| Aysén | — | 2 | 1 | 1 (MAPU) | 6 | 10 |
| Magallanes & Ch. Antarctica | — | 1 | 2 | — | 2 | 5 |
| Total | 93 | 167 | 288 | 48 (2IC,17MAPU, 13PR,2PDC,3PN, 3CAR,7EJ,1FACH) | 609 | 1205 |

*Note*: The *Corporación de Reparación y Reconciliación* (1996) identified 587 additional deaths corresponding to this period.

*Abbreviations*: CAR = Carabineros; EJ = Army; FACH = Air Force; IC = Christian Left; MAPU = United Popular Action Movement; MIR = Movement of the Revolutionary Left; PC = Communist Party; PDC = Christian Democratic Party; PN = National Party; PR = Radical Party; PS = Socialist Party.

*Source*: Data for Tables 2, 3, and 4 compiled from the case-by-case accounts of human rights violations contained in the official *Informe de la Comisión Nacional de Verdad y Reconciliación*, 2d ed. (Santiago: La Nación and Las Ediciones del Ornitorrinco, 1991).

This first wave of repression lasted until the end of 1973 and was marked by considerable regional variation in the selectiveness and modalities of repression (see Table 3). These patterns appear to have been a function of the personal disposition of the officer commanding each particular emergency zone, the degree of local organization of social movements, and the nature and intensity of local conflicts prior to the coup. In the mining regions of the north, which were traditional centers of organized labor activity, repression at first was relatively moderate. Some executions took place in fulfillment of war council death sentences, but disappearances and extrajudicial executions were rare. In mid-October, forms of repression changed when a special high-level army delegation was sent to review military justice and rectify the soft hand of provincial military authorities. The visit of this delegation coincided with the first extrajudicial executions in a number of cities in the north; among those executed were men who had already been tried and sentenced by military tribunals for offenses not punishable by death. Years after the termination of military rule, the judicial investigation into this special commission would have major ramifications on Chilean politics.[9] Yet, relative to the rest of Chile, the repression in the north tended to be selective, with few nonparty victims, deaths occurred by execution, and some effort was made to officially account

---

[9] On June 5, 2000, the Appellate Court of Santiago stripped then Senator Pinochet of his parliamentary immunity on the grounds that there existed well-founded suspicions of penal culpability in the cases arising out of executions which took place during the delegation's travels. Pinochet had delegated his authority as head of military tribunals in time of war to Gen. Sergio Arellano Stark, who was commissioned, along with a group of army officers, to review cases tried or pending before *Consejos de Guerra*, accelerate proceedings, and exhort more severe sentences. The group traveled to at least eight provincial cities by helicopter during October 1973. This mission became notorious because simultaneous to its presence, extrajudicial executions took place in five of the locales visited. These executions were officially explained as sentences handed down by *Consejos de Guerra* or escape attempts. In all, 72 men were executed: 4 in Cauquenes (October 4), 15 in La Serena (October 16), 13 in Copiapó (October 17), 14 in Antofagasta (October 19), and 26 in Calama (October 19). Five of the men in Calama and one in La Serena had already been tried and sentenced for offenses not punishable by death. Forty of the men executed were members of the Socialist Party, the rest were members of the Communist Party or the MIR. According to the *Comisión Nacional de Verdad y Reconciliación* (1991, 123), there is irrefutable proof that at least three members of Arellano's delegation were directly involved in the executions in La Serena, Antofagasta, and Calama. It is noteworthy that in each of these cities local officers, without the knowledge of the local commanding officer, were induced to act as accomplices, supplying troops and other equipment. All of the members of the delegation, with the exception of General Arellano, later became DINA agents. Verdugo (1989) reconstructs these events from the vantage point of the local garrison commanders, whom she interviewed. Despite the subordination of the officers involved to General Arellano, the 1991 truth commission held that Arellano neither ordered nor was cognizant of the executions before they occurred, as long claimed by his son (*Comisión Nacional de Verdad y Reconciliación* 1991, 122; Arellano Iturriaga 1985, 62). On June 10, 1999 General Arellano, along with four other officers, was charged and arrested for a number of offenses associated with the *Caravana de la Muerte*. At the time of writing, the judicial proceedings remain in progress.

**Table 3.** Fatalities Attributed by the Rettig Commission to Acts of State Repression, by Region, Month, and Cause of Death (September–December 1973)

| | September 1973 | | | | | October 1973 | | | | |
|---|---|---|---|---|---|---|---|---|---|---|
| | DD | EX | PV | O | Total | DD | EX | PV | O | Total |
| Tarapacá | 2 | 7 | — | — | 9 | 1 | 13 | — | 1 | 15 |
| Antofagasta | 3 | 9 | — | 1 | 13 | 1 | 56 | — | 1 | 58 |
| Atacama | — | — | — | 1 | 1 | — | 16 | — | 1 | 17 |
| Coquimbo | — | 1 | — | — | 1 | — | 16 | — | — | 16 |
| Valparaíso | 2 | 8 | 2 | 2 | 14 | — | 16 | 1 | 3 | 20 |
| R.M. Metrop. (Santiago) | 74 | 117 | 31 | 20 | 242 | 47 | 140 | 14 | 12 | 213 |
| B. O'Higgins | 1 | 2 | — | — | 3 | — | 2 | — | — | 2 |
| Maule | 9 | 8 | 1 | 1 | 19 | 18 | 17 | — | 1 | 36 |
| Bío Bío | 68 | 37 | 2 | 8 | 115 | 36 | 36 | — | 2 | 74 |
| Araucanía | 39 | 4 | — | — | 43 | 20 | 30 | 1 | — | 51 |
| Los Lagos | 18 | 9 | 2 | 1 | 30 | 9 | 79 | — | 3 | 91 |
| Aysén | 1 | — | — | — | 1 | 3 | 6 | — | — | 9 |
| Magallanes & Antarctica | — | 1 | — | — | 1 | — | 3 | — | 1 | 4 |
| Total | 217 | 203 | 38 | 34 | 492 | 135 | 430 | 16 | 25 | 606 |

*Note*: The 587 additional deaths identified by the *Corporación de Reparación y Reconciliación* (1996, 573) during these months include 233 executions, 79 disappearances, 213 victims of political violence, and 62 deaths that would be classified as "Other" in this table.

*Abbreviations*: DD = Detained-disappeared; EX = Executed; PV = Victim of Political Violence; O = Other (includes deaths attributed to irrational or excessive uses of force, abuses of power, and torture).

*Source*: See Table 2.

for these acts, usually attributing them to "escape attempts" (the infamous *ley de fuga*).[10]

In the Metropolitan Region of Santiago, September and October 1973 were the months of most intense repression. In the days imme-

[10] The *ley de fuga* (law of flight) refers to an actual legal category. ART. 374 of the CdJM authorizes soldiers to fire upon fugitive prisoners of war if they fail to obey a command to halt. However, according to the *Comisión Nacional de Verdad y Reconciliación*, escape attempts tended to be staged: prisoners were taken to a secluded spot, ordered to flee, and then fired upon. In every case of *ley de fuga* examined, the commission (1991, 23, 118) discounted the official explanation and classified the dead as victims of extrajudicial executions.

| November 1973 | | | | | December 1973 | | | | | Totals 1973 | | | | |
| DD | EX | PV | O | Total | DD | EX | PV | O | Total | DD | EX | PV | O | Total |
|---|---|---|---|---|---|---|---|---|---|---|---|---|---|---|
| — | 1 | — | — | 1 | — | — | — | — | — | 3 | 21 | — | 1 | 25 |
| — | — | — | — | — | — | — | — | — | — | 4 | 65 | — | 2 | 71 |
| — | — | — | — | — | — | 1 | — | — | 1 | — | 17 | — | 2 | 19 |
| — | 1 | — | 2 | 3 | — | 2 | — | — | 2 | — | 20 | — | 2 | 22 |
| — | 2 | — | — | 2 | — | 4 | — | 1 | 5 | 2 | 30 | 3 | 6 | 41 |
| 2 | 7 | 1 | 2 | 12 | 3 | 13 | 2 | 7 | 25 | 126 | 277 | 48 | 41 | 492 |
| 1 | — | — | 2 | 3 | — | — | — | — | — | 2 | 4 | — | 2 | 8 |
| 1 | — | — | 1 | 2 | 5 | — | — | — | 5 | 33 | 25 | 1 | 3 | 62 |
| 13 | — | 1 | 2 | 16 | 1 | 2 | — | — | 3 | 118 | 75 | 3 | 12 | 208 |
| 8 | 8 | — | 1 | 17 | 2 | 1 | — | — | 3 | 69 | 43 | 1 | 1 | 114 |
| — | 3 | — | — | 3 | — | 4 | — | — | 4 | 27 | 95 | 2 | 4 | 128 |
| — | — | — | — | — | — | — | — | — | — | 4 | 6 | — | — | 10 |
| — | — | — | — | — | — | — | — | — | — | — | 4 | — | 1 | 5 |
| 25 | 22 | 2 | 10 | 59 | 11 | 27 | 2 | 8 | 48 | 388 | 682 | 58 | 77 | 1205 |

diately following the coup, thousands of people were detained during mass searches of universities, industrial districts, and lower-class residential areas and were transferred to numerous makeshift detention centers, of which the largest was the *Estadio Nacional*, the soccer stadium built during the 1930s and the site of the 1962 World Cup final. According to a Red Cross estimate, eleven days after the coup the stadium held as many as seven thousand prisoners.

In Santiago over half of those killed did not belong to any political party, were under the age of thirty – there are many documented cases of deaths of male teenagers as young as fourteen and fifteen – and in many instances the cause of death was excessive use of force, abuse of power by state agents, or gunshot wounds inflicted under unclear circumstances.[11]

---

[11] The last type of cases were classified by the *Comisión Nacional de Verdad y Reconciliación* as victims of political violence.

Unlike in the north, no effort was made to officially account for executions after detention. Instead, bullet-ridden corpses appeared in the streets, in isolated areas, or in the waters of the Mapocho River. As was the case throughout the country, the overwhelming majority of fatalities occurred at the hands of army soldiers or *carabineros*, though the air force was responsible for some deaths in the capital.

In southern rural areas, particularly in provinces that had seen intense organization and conflict during the agrarian reform, the repression affected professionals and technicians employed by state agricultural and agrarian reform agencies, leaders of peasant organizations, and vast numbers of agricultural workers and peasants without party affiliation. The majority of the victims disappeared after detention, and much of the repression took the form of personal vendettas. In some areas, civilians accompanied uniformed personnel to identify those sought.

The chief difference between the first wave of repression and that which followed in 1974–1977 involved the modes of detention, the actors involved, and the selectivity with which victims were targeted. During the first months after the coup, the vast majority of arrests were made by uniformed army or *carabinero* personnel and no effort was made to conceal these arrests, which tended to occur during the day before witnesses. From 1974 onward, blatant arrests gave way to the covert methods referred to later in the discussion of the *recurso de amparo*. Similarly, victims were more carefully selected and the repression increasingly became the prerogative of special intelligence units, in particular the much feared *Dirección de Inteligencia Nacional* (National Directorate of Intelligence, DINA) and later the *Comando Conjunto*, a short-lived special joint security unit created by the air force in 1975 in response to the overwhelming power being attained by the DINA.[12] Political parties were successively targeted according to their perceived military and political threat to the armed forces. Thus, the Movement of the Revolutionary Left (MIR) bore the brunt of the DINA's

---

[12] The *Comando Conjunto* was dissolved in January 1977. Agents from the four military and police intelligence services participated in the *Comando Conjunto*, including for a short while members of the DINE, the army intelligence unit, though at all times air force intelligence officers predominated. From its inception, the group's objective was to dismantle the Communist Party organization in the popular and working-class districts of south Santiago. The very existence of the *Comando Conjunto* was unknown until 1984, when a former agent, Andrés Valenzuela, deserted and told his story to Mónica González, an opposition journalist. Until then it had been commonly believed that only the DINA had engaged in covert repression. On the *Comando Conjunto*, see González and Contreras 1991.

efforts during 1974 and the beginning of 1975, followed by the Social-ist Party (PS) in 1975, and the Communist Party (PC) in 1976, which was also targeted by the *Comando Conjunto* (see Table 4).[13]

Before examining the Judiciary's response to the repression, a few points should be made about the DINA. The DINA emerged out of an informal group of army majors and colonels who began operations on September 11, 1973 and quickly came to supplant the individual intel-ligence services of the different armed forces, such as the DINE and the SIFA, the respective intelligence organs of the army and the air force. In November 1973 the Junta decided to formally constitute the DINA (AHJG, 33, November 12, 1973), but the organization was not given legal form until June 1974 with the dictation of D.L. No. 521 (D.O., June 14, 1977). According to the known terms of the decree-law, the DINA was a professional military intelligence organization, directly dependent on the Junta, without operational capabilities. However, D.L. No. 521 contained a sole transitory article which stipulated that the final three articles of the decree-law were to be published as a restricted circulation annex to the official gazette. The second of these secret articles, ART. 10, authorized the Junta to avail itself of the DINA to carry out arrests and transfers of individuals ordered in exercise of the exceptional faculties given by the declaration of a state of siege.[14] Notwithstanding this reference to the Junta, once the Statute of the Junta (D.L. No. 527) was enacted within days of the formal creation of the DINA, the exercise of the powers conferred by a state of siege became a prerogative of the executive, not the Junta.[15] Thus, the DINA's sole formal, albeit secret, operational authority was tied to Pinochet, not the commanders in chief as a body, and in practice the DINA was identified with its head, Lt. Col. Manuel Contreras Sepulveda, who – if accountable to anyone – was subordinate to General Pinochet.

---

[13] Table 4 does not include all acts of state repression which resulted in death during the period from 1974 to August 1977. The *Comisión Nacional de Verdad y Reconciliación* documents ninety-nine additional dead whose circumstances of death largely corre-spond to the pattern of repression that marked the first wave of repression after the coup. Of these cases, according to the commission, forty-nine apparently were not polit-ically motivated. For accounts of these cases, see *Comisión Nacional de Verdad y Rec-onciliación* (1991, 485–504). During this same period, the commission reports only six politically motivated deaths among police and military personnel. Four of these deaths are attributed to clashes with MIR militants (*Comisión Nacional de Verdad y Reconcil-iación* 1991, 604–6).

[14] ART. 10, D.L. No. 521, *Trans. y Antec.* – D.L., vol. 19, f.217.

[15] No. 527, ART. 10, no. 14 D.O., June 26, 1974. Up until this point, pursuant to D.L. No. 228, ART. 1, the faculties conferred to the president by a declaration of a state of siege were exercised by the Junta.

**Table 4.** Fatalities Attributed by the Rettig Commission to Selective Repression by State Agents by Quarter, by Party Militancy (1974–1977)

| | Detained-Disappeared | | | | | | Other Military or Security Forces | |
| | DINA | | | | | | | |
| | MIR | PC | PS | N-M | O | Total | MIR | PC |
|---|---|---|---|---|---|---|---|---|
| 1974 – I | — | 2 | 4 | 1 | — | 7 | — | — |
| – II | 9 | — | — | — | 1ᵃ | 10 | — | — |
| – III | 74 | 19 | 13 | — | 5ᵇ | 111 | — | 4 |
| – IV | 54 | 1 | 3 | 1ᶠ | — | 59 | 1 | 1 |
| Total 1974 | 137 | 22 | 20 | 2 | 6 | 187 | 1 | 5 |
| 1975 – I | 30 | — | 3 | — | 2ᵈ | 35 | — | — |
| – II | 1ᶠ | — | 6 | — | — | 7 | 5 | 1 |
| – III | 1 + 1ᶠ | — | 3 | — | — | 5 | — | 3(2)ᵉ |
| – IV | 1ᶠ | 4 | — | — | — | 5 | 1 | 10(7) |
| Total 1975 | 34 | 4 | 12 | — | 2 | 52 | 6 | 14(9) |
| 1976 – I | 1 | — | 1 | — | — | 2 | — | 3(2) |
| – II | 6 + 1ᶠ | 17 | 3ᶠ | — | 4ᵉ | 31 | — | 9(2) |
| – III | 2 + 2ᶠ | 31 | — | — | — | 35 | — | 16(6) |
| – IV | 2 | 11 | — | — | — | 13 | — | 2(1) |
| Total 1976 | 14 | 59 | 4 | — | 4 | 81 | — | 30(11) |
| 1977 – I | — | — | — | — | — | — | — | — |
| – II | — | 2 + 4 | 1 | — | — | 7 | — | 1 |
| – III | — | — | — | — | — | — | — | — |
| – IV | — | — | — | — | — | — | — | — |
| Total 1977 | — | 6 | 1 | — | — | 7 | — | 1 |
| Total 1974–1977 | 185 | 91 | 37 | 2 | 12 | 327 | 7 | 50 |

*Notes*: The *Corporación de Reparación y Reconciliación* (1996) identified an additional 147 deaths attributed to human rights abuses and political violence during 1974–1977. These included 92 deaths in 1974 (23 disappeared), 30 in 1975 (7 disappeared), 16 in 1976 (5 disappeared), and 9 in 1977.

Number in parentheses indicate victims attributed to the *Comando Conjunto*.

a. One DINA agent

b. Three militants of the MAPU, one member of the PDC, and one PR militant.

c. General (R) Carlos Prats and Sofia Prats.

d. One member of the MAPU and one DINA agent.

e. Three MAPU militants and one IC militant.

f. Act of repression occurred in Argentina. Includes only cases attributed to official Chilean military or intelligence services.

*Abbreviations*: See Table 3.
*Source*: See Table 2.

| Detained-Disappeared | | | | | Other Forms of Repression | | | | | | |
| Other Military of Security Forces | | | | | | | | | | | |
| PS | N-M | O | Total | Total | MIR | PC | PS | N-M | O | Total | Total |
|---|---|---|---|---|---|---|---|---|---|---|---|
| — | 2 | — | 2 | 9 | — | — | — | — | — | — | 9 |
| — | 1 | — | 1 | 11 | — | — | — | — | — | — | 11 |
| 3 | 6 | — | 13 | 124 | 3 | — | 1 | 2 | $2^{fc}$ | 8 | 132 |
| 1 | 3 | — | 6 | 65 | 4 | — | — | 1 | — | 5 | 70 |
| 4 | 12 | — | 22 | 209 | 7 | — | 1 | 3 | 2 | 13 | 222 |
| 2 | — | — | 2 | 37 | 5 | — | 2 | — | — | 7 | 44 |
| — | — | — | 6 | 13 | 2 | — | 2 | 1 | — | 5 | 18 |
| 2 | 1 | — | 6 | 11 | 1 | 2 | 1 | 1 | — | 5 | 16 |
| 2 | — | — | 13 | 18 | 13 | 2 | 1 | 1 | — | 17 | 35 |
| 6 | 1 | — | 27 | 79 | 21 | 4 | 6 | 3 | — | 34 | 113 |
| 1 | — | — | 4 | 6 | 2 | — | — | 2 | — | 4 | 10 |
| 1 | — | — | 10 | 41 | — | — | — | — | — | — | 41 |
| 1 | — | — | 17 | 52 | — | 1 | 2 | 2 | — | 5 | 57 |
| — | — | — | 2 | 15 | 2 | — | — | — | — | 2 | 17 |
| 3 | — | — | 33 | 114 | 4 | 1 | 2 | 4 | — | 11 | 125 |
| — | — | — | — | — | — | — | — | — | — | — | — |
| 1 | 4 | — | 6 | 13 | — | 1 | — | — | — | 1 | 14 |
| — | — | — | — | — | — | — | — | — | — | — | — |
| 1 | 4 | — | 6 | 13 | — | 1 | — | — | — | 1 | 14 |
| 14 | 17 | — | 88 | 415 | 32 | 6 | 9 | 10 | 2 | 59 | 474 |

A highly secretive organization, the DINA carried out operations throughout Chile and abroad. At its peak, the DINA concentrated tremendous power, was beyond the reach of the law and the judiciary, and could inflict torment and duress on its victims with certain impunity. As Table 4 illustrates, the DINA was responsible for most of the deaths during the worst years of repression following the coup. This differential involvement of the various branches of the armed forces in the repression later would allow the commanders of the navy and the air force to assume stances critical of the repressive methods being used. From early on, the DINA's capacity to operate within the armed forces, particularly within the army, gave its members power beyond rank and seniority. This became one source of hostility to the organization among some military officers. There is considerable evidence of intense rivalry between the DINA and the SIFA, the air force intelligence service, particularly during the repression of the MIR in 1974 and 1975 (González and Contreras 1991). Unlike the DINA, the SIFA did not "disappear" its victims. General Leigh (Varas 1979, 78) claims that he withdrew virtually all air force personnel from the DINA once it became apparent that he had no power within the organization.[16]

Did the Judiciary provide any protection to the individuals targeted by the armed forces? As we will now see, the courts did little to halt the massive human rights violations of the first years of military rule. Shortly after the coup, the Supreme Court abdicated its authority to oversee the administration of military justice in time of war; and before the increasingly covert forms of repression the *recurso de amparo*, a variant of *habeas corpus*, proved totally ineffective.

## The Supreme Court and Military Justice

Although the Chilean Supreme Court in 1974 defended its faculty of reviewing the constitutionality of legislation, when it came to directly confronting the exception in its repressive and coercive dimensions the court backed off. In late 1973 and throughout 1974, in some of the most controverted decisions in its history, the court repeatedly abdicated its constitutional mandate to supervise and correct "all the tribunals of the Nation," declaring itself incompetent to rule on complaints (*recursos de queja*) regarding the military tribunals in time of war. In so doing, the court self-limited its own faculties, and set the boundaries between areas in which the courts would protect individual rights and those in which the military could repress and try its political opponents, unchecked by judicial oversight or review. In this

---

[16] On the organization and structure of the DINA, see *Colegio de Abogados* 1990, 126–36; *Comisión Nacional de Verdad y Reconciliación* 1991, 45–47, 449–58. Some of the most harrowing accounts of DINA methods have been provided by former militants of Left parties who, after being tortured, actively collaborated with the DINA. See, in particular, the testimony before the *Comisión Nacional de Verdad y Reconciliación* of Luz Arce Sandoval, a former socialist, published as "*Recuerdos del Infierno*" in *Página Abierta*, March 18, 1991, 22–41, as well as the testimony before the courts of former MIR militant, Marcia Merino, the infamous "*la flaca Alejandra*," reproduced in *Diario La Epoca*, July 21 and 22, 1991. Arce (1993) has also written a profound memoir about her experience.

manner, the Supreme Court was complicit in creating a dual judicial system: Civil and criminal cases that did not affect the extraordinary faculties of the military were adjudicated according to law in the ordinary court system, while "political offenses" – when and if tried – were handled by the armed forces in their own courts without any remedy before the Supreme Court.

### The Supreme Court and the Consejos de Guerra

From a comparative perspective, the extension of military jurisdiction in Chile – even prior to the coup – was extremely broad. Whereas the extension of military jurisdiction varies considerably across states and over time, the most important variables differentiating systems of military justice are whether military courts operate in peacetime and whether civilians can be tried in military courts. In the Chilean system of military justice, as regulated by the 1925 CdJM which replaced the 1839 *Ordenanza General del Ejército*, in both peacetime and time of war civilians as well as members of the armed forces could be tried in military courts for military and nonmilitary offenses.[17]

These courts differed substantially in jurisdiction, organization, and procedure during peacetime and time of war. The peacetime military tribunals were organized along lines analogous to ordinary civilian courts, trial procedure conformed to many of the rules of the *Ley de Organización de los Tribunales* and the *Código de Procedimiento Penal* (Code of Penal Procedure), and the Supreme Court expressly stood as the highest military court in peacetime. As regulated by the CdJM, during "state" or "time of war" military justice was administered by war councils (*Consejos de Guerra*) which functioned in the theater of military operations or areas of the country declared under state of assembly or siege. The conditions that activated the war councils were specified in Art. 73 of the CdJM: "From the moment in which a General

---

[17] Under Chilean law, civilians could be tried by military courts for such offenses as theft of military property, offenses or violence against police officers (*carabineros*), as well as offenses defined in special laws that give jurisdiction to the military courts (Astrosa Herrera 1985, 29). Prior to September 11, 1973, these laws included the *Law of Aeronautic Navigation* (D.L. No. 221, D.O., 30 May 1931), the *Law of State Security* (Law No. 12,927, D.O., August 6, 1958), and the *Law of Arms Control* (Law 17,798, D.O., October 21, 1972). The Junta enacted decree-laws which created additional offenses subject to military jurisdiction. The Chilean system of military justice is extensively analyzed in Astrosa Herrera 1985 and *Colegio de Abogados* 1990. Like the 1925 constitution, the Code of Military Justice was promulgated during a period of constitutional exception without any involvement of Congress.

in Chief of an army that must operate against a foreign enemy or against organized rebel forces is named, the competency of the Military Tribunals of peacetime will cease and that of the Military Tribunals of time of war will begin, in all territory declared in state of assembly or siege." Broader in jurisdiction than the military courts in peacetime,[18] these war councils were composed of military officers who – with the exception a single assessor (*Auditor*) – were not required to be lawyers and were convened by a general or commander in chief. The commander in chief stood at the summit of military jurisdiction and alone was empowered to approve, revoke, or modify the council's sentence, which was not subject to appeal. As in the popular imagery of court martials, "justice" by *Consejo de Guerra* was summary, opportunities for defense were constrained by the speed and secrecy of pretrial proceedings, and legal requirements for evidence and proof were minimal.[19]

After the coup the legal requisites for a state of war and the operation of war councils were satisfied by the Junta in D.L. No. 3, which declared that the Junta would be "General in Chief of the Forces that will operate in the emergency," and declared a state of siege throughout the country, thereby triggering pursuant to ART. 73 of the CdJM the activation of military justice in time of war (D.O., September 18, 1973). Although this decree-law named the Junta General in Chief, the everyday implementation of military justice was effected by division and brigade commanders to whom authority was delegated as permitted by ART. 75 of the CdJM (D.L. No. 8, D.O., September 19, 1973). In early October 1973 the CdJM was modified so that all authority associated with the administration of military justice in time of war could be delegated, including the faculty of approving sentences that imposed the death penalty (D.L. No. 51, D.O., October 2, 1973). Thus, within a week of the coup the war councils were legally in operation.

The potential for conflict between the Supreme Court and the *Consejos de Guerra* arose because ART. 86 of the 1925 constitution mandated that the Supreme Court exercise, in accordance with law, directive, economic, and correctional supervision over all judges and courts in the nation. The latter – correctional supervision – was the

---

[18] This jurisdiction also included ordinary offenses committed by soldiers and officers and was flexible, given that the heads of emergency zones could establish new offenses by dictating *bandos*.

[19] On the organization and procedures of the *Consejos de Guerra*, see Astrosa Herrera 1985, 125–39, 311–23; *Colegio de Abogados* 1990, 55–66; and *Comisión Nacional de Verdad y Reconciliación* 1991, 1:79–94.

potential source of conflict, as it involved overseeing the lower courts, rectifying any errors, and sanctioning judicial negligence or misuse of authority, including failure to follow proper trial procedure.[20]

Virtually within days of the first *Consejos de Guerra*, lawyers filed *recursos de queja* at the Supreme Court to seek redress from irregularities in military court procedure. The court did not delay in declaring that it would not intervene in the administration of military justice. On November 13, 1973, the Supreme Court for the first time declared itself incompetent to take cognizance of such appeals in "*Juan Fernando Sil Riveros.*"[21] The plaintiff in this complaint appealed to the Supreme Court to reduce a sentence handed down by a Valparaiso war council on the grounds that the military tribunal had misclassified the offense and had failed to consider extenuating circumstances – at stake was the difference between life imprisonment for espionage versus a five-year prison term for participation in an armed organization. Rather than consider the substance of the complaint, the full court invoked ART. 74 of the CdJM, which conferred full jurisdiction over military courts in time of war to the General in Chief, as ground for it to declare that it lacked jurisdiction to pronounce on rulings handed down by *Consejos de Guerra*. This jurisprudence in effect subordinated the constitution to ordinary legislation by allowing ART. 74 of the CdJM to supersede ART. 86 of the constitution. In a series of rulings throughout 1973 and 1974, the court repeated this position and denied that it held jurisdiction over the war councils. In mid-1974 one justice did, however, present a dissenting opinion affirming that the constitution took precedence over the Code of Military Justice and that the court held full authority to oversee military tribunals.[22]

The Supreme Court's refusal to oversee military justice in time of war was a clear case of the court limiting its own powers in abdication of its constitutional faculty, as well as a marked departure from the Chilean Supreme Court's historical jurisprudence. During the

---

[20] On the Supreme Court's constitutional faculty to supervise all lower courts, see Silva Bascuñán 1963, 3:416–22; Galté Carré 1965, 98–103; and Evans 1970, 154.

[21] The Supreme Court's ruling is reproduced in *Fallos del Mes*, September–October 1973, 180:222–25.

[22] Minister José María Eyzaquirre, who later served as president of the Supreme Court, presented the minority opinion in "*Sergio Roubillard González*," August 21, 1974. This opinion is reproduced in *Colegio de Abogados* 1990, 72.

Other Supreme Court declarations of incompetency are "*Silvia Lillo Robles*," Rol No. 6.603, January 16, 1974; "*Sergio Roubillard González*," Rol No. 7.633, August 21, 1974; as well as "*Jorge Garrido y otro*, Rol No. 10.397, September 21, 1976. For a general discussion, which concurs with the Supreme Court's jurisprudence, see Peña 1974.

nineteenth century on three occasions – in 1865, 1872, 1882 – the Supreme Court had challenged the pretense of military authorities to exercise unlimited and omnipotent powers during states of exception, particularly through their use of *bandos* to establish new offenses, and penalties, and to alter jurisdictions. Though on the first occasion during the 1865 war with Spain the government rejected the court's position, the government later sided with the court, particularly after the president's state of siege powers were defined and limited by the 1874 constitutional reforms and the *Ley de Organización y Atribuciones de los Tribunales*, the organic law regulating the organization of the courts, was promulgated in 1875. In 1882, during the War of the Pacific, the Supreme Court recognized an appeal to annul (*recurso de nulidad*) presented by defendants convicted by a Chilean *Consejo de Guerra* in Peru. This move led the General in Chief of the Chilean forces occupying Peru, Admiral Patricio Lynch, to initiate a jurisdictional conflict with the court before the Council of State. On this occasion, the Council of State confirmed the Supreme Court's authority to review the decisions of military tribunals in time of war, even of war councils operating in theaters outside of Chile. Significantly, the Council of State ruled that *Consejos de Guerra* decisions were acts of jurisdiction, not discretionary functions of military command; as such they remained subject to the Supreme Court's supervision and disciplinary jurisdiction.

This distinction between judicial acts and military command is clearly the substantive pivot upon which the question of the subordination or autonomy of the war councils to the larger judicial system turns. If the war councils do not exercise a judicial function, but exercise a command function, then autonomy would be warranted; otherwise the war councils should be conceived as part of the judicial system and subject to the supervision of the nation's highest court.[23] In 1882 the Council of State adopted the latter position. Although these nineteenth-century precedents predate the promulgation of the 1925 CdJM, Schweitzer, in the most exhaustive legal and historical analysis of this question, demonstrates that the code distinguishes between the military exercise of judicial functions and command and that the war council sentences are acts of jurisdiction (1975, 26–30).

---

[23] Astrosa Herrera (1985, 126–27) argues the former to conclude that the decisions of the war councils are not subject to review by the Supreme Court. For a critique of an earlier presentation of this position, see Schweitzer 1975, 29–30. The nineteenth-century precedent is also discussed by Sater (1986, 70–73).

In 1973 this self-limitation by the court and reversal of its earlier jurisprudence escaped neither the legal community, nor the members of the Junta. On the day of the first ruling, Silva Bascuñán voiced strong disagreement with the court's jurisprudence and insisted that the military courts were subordinate to the Supreme Court (AOCC, 16, November 13, 1973). Within the courts lawyers defending political prisoners immediately challenged the constitutionality of ART. 74, filing *recursos de inaplicabilidad* along with *recursos de queja* concerning war council decisions. According to one lawyer (Méndez Fetter 1979, 722–23), the Supreme Court invariably ruled on the complaint first, which closed the case and freed the Court from having to rule on the constitutional challenge because it was no longer associated with a live case. In December 1973, twelve lawyers, many of whom had provided defense in *Consejos de Guerra*, submitted a document to the Junta, the Supreme Court, the appellate court of Santiago, and the *Colegio de Abogados* – the national bar association – that outlined irregularities being committed by the military courts, asserted the Supreme Court's faculty of supervising all courts, and called for a suspension of the state of war, which they claimed was unnecessary given the absence of armed resistance within the country.[24] Though both the Junta and the Supreme Court returned the document without comment (AHJG, 67, January 11, 1974), the Junta three months later analyzed the matter of the Supreme Court and the *Consejos de Guerra*.

The early 1974 discussion within the Junta reveals that, notwithstanding the court's jurisprudence, the Junta had been informed and understood that the military courts fell within the court's correctional jurisdiction, even during time of war. In April 1974, Minister of Justice Gonzalo Prieto Gandara raised the need to review the Supreme Court's position and possibly modify the constitution to assure the court's participation in the administration of military justice (AHJG, 112, April 15, 1974, 9–12). Prieto held that despite an appearance of sympathy and cooperation, the Supreme Court was actually hedging to avoid sharing responsibility for military court abuses and infractions committed during the emergency. Prieto felt that without the court's participation, the armed forces would stand alone before the judgment of history –

[24] The document (reproduced in *Colegio de Abogados* 1990, 137–45) was signed by Eugenio Velasco Letelier, Pablo Vidales Baeza, Mario Verdugo Marinkovic, Luis Ortiz Quiroga, Juan A. Figueroa Yávar, Jaime Castillo Velasco, Gastón Cruzat Paul, Enrique Barros Bourie, Francisco Cumplido Cerceda, Andrés Aylwin Azócar, Adolfo Zaldívar Larrain, and Alejandro González Poblete.

which, interestingly, he expected to come some ten years later. A month earlier, the president of the Supreme Court, Justice Enrique Uruttia Manzano, in his address inaugurating the judicial year had stated that the court would supervise the military tribunals in time of war only if the constitution and law were modified to expressly grant this power. In Uruttia's words, "Such modifications are not of the competency of the Court, which must abide by the laws in force" (D.O., March 14, 1974, 4). Prieto, however, argued that such reforms were unnecessary since "the constitutional norm is very clear," and among other arguments he invoked the precedent established during the War of the Pacific (AHJG, 112, April 15, 1974, 10, 11). Still, the Minister of Justice insisted that the issue warranted careful study and modifications to the constitution if necessary to assure the Supreme Court's moral backing for the administration of military justice in time of war. At the time a study commission comprised of the chief legal counsel of each service was created; it eventually advised the Junta that Supreme Court participation was inadvisable (AHJG, 126, May 27, 1974, 5–6).

As a result of the Supreme Court's abdication of any authority to oversee military justice, notwithstanding the formal independence of the judiciary, the separation between the judiciary and the military government was nonexistent within the broad jurisdiction of military justice in time of war. Montesquieu's description of justice in despotic regimes – "the prince himself can judge" – applies to the war tribunals, since justice was being dispensed by officers hierarchically subordinate to the commanders in chief, who were creating the law. In many cases, defendants were tried for offenses created by decree-law[25] or whose cognizance had been transferred by decree-law to the military courts.[26]

---

[25] The principal instruments of legal repression created by the Junta immediately after the coup were D.L. No. 77, 81, and 175. D.L. No. 77 (D.O., October 8, 1973), defined Left political parties as illicit associations, dissolved them, and made it a criminal offense to reorganize these parties or effect Marxist propaganda. D.L. No. 81 (D.O., October 11, 1973) authorized administrative exile during time of war and made it a criminal offense to disobey a summons to appear before the authorities, to clandestinely enter the country, or to assist or shelter anyone committing these acts. D.L. No. 175 (D.O., December 10, 1973) modified ART. 6 of the constitution to allow the government during a state of exception to revoke the nationality of Chileans who from abroad engaged in grave attacks on the essential interests of the State.

[26] Thus, ART. 4, paragraph e) of D.L. No. 5 (D.O., September 22, 1973) transferred competency over infractions of the Law of State Security (Law No. 12,927) to military courts in time of war. This decree-law also increased penalties for specific infractions of the same law, the CdJM, and the *Ley de Control de Armas* (Arms Control Law) during time of war. Military jurisdiction over infractions to the Arms Control Law originated with the law under the Allende government (Law 17,798, D.O., October 21, 1972).

Similarly, penalties for most offenses were drastically increased by the armed forces in the first days after the coup.

Free from review by the Supreme Court, the military courts in time of war adjudicated unencumbered by external limits. During the years that war councils operated (1973–1978), over 6,000 individuals were tried in these courts. These trials were purportedly marked by a failure to observe even the permissive legal norms regulating military justice in time of war. According to critics, the sentences of the *Consejos de Guerra* were vitiated by numerous formal and substantial defects. Among other errors in law, common errors included: convictions without a description of the acts constituting the offense or of the evidence used to incriminate the guilty party; retroactive application of more severe penalties corresponding to time of war to acts committed prior to the legal activation of the war councils; conviction solely on the basis of a defendant's confession; disregard for extenuating circumstances; refusal to hear exculpatory witnesses; and incrimination using evidence attained by organs without investigatory authority.[27]

Notwithstanding this absence of any constraints, the Junta consistently sought to prevent any Supreme Court interference with military justice in time of war, as will be seen later in this chapter when the military's manipulation of its emergency powers is discussed. Similarly, within the Constituent Commission the question of whether or not to raise the Supreme Court's jurisprudence to constitutional rank by expressly excluding military tribunals in time of war from the domain of court supervision was discussed extensively in 1977. At the time Guzmán stressed the utility of the court's position, which conveniently allowed the Junta to maintain that the unsupervised activity of the military tribunals in time of war "was due to the Supreme Court's interpretation of laws in force, enacted prior to it, and not by the determination of the Government Junta itself" (AOCC, 331, December 7, 1977, 1849). However, this favorable situation was fraught with the potential for reversal: forbearance depended on the self-restraint and interpretation of another body, the court. Thus, the unconstrained operation of the military tribunals was contingent upon stability in the court's jurisprudence, and to preclude any such reversal, over a contrary recommendation from the president of the Supreme Court, the

---

[27] These irregularities are discussed in *Comisión Nacional de Verdad y Reconciliación* 1991, 92–94. Summaries of approximately three hundred war council sentences are reproduced in *Vicaría de la Solidaridad* 1990–1991.

Junta expressly excluded any Supreme Court supervision of military tribunals in time of war in ART. 79 of the 1980 constitution.[28]

## The Judiciary and the *Recurso de Amparo*

In light of the extent, ferocity, and, often, extralegal character of the repression in the first years following the coup, the Supreme Court's abdication of its correctional faculties over the *Consejos de Guerra* was perhaps less pernicious than its inability to protect personal liberty and security. During this period tens of thousands of militants and sympathizers of Left political parties and trade unions suffered illegal detention, duress, and torment, and, in thousands of cases, death at the hands of state agents without facing trial in either ordinary or military courts. Few, if any, of these individuals enjoyed effective protection of their constitutional rights to life and liberty, notwithstanding the judiciary's constitutional mandate to protect individual rights.

The Chilean judiciary has been sharply criticized for its inability to halt these abuses, and some have charged that the courts facilitated violations. Critics argue that, by passively processing *recursos de amparo* and complacently accepting official accounts regarding individuals thought subject to illegal detention and torment, the courts fostered a permissive environment in which the security forces could operate with certain impunity.[29] Regardless of the volition of judges, the judiciary's failure to protect human rights was in large measure a

---

[28] In December 1977 the Minister of Justice Mónica Madariaga insisted before the commission that it modify its initial formulation of this norm which expressly excluded only war councils in "time of external war." As she noted in a subsequent session, a majority within the Supreme Court was evolving toward a new jurisprudence whereby it would review rulings of military tribunals in time of war (AOCC 1913). Before the extension of the exclusion to include all military tribunals in time of war, then Supreme Court President José María Eyzaquirre, the author of the 1974 dissenting opinion, requested that for the record his opposition to the change be noted (AOCC 1903). The article stipulating the exclusion of military tribunals in time of war from Supreme Court superintendence was not modified in the July 1989 package of constitutional reforms which preceded the return to civilian government. For the 1977 discussion within the Constituent Commission regarding the Supreme Court and the military tribunals in time of war, see AOCC 937–38, 1166, 1307, 1849–50, 1861–63, 1897–1905, 1912–35.

[29] This charge was made by the *Comisión Nacional de Verdad y Reconciliación* (1991, 97), the official commission created in April 1990 to investigate those human rights violations that resulted in death during 1973–1990. For other critical accounts of the judiciary's performance on human rights, see *Vicaría de la Solidaridad* 1976, 1978, 1979; Méndez Fetter 1979; López Dawson 1985; *Comisión Chilena de Derechos Humanos* 1988; and Detzner 1988.

consequence of methods of repression deliberately designed and implemented to elude judicial control and penal responsibility. Before these illegal methods of repression, the judiciary's instruments of control were tragically insufficient.

In this regard, the judiciary's failure to aggressively protect the security of the thousands of individuals who overnight became targets of the most unprecedented, massive deployment of repressive force in Chilean history cannot be attributed to an absence of constitutional and legal precepts guaranteeing personal liberty and security, but to the inadequacy of these norms before repressive tactics which deliberately shunned the most elementary legal norms regulating arrests and detentions.

Personal liberty was sacrosanct in the many texts that form Chile's constitutional and legal tradition – under no circumstances could an individual be deprived of his or her freedom without legal justification. ART. 10, no. 15 of the 1925 constitution sanctified personal liberty, and the conditions of legal detention, trial, and imprisonment were meticulously defined in ARTICLES 11–15.[30] These constitutional guarantees

---

[30] Thus, among the list of guarantees that ART. 10 "ensures to all the inhabitants of the Republic," No. 15 specifies: "Freedom to reside in any part of the Republic, to move from one place to another, or to enter or depart from the territory, under the conditions that the legal requirements be observed, and excepting always prejudice to a third party; otherwise, no one can be detained, prosecuted, arrested or deported except in the manner as determined by the law."

Although they are standards of liberal constitutionalism, ARTICLES 11–15, given their importance, are also reproduced:

ART. 11. No one can be sentenced unless he be legally tried in accordance with a law promulgated prior to the act upon which the trial is based.

ART. 12. No one can be tried by special commissions, or otherwise than by the tribunal the law appoints and has previously constituted.

ART. 13. No one can be arrested except by order of a public functionary expressly empowered by law, and after such order has been made known to him, in legal form, unless he be surprised *in flagrante delicto*, and in this case for the sole purpose of being brought before the proper judge.

ART. 14. No one can be arrested, subjected to preventive detention or imprisoned except in his dwelling or in public places intended for this purpose.

Those in charge of prisons cannot receive therein anyone in the character of arrested, indicted or imprisoned without transcribing in their registers the detention order issued by an authority having legal capacity. They may nevertheless receive within the precincts of the prison for detention those brought for the purpose of being presented before the proper judge, but under obligation to render an account to the latter within twenty-four hours.

ART. 15. In case an authority orders the arrest of any person, he must, within the forty-eight hours following, make report thereof to the proper judge and place at his disposal the person detained.

were further regulated by law, and any infraction of these procedural rules was cause for civil and penal sanctions. ART. 16 of the constitution established the *recurso de amparo* to provide individuals subject to illegal detention or indictment with recourse to the judiciary to defend their personal liberty.[31] By law, when processing a *recurso de amparo* an appellate court could commission a judge to proceed to an individual's place of detention or imprisonment, hear them out, and, if warranted, order the individual's release or the rectification of the defects protested. Additionally, the court could order the individual brought before it (*habeas corpus*). Any delay or refusal to comply with such a request was ground for penal sanction, and whenever the court ordered a warrant of arrest or imprisonment revoked or an irregularity corrected, the preliminary findings were passed on to the public prosecutor's office, who by law was obliged to file a criminal complaint against the authors of the illegal detention or imprisonment; failure to do so was sanctioned with a fine and suspension from office.[32] Notwithstanding these punitive aspects, the primary purpose of the *recurso de amparo* was to provide immediate redress to protect individual liberty from arbitrary infringement.

Significantly, these individual guarantees and the *recurso de amparo* remained in force during constitutional states of exception. The declaration of a state of siege only empowered the president to restrict personal liberty, "to transfer persons from one department to another and to confine them in their own houses, or in places other than jails or intended for the confinement or imprisonment of ordinary criminals" (ART. 72, no. 17). These restrictions on personal liberty were discretionary acts of government that the president could use for reasons of

---

[31] ART. 16 of the 1925 constitution states:

Every individual who may be arrested, charged, or imprisoned contrary to the provisions of the foregoing articles may apply, for himself, or by anyone in his name, to the judicial authority designated by law, petitioning that the legal requirements be observed. This judicial authority shall order the individual to be brought before him and his order shall be exactly obeyed by all those having charge of the prisons and places of detention. Informed of the facts he shall declare his immediate release, or cause the legal defects to be corrected, or put the individual at the disposition of the proper judge, proceeding throughout in a brief and summary manner, correcting the defects personally, or referring them for correction to whomever it may concern.

Instructions for processing *recursos de amparo* were given by the Supreme Court to the appellate courts, which handled them in the first instance, in the *"Auto Acordado de la Corte Suprema de 19 de Diciembre de 1932,"* reproduced in Soto Kloss 1980, 315–18.

[32] The provisions regarding arbitrary detention and/or imprisonment are found in ART. 306–17 of the *Código de Procedimiento Penal* (Code of Penal Procedure).

state security, not judicial penalties – an individual could be subject to state of siege faculties without having committed any offense.[33]

Notwithstanding their discretionary character, these emergency powers were not a license for arbitrary detentions. Measures had to conform with the procedural formalities stipulated in the constitution and the law. In other words, they had to adhere to constitutional norms regarding the state of siege itself (ART. 72, no. 17), the manner of presidential action (ART. 75), and forms of legal detention (ART. 13). State of siege faculties, thus, could only be exercised by the president; his orders had to be issued as a written supreme decree, signed by the president and the appropriate minister; this order could go into effect only after the *toma de razón* by the *Contraloría General de la República*; the decree had to be openly presented at the moment of arrest; and the person so detained could be held only under house arrest or in a place where common criminals were not incarcerated. If any of these steps were not followed a *recurso de amparo* could with full justification be interposed on behalf of any individual under detention (Silva Bascuñán 1963, 2:360; and Schweitzer 1969, 205).

The Junta did not touch these norms after coming to power. Yet, despite the force of these norms during states of exception, the *recurso de amparo* proved totally ineffective as a safeguard of personal security and integrity of those persons persecuted after the coup. Thousands of *recursos de amparo* were presented during the first years of military rule, but virtually all of them were rejected. Of the handful accepted, many were subsequently overturned by the Supreme Court, others were ignored by the authorities, who never released the individual as ordered.

The typical appellate court procedure in handling a *recurso de amparo* was to request, by official letter, a report from the authority accused of affecting an illegal detention. Despite their authority to send a judge to the site of an arbitrary detention and to order *habeas corpus*, the appellate courts usually ruled without further investigation on the basis of the official response.[34] How the appellate courts ruled was

---

[33] For this reason, measures affected by virtue of a state of siege remained in force only while the state of siege was in effect, and is the reason why persons arrested in use of state of siege powers are to be held in places other than those used for the detention and imprisonment of common criminals (Silva Bascuñán 1963, 2:360–1; Schweitzer 1969, 207).

[34] The courts were not always so demanding. On September 14, 1973, Bernardo Leighton, the former Minister of the Interior to President Eduardo Frei and a prominent PDC leader, interposed by telephone the first *recurso de amparo* after the coup on behalf of Carlos Briones, Clodomiro Almeyda, Jorge Tapia, Claudio Jimeno, Oscar Waiss, Luis Armando Garfias, and Alvaro Morel, many of whom had been ministers to Allende, all

usually determined by one of two factors: (1) the Judiciary's long-standing jurisprudence that it lacked authority to evaluate the merit and modalities of the Executive's use of state of siege faculties, and (2) the intrinsic limits of the *recurso de amparo* before covert methods of repression. Depending upon whether or not authorities acknowledged an individual's arrest, one of these two factors came into play.

When government authorities officially acknowledged an arrest, the first factor provided grounds for rejecting a *recurso de amparo*. If the Ministry of the Interior informed the courts that the person in question had been arrested pursuant to faculties conferred by the state of siege, the courts invariably ruled the *recurso "improcedente"* (without merit) on the grounds that state of siege powers were lawful faculties and the courts had no authority to judge the Executive's use of them.[35] Thus, it was sufficient for the Ministry, via confidential communication, to acknowledge a detention and the number of the decree ordering the arrest for a *recurso de amparo* to be rejected. In these instances, the separation of powers, which forbade the judiciary from interfering with the faculties of other public authorities, was invoked by the courts before arrests ordered by virtue of the state of siege. As with the constitutionality of decree-laws, this jurisprudence was not contrived after the coup. It merely reiterated a position which the courts had repeatedly and consistently upheld during earlier states of exception, although this jurisprudence was already the subject of controversy among some Chilean legal scholars.[36]

Once, in March 1974, the appellate court of Santiago did go beyond the traditional jurisprudence and partially accepted a *recurso de amparo* presented on behalf of a minor. On this occasion the court con-

---

of whom were lawyers. The appellate court of Santiago dismissed this petition on the mere grounds that a state of siege had been declared, which conferred authority to detain the persons cited *"en algún Regimiento"* (in some Regiment). Whether and where these men were being detained was not ascertained. The resolution is reproduced in *Colegio de Abogados* 1980, 178–80.

[35] On appeal, the Supreme Court confirmed such rulings. See, for example, *"Bruno von Ehrenburg Pincheira y otros"* in *Fallos del Mes*, March–April 1974 (184–85): 29; and *"Luis Alejandro Fuentes Díaz,"* in *Fallos del Mes*, March–April 1975 (196–97): 32.

A *recurso de amparo* would also be rejected if the Ministry responded that the person was under indictment and facing criminal charges before the military courts.

[36] These critics questioned the limits of the Executive's prerogative and suggested that the courts did have authority to examine the justification and facts invoked in using state of siege measures. Compare Silva Bascuñán 1963, 2:332 with Schweitzer 1969, 205–7, and see the later discussion in Bidart Hernández 1986 and Mera F., González, and Vargas V. 1987, 25–27. For a general discussion of this problem with regard to acts of administration, see Fiamma 1977a.

ceded that state of siege powers were discretionary Executive powers, yet ruled that this discretion "has its limit where this power deviates towards measures that are arbitrary in regards to their ends or the persons to whom they are applied." One week later, the Supreme Court overturned this ruling and reaffirmed the established position concerning arrests under a state of siege: "the assessment of the reasons in virtue of which the arrest is ordered, in these cases, is exclusively the concern of the authority that decides it."[37] Under the guise of the separation of powers, the Supreme Court thus extended a virtual blank check to the military regime during states of siege and abdicated its jurisdiction to control the formal legality of state of siege measures. On the basis of the same principle, the Supreme Court also sanctioned the use of administrative solitary confinement even though by law solitary confinement was permissible solely upon order of a judicial authority. Thus, in July 1974 when a *recurso de amparo* presented on behalf of the Secretary General of the Communist Party of Chile, former Senator Luis Corvalán, sought the termination of his solitary confinement, the Supreme Court grounded its rejection of the appeal on the principle of the separation of powers. It stated, "just as the arrest itself and its duration depend on the exclusive judgement of the Executive, it is also logical that the manner in which it is enforced depends on the same authority" (*Fallos del Mes*, July 1974 [187]:132).

The second factor, the inefficacy of the *recurso de amparo* before covert forms of repression, became evident when an arrest went unrecognized by state authorities. In these cases, it was sufficient for the Ministry of the Interior to reply that the person solicited had not been detained "by order emanated from this Ministry."[38] In addition to such

---

[37] The appellate court's resolution is exemplary for its legal argument and rigorous defense of the applicability and scope of the *recurso de amparo* during a state of siege. The petition was presented on behalf of a fifteen-year-old boy, who had been arrested on December 19, 1973, held in solitary confinement for twenty-eight days, and subsequently transferred to the infamous *Estadio Chile*, where he was being held and ill. In addition to noting formal defects in the boy's detention, which were cited as grounds for protecting him, the court held that the prolonged arrest of the minor exceeded the scope of the discretional faculties conferred by the state of siege given his age and his scarce capacity to threaten state security. It ordered that he be put at the disposition of a juvenile court judge. For the rulings of both courts, see *"Luis Adalberto Muñoz Meza (amparo),"* in *Revista de Derecho, Jurisprudencia, y Ciencias Sociales y Gaceta de los Tribunales*, 1974, 71, second part, third section, 197–200.

[38] For examples, all of which involved individuals who either disappeared or were killed after detention by state agents, see *Comisión Nacional de Verdad y Reconciliación* 1991, 177, 210, 219, 371, 372, 375, 376, 380, 417, 505, 507, 529, 536, 542, 544, 545, 547, 552, 563, 568, 571, 572, 575.

straight-out denials of detention, official responses also assumed other variants: A detention might be officially recognized, but it would be claimed that the detainee had later been released. In some cases, it was claimed that the person had subsequently left the country, or else had never been detained but had left Chile. These types of responses became a ritualistic formula and invariably resulted in a rejection of the *recurso de amparo* as the courts operated under the assumption, albeit fictitious, that unless a decree ordered an arrest, no arrest had taken place.

However unrealistic this assumption – given the high number of irregular arrests – it does point to the principal shortcoming of the *recurso de amparo*: This instrument can only be an effective remedy against illegal detention if state agents acknowledge that a person is under arrest and permit the modalities of arrest to be subject to judicial scrutiny. Implicit in the design of the *recurso* is the assumption that even unlawful arrests involve some degree of deference to established legal forms. From this perspective, the arbitrariness that the *recurso* seeks to rectify consists of deviations from or misuses of regular modes of arrest, not the total disavowal of these forms. This becomes clear when one looks at the legal regulation of the *recurso de amparo*. All of the abuses that this instrument is to remedy are spelled out in the *Código de Procedimiento Penal* (ART. 306) in reference to the order of arrest or the order of imprisonment. An arrest is consequently arbitrary because it is either ordered: by an authority that lacks this faculty, in a situation where arrest is not called for by law, in infraction of procedural formalities, or without sufficient merit to warrant arrest.

As a result of this coupling with legal forms of detention, the *recurso de amparo* was intrinsically inefficacious before modalities of arrest and repression designed to secure impunity by concealing not only the identity of the perpetrators but also any trace of the arrest itself and the subsequent fate of the victim. Once the first wave of open repression following the coup subsided, which had involved hundreds of extrajudicial executions and disappearances after arrests by uniformed military and police personnel before witnesses in public, covert forms of detention became the norm as the DINA came fully into operation in mid-1974. These arrests generally occurred under cover of night and curfew or, if during the day, on crowded streets where passersby were unlikely to identify the victim. Agents moved about in unlicensed vehicles, civilian dress, and did not present identification or orders of arrest. DINA detainees were held in secret detention centers, subjected to tortures, and disappeared for varying periods of time – ranging from various days, weeks, months, or in hundreds of cases, to this day – as the fact of a person's arrest would be persistently denied by authorities as long as they were being held by the DINA.

In the face of these methods of repression, the inefficacy of the *recurso de amparo* became notorious. The director of the DINA, Col. Manuel Contreras, systematically refused to cooperate with the courts when they sought information regarding individuals thought to be in custody of the DINA. Contreras typically referred petitioners to the Confidential Department of the Ministry of the Interior or to the *Secretaría Ejecutiva Nacional de Detenidos*, whose mission was to supply such information. In some cases he added, "If the competent Authorities have informed you that they have not detained the person sought, that is the official information."[39] Relations between the appellate courts and the DINA apparently became so irritating that the Minister of the Interior and the president of the appellate court of Santiago met with Contreras in early 1975 to discuss relations. A Supreme Court resolution followed which, in so many words, instructed the appellate courts to cease directing queries to the DINA and to channel all requests for information to the Ministry of the Interior.[40] Although this agreement, which was later harshly criticized by human rights lawyers, probably amounted to little more than express recognition of the judiciary's powerlessness before the DINA, it rendered virtually seamless and impenetrable the obstructions in the way of effective judicial

[39] This response was contained in DINA (R) No. X3550/542, of March 18, 1975, a reply to the president of the appellate court of Santiago's request for information regarding Máximo Antonio Gedda Ortíz. Clearly this was not the first time that the appellate court received this reply from Contreras: A March 12, 1975 Court resolution to the DINA advised that regardless of ". . . whoever may be the authority to whom the Director is subordinate, he is under the legal obligation to inform this Court about the aforesaid circumstances." Photocopies of the official documents cited are reproduced in *Vicaría de la Solidaridad* 1976, Annex 1c. Gedda Ortíz, a leader of the MIR, had been arrested by the DINA on July 16, 1974 and was last seen in *Londres No. 38*, a secret detention center. In 1991, the official commission investigating human rights abuses reported that it was convinced that Gedda Ortíz's disappearance was the work of state agents (*Comisión Nacional de Verdad y Reconciliación* 1991, 507).

[40] This resolution was taken on March 27, 1975 and communicated to the appellate courts by the president of the appellate court of Santiago. This document is reproduced in *Vicaría de la Solidaridad* 1976, Annex 2b. In June 1976, upon the request of the Minister of Justice, these instructions appear to have been reiterated by the Supreme Court (Méndez Fetter 1979, 724; Frühling 1982, 54).

**147**

oversight of detentions: The Minister of the Interior, whether out of duplicity or ignorance,[41] rarely acknowledged arrests made by the DINA[42] – and when, for whatever reason, a particular arrest was finally recognized and validated, this tended to occur months after the *recurso de amparo* had been presented.

Thus, even though the Judiciary formally retained and exercised its mandate to protect constitutional rights of liberty and security from arbitrary infringement after the coup, the instruments it possessed, even when used aggressively, were largely ineffective before the institutional mutations affected by military rule. Prior to the coup the *recurso de amparo* was a mechanism internal to the judicial system whereby the appellate courts oversaw the lower courts and prison authorities, and in doing so protected individuals from errors or abuse.[43] All of this changed drastically with the military coup, as the

---

[41] It is not wholly implausible that the Minister of the Interior in many instances was genuinely ignorant as to whether an individual had been abducted by the DINA or any other intelligence service. In May 1974, then Minister of the Interior, Gen. Horacio Bonilla, informed the Junta of the problems arising from arbitrary arrests: ". . . as Minister of the Interior, I do not know who is under arrest in Chile. Each service, each Institution takes matters upon its own account and doesn't give notice; and then questions are posed to the Minister of the Interior and I do not know what to answer." To rectify this situation the Junta agreed to inform the Minister of Defense that thereafter all detentions effected by military intelligence services or military courts had to be communicated to the Minister of the Interior. It was also stated that arrests should conform to legal procedures (AHJG, 112, April 15, 1974, 12). As this last order was systematically violated, there is little reason to believe that the first order met with any greater compliance, particularly since to do otherwise would have undermined the system of covert repression.

[42] On rare occasions this cycle of denials broke down, though this didn't necessarily afford greater protection for an individual arbitrarily detained. These breakdowns occurred when an agency other than the DINA or the Ministry of the Interior – *Investigaciones, carabineros*, a commander of a regiment or a zone under state of siege, for example – informed that their institution had participated in an individual's arrest and had subsequently turned the person over to the DINA or was still holding them at the DINA's disposition – this occurred on occasion with the *Casa de Observación de Menores*, a detention home for minors. Separate queries to the Minister of the Interior generally would elicit a string of denials. In some instances, after months, the minister was forced by such contradictions to acknowledge and validate an arrest. Documentation regarding a dozen such cases is reproduced in *Vicaría de la Solidaridad* 1976, Annex 1 and 6. Contreras (1988, 53–58) reconstructs the convoluted and futile paper trail of one case in which a regiment commander intimated to the courts the DINA's responsibility in the disappearance of eight militants of the MIR. The officer's garrison had been the base of operations for the special team of DINA agents involved.

[43] This was true insofar as most arrests, except those that took place at the scene of a crime in progress, had to be ordered in the course of criminal investigations by a judge and individuals were detained or imprisoned in institutions subordinate to the Ministry

courts increasingly had to process *recursos de amparo* interposed on behalf of individuals detained or being held by authorities external to the judicial system and beyond the scope of its jurisdiction.

The obstacles inherent in this situation are amply documented by a former Santiago appellate court justice, José Canovas, in his memoirs (1989, 74–78). Canovas recounts that in 1974, as president of the appellate court, he met with then Minister of the Interior Gen. Horacio Bonilla to discuss difficulties with the *recurso de amparo*. Canovas informed Bonilla of the legal norms in effect, the government's failure to comply with them, and presented draft legislation modifying the handling of *recursos de amparo* during states of exception. Though Canovas does not provide details of this project, he does describe a later project he presented to Minister of Justice Miguel Schweitzer (minister from April 1975 through March 1977). This project confirms that the Judiciary had little power over actors external to it: Canovas proposed to transfer jurisdiction over *recursos de amparo* to the military courts during states of exception. Despite Schweitzer's interest, nothing happened. Canovas (1989, 75) attributed this outcome to the Minister of Justice's certain understanding that such a reform would have meant acknowledging that "during these states [of exception] the ordinary judicature is burdened with the responsibility, but is left with its hands tied." On the first occasion, Bonilla, via the Minister of Justice, requested that the Supreme Court itself revise guidelines on the *recurso de amparo*; the Supreme Court, in turn, merely transcribed Bonilla's communique and reiterated the standard legal references regarding the *recurso de amparo*.[44]

Under these circumstances and in the absence of ancillary checks, such as congressional oversight and impeachment, the courts retained very little leverage to assure compliance with legal norms regarding arrests and remedy and sanction infractions of these norms. On a number of occasions the judiciary did defend its ordinary jurisdiction

---

of Justice. In these circumstances, not only could the courts initiate criminal proceedings, they could also influence the career paths of judges or functionaries who failed to comply with court orders pertaining to *recursos de amparo*. Similarly, systematic abuses by members of agencies external to the Judiciary, such as, for example, *carabineros*, could give rise to congressional investigations and the impeachment of any minister found responsible.

[44] Bonilla's June 17, 1974 request to the Minister of Justice and the Supreme Court's instructions are reproduced in *Fallos del Mes*, August 1974 (189):159–60. Canovas later achieved notoriety for his tenacity as special investigating judge (*Ministro en Visita*) in the "*caso de los degollados*" – the March 1985 murder of José Manuel Parada, Manuel Guerrero, and Santiago Nattino, three Communist Party militants.

against external encroachment.[45] However, when faced with irregularities committed by state agents, the judiciary proved largely incapable of limiting extralegal acts, regardless of whether these were substantive or procedural infractions committed by war councils or criminal violations of constitutional guarantees at the hands of the security forces.

It is important to note that the freedom from judicial constraints in the realm of repression differed in character from the sources that allowed the Junta supremacy before the Supreme Court's powers of judicial review. With regard to the latter, the sovereignty of the Junta was assured by the modification of nominally higher norms to override or preclude effective constraints by the court. Conversely, in regard to repression, power was absolute because it was exercised arbitrarily, without concern for the legal formalities regulating arrests. In this context, any mechanisms of legal control held by the judiciary were inherently ineffectual. As a result, limitations upon the military government's use of repressive force had to arise not from the institutions constitutionally empowered to check such abuses but from within the military junta itself.

## Law and the Boundaries of Prudential Self-Limitation

Within a year of seizing power, in the face of mounting international criticism, the Chilean armed forces took first steps toward restricting by law their extensive emergency powers. Up until the state of siege was lifted in October 1978, such measures were enacted virtually every September as the commencement of the UN General Assembly approached. These modifications to emergency powers did not involve the creation or strengthening of institutions external to the Junta that might limit the use of state of siege faculties or the actions of the secu-

---

[45] An interesting example is the Supreme Court's March 28, 1974 resolution (Rol A-59-73), in which the full Court ruled that Division commanders' authority to issue *bandos* during time of war did not extend to commissioning ordinary judges – by *bando* – to serve as legal advisors (*auditores*) to the local military tribunal. The commander of the sixth army division in Arica had tried to do so. For the ruling, see *Fallos del Mes*, March–April 1974 (184–85):33–35. Later, in April 1974, the Supreme Court unanimously opposed a proposed constitutional reform to create a special Prosecutor General of the Republic with powers of investigation far exceeding those of the courts. This nonjudicial organ was to be dependent solely on the Junta. In the opinion of the Justices of the Court, as well as the members of the Constituent Commission, this reform if it had prospered would have implied the certain demise of the Supreme Court. This proposal is discussed below in more detail.

rity forces. The Junta's public claims to the contrary, these changes were carefully concocted ruses. The object was to deceive the international community by manipulating the nomenclature and scope of powers of different legal states of exception. Such maneuvers involved the deployment of a combination of legal stratagems to present an appearance of restraint and self-limitation while actually retaining extensive emergency powers and protecting the repression from judicial oversight.

Notwithstanding the Junta's externally unlimited prerogative powers, there were clear limits as to how far law, even decree-law, could plausibly be manipulated. These limits were set by certain widely accepted understandings regarding the rule of law. These standards were not enforced by institutions, but were prudentially accepted by the Junta. No institutional device compelled the Junta not to transgress these standards. Rather, in these cases the Junta forsook desired objectives after realizing that openly transgressing certain legal norms would be politically counterproductive. These dynamics were particularly evident in early 1974 as legal obstacles frustrated the Junta's plans to try top members of the Allende government. At this juncture, despite their conviction that these men were responsible for taking the country to the brink of disaster, the Junta acknowledged that in the absence of evidence these men could be tried only at the risk of making a parody of the law. The rule of law, which the armed forces had pledged to restore, implied certain standards, in particular the prohibition of any retroactive application of newly created offenses, which could only be transgressed at the cost of antagonizing significant supporters, such as the Supreme Court and the Constituent Commission.

Before these potential costs, the Junta in 1974 renounced its objective of trying prominent figures of the Allende government. Still, the limits of this type of prudential self-restraint must be underlined. In this instance, the Junta abstained from publicly violating central principles of the rule of law because of the perceived costs associated with any such transgression. Yet, this acknowledgment of the standard did not mean that such standards would be upheld when their violation was not costly or not likely to be perceived. The decision not to try the members of the Allende government did not lead to an improvement in the human rights situation on the ground. Rather, the effects of recognizing these constraints may well have been pernicious, as from this point on the repression increasingly took extralegal forms. Nor, as we will see, did acknowledgment of these principles prevent the Junta from subsequently seeking to manipulate the law to appease international critics while retaining for the regime broad repressive powers.

## 1974: The Trials that Never Were

After the coup, only the air force carried out a major public show trial of Allende officials and air force officers. This fact is sometimes interpreted as an indication of General Leigh's independence (Varas 1987, 46, n.6); nevertheless, within weeks of the coup the military junta decided to try all high officials of the Allende government. On October 3, 1973, the Junta agreed to instruct the Minister of the Interior "to prepare the background material to pursue a trial for treason to the Homeland (*Patria*) of those implicated of the former government and not only of Senator Luis Corvalán as has been appearing in the press in the capital" (AHJG, 14, October 3, 1973, 2). Shortly thereafter, an investigatory commission was formed within the *Consejo de Defensa del Estado* (Council of Defense of the State), the foremost state legal advisory body, to coordinate investigations within the different ministries and state institutions and to process evidence collected by the intelligence services.[46] As Admiral Merino noted some months later, the object was to put on trial "a system that had carried the country to economic calamity, to the total demoralization and de-motivation of its citizens, and, above all, to the brink of civil war, with all of the implications that this has for the destruction of a State" (AHJG, 76, January 21, 1974, 1). Notwithstanding these intentions, which were shared by all the members of the Junta, the trials never took place.

In part, the Junta's attempt to try government officials indirectly contributed to the dictatorship's international difficulties, which in turn gave urgency to the resolution of the issue of trials. This international pressure was a by-product of delays in the investigation that arose because the intelligence services and the ministries were not cooperating with *Consejo de Defensa del Estado* requests for documentation and evidence needed to piece together a case for a comprehensive trial.[47] These difficulties in putting together the evidence for a trial

[46] Historically, the *Consejo de Defensa de Estado* served two purposes: to defend the State's patrimonial interests and to provide the government with high-level independent legal counsel. The council consisted of twelve career functionaries, who were irremovable from office (except with Senate approval), and tended to be among Chile's most prominent and distinguished professors of law. On this organ, which was founded in the late nineteenth century, see Novoa Monreal 1978, 72–76.

[47] From the accounts in the Junta it seems that the principal problem delaying the *Consejo de Estado*'s investigation was the DINA's failure to cooperate (AHJG, 76, January 21, 1974, 1–8). These difficulties prompted Guillermo Pumpin, another *Consejo* lawyer, to propose that the Junta create a high-level committee with decision-making authority presided over by a high-ranking active service officer, who – backed by the clout of his

exacerbated the international situation because the military was deliberately holding back on granting the safe-conduct passes that would have allowed the many individuals crowding different embassies to leave the country. This was being done to give the military tribunals time to assess whether evidence warranted later extraditions.[48] As these delays dragged on, international pressure mounted for the release of those under detention, particularly the many former ministers of the Allende government who were being held under extremely harsh conditions on Dawson Island in the Strait of Magellan.

Before this pressure, in early April 1974 General Leigh insisted that the locus of the investigation be shifted to the different branches of the armed forces and *carabineros* to accelerate proceedings. The division of investigatory duties agreed to reveals the broad scope of the trials that the Junta wanted to hold: (a) the army would investigate the illegal manufacture of arms within state firms, activities harmful to National Security, and the provision of industrial secrets to foreign countries; (b) the navy would investigate the illegal entry and permanence of foreigners, the illegal importation of arms, as well as illegal acts involving Soviet fishing ships; (c) the air force would investigate the organization and activity of left-wing paramilitary groups, the "*Plan Zeta*," and irregularities committed in the Civil Registry and the Identification Service to facilitate electoral fraud; and (d) *carabineros* would investigate irregularities committed by intendents and governors, spying within telecommunications, and the formation of guerrilla groups. The responsibilities of the *Consejo de Defensa del Estado* were limited to investigating the state monopoly on auto sales, illegal

---

rank – would intercede directly before the intelligence services. This officer would also take charge of any findings that were not constitutive of penal offenses but would be of relevance to a political-historical trial. This proposal did not prosper. Instead, the Junta decided to organize a General Staff to advise the commission and cited the heads of the intelligence services and the DINA to a latter session (AHJG, 91, February 12, 1974, 1–3). At this meeting the intelligence chiefs reported on their relations with the *Consejo*, and the Junta decided to have the DINA appoint a liaison to coordinate relations between the services and the *Consejo* (AHJG, 94, February 18, 1974, 1–2).

[48] By mid-1974, these delays had resulted in a sharp deterioration in relations with Colombia and Venezuela, and tensions with other countries. In addition to being concerned with the situation of *Unidad Popular* leaders under detention, these countries were pressuring on behalf of arrested nationals and dual-citizens, as well as the many refugees crowding their embassy residences. The Mexican government gained exit for those on its embassy grounds only after negotiating extensive concessions to the military government; these promises were never fulfilled as Mexico broke diplomatic relations shortly after the releases in November 1974 (Muñoz 1986, 21). For an account of these problems from the perspective of an Italian diplomat, see de Vergottini 1991.

takeovers, irregularities in the state agricultural and agrarian reform agencies, the black market, and irregularities in *CORFO*, the state economic development agency (AHJG, 111, April 11, 1974, 1–2). In accordance with this division of labor, each service was ordered to appoint military investigating judges to initiate trial preparations so that within thirty to forty-five days those persons not under indictment could be expelled from the country.

Some days prior to this reorganization of the investigations, in late March 1974, Pinochet sent a project of constitutional reform intended to overcome the persistent obstacles delaying the trials to the Supreme Court and the Constituent Commission for review.[49] The debate on the project revealed the severe internal consequences that the military regime would face if it openly contravened by law – even indirectly and surreptitiously – fundamental guarantees regarding personal liberty.

The reform proposed to create a General Prosecutor of the State (*Procuradaría General del Estado*), directly dependent upon the Junta, to investigate crimes against internal and external State security and the economic interests of the State. Among other powers this bill granted the General Prosecutor authority to summon and detain individuals in the course of its investigations for as long as thirty days before releasing them or turning them over to the courts. During this period, detainees could be held incommunicado (ART. 4) and any private citizen or public functionary who refused to collaborate with the prosecutor could also be legally detained.[50] If at the end of an investigation no grounds for criminal prosecution were found, the results would merely be archived (ART. 4). Finally, the reform proposed to place the *Consejo de Defensa del Estado* under the *Procuraduría*, rather than the Ministry of Justice (ART. 10).

This proposal caused an uproar within the Constituent Commission (AOCC, 34, April 23, 1974, 3–21). In the presence of the presidents of the Supreme Court and the *Consejo de Defensa del Estado*, the commission's members vehemently condemned the project, which they argued was absolutely at odds with the rule of law and of likely totalitarian consequences. Not only did this bill grant a judicial function to a nonjudicial organ but, they objected, the *Procuraduría* was to hold preliminary investigatory powers in excess of those held by the courts,

---

[49] The project is reproduced in AOCC 25, March 25, 1974, 23–25.

[50] These individuals were to be arrested for up to five days, a period which was to be renewable for as long as the person remained defiant (ART. 5).

would operate without the oversight of any judicial authority, and would imply an open violation of the constitutional guarantee of personal liberty, since the individuals detained in the course of its investigations were afforded no mechanism to take recourse against arbitrary acts nor pursue penal responsibility against their authors. As Sergio Díez, a prominent member of the commission, argued, "if this project becomes reality, it will imply the absolute end of constitutional guarantees . . . as well as the disappearance of the power of the Judiciary" (AOCC, 34, April 23, 1974, 8–9). To further bolster his position, Díez also developed a line of argument which would later figure prominently in the Constituent Commission's deliberations over institutional design. This perspective stressed the relative stability of law and the uncertainty of the democratic process. As Díez insisted, the Junta was not only legislating for a transitory period, it was creating "permanent norms that in the future can be used by other groups with purposes opposite of those that motivate the Government Junta."[51] Such was Díez's indignation with the proposal that he also requested that the commission submit a transcript of its debate along with its written reply to the Junta so "if in the future this document comes to be leaked and falls into the hands of the enemies of this Government, it be known, that those who support the Junta, such as those who have spoken . . . have rejected it categorically and with good foundation" (AOCC, 34, April 23, 1974, 9).

The fear that this project's confusion of executive and judicial faculties might mark a turn to an "extreme totalitarianism" led Jaime Guzmán, who claimed to know the project's author, to expend considerable energy arguing that the project was really only intended to overcome obstacles besetting the investigation of offenses committed by the Allende government. Still, in its response, the commission set forth its criticisms at length, informing the Junta that the reform was highly inadvisable, and, if enacted, would be turned against the government by its international communist adversaries.[52]

---

[51] Díez invoked the precedent of decree-laws dictated during Gen. Carlos Ibáñez's first presidency. Although an inaccurate reference, Diez was referring to Allende's use of earlier decree-laws to expropriate firms by administrative decree. These decree-laws date to the short-lived "Socialist Republic" of 1932. This course was adopted to overcome the *Unidad Popular*'s lack of a sufficient majority to legislate in Congress. Novoa Monreal (1992), a staff member of the *Consejo de Defensa del Estado* since the early 1950s and the legal mastermind behind the Allende strategy, convincingly demonstrates that these highly controversial measures were nonetheless lawful.

[52] This reply, as well as the Supreme Court's response, are included as annexes to the minutes of the session already cited.

In the end, the General Prosecutor's office was never created and by May 1974 only the air force had begun a large public trial.[53] Toward the end of April it was reported (*New York Times*, April 30, 1974) that within a week the most important members of the *Unidad Popular* government were to be brought to Santiago for trial, an intention reiterated soon thereafter by the Minister of the Interior (*New York Times*, May 10, 1974). Still, the trials never took place.

Insurmountable legal barriers were just as crippling an obstacle for mounting a large public show trial as the logistical problems examined. As the Minister of Justice and the president of the *Consejo de Defensa del Estado* early on warned the Junta, there were no penal offenses on the books for which high officials of the Allende government were culpable (AHJG, 76, January 21, 1974, 3; 91, February 12, 1974, 3). Unless it could be demonstrated that these officials were involved in the commission of criminal offenses, such as treason, the violation of constitutional rights, usurpation of functions, misappropriation of public funds, or extortion, the acts for which the armed forces wished to try these men – the propagation of generalized economic and political chaos – could at best be cause for a political trial "for having gravely compromised the security or the honor of the nation" (ART. 39, no. 1, b, 1925 constitution).

The formal legality of the Allende government's actions, however, placed the armed forces in a terrible bind.[54] If the Junta enacted new criminal offenses by decree-law, these would have to be applied retroactively, a deviation from universally accepted legal principles which would have undoubtedly antagonized the Chilean and international legal communities. Yet, the pursuit of a political trial was no more viable. Pursuant to the constitution, ministers of state, as well as other state officials, could be accused by the Chamber of Deputies and judged by the Senate. When successful, these impeachment proceedings resulted only

[53] On the air force war councils, see the accounts of Luis Alvarez Baltierra, "Consejo de guerra: El proceso del Plan Zeta," *Ercilla*, April 24, 1974, pp. 9–13; "Consejo de guerra: Procesos en la etapa final," *Ercilla*, May 29, 1974, p. 13; "Consejo de guerra: El fiscal y la defensa," *Ercilla*, June 12, 1974, pp. 9–11; and Consejo de guerra: Historia del 'Plan Setiembre'," *Ercilla*, August 7, 1974.

[54] Lorenzo de la Maza, the president of the *Consejo de Defensa del Estado*, for one, must have been fully aware that the Allende government did not violate the law when implementing its economic policy. De la Maza was a member of the *Consejo* in November 1970 when it unanimously subscribed a legal brief confirming the legality of an administrative expropriation of a textile factory. The validity of these measures was also affirmed by the *Contraloría* when they reviewed their legality (Novoa Monreal 1992, 62–68).

in removal from office: Any civil liability or punishment was the jurisdiction of the ordinary courts.[55] Thus, even though the constitutional grounds for impeachment included acts not constitutive of criminal offenses, pursuing a political trial would have been pointless: Not only had the Junta dissolved the organs competent to initiate and hear such proceedings, it had already achieved the only effect possible in the absence of criminal charges when it overthrew the Allende government.

Unless the Junta was willing to flagrantly trample universally accepted principles of criminal justice, the only alternatives were to hold prominent government officials under arrest using state of siege faculties or to expel them from the country.[56] The military did both, but it never put them on public trial. When this determination was taken is unclear. In the minutes of the Junta's sessions, the last recorded mention of the need to quickly initiate trials was in late August 1974, when Admiral Huerta, then Ambassador to the United Nations, raised the issue. Nevertheless, by this date it was clear that the military did not have a criminal case against top officials of the Allende government. As General Pinochet acknowledged during the same session, "for what these persons have done, our Codes do not establish penalties or they are very small" (AHJG, 150, August 29, 1974, 8). This point was reiterated about a week later during the review of a report by a commission of retired admirals and generals which evaluated the documents seized by the intelligence services. The Minister of Defense noted that military tribunals had convicted only lower-level militants for illegally importing arms and organizing guerrilla groups. Otherwise, there was no evidence to implicate high government officials, though he did insist that they bore "moral responsibility" for these crimes (AHJG, 154, September 6, 1974, 1).[57]

---

[55] For analyses of Chilean law on constitutional accusations and political trials, see Silva Bascuñán 1963, 3:70–82, 91–113, 123–35; and Evans 1970, 64–68, 77–81.

[56] In August 1974, General Leigh argued that expulsion was the only solution. He suggested that a fact sheet be drawn up for each of the political prisoners still in detention – he explicitly mentioned Orlando Letelier, Allende's last Minister of Defense, and Daniel Vergara, former Under Secretary of Interior – listing the charges against them. This information could then be made known throughout the world. Later, by decree-law the Junta would expel these people from Chile on the basis of the charges formulated against them (AHJG, 144, August 5, 1974, 2). It is unclear whether this proposal was considered seriously. The Junta tactfully never followed this course, as it too would have made a mockery of justice. Rather, expulsions took place under provision of ART. 2 of D.L. No. 81, which surreptitiously expanded state of siege faculties to include administrative exile during time of war. On this decree-law, see note 25, page 138.

[57] At the same meeting Col. Jorge Espinoza, the officer in charge of detention camps, informed the Junta of the number of individuals then being held: 1,131 persons were

The Junta accepted these political constraints. Ironically and tragically, recognition of the internal and international potency of fundamental principles of criminal justice did not afford political adversaries of the armed forces any greater security or protection. It merely set the boundaries for what could be done in public. Whether a consequence or merely a coincidence, the process leading up to the decision not to hold trials coincided with a turn toward covert modes of repression which in many instances made the issue of trials irrelevant. Nor did these constraints prevent the Junta from strategically manipulating the law with the purported objective of restraining and limiting its vast emergency powers while, in fact, preserving and expanding them. The Junta responded to international pressure to improve the human rights situation, yet at least during the first three years of military rule, the commanders used their unrestrained legislative powers to enact decree-laws that at best effected cosmetic changes in the situation.

## The Cosmetic Self-Limitation of Emergency Powers

In an effort to stave off international sanctions, in September 1974 the Junta began to modify by decree-law the broad emergency faculties conferred by constitutional states of exception and its own earlier legislation – a tactic it would use whenever punitive measures by the United Nations or other international organizations appeared imminent. Such reforms were deliberately crafted to appear as genuine steps toward improving the human rights situation. Typically, lower ranking states of exception were declared to give an appearance of less severe emergency powers, or else procedures were enacted which purportedly protected the rights of individuals detained by virtue of states of exception. These measures tended to be carefully crafted gems of legislative technique. By employing a combination of legal subterfuges, decree-laws were drafted whose political intent and actual effects were very different from those announced or suggested by the content of the decree-law itself. Unless one was versed in the intricacies of Chilean constitutional and penal law, at least initially, the real significance of these measures would not be self-evident. A number of stratagems were employed to this effect, such as: the avoidance of amendments to

in detention camps, another 2,979 had been tried and convicted, and 3,220 other persons were facing proceedings. In all 1,800 military trials had been completed, 1,900 were in process, 19 were before ordinary courts, and the *Consejo de Defensa de Estado* was studying the initiation of another 19 cases (AHJG, 154, September 6, 1974, 2).

the constitution since explicit modifications drew international attention and were likely to be interpreted as a manipulation of faculties;
the use of obscure legal references to avoid openly indicating the substantive content of a norm; and the withholding for subsequent promulgation of articles that might belie the actual intent of the legislation.

Such gambits were behind General Pinochet's September 11, 1974
announcement that the state of siege in "time of war" was being terminated and lowered to the grade of Internal Defense, which had just
been created by D.L. No. 640.[58] This decree-law had been drafted in
anticipation of the attacks the Junta expected to face in the upcoming
General Assembly of the United Nations. The political purpose of this
decree-law was first intimated at a Junta session dedicated exclusively
to developing a strategy for the special delegation accompanying Chile's
Ambassador to the United Nations, Admiral Ismael Huerta (AHJG, 150,
August 29, 1974, 1–10).[59] Among other concerns, the principal problem
the Junta faced was how to credibly maintain that the internal situation had been normalized while at the same time continue upholding
a juridical state of war.

General Pinochet provided the essence of the eventual solution:

As one says, we have changed; we are travelling in a Mercedes Benz
mini-bus (*micro*) and we switch to another Mercedes Benz but we
label it Pegaso [the Spanish automotive firm]. We continue the same.
The name changes that's all. This is under study . . . The Supreme
Court does not participate which was the most important thing. It
continues the same, with the same judicial procedures and the civil
tribunal participates for effects of applying the law. It is the same,
but outwardly we can say that we have burnt this stage of war, we
have lowered the tension, and we pass to a State of Siege in the first
degree, State of Internal Defense. (AHJG, 150, August 29, 1974, 6–7)

The specifics of this project were worked out a week later with
the help of General Pinochet's and General Leigh's respective legal
advisors, Mónica Madariaga and air force Col. (J) Julio Tapia Falk, as
well as Jaime Guzmán (AHJG, 153, September 5, 1974, 1–9). The

---

[58] D.O., September 10, 1974. The lowering of the rank of the state of siege went into effect
the same day by virtue of D.L. No. 641, D.O., September 11, 1974. The classification
of the state of siege as in "time of war" dates to D.L. No. 5.

[59] The members of the delegation were: Gonzalo Prieto, by then ex-Minister of Justice;
Mario Arnello, an extreme right nationalist; Sergio Onofre Jarpa, a former Senator for
the National Party; Guillermo Bruna, former Undersecretary of Justice under Prieto;
and Sergio Rillón, the navy justice officer.

deliberations leading to this decree-law illustrate one tactical motivation behind the Junta's legalism: By manipulating preexisting legal categories, the armed forces could claim to be working within the bounds of Chile's established constitutional and legal tradition and thereby deflect charges that they were manipulating the law at will. This line of defense would be used up until the final days of the military government: In deploying repressive force the military was legitimately exercising legally valid powers established prior to the coup.

To remain true to this scheme, the Junta decided to create different gradations of state of siege, rather than institute a new state of exception alongside the state of siege. As Madariaga and Guzmán advised, the creation of a new state would require modifying the constitution and would produce an entity unknown abroad. As they noted, internationally a "state of siege" was "very presentable" – Colombia and Argentina were cited as countries that had been under continuous states of siege for years and years without external repercussion (AHJG, 153, September 5, 1974, 4–5). To avoid modifying the constitution the Junta decided to retain the traditional states of emergency in ART. 1 of D.L. No. 640 and to create four gradations of state of siege in a later article, which were distinguished by the powers they conferred and the circumstances warranting their declaration. Guided by the same motivation, the Junta also retained the constitutionally vacuous yet traditional *Estado de Asamblea* (State of Assembly).[60]

Although General Leigh at first was against including any reference to internal war among the new gradations, such a reference was retained since, as Guzmán noted, "It's a little tough to have lived the whole year in one State, then suddenly it is legislated upon and it doesn't exist." Guzmán also observed that by maintaining a category of internal war the Junta could declare a state of siege in the grade of Internal Defense and not appear to still be using its most extreme powers (AHJG, 153, September 5, 1974, 6, 7).

This apparent reduction notwithstanding, through the use of deliberately obscure references, the two intermediate levels – Internal Defense and Internal Security – came to have identical juridical effects as the declaration of a state of siege in time of war. ART. 2 of the decree-law alluded to time of war only obliquely by referring to ART. 418 of the CdJM (which defines "state of war" and "time of war"), whereas

---

[60] The *Estado de Asamblea* was applicable during war with other states but granted no powers. As described by General Leigh's legal advisor, Colonel Tapia, the state of assembly was as an "aftertaste of the constitution of 1833" (AHJG, 153, September 5, 1974, 1).

ART. 7 stated that during a state of siege in the degree of Internal Defense, "there will apply the legal dispositions contained in Title III of Book I and in Title IV of Book II of the Code of Military Justice, and, when it applies, the penalties corresponding to time-of-war." Though this last clause might suggest something other than time of war, the respective headings in the CdJM of the Titles invoked are revealing: "Of the Military Tribunals in time-of-war" and "Of the Penal Procedure in time-of-war."[61] Thus, during both states of siege the military tribunals in time of war were to continue operating, with penalties lowered one degree during the grade of Internal Security (ART. 8, D.L. No. 640).[62]

In this manner, a juridical foundation was created which allowed the Junta to supersede the politically unacceptable designation "state" or "time of war" without having to restrict its broad emergency powers nor allow the Supreme Court to intervene in the administration of military justice. This nominal ratcheting down of the state of exception required modifications of other decree-laws to preserve emergency powers that had been initially enacted restrictively by confining their applicability to "time of war." However, given the Junta's facile legislative powers, these modifications were easily enacted at later dates when they were unlikely to draw international attention. Thus, one month after D.L. No. 640 was decreed, D.L. No. 81 was modified to enable administrative exile during any state of siege regardless of gradation. This method whereby exceptional faculties were successively normalized whenever states of exception or repressive practices had to be formally mollified became a common legal tactic.[63]

Notwithstanding these moves, the military government remained under considerable pressure to take effective measures to improve its human rights record, release political prisoners, and permit some mechanism for appealing military tribunal decisions. During the last

---

[61] This equivalence was made explicit eight months later when ART. 7 of D.L. No. 640 was modified to also apply to states of siege in the grade of Internal or External War (ART. 8, D.L. No. 1,009, D.O., May 5, 1975).

[62] Formally, the declaration of one grade of state of siege rather than the other depended on the subject provoking the internal commotion: active, organized rebel or seditious forces warranted a state of siege in the grade of Internal Defense; a state of siege in the grade of Internal Security was applicable when confronting "unorganized" forces.

[63] Later, when the DINA was dissolved in August 1977, references to the state of siege contained in D.L. No. 81, as well as in two other decree laws, became applicable to the State of Emergency, an extraconstitutional state of exception which dates to the Law of Internal State Security of 1957 (ART. 2 of D.L. No. 1,877, D.O., August 13, 1977). D.L. No. 1,877 was enacted in express use of the constituent power, and, under the guise of complementing the 1957 law, also granted the president authority to arrest individuals at his prerogative for up to five days in their homes or facilities other than jails.

months of 1974, foreign relations dominated the government's deliberations. After the September 11 announcements, the Junta met virtually every two weeks in extended sessions to hear reports on the international situation and bilateral relations from delegates and ministers who had just returned from trips to Europe and the United States to confer with government officials, businessmen, and journalists or to attend international meetings.

Upon returning to Santiago, these representatives invariably stressed the need to improve the quality of diplomatic appointees, develop better contacts abroad, and build ties to states in Africa, Asia, and the Middle East. Fernando Leniz, the Minister of Economic Coordination and Reconstruction, for example, insisted that U.S. public attention upon human rights in Chile was grounded in genuine religious and ethical concerns and wasn't part of the campaign by world communist parties to isolate Chile and precipitate the collapse of the military government. As he related to the Junta, individuals abroad had explained why the human rights situation in Chile was receiving such extensive press attention, "they told me that the past of Chile is a past that is too interesting and important for them not to follow what happens here with much more care than they do regarding events in other countries. They add that we are neither Bolivia, nor Mexico, nor any other country that has had a stormy past" (AHJG, 177, December 11, 1974, 3). In this context, officials suggested that "moves" such as releasing well-known political prisoners might bolster the bargaining position of the Chilean government and also create space for those foreign government officials who sympathized with the military's economic policies but who could not openly assist the regime because of political considerations.[64]

Despite a series of measures in early 1975,[65] any easing of international pressure was lost as the government proved incapable of sus-

---

[64] For example, during a visit to West Germany, the German Minister of Economics sternly told Raúl Saez that Germany would not disburse a $21 million loan agreed to during the Popular Unity government as long as José Clodomiro Almeyda, the minister who had signed the loan, remained in jail (AHJG, 180, December 27, 1974, 3–6). Saez refused to negotiate with the minister, but shortly after reporting this to the Junta, Almeyda was sent into exile and the loan was released (*Latin America*, January 17, 1975).

[65] In May 1975 a procedure was instituted to commute prison sentences of the military tribunals to exile. Further measures were also taken to "self-limit" discretionary faculties under the state of siege. D.L. No. 640 was modified so that peacetime procedures of military justice with Supreme Court participation would go into effect once the state of siege was lowered to the level of Internal Security or lower (ART. 8, D.L. No. 1,009, D.O., May 5, 1975). This move was largely nominal, as the following article excepted specific offenses described in the Law of State Security and left them under the jurisdiction of military tribunals in time of war.

taining any credibility for its promises to improve the human rights situation. In July, Pinochet reneged on his pledge to allow a visit by the UN Human Rights Commission the day before the group was to arrive in Chile, precipitating a deterioration in relations, particularly with the United States.[66] This adverse international situation meant further difficulties in obtaining credits from multilateral organizations, in renegotiating the foreign debt, in acceding to foreign bilateral credits and assistance, and further kindled efforts to organize an economic boycott of Chile. As the 30th UN General Assembly approached, for the first time the Junta seriously considered the worst-case scenario that Chile might be expelled from the United Nations (AHJG, 226, August 18, 1975, 1–38).

Before this scenario the Junta engaged in an exhaustive analysis of the internal and external situations, and reviewed and evaluated a number of alternative courses of action. The strategies considered differed according to the intensity and pragmatism of the Chilean response to anticipated Soviet attacks in the UN General Assembly. Two aspects of this discussion should be stressed. First, the specific measures considered were expected to leave unaffected the "internal security situation." In fact, the general rule was to first submit possible measures to the DINA so that it could evaluate whether the proposed measures would compromise internal security. This review greatly narrowed the number of feasible tactics: As the Minister of Foreign

---

A state of siege at the grade of Internal Security was first declared in D.L. No. 1,181 (D.O., September 11, 1975). It was renewed at this level every six months until September 10, 1977, when it was dropped to the grade of Simple Interior Commotion. As is discussed in the following chapter, the state of siege was allowed to lapse six months later.

[66] The reason for the reversal is unclear. At an earlier Junta meeting, Sergio Díez reported on the situation at the United Nations and spoke of the subsequent visit as if it would proceed (AHJG, 193, May 23, 1975, 3–6). Diez intimated (3) that conditions were to be negotiated, but the records contain no further reference to this. Pinochet (1990, 2:87) acknowledges that a majority around him favored the visit and presents the reversal as a personal resolution to protect the national dignity of Chile. The visit by the UN Commission on Human Rights had been promoted by Great Britain, West Germany, France, Holland, and Austria. At the May 1975 General Assembly of the Organization of American States (OAS), Chilean delegates successfully used the UN visit as a card to circumvent proposals for an on-site investigation by the Interamerican Commission of Human Rights and any discussion of the human rights situation in Chile or the OAS's first report. As a result, according to Foreign Minister Rear Adm. Patricio Carvajal, the human rights situation would not be addressed for one year (AHJG, 205, June 13, 1975, 1). The United States had supported postponing the OAS visit (Sigmund 1993, 103). The decision to allow the visit also contributed to improving Chile's situation in a number of international forums.

Relations noted, "after filtering them this way we were left only with the general conclusions and a few concrete measures" (AHJG, 205, August 17, 1975, 16). The proposals that remained consisted of: anti-terrorist legislation modeled after West German and British statutes; dropping the state of siege a notch so that military tribunals in peacetime would operate and appeals could reach the Supreme Court; lifting or easing the curfew; releasing more prisoners into exile; and announcing the formation of a national commission to study the human rights problem. None of these measures were foreseen as substantially affecting the regime's capacity to control the internal situation.

Second, steps were evaluated in terms of whether they would strengthen the position of foreign personages sympathetic to the military regime. The interest of the Junta, to use the military's argot, was to "send weapons to our friends." The primary concern was not to address the underlying situations which gave cause for international pressure, such as the continued problem of disappearances.[67] Still, junta members did think that they were addressing such causes, only they identified them differently – as the corrosive impact of Soviet imperialism and Marxism, which abroad appeared in the guise of the solidarity movement and in Chile took the form of the Left parties which had taken the country to the brink of disaster in 1973. This situation justified, in the Junta's view, exceptional measures internally and an aggressive anti-Soviet stance abroad, a diagnosis uncomfortably out of step with Henry Kissinger's policy of detente.

Despite this common approach to the international situation, the discussion also revealed signs of differentiation among the junta members regarding responsibility for the acts of repression which were the source of international pressure. At one point, General Leigh warned that Chile was going to receive severe attacks for the "lists of *miristas* killed abroad." Leigh was referring to the "lists of the 119," the July 1975 publications in Argentina and Brazil of lists of Chilean Leftists purportedly killed in internecine struggles outside of Chile. Leigh cautioned, "I wouldn't want to be in the pants of the members of the Chilean Embassy to the United Nations with regard to how they will

---

[67] During an exchange on how to improve relations with the foreign press, Carvajal acknowledged that most requests for information concerned the disappeared. In response, the head of *carabineros*, General Mendoza – in probably the only indiscretion contained in the *Actas* – stated, "In my opinion that is not the story that interests them, because this matter of the dead is overly played out. . . . For them the deaths are no longer stylish, since they [the journalists] are people that are helping us. For the attacker the dead are important" (AHJG, 226, August 18, 1975, 30).

defend this," intimating his distance from this act, which is widely thought to have been a DINA operation (AHJG, 205, August 17, 1975, 24).

During this strategy session, an officer (AHJG, 205, August 17, 1975, 20–21) mentioned in passing a tactic that would come to stand as the centerpiece of the military government's maneuvers to stave off international pressure: If the military promulgated a part of the Constituent Commission's work, particularly the sections on rights, it could claim to be on the path to constitutional normalcy. Though this idea was not extensively discussed, the possibility of promulgating *Actas Constitucionales* met with general approval. On September 11, 1975, the second anniversary of the coup, General Pinochet announced that the Junta would dictate a series of constitutional acts, as well as create a civilian Council of State to advise the president,[68] and institute a lower grade state of siege. These *Actas Constitucionales* were to be promulgated before the end of the first semester of 1976 and address the following three areas: fundamental bases of the new institutionality; nationality and citizenship; rights, constitutional guarantees, and regimes of emergency (*El Mercurio*, September 12, 1975).

As this chapter has shown, despite the fact of limits within the Junta, the dictatorship's power to impose punishments upon society was unlimited by standing rules. The institutional powers held by the judiciary were wholly ineffectual constraints. On the one hand, the Supreme Court abdicated its authority to oversee the military tribunals in time of war, thereby permitting the creation of a dual legal system in which opponents of the regime were tried in special courts free from any judicial oversight. Whereas on the other hand, the standing instrument for defending individual rights, the *recurso de amparo* was of no

---

[68] The Council of State (*Consejo de Estado*) was created by *Acta Constitucional No. 1* (D.L. No. 1,319, D.O., January 9, 1976) as an exclusively advisory body to the president. Former presidents were members by right, while sixteen other individuals were appointed by the president in representation of a range of social and state institutions. The creation of the Council of State did not in any way limit Pinochet's executive power: Consultations were optional and council recommendations were nonbinding. Although the government publicly heralded the council as a sign of its commitment to expand civilian participation as circumstances permitted, the political intent behind the creation of the Council of State was to lure former President Eduardo Frei Montalva (1964–1970) into a voiceless chamber, where the secrecy of consultations would oblige him to mute his criticism of the military government (AHJG, 256, December 29, 1975, 1–13). Frei did not fall for this gambit. The only two other surviving ex-presidents, Gabriel González Videla (1946–1952) and Jorge Alessandri Rodríguez (1958–1964), did participate in the council. Alessandri was appointed President of the Council of State.

force before methods of repression that deliberately sidestepped legal procedures of arrest and detention. In this context, restrictions on arbitrary repression could only come from within the Junta. As we have seen, initially the regime responded to international pressure with cosmetic legal changes. However, recourse to promulgating a partial constitution as a further attempt to deflect international pressure proved to be a strategy that inadvertently precipitated sharp conflicts within the Junta, whose eventual resolution took the form of the 1980 constitution.

# Chapter Five

## Constitutionalization without Transition: Prompting the Dual Constitution of 1980

When the members of the Junta decided to promulgate partial constitutional acts – the *Actas Constitucionales* of 1976 – they inadvertently set in motion a sharp internal debate over institutions and dictatorship that culminated only in 1980 with the promulgation of a constitution. At the outset, the Junta embraced constitutional "self-limitation" as a stratagem to stave off international critics without abdicating power. Nonetheless, the cosmetic manipulation of constitutional forms triggered intense conflicts over the advisability of continued military rule and alternative scenarios of transition. The repercussions of contingent acts, particularly the recoil of the September 1976 car-bomb assassination of Orlando Letelier and Ronni Moffitt in Washington, D.C., and recurring conflicts over the use of dictatorial power further fueled these exchanges. After a drawn-out process, agreement was reached to enact a "definitive" constitution, and in July and early August 1980 the Junta worked out the final text on the basis of proposals drafted by the Constituent Commission and the *Consejo de Estado* (Council of State), the advisory council created in 1976. The eventual text stipulated the organs and powers that would form a postmilitary "protected" democracy, a timetable and steps for moving to this civilian regime, and the structure of military power during the interim, and was ratified by plebiscite on September 11, 1980 and went into effect six months later.[1]

This chapter analyzes the political dynamics that prompted the promulgation of the 1980 constitution. The following two chapters will examine the substantive content of the constitution and its impact upon military rule and the transition to civilian rule. Contrary to the

---

[1] According to the official tally, 67.54 percent of valid votes were cast "Yes" and 29.62 percent were cast "No." Allegations of fraud were immediate and discounted by the government. On these charges, see note 10, page 173.

conventional wisdom that the 1980 constitution was designed and dictated by General Pinochet, I will show that the constitution was rather the product of a compromise: It settled ongoing conflicts within the Junta over the duration of military rule and the character of the regime to follow. Furthermore, the content of the constitution did not embody the ideal of any one faction or junta member. As will become apparent when the content of the constitution is examined in Chapter 6, the charter does not embody any single position which emerged during the 1977 debate over the structure of the Junta, its relationship to the "new institutionality," and the termination of military rule. No member of the Junta unilaterally imposed their preferred institutional framework, timetable, or scenario of transition, least of all Pinochet, who as we shall see would have preferred to rule with no constitution at all or else one radically distinct from that promulgated.

This analysis will proceed as follows. The first section presents the basic outlines of the structure and content of the 1980 constitution. This overview provides a context for introducing the standard explanation of why the constitution was enacted and for posing further questions. The second section addresses some of the difficulties inherent in analyzing the constitution-making process, and the third section reconstructs the conflictive process that led the Junta to enact the constitution.

## The 1980 Constitution and Its Discontents

After almost four years of intermittent on-again-off-again conflict over institutions and the prudence of extended dictatorship, the Junta settled on a charter which somewhat surprisingly left untouched the existing organization of military power as defined in 1974–1975 and postponed competitive elections for nine years, an interlude longer than the armed forces had been in power. The 1980 constitution neither set in motion a transition nor inaugurated a liberalization of the military dictatorship.[2]

---

[2] Nonetheless, it is inaccurate to maintain that the constitution precluded any liberalization until the plebiscite. Transitory Disposition 10 stipulated that all forms of political or party activity were prohibited *until* the organic constitutional law on political parties went into effect. However, the Junta was free to enact the political party law at any point and its enactment would have triggered a *de jure* resurgence of political activity. Furthermore, the Junta retained the power to modify the constitution (subject to plebiscite), and, therefore, could have modified this prohibition at any point to initiate an opening. As we will see in the following chapter, the Junta divided over when to enact the political party law. The bill (Bulletin 496-06) entered the legislative system on June 5, 1984 but the law was not promulgated until March 23, 1987.

This mode of dictatorial stabilization through constitutionalization was achieved by combining permanent articles and transitory dispositions in the constitution. In effect, the 1980 constitution contained two constitutions in one.[3] In fourteen chapters and 120 articles,[4] the permanent body of the text structured a "self-protected democracy," composed of what are essentially Republican institutions – an elected bicameral legislature and president – bolstered by a number of mechanisms designed to protect the institutional order from subversion from within. These innovations upon Chile's constitutional tradition included: a constitutional ban on Marxist parties (the infamous ART. 8); a reinforced bill of rights and the institution of a new remedy for their protection (the *recurso de protección*); a delimited maximum domain of legislation, adapted from the French 1958 constitution; a set of nonelected members to moderate the elected majority in the Senate; a revived Constitutional Tribunal, with a new composition weighted in favor of members designated by nonpolitical organs; the insulation of military appointments from political manipulation; the elevation of the armed forces to the status of guarantors of the institutional order; and more demanding requirements for modifying the constitution, including delays for entrenched articles.

The second "constitution," set out in twenty-nine transitory dispositions (T.D.), took precedence over the permanent articles during a first presidential term which was to begin once the constitution went into force six months after its ratification by plebiscite (T.D. 13), that is, on March 11, 1981.[5] Through a process of subtraction and substitution, the transitory clauses reinstated the status quo of dictatorship: General

[3] Somewhat surprisingly, I know of no English language commentaries on the 1980 constitution written during the military period. This void largely reflects the widespread assumption that the military's constitution would not survive a transition to democracy. Only now is the text receiving slightly more attention, though mainly as a limit on democracy in Chile. For an English language translation of the text, see Blaustein, Calvo Roth, and Luther 1980.

[4] The chapters are: (1) Bases of Institutionality; (2) Nationality and Citizenship; (3) Constitutional Rights and Obligations; (4) Government (Presidency); (5) National Congress; (6) Judicial Power; (7) Constitutional Tribunal; (8) Electoral Justice; (9) Office of the Comptroller General of the Republic; (10) Armed Forces, Forces of Order and Public Security; (11) National Security Council; (12) Central Bank; (13) Government and Internal Administration of the State; (14) Reform of the Constitution.

[5] The date of activation of the constitution was specified in the Final Article of the constitution. Two transitory dispositions, T.D. 9 and T.D. 23, became effective immediately with ratification. These clauses respectively concerned the initial designation of members to the Constitutional Tribunal and the selection of a subrogate president in the event that Pinochet be absolutely disabled from serving as president during the interim between the plebiscite and the constitution coming into force.

Pinochet was to remain in office during the eight-year presidential term, and the four-member Junta was to continue to exercise legislative and constituent powers, as always in accordance with the unanimity rule. With only slight modifications, the transitory dispositions reconstitutionalized the organizational constitution of military rule which had been codified during the first years of dictatorship (D.L. No. 1, 128, 527, and 788).

The most significant modifications to this prior framework were the immediate installation of the Constitutional Tribunal, a new requirement that modifications to the constitution also be subject to plebiscitary ratification, and, for the first time, a term limit for military rule. Although the constitution left open the possibility of a second presidential term for Pinochet – if nominated by the Junta and approved in a ratifying plebiscite (T.D. 27) – regardless of the outcome of the presidential plebiscite, the constitution structured a process whereby in March 1990 military rule would end, the Junta would cease to exist, and an elected, civilian Congress would be inaugurated. T.D. 27, 28, and 29 anticipated two alternate paths to the full implementation of the constitution, with the outcome of the plebiscite triggering which path would be followed. If the citizenry approved the Junta's candidate, then the president-elect would assume office and the constitution would go into full effect, except that the Junta would continue operating until the inauguration of an elected Congress one year into the presidential term. General elections for deputies and senators were to be convoked nine months after the inauguration of the president (T.D. 28). If the Junta's candidate was defeated, as eventually happened in 1988, the incumbent's (Pinochet's) term would be extended one year, and ninety days before the end of this extension competitive presidential and congressional elections would be convoked, subject to the permanent provisions of the constitution (T.D. 29). In this case, as well, the Junta would function until Congress opened.[6]

---

[6] The constitution structured considerable uncertainty regarding when the ratifying plebiscite would take place. T.D. 27 allowed the Junta maximum discretion in setting the date: The only temporal qualification was that the Junta meet to choose a candidate *at least* ninety days before the end of the first presidential term. Otherwise, the plebiscite could be held at any point without violating the constitution. Again, setting the date of the plebiscite was also subject to the unanimity rule. For purposes of the plebiscite, T.D. 27 also suspended the constitutional prohibition on presidential reelection (ART. 25, para. 2), thus leaving open the possibility of a Pinochet nomination. However, regardless of who the Junta proposed, in the event of a defeat in the plebiscite, Pinochet would be ineligible for a second chance in the open presidential election since this contest was subject to the permanent norms of the constitution (T.D. 29). Any Pinochet candidacy in this election would have required a constitutional reform.

At the moment of promulgation, however, the dualism of permanent and transitory articles rendered the permanent body of the 1980 constitution largely nominal and declarative: The normative framework of a civilian regime and the steps leading up to it stood only as promises – and not very credible ones – since the semantic constitution contained in the transitory articles not only reasserted the status quo of dictatorship but also granted the president new and broader discretionary, repressive powers, available irrespective of whether a state of exception was in effect. These powers were granted by the much criticized T.D. 24, which authorized the president to: (1) detain persons for up to five days in their own homes or places other than prisons (this term could be increased to fifteen days in the event of serious terrorist acts); (2) restrict freedom of assembly and limit the creation and circulation of new publications; (3) expel from Chile or prohibit from entering the country any individual propagating Marxist doctrines or effecting acts contrary to Chilean interests or that constitute a threat to internal peace; and (4) banish (*relegar*) individuals for periods up to three months to specific urban localities within Chile. These powers could be used for renewable six-month periods whenever there occurred "acts of violence aimed at altering public order or there exist danger of disturbance to internal peace" (D.T. 24). The determination of whether these conditions held was the exclusive prerogative of the president. T.D. 24 also closed off any intervention by the courts by expressly stipulating that these measures were not susceptible to any judicial remedy.[7]

The constitution as structured in the T.D.s hardly augured any changes in the dictatorship. As Hernán Montealegre (1980, 6–7), a prominent opposition lawyer, noted in a public lecture given just prior to the plebiscite to ratify the constitution, transition implies moving beyond one stage and taking steps toward another, yet the transitory articles only radicalized the "emergency" purportedly being surpassed without providing any channels for citizen participation. In his words (1980, 15–16), "Far from being a constitution of national unity, of internal peace, of harmony of a government with its people, the government's conviction that the coming years will be the very opposite,

---

[7] Given the extent of these powers and the attempt to preempt the use of constitutional mechanisms for protecting rights, T.D. 24 immediately became the target of the Center and Left opposition parties, who demanded that the government desist from using the article and presented legal challenges. For an analysis of the constitutionality of T.D. 24, see Ríos Alvarez 1983 and Silva Bascuñán 1986, 98–99.

a period of confrontation, shines through the transitory dispositions. Otherwise, it is impossible to explain why the government anticipates confrontations by providing exceptional powers which it didn't even have during the period of emergency."

In terms of the comparative analysis of constitution making (Elster 1997), the 1980 constitution was one of the class of internally imposed constitutions. It was drafted in secret and enacted by a sovereign law-maker, the Junta, without any popular participation through an elected constituent assembly. The adoption of the constitution was accompanied by a plebiscite, but the legitimacy of this act was impugned by the Center and Left opposition since the plebiscite took place amidst a state of emergency, with all political parties outlawed, no alternatives presented to voters, no statement of the juridical consequences of a defeat, and, most significantly for the opposition, no voter registration rolls, and no independent electoral oversight or counting.[8]

To vote in the plebiscite, Chileans and resident foreigners over the age of eighteen had only to present their national identity card and could vote at any polling site regardless of their place of residence. Mayors directly appointed by the executive constituted the voting tables, oversaw the voting, and effected the initial counts; ad hoc regional and national tellers' colleges designated for the plebiscite completed the regional and national counts. These counts followed a peculiar counting rule: Blank ballots were to be counted as "Yes" votes in favor of the constitution.[9] The ratificatory plebiscite thus occurred under conditions of questionable impartiality, leading the

---

[8] Opposition figures impugned the legitimacy of the military's constituent process from the outset. In August 1978 a constitutional study group formed to discuss an alternative project of constitutional reform – the *Grupo de Estudios Constitucionales*, better known as the *Grupo de los 24*, after its twenty-four members – brought together prominent constitutionalists and former members of Congress from across the political spectrum. The group initially demanded the election of a constituent assembly (Adelmar 1978; Rodriguez 1979), but as this demand proved unlikely, it shifted to the requisite conditions for a fair plebiscite (Cumplido 1980; Pozo 1980). Principal among these was the reconstitution of the voter registries which the military destroyed in 1974 on the ground that they had been corrupted by Allende. As these critics noted, inscription in electoral registries was a condition for citizenship with the right to vote in both the 1833 and the 1925 constitutions, and the Junta had not derogated the pertinent norm in the 1925 charter (ART. 7) nor other statutory norms regulating elections. In a public declaration, Gustavo Leigh, by 1980 no longer a Junta member, rejected the plebiscite on similar terms. See *El Mercurio*, September 8, 1980, C2.

[9] The plebiscite was structured by D.L. No. 3,465, D.O., August 12, 1980. The counting rule was specified in ART. 20. For accounts of the plebiscite, see Cumplido 1983, 32–46 and Andrade Geywitz 1984. Also see the documents reproduced in *Chile-America* 64–65, September 1980, pp. 19–53.

opposition to disqualify the act as a valid test of support for the new constitution.[10]

Both in its origins and mode of ratification, the 1980 constitution appeared to be nothing more than an imposition by force, a coercive act, which in accordance with principles of public law was juridically null and void. From this perspective, the validity of the 1980 constitution was no different than that of any other decree-law: The constitution was de facto and its practical efficacy was solely a function of the relations of force sustaining it (Cumplido 1983, 46).[11] At its promulgation the 1980 constitution appeared to be merely a device to prolong military rule – and given the regime's proclivity toward organizing plebiscites on its own terms the constitution appeared to portend at least sixteen years more of military rule. The permanent text, thus, was merely nominal because ineffective, whereas the transitory dispositions, the effective constitution, rendered the constitution semantic because it only codified the prevailing power monopoly.

Notwithstanding its character as an imposed constitution and its effect of perpetuating military rule, the constitution should not be portrayed as the fancy of Pinochet, despite the many academic analyses which subsume the constitution to the interpretation of the regime as

---

[10] A few years after the event, Eduardo Hamuy (1985), the father of social scientific survey research in Chile, reported the results of an informal audit carried out on September 11, 1980. With a team of 600 volunteers, voting and counts were observed at 981 randomly selected voting tables in the Greater Santiago area (about 10 percent of the 10,552 tables at 170 voting sites). Hamuy reported five types of observed fraud or irregularity: miscounting of votes ("No" and null votes counted as blank or "Yes," or nullified "No" votes); inconsistencies in the number of votes counted and the number of voter signatures recorded (excess or missing votes); nonpublic counts; persons voting more than once; and a category of other irregularities. Hamuy could not quantify the absolute magnitude of fraud, but did report the percentage of tables at which fraud allegedly took place – 39.7 percent. Given this magnitude, he maintained that the actual result of the plebiscite in the Greater Santiago area must have been very different from the official results, with the "No" more than likely winning in communes where the "Yes" vote was relatively low (Nuñoa, Quinta Normal, and Renca). Hamuy's conclusion (1980, 236–37) is worth citing: "It is within the realm of probability that without electoral fraud the plebiscite would have gone against the government in the Greater Santiago area. Thus, we feel that it is probabilistically justified to doubt the legitimacy of the 1980 constitution and, even, to deny it (*negarlo*)."

[11] In fact, the constitution was enacted as a decree-law (D.L. No. 3.464, D.O., August 11, 1980). As the "Whereas" clauses of the decree-law stated, the Junta, in exercise of the constituent power, approved the new constitution, *subject to ratification by plebiscite*. No prior norm, antecedent to the coup, nor of the Junta's own making, obliged the Junta to submit the constitution to ratification by plebiscite since the Junta had formally arrogated constituent powers. In this sense, the ratification of the constitution by plebiscite involved an implicit modification of D.L. No. 788.

a personalized dictatorship. Viewed from this perspective the constitution emerges as functional to Pinochet's needs, corresponds to his preferences (Ensalaco 1994, 411–12), and reflects Pinochet's hope of remaining in power "with popular legitimation, without modifying the authoritarian structure of the regime" (Linz 1992, 454).[12] However, as I will argue throughout the rest of this work, the interpretation of the 1980 constitution as "Pinochet's constitution" is fundamentally misleading and of little or no explanatory value.

The 1980 constitution was indeed authoritarian in its origins and imposed from above by a military government headed by General Pinochet, but this is the only sense in which the constitution can be identified with Pinochet, that is, as stylistic shorthand for "the constitution enacted and imposed by the military government." Pinochet *is* indeed the only individual referred to specifically by name in the constitution (T.D. 14), but the constitution is not *his* in any exclusive sense of the possessive pronoun – neither in regard to the origins of the constitution, its substantive content, nor the eventual mode of its implementation during 1981–1989. Furthermore, although the constitution contained provisions that extended military rule, the main body set out the contours of a regime qualitatively distinct from the military government. It was not the constitution that would have emerged from an elected constituent assembly, but, at least in principle, the main body of the constitution did structure a democracy, albeit with protections and exclusions, however objectionable and controversial.

## Making Sense of the Making of the Dictatorship's Constitution

Given the Junta's strategic interest in concealing internal differences as well as the nonpublic, unregulated character of the constituent process itself, it is not surprising that we know very little about the making of the 1980 constitution. The formal stages in the preparation of the draft – if not the deliberations at each stage – have been clear all along: In October 1978 the Constituent Commission submitted its *anteproyecto* to the president; the draft was then sent to the Council of State for review; in early July 1980 once this review was completed

---

[12] In a similar vein, Constable and Valenzuela (1991, 136) maintain, "After years of building piecemeal legal control over the country, Pinochet needed to establish a comprehensive body of laws that would legitimize his rule and enshrine his authoritarian powers in a manner more befitting Chile's legalistic traditions." For other examples of the "personalization of power" approach to the constitution, see Garretón 1986, 158–63; Valenzuela 1995, 50–54; and González Encinar et al. 1992.

the two drafts went directly to the Junta, where the final text was hammered out in daily, marathon sessions until the final version was completed and approved on August 10, 1980.[13]

Yet, an account of constitution making that focuses solely on these identifiable stages is flat and incomplete because it fails to address many difficult questions concerning the constitution-making process. As advisory bodies, neither the Constituent Commission nor the Council of State had authority regarding the timing of promulgation nor the content of the new constitution.[14] The minutes of these bodies provide fascinating insights into how prominent conservatives perceived institutions and redemocratization, as well as the motives and understandings behind the many articles that did make it into the constitution, but they do not explain why or when the Junta made the political decision to enact a new constitution. Nor are public speeches and announcements very helpful. A narrative account of the signposts marking the public emergence of the constitutional question is of limited value unless we can somehow decipher the significance of public acts in a context of secret interactions. Even though we can identify known "constitutional events" – such as the *Actas Constitucionales* of 1976,[15] the *Discurso de Chacarillas* of July 9, 1977,[16] President Pinochet's November 1977 memo to the Constituent Commission, or the president's April 1978 speech announcing the future promulgation of a single, definitive constitution – these utterances and legal enactments do not in themselves reveal their strategic significance. The nonpublic nature of dictatorial deliberation and decision makes it extremely difficult to sort out the motives, targets, and character of these moves. Any chronological reconstruction, therefore, begs the question of the status of the events included in its narrative. Without

[13] The Constituent Commission's *Anteproyecto de Constitución Política* was published in *El Mercurio*, October 19, 1978. The *Consejo de Estado*'s *Proyecto de Nueva Constitución Política* was published in *El Mercurio*, July 9, 1980. These and other documents related to the constituent process are reproduced in *Revista Chilena de Derecho* 8, 1981, 137–491. Andrade Geywitz (1984) provides a useful account of the formal stages.
  Hereafter the following abbreviations will be used to refer to these draft constitutions, followed by the number of the article cited: *AdCP* – *Anteproyecto de Constitución Política*; *PdNCP* – *Proyecto de Nueva Constitución Política*.

[14] For this reason, analysts who reproach the military government for not accepting the Council of State's recommendations are off base, as are those who interpret differences in the content of these drafts as an indication of internal contradictions within the regime.

[15] On these partial constitutional acts, see page 181.

[16] In this speech Pinochet, for the first time, publicly presented a scheme and timetable for a transition. This formula is discussed below, see note 45, page 203.

this ground, postures and moves may easily be confounded with deci-sions and outcomes, and disconnected, secondary, incidents are con-flated with truly significant events.[17]

Nevertheless, most accounts of the 1980 constitution ignore these problems inherent to the study of nonpublic regimes. In the personal-ization of power approach, the obstacles set by secret rule are obvi-ated by the assumption of monism. Once the regime is portrayed as reducible to a single actor, there is no point delving beyond the sur-face of public acts. This observation holds for both critical and promil-itary accounts of the Chilean dictatorship. In the former, Pinochet's announcements are accepted at face value and any twists and turns are criticized or explained away as instances of autocratic caprice, as merely further moves to prolong Pinochet's personal rule.[18] The official account is formally identical, though of a different sign: It portrays suc-cessive institutional acts or announcements as progressive steps – and shifts and reversals, when they are recognized, as convenient adjust-ments – to further the armed forces' original mission of economic reconstruction and the restoration of democracy. Thus, in the final offi-cial account of the military presidency the work of the Constituent Com-mission, the *Actas Constitucionales*, the *Discurso de Chacarillas*, the *Consejo de Estado*'s review, the final drafting within the Junta, and the September 1980 plebiscite emerge as continuous moments in the exe-cution of the armed forces' mission of "reconstructing democracy, cleansed of the defects that facilitated its destruction" (*Presidencia de la República* 1990, 1:24). In both versions, a prior teleology drives the constitution-making process, and each announcement, act, or draft emerges as a progressive step on a virtually seamless path to the 1980 constitution.

*Puzzles in the Constitution*

Nevertheless, the structure and content of the constitution itself suggest a number of puzzles that are lost in the black and white cer-tainty of oppositional and proregime accounts. First, why was a con-stitution enacted at all, particularly since the military *apparently* had

---

[17] This is the problem with chronological reconstructions of the dictatorship which purport to explain everything and in the end explain nothing. These histories tend to blur underlying causes, choices, key junctures, and unintended consequences into a litany of episodes whose interconnections are never explored. This type of narrative appears to be a particular occupational hazard among journalists.

[18] For examples, see the works cited in note 12, page 174.

no intention of embarking on a transition? As we have seen in earlier chapters, the Junta already had agreed to its own rules and had worked out potential issues with the judiciary. Furthermore, the transitory articles enacted did not significantly depart from this prior organization. Why then the dualism of permanent and transitory articles? If the constitution was merely an exercise in legitimation, why the meticulous attention to the content of the permanent articles? If, on the other hand, institutional questions were pressing by 1977–1978, then why was there no liberalization or transition in subsequent years?

Given the unwillingness of the participants to reveal the different beliefs, strategies, and moves whose interplay culminated in the decision to enact a constitution, it may be impossible to fully answer these questions.[19] Even if the complete archives of the Junta were accessible, there may not be an adequate record of the top-level decision-making process leading to the constitution, just as there is no documentation of the Junta's work on the final draft in July 1980. In the Junta's archive of legislative histories, the entry for D.L. 3,464 (the constitution) contains a single sheet which states only, "The history of this D.L. appears in a special volume" (*Trans. y Antec. – D.L.*, vol. 243, 42). My attempts to locate this volume were futile – though I did once uncover a volume containing a comparative concordance of the two drafts and the 1925 constitution. Nevertheless, it is not likely that in the future any record beyond possibly such preparatory materials will emerge. During a 1981 Junta discussion regarding whether the Junta should allow a private individual access to one of the legislative histories, then Secretary of Legislation, *Capitán de Navío* Aldo Montagna, reminded those present that no record had been kept of the Junta's sculpting of the final text of the constitution: "The Political Constitution of the State has none [legislative history] for its establishment in the Junta and that you know perfectly well. It has a history, sure, in the Council of State and in the Ortúzar Commission. There are antecedents that make it possible to study it, but there doesn't exist any history of

---

[19] General Pinochet's memoirs (1990), for example, provide absolutely no insight into the internal decision-making process. The reader finds no rumination – no matter how self-serving – over choices and difficult situations. These volumes are essentially a rehashing of what appeared in the press, documenting Pinochet's every public move and speech, without providing any new insights into the man or even an accurate version of the institutional process as it publicly unfolded. For example, the account of the 1976 anniversary speech fails to mention the promulgation of *Actas Constitucionales No. 2–4*, and similarly the transition plan specified at *Chacarillas* in 1977 is not accurately represented (1991, 2:123, 145–46).

the modifications introduced by the Junta, which were many." (AHJG, 81–19, July 9, 1981, 11).

Documentation of the internal debates that prompted the decision to enact the constitution may remain just as scarce. After 1976, with the routinization of the legislative process, the minutes of the Junta's sessions almost exclusively chronicle deliberations on legislative matters, and for certain particularly sensitive agenda items there is no substantive record at all.[20] Furthermore, any junta member could request to have a discussion suspended and taken up again in a "Private Session" without advisors present – the verbatim history of these arguments and conversations has necessarily vanished. Since there was no established procedure or forum for raising the constitutional question, which in any case was peripheral during the first years, it is very likely that internal pressure to enact a constitution mounted in these "private" encounters for which there are most likely no complete records.[21]

As a result, some aspects of the constitution-making process may never be fully clarified. Nevertheless, in the course of my research, I discovered too many pieces of the puzzle that do not fit the conventional account and that suggest alternative motivations for military constitution making. Though the causal connections between events are not always clear, the record of the Junta's drafting of the *Actas Constitucionales* in 1976, the position papers on institutionalization found among Jaime Guzmán's papers, the minutes of the Constituent Commission and the *Consejo de Estado*, and other documents provide elements for a more nuanced sense of the strategic context of constitution making. On this basis plausible answers can be developed for the questions outlined above. After anticipating these answers, I will elaborate my argument by considering alternative versions in light of the now available evidence.

## The Strategic Context of Constitution Making

Why did the military enact such an elaborate constitution if the regime had no intention of embarking upon a process of liberalization

---

[20] Even though the Junta's sessions were secret and the *Actas* long shrouded in mystery, the Junta took additional precautions before discussing particularly sensitive topics. For example, before considering bills concerning issues of national defense, nonessential officers and counsel were asked to leave the room and the tape recorders were turned off. In these instances, the *Actas* merely record the agenda item and identify the individuals who remained for the discussion, but contain no further record.

[21] Still, I suspect that secret records were kept of agreements reached at such top secret meetings, precisely to preclude later conflicts over the content of each decision.

or transition? It appears that the constitution was enacted in fulfill-ment of a prior agreement – reached, after much conflict, probably, in 1977 or 1978 – that the armed forces would not attempt to institute a permanent authoritarian regime. This settlement followed repeated bids by Pinochet to further centralize power, which again involved weakening the Junta. These blocked attempts suggest at least one reason for reconstitutionalizing the prior organization of military rule in the transitory articles: to debar any future renewal of dis-cussion of this issue. Thus, the dualism of permanent and transitory articles.

The conflicts that prompted constitutionalization turned on the char-acter of the successor regime (which essentially involved a struggle over the nature of the military regime itself), not the need, at least in the short run, for continued military rule. Although perceptions of how long the armed forces should remain in power varied, during the second half of the 1970s all sectors were leery of any immediate abdi-cation of government, as military officers and their advisors feared returning power to the same political forces that had driven the 1972–1973 crisis. Therefore, no immediate transition was contem-plated, and although formulas for liberalization were considered, they appear to have been precluded for precisely the same reason that the prior semantic constitution of military rule was retained: As we will see, each of these intermediate formulas at the time implied modi-fying the structure of the Junta. Given the other junta members' aversion to granting Pinochet absolute control, liberalization was unacceptable insofar as it implied a weakening of the Junta, and as a result the organization of power during the transitory period remained largely identical to the period which the regime allegedly was stepping away from.

Thus, the 1980 constitution represents a settlement which stabilized military rule in the short term by reasserting the interforce status quo and by postponing any transition or liberalization of the military regime, but also closed the debate over the duration of military rule by specifying the contours of a postmilitary regime and a timetable for its realization. However, as we will see in Chapter 7, the indeterminacy of many politically significant precepts – which in most cases were left for later specification in organic constitutional laws – provided a source of ambiguity that allowed virtually all sectors within the regime to view the constitution as a vehicle for the further pursuit of their own particular institutional aspirations during the transitory period. As a result, the 1980 constitution was self-enforcing: It structured incentives for all junta members to participate in the implementation and further specification of the constitution's content.

## Prompting the Decision to Enact a New Constitution

The sequence of events and the structure of the constitution belie accounts that stress the unbroken democratic mission of the armed forces, the impact of foreign pressure, or Pinochet's designs to perpetuate himself in power. First of all, even though the armed forces from the outset vowed to restore "*chilenidad*, justice, and the institutional order [which were] torn asunder by the crisis,"[22] this pledge remained peripheral and abstract until conflicts over the consequences of military rule itself forced the Junta to define a common position on regime succession. In fact, much of the internal tension that emerged during 1977–1978 arose precisely because the Junta had not established any procedure for resolving differences over the duration of the regime and the nature of a new constitution. The Junta had established the Constituent Commission within days of the coup, but its mandate was limited to preparing a draft constitution. Likewise, the organizational constitution of military rule agreed to in 1974 formally specified how constituent powers would be exercised, but in reference to the 1925 constitution, not the creation of a wholly new constitutional order. In the context of de facto rule, setting aside this last constraint was merely a matter of will; still the Junta as a body never set a timetable or a procedure for jointly resolving the political question of what eventually to do with the constitution as a whole. Nor was the decision to enact the constitution essentially a response to foreign pressure. From 1975 onward, the Junta did turn to constitutional measures in an attempt to ameliorate the regime's international isolation, and later much of the urgency of the constitution-making process was given by fear of how a further deterioration in Chile's international position might affect the stability of the regime. In this sense, diplomatic considerations were clearly a factor in the eventual decision. However, this factor was mediated through the Junta and the decision to enact a constitution emerged out of the subsequent conflicts within the regime over alternative responses. Sectors close to Pinochet consistently advocated entrenchment in the face of pressure. Constitutionalization was neither imposed nor the only move open to the military government. Furthermore, the promulgation of the constitution took place only after the military

---

[22] D.L. No. 1, D.O., September 18, 1973.

regime had surmounted the most severe, potentially destabilizing, external pressures in 1978 and 1979.[23] Nor does foreign pressure explain the content of the constitution, which was fundamentally crafted looking backward at internal political-institutional problems that emerged in the 1960s and 1970s.

Nor can the promulgation of the constitution be explained as a unilateral move by Pinochet to perpetuate himself in power. In the process leading up to the constitution Pinochet did attempt to further centralize power, but these bids for absolute power were blocked and only served to ignite the institutional debate. It was only after the navy and the air force rejected an army proposal to restructure the Junta that transition formulas began to be discussed within the regime, and, although the constitution granted Pinochet another eight years as president, the constitution did not embody Pinochet's project of permanent military rule.

### The Actas Constitucionales of 1976

The constitutional question was pushed onto center stage inadvertently by the Junta's ploys in 1976 to stave off international critics by promulgating three *Actas Constitucionales* (Constitutional Acts, hereafter *A.C.*). As was seen in the preceding chapter, this strategy arose out of a brainstorming session in anticipation of the 30th UN General Assembly. In his September 11, 1975 speech, Pinochet announced that six or seven constitutional acts would be promulgated, with the first three due during the first semester of 1976. In the end, after delays, only three in the series of acts were ever promulgated, all on September 11, 1976, one of which, A.C. No. 4 on emergency powers, never went into effect.

Unlike the *Atos Institucionales* enacted by successive military presidents in Brazil or Franco's *Leyes Fundamentales*, the Constitutional Acts were not intended to regulate or create new dictatorial powers.

---

[23] In January 1980, in a document prepared for the Minister of the Interior, Jaime Guzmán (1980) argued that changes in the international situation presented the government with "an extraordinarily stable and solid" political situation, which freed the government to concentrate on "its own creative task." Along these lines Guzmán mentioned the continued implementation of neoliberal reforms in labor relations, social security, education, health, and agriculture, as well as the promulgation of a new constitution. The international problems that Guzmán identified as having been "definitively surpassed" were U.S. pressures regarding the Letelier assassination, the AFL-CIO's threat to boycott Chilean trade in 1979, and tensions with Argentina over the Beagle Channel.

In theory, they were going to allow the regime to restore constitutional certainty (they were to contain only norms of constitutional rank), and to begin to gradually anticipate the future constitutional order in less conflictive areas. For some advocates, such as Jaime Guzmán, the constitutional acts were of major significance as an assertion of the Junta's constituent authority to enact its own constitution, since the acts were going to systematically and definitively derogate the 1925 constitution. This scheme of partial and gradual implementation of a new constitutional order was justified on the basis of an evolutionary, materialist conception of institutions. From this perspective, institutions had to concord with "reality": since conditions had not evolved sufficiently to envision the future organization of state powers and the methods for their generation, institutions could be established only on a gradual, provisional basis in areas compatible with the continued emergency.[24] In this conception, the military regime was to take first steps on the constitutional path to normalcy while leaving untouched the structure of the dictatorship until conditions allowed for further changes.

The practical viability of this strategy of constitutionalization on the installment plan was immediately questioned within the Constituent Commission. The question once again was the relationship between the present and the future. Could constitutional norms structured with a view to the immediate concerns of the Junta in any way provide a foundation for a later democratic order, or were they necessarily only a diversion from the task of working out the structure of a future democracy? This debate and the corresponding internal divisions broke out immediately with Pinochet's announcement, particularly since he had also announced that the Constituent Commission would collaborate in the preparation of the *Actas Constitucionales*.

As he had earlier, Silva Bascuñán argued forcefully against shifting attention from the commission's primary mandate (AOCC, 153, September 23, 1975, 1–25), and the issue resurfaced each time the commission set to work on the *Actas*. Within months, the group nearly tore itself apart when Enrique Evans, exasperated by the snail's pace of progress on the draft for the actual constitution, demanded that an internal deadline be set for completing a first draft.[25] In the course of the prolonged debate that followed, Sergio Díez and Jaime Guzmán

---

[24] For this justification of the *Actas Constitucionales*, see Jaime Guzmán 1975.

[25] Interestingly, the deadline Evans proposed, October 21, 1976, fell within days of the date that Allende's presidential term was to have expired – November 3, 1976 (AOCC, 177, December 30, 1975, 5). This demand for a deadline precipitated an extended discussion (AOCC, 178, January 6, 1976 and 179, January 7, 1976).

argued that the Commission had no alternative but to cooperate in the preparation of the *Actas Constitutucionales* – to do otherwise would be to abdicate any influence over decision making regarding the future institutional evolution of the regime. According to both, within the executive this discussion was being dominated by proponents of extended military rule. Sergio Díez related that the government was being advised by extreme right-wing civilians who were "extremely dangerous since they don't like elections, as they know that they will never be elected . . . [and] prefer the subterranean work of the little man who spins a web of rumors and intrigues to survive, prosper, and attain a position that he would never reach on personal merit alone." Díez noted that many of these advisors had worked within the COAJ legislative advisory group, for which reason he celebrated the formation of the *Comisiones Legislativas* (AOCC, 179, January 7, 1976, 13). Guzmán made the same point somewhat more obliquely, arguing that the real fate of any constitutional draft would "depend fundamentally on how the emergency is guided." If the "emergency" followed a course at odds with the commission's perspective, the group's work would be rendered useless (AOCC, 179, January 7, 1976, 14–15). In the end, work proceeded on the *Actas*, with Silva Bascuñán abstaining from the group's work whenever the commission's deliberations concerned the *Actas Constitucionales*.

In practice, this piecemeal strategy of "bottom-up" constitutionalization proved stillborn. The Junta's reworking of the draft constitutional acts prepared by the Constituent Commission largely confirmed Alejandro Silva's objection that these acts could only address contingencies arising out of the extraordinary situation of military rule and would not give rise to a constitution framing and organizing public powers within a democratic state. Any number of articles which had been carefully crafted in the Constituent Commission to ground the Junta's authority to dictate a new constitution or to entrench safeguards against attempts to utilize democracy for extraconstitutional purposes were excised or substantially weakened in the Junta. The members of the Junta and their advisors were extremely wary of inadvertently enacting precepts limiting the government's prerogative. The verb *entrabar* (to obstruct) was used to discuss such clauses, which were referred to as *amarres* (binds). Whenever junta members or their counsel felt a norm might limit existing powers of the military regime, or subject the Junta to further criticism by exposing a "target" (*blanco*) to its enemies, or provide a loophole through which the constitutionality of the political recess could be challenged in the courts,

**183**

immediate political concerns took precedence over the broader intention underlying the article under review.

This dynamic can be seen in the fate of the article on sovereignty (eventually ART. 4) which had been included in the draft for A.C. No. 2 (*The Essential Bases of Chilean Institutionality*), an essentially dogmatic chapter intended to set out the basic principles and conceptions of law from which the rest of the constitution would follow. The article on sovereignty had been crafted to link the Junta's *exercise* of sovereignty to its *original* source, the Nation, and stated: "Sovereignty rests in the Nation and is exercised by the authorities who *at its [the Nation's] fair and legitimate request assumed the direction of the Republic, on 11 September 1973*" (AHJG, 280, September 3, 1976, 16, emphasis added). This wording was particularly dear to Jaime Guzmán, who argued that since the legitimacy of the regime derived from "the Eleventh" (the coup), not the 1925 constitution, the Junta had to profess a source of its own legitimacy to establish a new order. Nevertheless, Admiral Merino and naval counsel strongly objected to the phrase italicized above. They insisted that it would be harshly denounced in the United Nations. After much debate the phrase was dropped despite Guzmán's insistence that the clause's value far offset "adding a drop of water" to the ocean of criticism abroad (20–22, 33–34). As a result, ART. 4 of A.C. No. 2 specified the locus of sovereignty and the manner of its exercise, but not the subject who wielded it.[26]

In a similar manner, a reference to the rule of law (*Estado de Derecho*) was struck (AHJG, 280, 14), even though the Constituent Commission had debated this clause extensively and had unanimously agreed to mention the principle since it was understood to imply the antithesis of a "totalitarian state" (AOCC, 47, June 20, 1974, 17–31). The same fate befell a clause drafted by the Constituent Commission as an antidote to the principal offense claimed to have been committed by the Allende government: "the deviation of power" (*desviación del poder*), the formally legal use of technicalities and loopholes (*resquicios*) for purposes contrary to the original intent and "spirit" of the law (AOCC, 51, July 4, 1974, 3–12). A phrase stating that "Good faith is always a requisite of acts of authority" was drafted to protect

---

[26] ART. 4 of A.C. No. 2, thus, merely states: "Sovereignty rests essentially in the Nation and will be exercised in observance of the Act of Constitution of the Junta of Government and all provisions which have been or may be enacted under it." The corresponding article of the 1925 constitution, ART. 2, states: "Sovereignty rests essentially in the Nation, which delegates its exercise in the authorities that this Constitution establishes."

against such lawful "abuses" of power, but was deleted at Ortúzar's suggestion since it might hinder the military regime by forcing it to demonstrate its own good faith before the *Contraloría* (AHJG, 280, 24). Just as Silva had warned in the Constituent Commission, the immediate concerns of the Junta consistently took precedence over norms designed to protect the anticipated future constitutional order.

Unbeknownst to the participants in these deliberations, the attempt to structure a set of constitutional acts would have consequences far beyond the immediate objective of bolstering the dictatorship before international pressure. These consequences would become a major factor in the decision to enact a single, definitive constitution structuring a postmilitary institutional order. In fact, it was the logic of constitutional forms, of establishing higher ranking norms, that led to this outcome by forcing the Junta to restudy its own organization and ended up stimulating renewed conflicts over the structure and duration of military rule. Before examining this dynamic we should highlight some of the alignments and difficulties that emerged during the final drafting of A.C. No. 2–4, as they are of fundamental importance for understanding later developments.

### The Quiet Dissidence of Admiral Merino

Typically, Gen. Gustavo Leigh, the commander of the air force, is portrayed as the dissident member of the Junta. As a result, the involuntary removal of Leigh from the Junta in June 1978 is usually interpreted as the final step in Pinochet's consolidation of personal power, which supposedly left him free to impose his constitutional project without opposition. However, this interpretation holds only because the constitutional and dissenting opinions of the commander in chief of the navy, Adm. José Toribio Merino, rarely escaped the hermetic confines of the Junta: Merino was often just as severe and intransigent as Leigh, and given his positions on the unfolding institutional debate it is hard to imagine that he would have acquiesced to Leigh's ouster without exacting some agreement from Pinochet regarding the resolution of the constitutional issue. This observation is merely a conjecture, but it should be noted that the cleavages that emerged within the Junta tended to be cross-cutting: Economic questions usually aligned Merino with Pinochet against Leigh's opposition to neoliberal reforms, whereas Merino far more consistently than Leigh opposed any move that signaled a sharp turn away from Chile's constitutional tradition and often aligned with Leigh on political-institutional questions (though on occasions Merino stood alone in his disagreement). Merino most likely supported Leigh's ouster as an opportunity to proceed with structural reforms that had been blocked by Leigh, but he was no advocate of entrenching authoritarianism on a permanent basis.[27] Both commanders could be staunchly independent and intransigent in the defense of their positions.

These long-standing dynamics were evident during the review of the *Actas Constitucionales*; the minutes for these sessions reveal that Merino was the stickler who harshly challenged and sometimes sarcastically ridiculed proposals and concepts that he found objectionable or counterproductive.

One of the most difficult problems encountered in these sessions was how to uphold constitutional rights and guarantees in A.C. No. 3 without opening the door to a legal resurgence of political party and union activity. A.C. No. 3 contained norms covering all rights traditionally recognized in the constitution. The draft from which the Junta worked had been prepared by the Constituent Commission, whose chief concern had been to strengthen the protection of rights allegedly violated during the Allende government – property rights and freedom of expression, assembly, and education.[28] In preparing these articles the Constituent Commission followed the 1925 constitution and drew on other constitutions and the Universal Declaration of Human Rights for comparative purposes (AOCC, 84, November 4, 1974). Many precepts were retained virtually verbatim from the 1925 constitution, particularly the guarantee of personal liberty and the procedural guarantees regulating arrest, which were moved forward to improve the logic of presentation. The only constitutional guarantees not expressly regulated in A.C. No. 3 were those contained in the statute of political parties (ART. 9) which had been added to the Constitution

---

[27] By September 1976, proposals had been worked out to open the door to privatization of education and mining property. But these clauses, to be contained in A.C. No. 3 on rights, were vetoed by Leigh. As a result of Leigh's opposition, these matters were left to later regulation in special statutes (ART. 1, No. 14, and ART. 1, No. 16, respectively). In the interim, existing constitutional precepts remained in force, as indicated by transitory articles. On education and mining, respectively, see AHJG, 280, September 3, 1976, 125–33; 281, September 9, 22–28.

[28] The most significant departures from Chilean constitutional tradition, as well as the norms that elicited the most controversy within the Commission, were the introduction of prior limits on freedom of expression and a paragraph that declared all acts involving the dissemination of doctrines contrary to the essential bases of the state illicit and unconstitutional. This last clause was included against the votes of Evans and Silva and eventually became ART. 8 of the Constitution which in effect banned Marxist-Leninist parties.

as part of the January 1971 reforms – the *Estatuto de Garantías* – agreed upon just prior to Allende's taking office. This article established unrestricted freedom of party organization. Otherwise, the Act provided guarantees for all rights, liberties, and equalities traditionally protected by the Chilean constitution, including the *recurso de amparo*, and the Act created the *recurso de protección*, a new judicial remedy to protect a broader range of rights than those covered by the *recurso de amparo*.[29]

Immediately the tension between recognition of such a broad range of rights and the intention of maintaining the recess on political activity drew the attention of Junta legal counsel. Somewhat surprisingly, the internal debate over ART. 9 of the Constitution emerged in reference to the "democratic parties" that had been declared in recess, not the Marxist parties (AHJG, 280, September 2, 1976, 36–46). The gist of the problem, as identified by naval legal advisor Capitán de Navío (J) Sergio Rillón was that, although the illegality of the Left parties (D.L. No. 77) might prove constitutional references to "organized social groups" in A.C. No. 2 and to the right of association in A.C. No. 3 would derogate D.L. No. 78, which declared all other parties in recess. Furthermore, since D.L. No. 77 (the decree-law which prohibited the Marxist parties) and D.L. No. 78 had been enacted in reference to the internal security law, not the state of siege, these restrictions would not be upheld by constitutional states of exception. Unless the validity of D.L. No. 78 could be assured, a legal resurgence of the parties would be unavoidable. One solution was to include a transitory article acknowledging the continued validity of the two decree-laws, but this alternative was discounted since it might, by omission, diminish the validity of all other nominally constitutional decree-laws that were not so recognized – a first intimation of how difficult it would be to close the constitutional circle. This left the facile solution, proposed by Pinochet's legal advisor, of expressly derogating ART. 9 of the constitution (AHJG, 280, September 3, 1976, 38).

This proposal led Merino and naval legal counsel to a stance sharply at odds with other officers who were willing to flaunt the Junta's facile constituent powers to resolve this conundrum. In the extended arguing that followed over the convenience of doing away with the parties, naval justice officers were pitted against Pinochet and his counsel. The

---

[29] Original proposals for such a writ had been drafted during the Allende government by Sergio Díez and Sergio Onofre Jarpa to provide a remedy against government requisitions of private property. The 1980 constitution retains the *recurso* as ART. 20.

naval officers repeatedly pointed out that the Junta had never internally or in any public declaration or decree questioned the existence of political parties. At most, they had criticized how the parties operated but never their right to exist. Pinochet, emboldened by Uruguayan proposals to abolish parties, wanted to eliminate parties (AHJG, 280, September 3, 1976, 23, 32, 36, 38–39, 43; and 281, September 9, 1976, 168). Though his Minister of Justice counseled that derogation might "illegitimately be considered totalitarian," when Ortúzar advised that it wasn't a good time to suppress the parties, Pinochet's dismay was apparent. He commented, "It's never going to be convenient Don Enrique. Never. One thing or another is always going to come up" (AHJG, 280, September 3, 1976, 40). Leigh initially opposed the prohibition of all parties (AHJG, 280, 44) but shifted position, eventually supporting dissolution – as long as it was done as a simple decree-law, not a constitutional reform (AHJG, 281, September 9, 1976, 49). Nevertheless, the navy's intransigence forced the debate back to a search for ways to expressly maintain restrictions on ART. 9 in a transitory article. Thus, even though, as Pinochet noted, there were three votes against one, ART. 9 was only suspended "in accordance to the law" by transitory article 7 of A.C. No. 3. Intransigent naval opposition blocked this proposal to flat-out derogate ART. 9 of the constitution which since 1971 had established unrestricted freedom of party organization.[30]

Merino's independence from Pinochet and Leigh also was expressed in the deliberations over A.C. No. 4 on emergency powers.[31] Throughout these debates Merino ridiculed the pretension that the Junta could outwit the international community by again manipulating the nomen-

---

[30] The navy's position correctly reflected the existing political and juridical status quo: The regulation complementing D.L. No. 78 defined recess as "the situation of inactivity that affects them [the parties] in all matters tending to the attainment of the ends that are characteristic of them, without this denoting in any case the suppression of their existence as such" (ART. 1, D.S. No. 1,921, Ministerio del Interior, D.O., January 21, 1974). This decree froze party leaderships and stipulated that national and provincial party governing bodies could meet only to administer party properties.

[31] The draft of the Act on emergency powers had been prepared by the Commission to Redact a National Security Code. This commission (the *Comisión Redactora del Código de Seguridad Nacional*) was created in September 1974, and was presided over by Ortúzar. Another member of the Constituent Commission, Jorge Ovalle, also worked on the commission. For the names of other members, as well as the members of a half dozen other advisory bodies created to study reforms to the different legal codes, see *Gaceta Jurídica* 1976. The national security code was drafted, but never enacted. There is no recorded discussion of the code in the *actas* of the Junta's sessions. The only substantial mention in the Junta minutes is in 1975 when Ortúzar presented a preliminary report on the conception and structure of the code (AHJG, 222, August 12, 1975).

clature of states of exception. Merino sharply expressed his ire before a proposal to create a new "lower" state of exception, a "state of latent subversion." Before Ortúzar could even finish his introductory comments to the act on emergency powers, Merino demanded an explanation of the political and juridical meaning of "latent subversion," a term which he stated was meaningless to him (AHJG, 280, September 3, 1976, 172). Ortúzar and Guzmán responded that the state had been devised at Pinochet's behest to allow continued restrictions of rights without having to maintain the state of siege which was becoming increasingly untenable in the absence of any apparent internal commotion. This response did nothing to placate Merino. After noting that certain states of commotion were accepted around the world, Merino, in what can only have been a tone of sarcasm or anger, asked, "In regards to the state of latent subversion, which has such a pretty name, is there any other place in the world where they have discovered a little word like that?" The response was, "no," qualified by claims that numerous countries would copy it and that the provision would be extraordinarily useful for defending Chile in the UN (AHJG, 280, September 3, 1976, 175). Merino responded,

> In other words we can assume that the world will accept, by the work of the Holy Ghost and your brilliant minds, a new system that is neither the state of siege, nor that of war, nor that of commotion, but one of internal subversion [sic]; that they will accept that for the purpose of preserving the lives of citizens, liberties are curtailed, that this is admissible, and that in regards to human rights it is not scandalous. And I repeat the word "scandalous" because it has been said to me in the United States and Brazil in reference to certain norms and ways that we have been operating. (AHJG, 280, September 3, 1976, 176)

Before Merino's intransigence, the state of latent subversion was stillborn.

From Merino's perspective A.C. No. 4 was a step backwards in terms of international presentation and obliterated 80 percent of the progress made in ACs Nos. 2 and 3 (AHJG, September 9, 1976, 281, 55). In this context, he obstinately opposed extending emergency powers to encompass the gamut of nominally constitutional repressive powers decreed by the Junta. Significantly he referred to these faculties as "fabrications enacted after 1973." Throughout this discussion, Merino made it clear that his constitutional benchmark was the text as it stood at the moment of the coup, not the semantic constitution as defined by D.L. No. 788.[32] For example, Merino (AHJG, 280, September 3, 1976, 204) argued, "You cannot restrict the right of association, freedom of labor, censor correspondence and communications, as put forth, nor stipulate the requisition of goods nor establish limitations on the right to property. Never has this ever been in the constitution." In the end, A.C. No. 4 contained the broadened range of emergency powers that Merino objected to, but only after extensive reworking of the article to improve its presentation. A.C. No. 4, however, never went into effect, as the Junta failed to enact the complementary legislation required for it to go into force.

There were many facets to the naval commander's constitutional dissidence. However, the principal difference was that Merino and his advisors were far more apprehensive of and sensitive to the consequences of antagonizing the international community than Pinochet, Leigh, Ortúzar, or Guzmán, who were more concerned with internal security and the need to preempt any legal challenges to the constitutionality of existing tools of repression. This difference was stated bluntly by Merino during the extended debate over the unconstitutionality of the Law of State Security (Law 12,927), "Let's make ourselves understood in Chilean. What are we interested in? What our Courts say or the international judgement, which tomorrow can boycott the entire country?" A few minutes later, Merino asked what the International Labor Organization would do in response to provisions restricting labor rights during a state of siege. After one advisor responded, "Nothing," Guzmán added, "Nothing good for us is going to happen." To which Merino replied, "Yes, but let's avoid having bad things continue to happen to us" (AHJG, 280, September 3, 1976, 204, 206).[33]

Merino's stance also involved subtle and not so subtle intimations that the methods of repression being practiced in Chile were excessive

---

[32] The constitution in force at the moment of the coup provided for only two constitutional states of exception, the state of assembly and the state of siege (ART. 72, No. 17). Under qualified circumstances, Congress could also enact Laws of Extraordinary Powers granting the president authority to restrict personal liberty, impose prior censorship, and suspend or restrict freedom of Assembly (ART. 44, No. 12). Although this article prohibited any other legislative suspension or restriction of rights, Congress in 1958 enacted the Law of State Security (Law 12,927) which included provisions allowing the president to declare all or part of the country in a state of emergency. The emergency powers conferred by such a declaration far exceeded those of the state of siege, and legal scholars generally viewed the state security law to be unconstitutional. This opinion was also held by the Constituent Commission (AOCC, 2408–12).

[33] For further statements of this position, see AHJG, 280, September 3, 1976, 198–206; 281, September 9, 1976, 53–62.

and disproportionate to any existing threats to internal security. This stance is well captured, though allusively, in the words with which Merino launched his salvo against extended state of siege powers: "No one can say that, to the extent that we have lived, we haven't learned; and in learning one must go forward, forgetting things, to put them in their proper order" (AHJG, 280, September 3, 1976, 196).

Merino's constitutional position was not solely prudential. At many points during the review of the three bills, Admiral Merino expressed his reverence for Chile's constitutional tradition, insisting that phrasings of no practical importance be maintained because of their beauty and venerable history. For example, over objections that the word was of no consequence, Merino had the adjective "intrinsically" (*esencialmente*) restored to the article on sovereignty – "sovereignty is vested intrinsically in the Nation" (AHJG, 280, September 3, 1976, 18, 35). Similarly, Merino objected to a modification of the paragraph on equality before the law which suppressed the phrase, "In Chile there are no slaves, and he who sets foot upon its territory becomes free" (AHJG, 280, September 3, 1976, 69). This construction dates to the 1833 constitution, and its suppression was debated in 1925 but it was then retained as part of national tradition (Silva Bascuñán 1963, 2:211). Although the sentence did not appear in A.C. No. 2, the phrase was later reinstated in the 1980 constitution (ART. 19, no. 2).

Contrary to his public appearances, within the confines of the Junta Merino voiced a position of constitutional conservatism and in many instances was more critical of regime practices than General Leigh. Merino's independent stance should not be underestimated as in the conflicts that led up to the decision to enact the constitution the navy intransigently opposed attempts to institute military authoritarianism on a permanent basis. Notwithstanding the commonplace that Leigh was the dissident within the Junta, Pinochet faced strong independent positions from both the navy and the air force.

### The Constraint of Constitutional Forms

Ultimately it was the logic of constitutional forms itself that precipitated the demise of the *Actas Constitucionales* by inadvertently renewing conflicts over the structure of the Junta. During the study of the three constitutional acts, the Junta and its legal advisors kept stumbling upon the need to maintain a shadow constitution beyond the acts. As they quickly discovered, if they closed the constitutional circle and established the supremacy of constitutional norms – even their own – the

Junta might inadvertently derogate any number of legal precepts and unintentionally deprive themselves of powers. This hazard became particularly apparent in the course of the review of A.C. No. 4, which systematized existing legal emergency powers into a single text. By giving prominence to the *Actas Constitucionales*, the Junta risked diminishing the force of all nominally constitutional decree-laws that remained outside of the acts. Thus, even though the Junta did not want to openly assert the juridical structure of military rule (contained in D.L. No. 1, 128, 527, and 788) in the *Actas Constitucionales*, in the course of their preparation members of the Junta came to recognize that some organization of power had to be elevated to the level of *Actas* in order to brace their own constitutional authority.

Earlier, during the discussion of A.C. No. 2, Pinochet had suggested that the Junta convert all decree-laws of constitutional rank into Constitutional Acts as a first step which would allow the Junta henceforth to designate its legislative acts simply as "laws." Such a tack would allow the Junta to avoid any reference to "decree-laws" in A.C. No. 2 (AHJG, 280, September 3, 1976, 15). To this end, Pinochet advocated the inclusion of a transitory article stipulating that the conversion be completed by September 1, 1977. The original wording proposed by Pinochet was, "Within the period of one year decree-laws that are of constitutional rank should take the form of *Actas Constitucionales*" (AHJG, 280, September 3, 1976, 30). The following day, Navy Capt. Aldo Montagna, the secretary of legislation, impressed upon the Junta the dangers implicit in purporting to raise all nominally constitutional norms to the level of constitutional acts: "Everything that is not included in *Actas Constitucionales* is going to appear stripped of the constitutional character that they might have for any circumstance not anticipated." He noted that any transitory article that affected D.L. No. 788 would give rise to a "tremendous snare if we don't pay detailed attention to everything that might have constitutional scope." Finally, the transitory article was reworded to encompass only degree-laws that had modified the constitution in respect to public powers and their exercise (AHJG, 281, September 9, 1976, 11–12); by Transitory Article 2 of A.C. No. 2 all such decree-laws had to take the form of constitutional acts within one year.[34]

---

[34] Pinochet's comments on self-limitation with regard to setting a deadline are revealing. When asked by Ortúzar if it was necessary to bind himself with a deadline, Pinochet (AHJG, 280, September 3, 1976, 30) responded, "I want to bind myself, although I never do." He insisted that a deadline was necessary, otherwise the conversion would never take place.

In this manner, though they had been embraced as a stratagem to avoid having to prematurely address problems of institutional design, the *Actas* ended up placing the organization of public powers on the agenda, but now in reference to the existing organization of military rule – not the "new institutionality" that would emerge from military rule. Insofar as the relationship between the two was unclear, the *Acta Constitucional* on the Junta set the stage for sectors within the government to push for a hard-line response to the regime's continued international isolation. These moves renewed conflicts over the structure of the Junta and the duration of the regime, and revealed the lack of any consensus within the armed forces behind a permanent authoritarian alternative.

## Permanent Military Rule and the Emergence of "The Transition"

Although the pretext for posing anew the character of military rule was Transitory Article 2 of A.C. No. 2, the context of the debate over the *Acta Constitucional de la Junta de Gobierno* and the subsequent institutional question was shaped by a confluence of difficult challenges to the military regime – continued diplomatic isolation, foreboding developments among the political parties, particularly signs that the PDC was shifting toward forthright opposition, the first strains in what would become intermittent border tensions with Peru and Argentina, and the gradually mounting pressure in the aftermath of the September 21, 1976 car-bomb assassination of former Allende Minister Orlando Letelier and his assistant, Ronni Moffit, in Washington, D.C.[35]

---

[35] Orlando Letelier, a member of the Socialist Party, had been Minister of Defense at the time of the coup and had served as Ambassador to the United States during the Allende government. At the time of his assassination the British weekly *Latin America* (October 1, 1976) described Letelier as "perhaps the most effective international lobbyist for the UP," and noted "the Chilean exile community recognizes that his death leaves a very difficult slot to fill, on both sides of the Atlantic."

During the first years after the coup, assassination attempts abroad during the month of September became an alarming tradition. On September 29, 1974, former commander in chief of the army Carlos Prats and his wife Sofia Prats were killed in a car-bomb explosion in Buenos Aires. In September 1975, one of the founders of the PDC, Bernardo Leighton and his wife were shot during a bungled attempt in Rome. At the time, Leighton, a prominent leader of the left wing of the party, had been active in building bridges to the Left in exile. In October 1974, the government prohibited Leighton's return to Chile because of his opposition work. Contemporary profiles of Prats, Leighton, and Letelier suggested that each had been targeted because of their stature as prominent, well-liked and respected opposition figures, who might span divi-

In the course of 1977 and 1978 these different variables waxed and waned in intensity, at times feeding rumors and expectations of an imminent collapse of the military government, particularly once solid evidence was established that tied the DINA to the Letelier assassination when two key suspects were identified in Santiago in March 1978. The government initially took a formally hard-line response to these developments, which did nothing to improve the regime's international situation and appears to have only exacerbated internal tensions over the course of the regime. These dynamics reveal some of the contradictory political constraints faced by the dictatorship as well as the limits of their efficacy as restrictions.

The hard-line turn took public form in January 1977 when the government closed the PDC-owned radio station, *Radio Balmaceda*. Subsequent events exemplify Hobbes's claim that autocrats may suppress legal constraints when they trouble them. Just as Christian Democratic lawyers were availing themselves of the newly created *recurso de protección* to have the Santiago Appellate Court reverse the closure, the Junta amended A.C. No. 4 and rendered inadmissable the use of the *recurso de protección* during states of exception.[36]

This unexpected modification, without consultation, provoked a crisis within the Constituent Commission, which deepened once further steps to stifle the PDC were taken. At its first session upon reassembling after summer vacations, the Constituent Commission met in secret session to discuss D.L. No. 1,684 (AOCC, 274, March 8, 1977, 719). As the minutes for the following session reveal, the commission

sions separating the center and the Left, form a national unity government, and, in the case of Prats, possibly head such a government. For these impressions see *Latin America,* October 4, 1974, October 11, 1974, October 10, 1975, September 24, 1976.

Judicial proceedings have implicated or convicted DINA officials and agents in each of these cases. In May 1995 the Chilean Supreme Court confirmed the convictions of Army General (R) Manuel Contreras, the former head of the DINA, and Army Colonel Pedro Espinoza as authors of the Letelier assassination. They were sentenced to seven and six years imprisonment, respectively. On the tensions surrounding the imprisonment of Contreras and Espinoza, see Cavallo 1998, chap. 27. An Italian court tried and convicted Contreras *en absentia* for involvement in the Leighton attempt; he was sentenced to twenty years imprisonment. As mentioned in Chapter 2, in November 2000 an Argentine court convicted Enrique Arancibia Clavel as an accessory in the Prats assassination, which the court concluded had been carried out by the DINA.

[36] D.L. No. 1,684 (D.O., January 31, 1977), decreed in express use of the Junta's constituent power, derogated and replaced ART. 14 of A.C. No. 4. By this norm, the *recurso de protección* became inadmissible not only during the states of exception defined in A.C. No. 4 but also during any state of emergency declared pursuant to the Law of State Security. The *actas* of the Junta's sessions (AHJG) contain no record of deliberations on this measure.

then decided to issue a public statement to clarify that neither it nor its members had participated in the drafting of the amendment and that the commission's original formulation of ART. 14 of A.C. No. 4, which permitted the use of the *recurso de protección* during states of emergency, had been intentional and not an oversight (AOCC, 275, March 10, 1977, 722–25). Some days later, Sergio Díez elaborated this point for the record. Díez's comments indicate civilian preoccupation with abuses of emergency powers and reveal that prominent members of the traditional Right were advocating judicial oversight of their use:

> [I]nsofar as there exist emergency situations and, as a consequence, the powers the Executive presently holds, it is necessary that the Judiciary have the authority to examine whether these measures have been taken in accordance with the law or not . . . to analyze whether or not the Executive is acting within the norms set by the emergency laws; comprising, moreover, that in an extreme case, which is not presently at hand, the courts may, by means of these remedies, decide and even apply the theory of the abuse of process (*abuso de derecho*). (AOCC, 277, March 17, 1977, 727–28)

The crisis within civilian advisory bodies to the military regime deepened as the Junta enacted legislation (D.L. No. 1,697, D.O., March 12, 1977) to dissolve the political parties of the Center and the Right, which after the coup had only been declared in recess (by D.L. No. 78), and imposed additional penal sanctions on individual political activity. The minutes of the Junta's meetings do not include documentation specifically pertaining to this decree-law. However, the record of the debate over a bill presented shortly after the promulgation of A.C. No. 2–4 suggests that the dissolution of the parties in 1977 may have been another instance in which the Junta adopted more extreme measures after anticipating criticism from within its base of support if it enacted legal instruments that trampled generally recognized legal principles. In this case, as Leigh's criticisms indicate, alternative solutions also threatened to disrupt the balance of power among the junta members.

The executive introduced the bill in question to close a loophole in D.L. No. 78 that rendered the decree-law ineffective as a judicial ground for repressing individual violators of the political recess (AHJG, 284, October 6, 1976, 9–26, and 285, October 7, 1976, 19–26). D.L. No. 78 was of limited value as an instrument of legal repression because to convict someone of violating the recess, proof had to be supplied that the defendant had acted as an agent of a specific party; without evidence of this connection, the defendant would go free regardless of evidence that he or she had committed the "political" act in question. Substantiating this connection, apparently, was almost impossible given the underground operation of the parties. The bill circumvented this problem by allowing the Ministry of the Interior to establish the fact of an individual's connection to a party merely by assertion in a ministerial resolution to this effect. Mendoza and Leigh objected that this solution openly forced the hand of the courts and would cause an uproar among judges, defense lawyers, and critics abroad (AHJG, 284, October 6, 1976, 13–17). Provisions to delegate extremely broad legislative authority to Pinochet for one year to modify the recess at will were also shot down by Leigh. He objected, "This is going to bring upon us an enormous loss of prestige, since it implies that we will demonstrate that, in fact, in Chile we decree *Actas Constitucionales* but then transform the Head of State into an absolute dictator, who by Decree with Force of Law can do whatever he wishes with the political parties" (AHJG, October 6, 1976, 284, 21).

In the following session a new bill was presented, at which point the documentation on this issue ends. This background suggests that before a deteriorating international situation and increasingly active opposition by a former proregime party, the PDC, a hard-line turn may have appeared less costly than other measures likely to antagonize individuals and institutions still supporting the dictatorship or to imply shifts in the balance among the armed forces. Without further evidence, this interpretation must remain at the level of conjecture.

However, regardless of the motivations, the ramifications of outlawing the PDC were immediate within the Constituent Commission and the Council of State. Enrique Evans and Alejandro Silva Bascuñán resigned, precipitating new appointments to the Constituent Commission.[37]

[37] Evans and Silva's letters of resignation are reproduced in AOCC, 740–41, 751–53. The rest of the commission sought unsuccessfully to convince Evans and Silva to temporarily suspend their resignations in the hope that the situation with the parties might be mitigated (AOCC, 742–46, 753–58).

Two months later, in May 1977, Jorge Ovalle Quiroz resigned from the commission (AOCC, 1140). On June 9, 1977, at a ceremony attended by President Pinochet and his Minister of Justice, Mónica Madariaga, three new commission members were sworn in: Luz Bulnes Aldunate, Raúl Bertelsen Repetto, and Juan de Dios Carmona Peralta (AOCC, 1152–58). Bulnes and Bertelsen were law professors. Carmona was former Minister of Defense to Eduardo Frei, but had been expelled from the PDC after accepting appointment to the Council of State in 1976. Ironically, in the commission Carmona adopted a stance similar to Silva Bascuñán; he consistently argued against *actas constitucionales* in favor of preparing a draft constitution. For references on this point, see note 56, page 209.

Simultaneously, the Subcommission on Electoral Laws and Political Parties suspended its activities (AOCC, 830). Within the Council of State the measure also sparked harsh criticism. At the first session after the dissolution of the parties, former president Alessandri informed the council that he had learned of the measure through the press and that he had suspended council sessions until he could first confer with Pinochet. At this meeting, he reported, he informed Pinochet of his opposition to the measures and had insisted that the DINA's activities be moderated. In the ensuing council discussion, members complained of being consulted only on secondary matters and not on major lines of government action. Alessandri also noted that the dissolution of the parties was apparently the result of a struggle between what he referred to as *militarista* and *civilista* groups within the executive (ACdE, 14, March 29, 1977, 44–47).

However, the hard-line turn was largely a formality, as a crackdown on the PDC did not immediately follow.[38] In a document written some months after these events, Guzmán [1977a, 3] indicates that Pinochet's March 18, 1977 speech, announcing the future creation of a designated legislative chamber, had been given to allay fears among government supporters that the military was taking a turn toward arbitrary, totalitarian rule.

It is difficult to tell exactly how these twists and turns dovetailed with the emerging conflict over the *Acta Constitucional* on the Junta, as there is sparse documentary evidence with which to reconstruct the controversy over the AC on the Powers of the State, virtually no secondary references, and the timing of debates and decisions is unclear. Nevertheless, the available documentation reveals that conflicts over the constitutional act paralleled these attempts to press a harder line, but that among the commanders of the armed forces there was no consensus to confront the dictatorship's internal and international difficulties by openly committing to an authoritarian regime as the regular structure of government in Chile.[39]

---

[38] Regarding the absence of a crackdown on the PDC, the *Latin American Political Report* (London, May 6, 1977) noted, "The Christian Democratic Party . . . continues to exist in a kind of limbo; the expected wave of repression against its members has never materialized . . . and there are no reports that any of its property has been confiscated."

[39] I have on file four documents on the revision of D.L. No. 527 (the Statute of the Junta, decreed in June 1974): one each from the navy, army, and air force, and a handwritten summary of positions drawn up by Guzmán. Cavallo et al. (1989, 152–54) also provide a brief account.

## The Acta Constitucional de la Junta de Gobierno

The navy submitted the first draft proposal for this act in mid-October 1976.[40] Its proposal essentially reaffirmed the division of powers codified in D.L. No. 527, defended the original position of the Junta, and introduced additional checks to prevent the president from straying from Junta agreements. These included limiting the president to four years in office, with a proviso for one additional term upon reelection by the Junta, as well as the requirement of written Junta agreement as a condition for the validity of a number of executive acts.

In the preamble to its draft, the navy justified its position by invoking the nineteenth-century tradition of Diego Portales – strong government, order, and authority combined with impersonal rule and formal legality – a tradition which the government often invoked. The draft proceeded to assert the primacy of the Junta as a body and the limits of Pinochet's title to executive power. In its review of the legal antecedents for the draft *acta*, first the navy reasserted that the Junta was the locus of executive as well as legislative and constituent powers, and that in a "gesture of disinterested patriotism" the other junta members had granted to the President of the Junta only the *exercise* of executive powers. In the final "Whereas" clause of the preamble (No. 10) the implications of the Portalian notion of effective authority fused with legality were stated: The president should be given all powers necessary for an "efficient, agile, just, authoritarian discharge of its mandate," but the Junta should also "set the counterbalance which that regime had – that is – a severe respect for the law and the impossibility of perpetuating himself [the president] in Power." These counterbalances were specified in the body of the act. They consisted of limiting the president designated by the Junta to a four-year term, with allowance for reelection to one additional term (ART. 1), and of binding the president to implementing Junta decisions in accordance with written conditions, timetables, and formalities that were to be preserved in a written record of the decision. Furthermore, any executive acts that required the Junta's agreement (these were broadened in ART. 11 beyond those specified in ART. D.L. No. 527) were to be valid only if they indicated the date and number of the *Acta* of the Junta's written agreement; otherwise the *Contraloría* had to represent their illegality (ART. 2).

---

[40] The document, which I have on file, is titled "*Acta Constitucional No. De los Poderes del Estado.*" This document is undated, but the photocopy I possess has scribbled on it, "Remitted by the Navy of Chile on 14-X-76."

The navy's draft did not mention any deadline for the termination of military rule. However, clearly, the navy's position was to maintain the institutional status quo and to reinforce the position of the other Junta members before Pinochet. The navy proposal stands in stark contrast to the two documents distributed by the presidency on January 4, 1977, a justificatory "Memorandum" and a bill entitled "Statute of the Government of Chile."[41]

In the guise of perfecting an enduring military authoritarian regime, the president's proposal unmistakably was another bid to establish Pinochet's personal supremacy over the Junta. Pinochet's memorandum portrayed the reform of the Junta as the completion of the new institutional order – the broad contours of which it claimed were already given by the existing organization of military rule. Thus, the document was entitled "Statute of the Government of Chile." To justify this title, point four of the memorandum noted that to refer to the government as the *Junta de Gobierno* "gives the impression that the Nation possesses a Government with transitory characteristics and not permanent goals." To underscore Pinochet's position that dictatorship was not an exception but the appropriate form of government, the fourth "Whereas" clause stated, "The period of transitoriness has come to an end and it is necessary to present the Government of the Nation with a stable character."

Against this backdrop, the changes Pinochet proposed were presented as correcting flawed traditional practices that had been codified in D.L. No. 527 out of haste and the need to reach agreement at that time (June 1974) "to prevent the rupture which today, after three years have elapsed, may occur (pt. 5)." Such thinly veiled threats spotted the memorandum, with Pinochet intimating grave and unforeseeable consequences if the scope of the president's powers were not clarified. After noting that continued uncertainty regarding the nature of executive power could produce grave situations, the memorandum noted, "This, as I have indicated, could even be cause for bloody acts with absolutely negative results for Chile and even for those who triumph

---

[41] The document that I have on file, stamped "Secret," is a numbered copy, but is undated. The date cited is the reference from General Leigh's response. The cross references in Leigh's document fully concord with the army proposal, which Leigh identifies as *Oficio CASMIL (R) No. 3100/2 de 04.ENE.77*. It is unclear who wrote the army documents. Guzmán drafted innumerable documents for the presidency during these years. However, these texts lack the sophistication, precision, and careful argument characteristic of Guzmán's writings; in addition, the content of the document is totally at odds with Guzmán's position on military rule.

in the armed incident that personal blindness or ambition could lead to (3)."

The modifications proposed structured a strongly presidentialist regime that allowed Pinochet to predominate over the Junta. Again, majority decision making with a swing vote going to the president replaced the unanimity rule but, unlike the attempt to impose this rule during the drafting of the 1974 Statute of the Junta, this time no distinction was made between legislative and constituent acts – majority decision was to extend to modifications to the constitution, thereby allowing Pinochet to also modify the constitution at will. With regard to the office and powers of the presidency, executive powers were to be exercised exclusively by the president. Requirements that specific powers could only be exercised with the agreement of the Junta were suppressed, including those for powers that traditionally had required senate approval. The office was tied to the commander in chief of the army, and the president was also authorized to designate a vice president to supersede him in the event of illness, and to hold down the fort when he travelled abroad or in any other situation temporarily impairing him from fulfilling his duties (Art. 14).[42] The draft did not set out a procedure for the "definitive replacement" of the President, but the accompanying memorandum stipulated that a procedure would be "legalized" within ten days of the act's promulgation (Art. 18). Under the terms of Pinochet's proposal, this delay implied that this decision would be decided according to majority decision making, allowing the army to easily impose its preferred solution.

With regard to the decisive question of the relationship between the president and the branches of the armed forces, Pinochet's memorandum held that the president – by virtue of office – was *generalissimo* (supreme commander) of the armed forces and *carabineros* (pt. 7). In other words, Pinochet was to hold the traditional presidential power of designating and removing the commanders in chief of the other services at will. This demand was presented as one dimension of the more general claim that executive power should be exclusively exercised by the president and was followed by the threats already cited. To this end, Art. 12 of the draft gave the president the power to confer the highest ranks within the armed forces, yet now *without* Junta agreement. Without this constraint, which had been codified in D.L. No. 527,

---

[42] This was a departure from Art. 16, D.L. No. 527, which tied surrogation to the order of precedence among the members of the Junta. This earlier formula was maintained in the 1980 constitution (T.D. 16).

Pinochet would have been able to manipulate the apex of the chain of command in each service and alter the composition of the Junta as legislature. These powers thus could be used to assure a compliant body in the Junta. When coupled with the proposal for majority decision making, the implications are obvious.

Air force commander Gustavo Leigh's reply came months later, only after Pinochet had apparently presumed that Leigh's silence indicated approval for Pinochet's proposal.[43] Leigh responded with a carefully argued, five-page, point-by-point rebuttal. In it Leigh highlighted the proposal's numerous procedural and substantive departures from prior Junta agreements and commitments. Regarding procedure, Leigh reminded the president that the constitutional act pertaining to public powers was a matter of law and therefore required the approval of the Junta which held legislative and constituent powers. Further, Transitory ART. 2 of A.C. No. 2 stipulated only that the Junta convert already existent decree-laws regulating constitutional matters into constitutional acts. Although the Junta might enact slight modifications in the process, Leigh stressed, "the basic philosophy and spirit . . . (1)" of the decree-laws could not be changed. With regard to the substance of Pinochet's proposal, Leigh disagreed forcefully with the suggestion that military rule ought to be permanent in any way, a suggestion that he described as strange because never in its history had Chile had anything akin to a permanent government. In Leigh's opinion, the legacy of a government resided in the laws that it promulgates, as these may perdure in time. To suggest permanent military rule was to contradict the Junta's repeated statements that it would withdraw from power once it fulfilled its objectives.

Leigh found Pinochet's analysis of the structure of the Junta "truly disconcerting (3)." Leigh reminded Pinochet that executive power had been put in his hands "by decision of the *Junta de Gobierno*, which cannot be interpreted as an acquired right of the commander in chief of the army . . . (3)." Upon coming to the threats accompanying this point, Leigh halted his analysis, stating that Pinochet's objective was clear and that the document required no further analysis:

[43] This is referred to in the text of Leigh's reply. The document, which I have on file, is undated and consists of an official letter from Leigh to Pinochet. When exactly General Leigh's reply was drafted or presented to Pinochet is unclear. It includes a reference to Pinochet's March 18, 1977 speech. This suggests that the letter was drafted after that date but prior to July 10, 1977, the date of Pinochet's *Chacarillas* speech. Presumably, Leigh would have referred to the latter speech had the letter been written after these announcements.

> The real essence of the Project proposed by *V.E.* (*Vuestra Excelencia*, Your Excellency) is to concentrate total and absolute Power in the Person who exercises Executive Power, a phenomenon which openly contradicts such documents as the Act of Constitution of the *Junta de Gobierno*, the Declaration of Principles of the Government of Chile, remarks expressed by the Members of the *Junta de Gobierno* in different speeches, and most recently the speech pronounced by *V.E.* on 18 March 1977 (4).

Under any such arrangement the Junta would cease to wield any effective power. The differences between the navy and the air force positions and those of Pinochet are self-evident. The navy appears to have also responded to Pinochet's proposal, but I was unable to locate the document. According to the one secondary source that discusses these events, the navy's rejoinder contained even harsher language than found in the air force document (Cavallo et al. 1989, 154).

In any event, Pinochet's proposal to restructure the organization of the Junta precipitated a deep internal crisis among the armed forces. The depth of this crisis is revealed by the fact that, in a departure from usual practices which restricted deliberations to the Junta members and their immediate legal counsel, the high commands of each of the other branches met to discuss Pinochet's proposal. A handwritten document, drawn up by Guzmán (1977b), records the position of the high command (officers with rank of admiral or general) in each of the other three services.[44] The document is organized according to the four central reforms proposed by the president (tying the presidency to the army; allowing the president to designate a temporary surrogate as necessary; removing all requirements of Junta agreement or opinion when exercising specific executive powers; and dropping the unanimity rule).

In all three services the top-ranking officers rejected the proposal virtually unanimously. The navy was the force most cohesively united around a single position. Aside from one Admiral (Patricio Carvajal), who consistently advocated "to not innovate" upon the status quo, the eleven other admirals backed the navy proposal discussed above,

---

[44] It appears from the document that Guzmán attended separate meetings for each force. The document is not dated. Personnel at the archive have incorrectly cataloged the document as from 1974, presumably because of the title's reference to D.L. No. 527 (the Statute of the Junta) of that year. However, the document contains a reference to D.L. No. 1,639 which was enacted December 30, 1976, and the concordance of cross references establishes that the document concerns the 1977 controversy over the constitutional act on the Junta.

which seems to have been previously approved by the *Consejo Naval*, the council of admirals. Positions among the fifteen air force generals were more varied, though the generals overwhelmingly opposed the proposal and unanimously rejected fusing the presidency to the army; however, one air force general did support the adoption of majority decision making. Whereas there is no indication that the admirals explicitly raised the issue of the termination of military rule, an unspecified number of air force generals endorsed setting a deadline for completing the government's task and calling elections. Officers within *carabineros* divided equally among generals who did not state an opinion and generals who advocated leaving the status quo intact. Once again, Pinochet's bid for absolute control was an aspiration of army officers alone.

On the last page of Guzman's tally, a number of observations are jotted down. These state that the institutional status quo is to remain as is and briefly outline a plan for a transition. The scheme is virtually identical to the transition plan later announced by Pinochet on July 9, 1977 in the so-called *Discurso de Chacarillas*.[45] This plan did not reflect a joint position of the armed forces. Nevertheless, the internal, nonpublic meaning of the speech should be clear: The constitutional act on the Junta as proposed by Pinochet would proceed no further as there was no consensus to restructure the Junta and establish a nonelected authoritarian regime as the "normal" institutional order of Chile. Legally, the constitutional act on the Junta died in August 1977

---

[45] In this speech, Pinochet for the first time outlined a plan for the creation of a *new democracy* in three stages: *recuperation, transition, consolidation*. The first stage, that of recuperation, was to end no later than December 31, 1980 and was to involve the continued concentration of all political power in the armed forces and *carabineros*. The major task of this phase would be to enact key legislation and complete the dictation of the *Actas Constitucionales*. The following four- or five-year transition stage (to begin in 1980) was to be characterized by a change in the role of civilians, who were to "pass from collaboration to participation" through the creation of a civilian legislative chamber, two-thirds of whose members were to be appointed by the Junta (the other third would serve by right or by presidential appointment). During the "transition" the presidency was to remain in the hands of the president of the Junta, and the powers of the Junta as a body were to be reduced to the exercise of constituent powers, though each member would be able to initiate legislation and initiate an absolute veto of any legislation deemed to endanger national security. The passage from transition to consolidation was to be marked by the electoral generation of the nonappointed two-thirds of the chamber, the designation by the chamber of the new president, who would serve a six-year term, and the enactment of a single, complete constitution. In this last stage, the constitutional role of the armed forces and *carabineros* was to consist of guarding the essential basis of the new institutionality and national security. For the text of the speech, see *El Mercurio*, July 10, 1977.

when Tr. ART. 2, A.C. No. 2 was modified to eliminate the deadline for converting all nominally constitutional decree-laws affecting state powers into constitutional acts.[46]

## The "Period of Transition": Constitutionalization without Elections and without Liberalization

The divisions revealed by Pinochet's proposal for permanent military rule shifted the intraregime struggle onto the terrain of defining the future constitutional order and the terms of a transition. This new context opened a space for pro-institutional civilians advising Pinochet to drive home the importance of devising a new political-institutional regime and a strategy to assure its permanence and stability. Jaime Guzmán was the chief advocate and the most important architect of "institutionalization." From the very beginning, he self-consciously formulated conceptions of "transition" that eschewed elections in the short and medium terms. Nevertheless, this shift in the internal debate over the trajectory of the dictatorship set another dimension upon the military-institutional debate. Whereas the conflict over the reform of the Junta turned on the immediate organization of military rule, now the emphasis – at least, in some quarters – shifted toward how to establish and entrench political-institutional mechanisms that would bind future civilian actors and preclude any recurrence of the 1972–1973 organic crisis. Once the option of hard-line authoritarian entrenchment proved without support within the armed forces, forward-looking political-institutional strategies came into play with strategies for sustaining military rule in the short run.

These two dimensions were not wholly compatible. The tension between designing and securing a constitution capable of binding civilian actors and buttressing the immediate authority of the military regime had been recognized as early as November 1973 when Silva Bascuñán and Guzmán argued over whether the Constituent Commission ought to provide the Junta counsel on contingent constitutional problems. As then became evident, constitutionalization of the dictatorship and instituting a reformed constitution to structure a post-military order might be imperatives that pulled in opposite directions. The many modifications to the draft constitutional acts in 1976 largely confirmed Silva Bascuñán's position that immediate concerns of the dictatorship would take precedence over provisions designed for a civil-

---

[46] D.L. No. 1,873, D.O., August 23, 1977. The deadline was to expire September 18, 1977.

ian future. After the 1977 controversy over restructuring the Junta, the predominant pole shifted toward the design of a constitution. However, the tension remained. The collegial character of the Junta, particularly after the 1977 confrontations, placed a fundamental political constraint upon any strategy of constitutionalization: Any innovations had to leave intact the existing structure of the Junta. This constraint explains the only partial implementation of Guzmán's preferred strategy which involved liberalization of the regime through the institution of a designated Congress prior to the full implementation of the constitution. Insofar as a designated Congress implied a reduction in the powers of the Junta, this aspect of Guzmán's strategy proved untenable. However, Guzmán's argument for a constitution warrants attention as it underscored the importance of introducing and consolidating a constitution prior to any transition to civilian rule.

Guzmán's position was articulated in a series of internal position papers drafted in 1977 and 1978.[47] Guzmán devised his strategy to resolve a series of dilemmas posed by the historical form of political conflict in Chile and comparative experiences of authoritarian and military rule. From other cases of authoritarianism Guzmán drew the lesson that military rule was inviable over the long run. Consequently, he argued, long-term stability could be secured only through effective, impersonal, juridical institutions. Military regimes that failed to introduce new political-institutional regimes invariably eroded from within and withdrew from power without altering the prior configuration of institutions or political forces. The difficulty in Chile, however, was that the depth of the prior crisis, as well as the strength of the parties, precluded any introduction of institutions and return to civilian rule in the short term. Nevertheless, Guzmán argued that the definition of a new regime could not be postponed. If it were, the regime risked an eventual loss of initiative and being forced to respond to pressure, which would turn it into an object of events.[48] In this case, most likely the same political class and institutions that had produced the earlier crisis

---

[47] The most important of these documents are Jaime Guzmán 1977a and 1978. The second document essentially restates the initial strategy but in terms of a single constitution with transitory articles rather than a series of constitutional acts. Guzmán was also the author of the *Discurso de Chacarillas*, as confirmed by the many drafts of the speech found in the 1977 Transition File at the same archive.

[48] Writing in mid-1977, after the political strike wave of 1976, the legalization of the Spanish Communist Party, the self-dissolution of the Francoist *Cortes*, and about the time of the June elections for a constituent Congress, Guzmán noted that what was happening in Spain was a good example of what should be prevented from happening in Chile (1977a, 2).

would be restored. The logic of the situation, thus, circled back to the need for extended military rule. However, the circle was vicious, as Guzmán insisted that long-term military rule too was inviable: Ongoing military involvement in contingent political affairs invariably would result in political deliberation within the armed forces, the formation of factions, and an erosion of hierarchical discipline – factors which eventually would force a decision to withdraw to preserve the services as institutions.[49] In the long run, the only way out of this predicament was to gradually establish and consolidate a new institutional regime that would place the armed forces beyond politics. This undertaking, Guzmán insisted, could not be postponed; institutions had to be defined prior to the emergence of mass pressure for a return to democracy, lest the government lose control of the process.

For Guzmán, the crux of the problem was the choice between governing within an effective, impersonal, juridical order or of relying solely upon the arbitrary will of those in power (1977a, 3–4). He analyzed this choice in terms of temporal trade-offs in power and stability. As he argued, arbitrary rule maximized short-term power at the expense of long-term stability. The government might find the "formula of the arbiter" – that is, a system of government without effective juridical limits of any sort – more attractive because it permits the government to overcome difficulties, to solve immediate problems without impediments, and to impose its will without counterbalances. However, Guzmán contended, beyond appearances, such a form of authority sacrifices medium or long-term stability, in concession to greater power in the short term (1977a, 3).

Governing within a binding juridical framework, on the other hand, necessarily implied being subject to limits and, at times, being blocked from implementing measures perceived to be for the good of all. In Guzmán's words, "There is no possible formula for a real juridical regime that does not give rise to limits upon the will of the governing" (1977a, 4). However, these constraints, Guzmán insisted, were actually a source of power, since in a country with such a deeply ingrained legalistic mentality among the population as Chile, government stability is strengthened to the extent that authority originates from and is framed within an impersonal, juridical order. In this context, if the military government exploited its extensive legislative, executive, and constituent powers, and modified norms and changed the system every

[49] Guzmán referred explicitly to Onganía's attempt to establish permanent military rule in Argentina.

time some act presented difficulties for the authorities, the very essence of juridical security would be destroyed, and the regime's medium- and long-term stability would be gravely eroded (1977a, 4).

However, the central point of Guzmán's document was that it was not sufficient to acknowledge the paramount importance of new institutions. The real challenge was to introduce them and assure their stability over time. This was the heart of Guzmán's understanding of institutionalization and transition: The new regime would be enduring only if new "civic habits" and a new generation of political actors were formed to sustain and support it. This training, he insisted, could only arise out of real civilian participation in decision making.[50]

This was the pedagogical and strategic significance of Guzmán's advocacy of a one-term designated Congress alongside continued military retention of the "essence of political power" (executive power in the president and constituent power in the Junta) during a five-year transitory period. Although elections could not be held immediately, civilians had to be given an arena for regular participation in decision making.[51] The government had to broaden its base of support. Otherwise, a purely military government would remain remote and alien from the population, devoid of channels allowing for civilian identification. On this point, Guzmán was extremely critical of the government's relationship to its own supporters and, in particular, of its recent policy toward the PDC. As he noted, instead of dividing the party, the military had united the PDC like never before and had made it impossible to attract former party militants or sympathizers to the government. He stated, "to push into the opposition every person who sympathized or worked in some manner alongside the Christian Democrats, is one of the gravest tactical errors the Government can make" (1977a, 8–9).[52] Securing the "new institutionality" required the

---

[50] Guzmán stressed the danger of allowing the "anti-marxist civilian sector (*civilidad*)" to lapse into political indifference. He insisted that whereas the Marxist parties would always be ready and organized when the moment comes, the training of the "anti-Marxist" sectors could only take place within a framework of real civic participation. On this ground, Guzmán contended, such a framework was irreplaceable if the goal is to prepare these new actors that are needed by the regime (1977a, 7).

[51] As we will see, Guzmán also maintained that elections should not be the sole mechanism for generating political authority. Thus, his advocacy of a partially nonelected Senate, which later would be inscribed in the 1980 constitution.

[52] In an earlier document written in preparation for a conversation with Pinochet, Guzmán (1976) noted that an increasing number of civilians were leaving the government discouraged, resenting ill-treatment and being undervalued. These sentiments were generating disinterest in – and even fear of – accepting government positions among civilians. He also noted that civilians were increasingly complaining of

opening up of channels whereby proregime civilian actors could gain political experience. In Guzman's conception a designated congress would provide this school of civic education.

Significantly, at this stage Guzmán developed strategic arguments for ratifying the eventual plan by plebiscite. The use of a plebiscite was understood as a limitation of the Junta's otherwise absolute constituent powers, yet this constraint was argued to be worthwhile given the strategic value of popular ratification. As Guzmán noted, the Junta could either directly use its constituent powers to implement the plan of institutionalization (which as yet was not conceived in terms of a single constitution) or submit the plan to the nation in a plebiscite (1977a, 15–16). The advantage of the plebiscite, Guzmán argued, was that popular approval would subsequently "invalidate any request for a new plebiscite or a general election prior to the fulfillment of the milestones foreseen in the plan itself." The drawback was that a plebiscite would make it "morally more difficult" to later unilaterally amend the plan (appending a requirement for plebiscitary approval of all modifications to the constitution later would formally overcome this obstacle).[53] Nevertheless, this inconvenience was further offset by supplying direct popular support for the plan, as well as for inaugurating the first legislature without elections.

In this manner, recourse to sources of agreement beyond the Junta for the first time appeared as a mechanism for bolstering the institutional order decreed from above and as a justification for introducing a limit upon the Junta's unilateral exercise of constituent power. Of course, as in all instances of referenda, how any popular consultation would be organized quickly came to the fore as a key question, both within the Junta and among the opposition parties. Guzmán's position was that any ratifying plebiscite would have to proceed solely with national identity cards, given the absence of electoral registries (1977a, 16).[54] From his perspective, the plebiscite also presented a mechanism

domineering behavior (*prepotencia*) by soldiers, as well as a sense of resignation that it was futile or dangerous to petition against such mistreatment. Guzmán warned that the emergence of broad antimilitary sentiments would isolate the armed forces and hasten the fall of the government.

[53] This solution first appears in the 1978 document "*Periodo de transición*," which reformulates the institutionalization plan in terms of a single constitution. In the constitution the requirement is stipulated in T.D. 21 (d).

[54] This form of ratification was a departure from the long-standing assumption within the Constituent Commission that any ratifying plebiscite would take place with a full electoral system in place. At its inception, the Constituent Commission set as a priority the formulation of a new fraud-proof system of electoral registration – based on a new iden-

for claiming support beyond the Junta, something which Pinochet would attempt to do with the January 1978 *Consulta Nacional* – at the cost of precipitating an extremely severe internal crisis, as Merino and Leigh refused to back a sham plebiscite to condemn another UN resolution against Chile.

Up until early 1980, Guzman's scenario of transition – with power sharing among an appointed civilian legislature, a military executive, and a constituent military junta – was the central focus of internal and public proregime commentary on institutionalization. This was the formula discussed within the Constituent Commission, and a variant of it later appeared appended to the Council of State's draft, which was presented publicly in early July 1980.[55]

### The Letelier Accelerant

Initially, institutionalization was conceived of in terms of a cluster of *Actas Constitucionales*. The packet, as specified in a November 1977 commission agreement (AOCC, 1793), was to include constitutional acts on: the *Contraloría General de la República*, the judiciary, the executive, the single legislative chamber, the security power (armed forces and national security council), constituent powers, and nationality and citizenship. Throughout the second half of 1977, the commission worked simultaneously on draft chapters and constitutional acts structuring judicial powers and the *Contraloría*, but these acts were never promulgated.[56] In March 1978 this strategy was reformulated after

---

tity card – and the reregistration of all citizens. These expectations faded into discouragement, particularly within the Subcommission on Electoral Laws and Political Parties, as recommendations to the Ministry of the Interior concerning the organization of such a system met with delays and indifference.

[55] The commission began to address the "transition period" after receiving Pinochet's November 10, 1977 missive "*Basic Orientations for the Study of the New Constitution,*" which basically instructed the commission to proceed along the lines contained in the *Discurso de Chacarillas* (AOCC, 1786–93). Throughout March 1978, the transition was discussed in the broader context of institutions (AOCC, 1987–90, 2005–46). However, the report and draft constitution submitted by the commission in October 1978 did not include recommendations concerning a transition. In March 1979, within the Council of State, Ortúzar, who was also a member of this body, explained that this omission occurred only because the commission had not received in time formal instructions to include such recommendations (AdCdE, vol. 1, 438).

[56] The proposed constitutional act on the judiciary was extremely controversial, as some commission members (particularly Juan de Dios Carmona) argued that it was politically inadvisable to legislate on the judiciary (AOCC, 1223–37) – a position shared by the full Supreme Court (AOCC, 1240–55). The commission members generally agreed that if a constitutional act on the judiciary was to be enacted, it should be promulgated

public breakthroughs in the U.S. Justice Department's investigation into the September 21, 1976 assassination in Washington, D.C. of former Allende minister Orlando Letelier and his assistant Ronni Moffit prompted intensified pressure and a crisis became imminent.

In the aftermath of the car bombing, the Justice Department's investigation lingered until March 4, 1978, when Michael Townley, a U.S. citizen, and Armando Fernández Larios, a Chilean army captain, were identified in Santiago as the men in the two leaked photos published in the *Washington Star* on March 3, 1978 and distributed worldwide by the wire services. These photos originally had been attached to two Paraguayan passports, issued at Pinochet's request in July 1976 by the Paraguayan president, Gen. Alfredo Stroessner. After a blatantly irregular request for entry visas, U.S. Ambassador to Paraguay George Landau took the precaution of photocopying the two passports, which he knew contained false identities and nationalities for two DINA agents, thereby preserving what would become a crucial key for the investigation. Once Townley and Fernández Larios were identified, the pieces of the investigation rapidly fell into place. Connections between Townley and the DINA emerged, as did evidence tying Townley to long suspected anti-Castro, Cuban nationalist groups in New Jersey.[57]

Within days of the identification of Michael Townley and Armando Fernández Larios, on March 14, 1978, the Constituent Commission quickly reworked the plan along the lines of a single constitution with transitory articles, as the designated congress suddenly assumed new urgency as a potential escape valve in a restructured regime. Amidst the commotion over the Townley and Fernández Larios identifications,

---

only after or along with acts on the other state powers. It should be noted that Carmona, a new member commissioned after the March 1977 resignations, like Silva Bascuñán, consistently objected to the *Actas Constitucionales* on the ground that the commission's task was to prepare a new constitution (AOCC, 1229–31, 1248–49, 1957, 2009).

The interdependency of institutions also stymied the strategy of partial implementation. In the course of work on the constitutional act on the *Contraloría*, the commission discovered that it was extremely difficult to structure mechanisms of legal and administrative control without any sense of how a future congress would be organized, the nature of its oversight functions, or the oversight and control functions that other organs might possess (AOCC, 1608–24, 1667, 1720–38, 1818–27).

[57] Early on, investigators pursued leads pointing to Chile, at first only as they pertained to Cuban exiles who been in the country prior to the bombing. By May 1977, leads linking the Cubans to the DINA were being examined. The first strong corroboration came in early July 1977, but solid evidence was obtained only with the March 1978 breakthrough and Townley's April 17, 1978 confession. The course of the investigation can be traced in Branch and Propper 1983. Eugene M. Propper, as Assistant U.S. Attorney, led the Justice Department's investigation. A synopsis of the case is provided by Sigmund (1993, 111–18).

Sergio Díez stressed, "at any moment an inescapable need for an organic formula of civil participation may arise" (AOCC, 2007). He advocated immediate work on a constitutional act to structure a civilian legislature. In the course of this session, however, it became increasingly clear that promulgating a single complete constitution with transitory articles was superior as a strategy of implementation to enacting a series of constitutional acts capped by a constitution at the end of the transitory period. This was so because institutions established by constitutional acts could easily appear only provisional, fall into disfavor, and give way to a restoration of prior institutions (AOCC, 2009, 2022) – which had always been Carmona's argument against the *actas*.

At the same session, Guzmán introduced an additional reason for opening the regime: It was necessary to ease pressure upon the judiciary and place a cushion (*un colchón*, literally, a mattress) between the government and the judiciary. He pointed out that the absence of any legitimate arena of political debate was forcing political contestation into the courts. As a result the government was "running unnecessary risks by sustaining . . . a latent possibility of a very severe confrontation between the government and the judiciary at any moment" (AOCC, 2024).[58] Guzmán's solution was the designated congress. As an alternative to decompress the situation, Carmona advocated the creation of a Constituent Assembly on the ground that a designated congress implied the virtual dissolution of the Junta (AOCC, 2011) and that such a legislature would be challenged as being a mere Junta fabrication (AOCC, 2028). Guzmán, however, turned Carmona's second point against advocacy of a constituent assembly, noting that a constituent assembly could be differentiated from the Constituent Commission or the Council of State only if it were generated through elections; but since elections were out of the question during the transitory period the constituent assembly too was inviable.

---

[58] Guzmán's argument regarding the need to relieve pressure upon the judiciary was corroborated in 1984 when opposition lawyers successfully argued that individuals had a right to protest before the Santiago appellate court. The court's ruling set the Ministry of the Interior on a collision course with the judiciary as the executive initiated a conflict of competencies against the court before the Junta. This extreme procedure was suspended only after the Supreme Court overturned the lower court decision. The resolution of such conflicts between political or administrative authorities and the higher courts was a traditional power of the Senate, which was maintained in the 1980 constitution (ART. 49, 3), and exercised during the transitional period by the Junta in accordance with T.D. 18, H. On this conflict, see AHJG, 14/84-E, June 29, 1984, 1–36; 17/84, July 17, 1984, 5–6; 18/84, July 24, 1984, 19–22; 19/84, July 31, 1984, 8–15.

The transition, Guzmán insisted, required a military president, not a military government: "In any case, it is absolutely necessary to acknowledge one fact: the transition requires a military President, it necessarily requires a limitation of the functions of the *Junta de Gobierno* in regards to those that it has today, and it requires, for that reason, the generation of civic-military Government" (AOCC, 2029).

On April 5, 1978, amidst the uncertainty and extreme tension generated by the internal struggle (pitting Contreras and DINA stalwarts against Army General (R) Odlanier Mena – the new intelligence chief, anti-Contreras sectors within the government and the armed forces, and the U.S. Justice Department) regarding Michael Townley's security and expulsion to the United States, Pinochet announced that the Junta would enact, subject to plebiscitary approval, a new constitution with transitory articles to regulate a period of transition prior to the constitution going fully into effect. During this transitory period, he stated, all permanent state organs would come into operation, including a legislative chamber, a constitutional tribunal, and an unspecified security organ, but there would be no electoral generation of the institutions that would exercise public powers.[59]

With growing evidence of government involvement in the Letelier assassination, Pinochet was beset from all sides – including sectors of his own general staff – and was forced to take steps toward institutional and juridical "normalization."[60] In addition to allowing the state of siege to lapse at the onset of the crisis, these steps included on April 14, 1978 the first-time appointment of a civilian, Sergio Fernández Fernández, as Minister of the Interior to head a predominantly civilian cabinet, and shortly afterward the enactment by decree-law of an amnesty to assure conscripts and officers directly implicated in acts of repression that they would not bear the costs of any transformations of the dictatorship.[61]

---

[59] *El Mercurio*, April 6, 1978. Pinochet also announced that the prison sentences of individuals convicted by military tribunals for offenses against state security would be commuted to banishment from Chile.

[60] According to the April 28, 1978 issue of the British weekly *Latin American Political Report*, thirteen army generals called for Pinochet's resignation in a March meeting of the general staff but were outvoted by the seventeen other generals.

[61] The state of siege expired on March 11, 1978, leaving only the state of emergency in effect. It wasn't until November 6, 1984 that a state of siege was again declared, well into the cycle of mass protests that began in April 1983. Prior to Fernández's appointment, only army officers – Gen. Oscar Bonilla and Gen. César Benavides – had headed the Ministry of the Interior. The amnesty law (D.L. No. 2,191, D.O., April 19, 1978) covered all criminal acts committed during the state of siege (September 11, 1973 through March 10, 1978), with the exception of the Letelier case, which was expressly excluded.

Simultaneously, the Constituent Commission stepped up the pace of its work. In a sign that a decision had been made earlier, the commission met for two days in late March to discuss the tasks remaining and to assign topics to each member to prepare studies on. No minutes were kept of these meetings. At the following session, on April 4, Ortúzar announced that Pinochet wanted the complete draft, with transitory articles, ready by the end of the year (AOCC, 2074). Henceforth, progress in preparing the constitution proceeded through the known stages: The Constituent Commission completed its work in October 1978; their draft was sent on the Council of State, which officially presented its proposal to the president in early July 1980; then, the Junta convened in marathon sessions to work out the final text.

In the interim, General Leigh was forced to resign from the Junta on July 24, 1978. There is no discounting the severity of this crisis. Leigh's removal from the Junta was accompanied by the resignation of virtually the entire high command of the air force – of the nineteen other generals forming the general staff, seventeen resigned. Gen. Fernando Matthei Aubel, the tenth ranking general, did not resign and assumed the rank of commander in chief. Despite this crisis, Leigh's forced resignation does not establish that the regime was a personalist dictatorship nor that Pinochet from that point on freely imposed his institutional design in the constitution, as has often been argued.[62] The pretext for Leigh's ouster was an interview published in the *Corriere de la Serra* in which Leigh spoke of the need to restore democracy within five years and stated that if proof were established of government involvement in the Letelier assassination, he would have to reconsider air force participation in the Junta. Other than the accounts of what happened on the day of Leigh's removal there is little hard evidence of what precipitated this crisis, nor of the position of the other junta members. However, a number of points suggest that the above claims are overstated. First, Leigh's principal offense may have been that he went public, particularly in the foreign press, and broke the unwritten convention that differences within the Junta remain behind closed doors. Second, the crisis that culminated in Leigh's ouster is consistent with the logic of unanimous decision making within a collegial organ. Unanimity itself can produce irresolvable conflict if persistent differences among constituents lead to decision-making paralysis, and historical accounts of unanimous decision making provide many

---

[62] On Leigh's destitution, see Cavallo et al. 1989, 222–32; Remmer 1989a, 131; Valenzuela 1991, 39, 50.

examples of the use of force to suppress dissidence (Heinberg 1932: 453–54). In this case, as already mentioned, there is solid evidence that prior to his destitution Leigh had vetoed and halted important privatizations supported by Merino and Pinochet. Merino may have therefore supported Leigh's removal from the Junta in order to proceed with the blocked reforms. But there is no evidence to suggest that Merino supported entrenching authoritarian rule nor a centralization of power in Pinochet. As I have noted repeatedly, Merino often sided with Leigh against Pinochet. Shortly prior to Leigh's ouster both commanders had vehemently opposed the January 1978 *consulta*, which Pinochet had initially sought to enact as a plebiscite. Furthermore, Leigh's removal may even have been legal under the terms of ARTS. 18 and 19 of D.L. 527 – the two articles that regulate removal and replacement of junta members.[63] Finally, it should be stressed that this crisis did not result in any modification to the unanimity decision rule, nor any attribution of powers of selection to Pinochet. Nor did it prevent Admiral Merino and General Leigh's successor, General Matthei, from henceforth developing and defending positions at variance with General Pinochet within the Junta.

In conclusion, it should be stressed that although external pressures gave urgency to the process of constitution making, they neither caused the decision to enact the constitution nor determined the constitution's content, as will be seen in the following chapter. The political decision to enact a constitution emerged out of conflicts over the duration and permanency of military rule that arose from Pinochet's repeated attempts to undermine the Junta. This history and the substance of the constitution also reveal that Pinochet's alleged dominance of the constitution-making process was largely a myth.

---

[63] The legal question turns on the meaning of "absolute impediment," which is one of the grounds for removal from the Junta listed in ART. 18. In a memorandum challenging the legality of Leigh's ouster (reproduced in Varas 1979, 167–70), Jorge Ovalle, a close legal advisor to Leigh, restricted the term to physical or psychological impediments. Ironically, however, early in September 1973, Ovalle, along with three coauthors, analyzed the same term in a legal brief (reproduced in Orden de Abogados 1980, 162–72) whose central argument was that the 1925 constitution authorized Congress to declare and remove Allende from office on grounds of absolute impediment (following ordinary legislative procedures, not the more demanding requirements for impeachment). In this context, in the absence of an explicit definition in the text, they argued, it was up to Congress to decide the scope of the term, which they interpreted broadly, as extending beyond solely physical incapacities. Following this interpretation, Leigh's destitution may have been consistent with the terms of D.L. No. 527, as the decree-law also does not define the term and authorizes "the rest of the titular members of the Junta to resolve on the doubt posed" (ART. 19, D.L. No. 527, D.O., June 26, 1974).

In both the celebratory and critical annals of military rule, Pinochet dictated the terms of the constitution because on November 10, 1977 he sent the Constituent Commission a memorandum entitled "Basic Orientations for the Study of the New Constitution."[64] However, for all its notoriety, the memo was at most a signal to increase the pace of work, not a decisive text in the constitution-making process. First, the document apparently was motivated by political considerations, not a decision to send forceful instructions to the Constituent Commission; otherwise it is difficult to explain why the memorandum was given immediate publicity before it was discussed within the Constituent Commission, which was not usual practice with instructions and consultations conveyed to the Constituent Commission.[65] Second, this memo, which instructed the group to proceed along the lines of the *Chacarillas* speech, contained only broad guidelines – most of which the commission had already developed on its own. The official minutes of the Constituent Commission also amply demonstrate that after receiving the missive, the commission continued to deliberate autonomously and that influential members, such as Guzmán, repeatedly insisted that the group should proceed independently of specific presidential recommendations (AOCC, 1697, 1990, 2035).

This point is readily borne out by a comparison with the eventual constitution. For example, the memo's suggestion to consider an indirect election of the president went nowhere (it was rejected virtually unanimously in both the Constituent Commission and the Council of State), nor did the Junta accept the transition formula of a designated congress even after both advisory bodies had endorsed it.[66] Here again, the collegial organization of the Junta and each commander's zealous defense of his institutional position within the regime blocked any strategy of liberalization that involved a diminution of the Junta's powers. Pinochet impressed this point upon Jorge Alessandri, the president of the Council of State, in a series of two meetings in late March and early April 1980. At these meetings Pinochet informed Alessandri that the Council's proposed transition schemes involving

---

[64] For examples, see Pérez Tremps 1984, 12; and Ensalaco 1994, 410–11.

[65] The text was published in *El Mercurio* on November 12, 1977 and first discussed within the Constituent Commission on November 15, 1977 (AOCC, 327). The memo is generally believed to have been written by Guzmán and Mónica Madariaga, then Minister of Justice.

[66] As noted above, the Constituent Commission backed a designated congress, but did not include any recommendations for a transition with its report and draft. The Council of State's proposal is discussed in the following note.

the dissolution of the Junta after it designated the members of the Chamber of Deputies (the Senate was to be overwhelmingly appointed by the president) had created a "delicate situation" for the president and that the disappearance of the Junta was unacceptable (AdCdE, vol. 2, 234–35).[67] Thus, the legal constraint given by the unanimity decision rule implied that in the short run any significant liberalization involving civilian control over legislation was precluded. As a result, at the moment of its promulgation the 1980 constitution would appear as little more than a cosmetic device for perpetuating the dictatorship.

[67] Alessandri's report of these meetings led to a debate within the Council as to whether under these circumstances it should recommend any transition formula at all. After Carmona warned that if the Council failed to make recommendations for a transition it might precipitate a crisis by giving the appearance that it was advocating an immediate implementation of the full constitution, the Council decided to rework its formula and restore minimal powers to the Junta (AdCdE, 2, 240–49). The restored faculties were still narrower than those proposed by Guzmán and were limited to replacing the president in the event an absolute impediment prevented him from remaining in office, participating in the exercise of constituent powers when modifying entrenched chapters of the constitution, and advising the president on the organization and distribution of the armed forces (PdNCP, D.T. 15).

# Chapter Six

# The Permanent Text: Constitutional Controls or Military Tutelage?

In August 1980, when the constitution was presented to the public, the charter could not be separated from its authoritarian origins and impact. The constitution had been imposed from above: Narrow, appointed bodies prepared preliminary materials behind closed doors; "the founders," four nonelected, military commanders, aided by their legal counsel, framed the final text; and the only participation citizens were allowed was to assent in a dubious plebiscite carried out amidst a state of emergency.[1] Similarly, the constitution did nothing to alter the dictatorial character of the regime: Despite some changes (discussed in the following chapter), the transitory dispositions left Pinochet in office as president for an eight-year term, gave him expanded repressive powers, and left the four-man military junta to legislate, as well as exercise other government functions. In its genesis and effects the 1980 constitution appeared as a masterwork of authoritarian constitution making: The main body structured a passable – if controversial – democratic edifice, while behind this façade the real structure of dictatorial power stood, braced by the authoritarian scaffolding of the transitory dispositions.[2]

This immediate effect occluded another dimension of the constitution: Its autocratic origins notwithstanding, the main body of the constitution was never intended to organize an authoritarian regime. Contrary to the conventional wisdom, the constitution was crafted neither to assure continuity in power beyond the transitory period nor

---

[1] On the ratification of the constitution and opposition criticisms of the process, see above, note 8, page 172.

[2] Initial appraisals of the constitution, consequently, wrote the document off as a cover for continued dictatorship. See, for example, Pérez Tremps 1984 and Schäfer 1984. Schäfer's critique is particularly off the mark, since many of the precepts he targets for criticism are not innovations introduced by the 1980 constitution but long-standing features of presidential government in Chile.

to grant the armed forces a permanent place from which to dominate civilian politics. The concept of constitutional safeguards set into the 1980 charter was institutional, not tutelary – as Guzmán was wont to insist the constitutional order was to be "self-protected," secured by organs internal to the political-institutional regime, not by an external guardian, such as the armed forces.

In this chapter I bring this hazy dimension of the constitution into focus. First, the concordance of the final text and the two preliminary drafts is examined to validate the relevance of the Constituent Commission's deliberations. Then the basic legal-ideological assumptions of the regime's civilian constitutional advisors are discussed. After which the institutional logic behind the 1980 constitution's most significant departures from the 1925 text are examined, in particular the motivations for introducing a partially, nonelectorally generated Senate, for augmenting the separation of powers with additional organs of constitutional control, and for limiting presidential authority to alter the chain of command within the armed forces – provisions which have led some to argue that the 1980 constitution structures a military-dominated regime.

## Two Drafts and a Constitution

As I have already intimated, any explication of the "original intent" of the military founders is made difficult by the lack of any record of the Junta's final drafting in July 1980. This lacuna was intentional. To expedite progress the Junta decided not to work through the regular procedures of the legislative commissions and to instead constitute a special, joint working group to prepare the final draft.[3] Consequently, the rich documentation routinely generated by the Secretary of Legislation and the Legislative Commissions was never produced. The same desire to expedite progress also led the Junta to work without the tape recorders running to facilitate a looser, more fluid exchange. As a result there are no minutes of the final deliberations and decision making on the constitution.[4] According to the participants in the final drafting, the

[3] In November 1977 the Constituent Commission proposed that its projects go directly to the Junta instead of through the system of legislative commissions (AOCC, 1793). According to then Secretary of Legislation Rear Adm. (J) Mario Duvauchelle, processing the constitution according to the regular legislative procedure defined in D.L. No. 991 would have delayed the adoption of the constitution for two to three years. Interview with Rear Adm. (J) Mario Duvauchelle, Santiago, Chile, June 22, 1992.

[4] Interview with former Minister of the Interior Sergio Fernández, Santiago, Chile, March 26, 1993.

preliminary final draft was drawn up by a special working group composed of the relevant cabinet ministers, the Secretary of Legislation, and the chief counsel of each service. On a chapter-by-chapter basis, in daily afternoon sessions, agreements were hammered out, and then presented to the Junta for review and decision the following morning. The main text was prepared independently of any work on the transitory articles, which were drawn up subsequently and separately.[5]

Despite the lack of materials documenting deliberations at the final stage of constitution making, a close comparison of the text adopted and the two preliminary drafts reveals that the Junta's modifications were not so consequential as to undermine the value of the existing documentation as a source for making sense of the institutional strategy behind the charter – notwithstanding many changes, the Junta maintained the basic organization and structure of powers as first defined by the Constituent Commission. The commanders in chief and their legal counsel adopted a number of secondary modifications suggested by the Council of State,[6] dropped some clauses advocated in both drafts,[7] and – with one or two significant exceptions – limited their

---

[5] Interviews with Rear Adm. (J) Mario Duvauchelle, Santiago, Chile, June 19, 1992; Gen. (J) Fernando Lyon, Santiago, Chile, November 23, 1992; and Sergio Fernández, Santiago, Chile, January 25, 1993. The participants in the special working group were: the Minister of the Interior, Sergio Fernández; the Minister of Justice, Mónica Madariaga; the Secretary of the Presidency, Gen. Santiago Sinclair; the Secretary of Legislation, Navy Captain (J) Mario Duvauchelle; and the *auditor* (chief counsel) for each service. The *auditores* were Army General (J) Fernando Lyon, Adm. (J) Aldo Montagna, Air Force General (J) Enrique Montero Marx, and *carabinero* Lieutenant Colonel (J) Harry Grunwald.

[6] In addition to a number of suggested changes in redaction, the Junta accepted the Council of State's recommendations to: retain eighteen as the voting age instead of raising it to twenty-one; require presidents to be at least forty years of age; maintain a regionally based Senate rather than adopt the Constituent Commission's recommendation of a national Senate; and reserve to Congress, rather than the president, the authority to pardon individuals convicted by the Senate in a constitutional accusation.

[7] A phrase declaring the equal rights of men and women was excised from the guarantee of equality before the law (ART. 19, no. 2). The Junta did, however, restore the traditional reference to the absence of slavery in Chile and a slave's immediate emancipation upon treading Chilean soil, which Merino had championed as integral to this clause during the 1976 review of A.C. No. 3. Neither commission had preserved this phrase.

Similarly, the members of the Junta did not grant the judiciary broader powers to annul unconstitutional statutes, as was proposed by both bodies. Each had structured a mechanism of annulment to operate after three consecutive, uniform Supreme Court rulings of inapplicability. The Constituent Commission gave authority to rule on nullification to the Constitutional Tribunal (AdCP, ART. 88, no. 12), whereas in the Council of State's version the norm would cease to possess legal force once the Supreme Court gave public notice in the *Diario Oficial* (PdNCP, ART. 80). The armed forces instead retained the established *recurso de inaplicabilidad* with its limited effects (ART. 80).

modifications to the details of precepts.[8] Perhaps the most controversial deviation from the two drafts was to grant participation to the National Security Council in selecting two of the seven members of the Constitutional Tribunal (ART. 81). Another important departure was the Junta's decision to maintain the state's exclusive, inalienable monopoly over mining property.[9] Surprisingly, however, contrary to some expectations – though not inconsistent with positions already seen within the Junta – the commanders in chief did not ratify every institutional prerogative scripted into the preliminary drafts.[10] Even after these modifications, the 1980 constitution set in place the institutional design elaborated within the Constituent Commission. Consequently, the voluminous documentation of this group's deliberations stands as a major, relevant source for understanding the institutional logic inscribed in the new constitution.

## The Understanding of "Constitution"

From its inception, the members of the Constituent Commission took it for granted that the purpose of a new "Political Constitution of the Republic" – the proper name for the Chilean constitution – was to structure a representative, democratic, republican form of government, with explicit constitutional guarantees protecting individual rights, a system of separate and divided powers, and regular, periodic elections to both the presidency and Congress. Still, these lawyers did not equate recon-

[8] In a number of articles, adjectival quantities were altered, sometimes with regard to time schedules for events, other times to the duration of sanctions, or the years of professional experience or time out of office required to satisfy the qualifications for specific posts. For example, the sanction for individuals who contravened ART. 8 was doubled, qualifications for elected office were made more demanding, the paragraph on political parties of ART. 19, no. 15 (the right of association) was made more restrictive, and in three or four instances where the two preliminary drafts consigned the regulation of a precept to law, the Junta specified regulation by a *ley de quorum calificado*, which required a higher majority for enactment and modification.
[9] For one account of the controversy over copper and the constitution, see Fontaine 1988, 125–28.
[10] ART. 9 of both versions defined terrorism as violating natural law and granted military tribunals jurisdiction over terrorist crimes. In the constitution, the Junta retained the definition but excised the jurisdiction. A related provision in both drafts, in the chapter on the judiciary, included "military courts of any time [war or peace] when they take cognizance of offenses qualified by the law as terrorist behavior" among the special courts expressly exempted from Supreme Court directive, economic and correctional supervision (AdCP, ART. 85; PdNCP, ART. 79). The Junta also removed this exemption. Nonetheless, some scholars (Constable and Valenzuela 1991, 137) ascribe it to the constitution.

stitutionalization with a restoration of the 1925 constitution – the trauma of the 1972–1973 constitutional crisis had revealed too many fault lines for any of them to advocate rehabilitating the prior constitutional edifice. Nevertheless, despite their willingness to innovate, none of the members of the commission sought to break with the traditional principles that had structured democratic, presidential government in Chile. Perhaps due to their immersion in Chile's deeply legalistic political culture, these jurists understood the prior crisis as a demonstration of the inadequacy of particular institutional mechanisms and not a failure of the general principles of democracy or constitutionalism.

This distinction between mechanisms and principles marked the line separating a conservative constitutionalist position from an extreme right antidemocratic position. The latter interpreted the *Unidad Popular* experience as the inescapable consequence of democracy and held that to restore democracy, even with modifications, was to invite a repeat performance of the Left in power. From this perspective, nationalist–far right ideologues were critical of the Constituent Commission's orientation from the outset, particularly after the appearance of the commission's preliminary memorandum presented to the Junta in late 1973.[11] A few years later, in both the Constituent Commission and the Council of State, one or two members would argue against universal suffrage; however, these positions were never influential. In the Constituent Commission, Raúl Bertelsen advocated that the president be elected by a restricted electoral body of a few thousand people (AOCC, 2081, 3217). In his view, universal suffrage was "dangerous for the stability of the democratic regime" (AOCC, 2270). During the Council of State's review of the Constituent Commission's draft proposal, Pedro Ibáñez and Carlos Cáceres consistently rejected the adoption of any system generated primarily through elections.

---

[11] Aside from one or two imprecise allusions to "organic" forms of participation, this statement of principles and anticipated institutional correctives was largely in line with previous constitutional reform proposals formulated by the conservative right. Note that Ortúzar, the president of the commission, had drafted one such project in the early sixties, when he served as Minister of Justice to President Jorge Alessandri Rodríguez. During a visit to the group in early 1974, Francisco Cumplido, later Minister of Justice in the first postmilitary government, commended the commission for its mainline democratic, constitutionalist orientation (AOCC, 24A, March 19, 1974, 10–13). The memorandum, "*Metas u objetivos fundamentales para la Nueva Constitución Política de la República*," is reprinted in Soto Kloss 1980, 11–31. For the nationalist far-right criticism, see the letter and article that Carlos Cruz-Coke sent to Pinochet in December 1973, reproduced in AOCC, 20, January 15, 1974, 10–13.

In a memorandum presented to the council in late March 1979, Ibáñez claimed that the commission's project "re-establishes the 1925 constitution" and as an alternative advocated what he described as an "autocratic" system, containing mechanisms of functional representation, which restricted the use of universal suffrage to the election of the Chamber of Deputies.[12] This proposal was met by severe criticism from all members of the council, except Cáceres. Carmona, who had been a member of the Constituent Commission, warned that the adoption of such a system would generate immediate pressure from democrats to put an end to the constitution structuring it, and this reaction, he thought, would assume violent forms since such actors would be without any channel of representation (AdCdE, vol. 1, 440). Former president González Videla openly qualified Ibáñez's proposal as "totalitarian and fascist," and insisted that its content be kept secret since any public diffusion would produce a severe national and international reaction (AdCdE, vol. 1, 440). At the following session, by a vote of 13 to 2 (Ibáñez and Cáceres), the council decided to table any further discussion of the proposal and consider its points only when they pertained to a specific norm under study (AdCdE, vol. 1, 460). Though Ibáñez and Cáceres insisted on their criticism of elections throughout the council's deliberations, they were consistently outvoted and at the end of the council's work on the constitution presented a joint minority opinion which reiterated their stance and presented Ibáñez's institutional proposals.[13]

Apart from these minority positions, in neither the Constituent Commission nor the Council of State was there any serious countenance of establishing authoritarian rule or a military-dominated order

---

[12] Deputies to the lower house, which was deliberately structured to overrepresent less populated provinces, were to be elected from single-member districts by absolute majority, with a second round. Senators, on the other hand, would not be directly elected but chosen by Regional Colleges composed of "no less than 200 nor no more than 1,500 persons who occupy the most important positions in the region." These positions were exclusively associated with professional associations, business and labor unions, education, and a variety of other social organizations. Similarly, Ibáñez advocated three alternate indirect methods of electing the president. These were selection by: (1) a restricted Council of the Republic composed of prominent figures; (2) election by a high quorum (67 to 75 percent) of the members of both Chambers, with the Council of State resolving by simple majority if the qualified majority was not reached; and (3) election by the Council of the Republic from among candidates proposed by no less than ten or twelve Senators. A copy of Ibáñez's memorandum is included in AdCdE, vol. 1, 447–58.

[13] See "Voto de Minoría en Informe Sobre Anteproyecto Constitucional," *El Mercurio*, July 10, 1980.

German constitutions (ART. 89, para. 5 and ART. 79, no. 3, respectively) to justify absolutely entrenching specific norms, such as ART. 8, by prohibiting their modification (AOCC, 2395, 2467, 2633–34). Guzmán was adamant that, unless entrenched, ART. 8 would be rescinded immediately by a civilian Congress (AOCC, 2466–67). To this end, the Constituent Commission's project contains a norm that declared inadmissable all bills aimed at modifying or circumventing the clause (AdCP, ART. 122, para. 2), which however was not adopted by the Junta.[18] Both ART. 8 and the attempt to entrench constitutional norms were departures from Chile's constitutional traditions, yet as the German and French constitutions demonstrated, such prohibitions and norms prohibiting their modification could be adopted without breaking with established conceptions of constitutionalism.

These assumptions about constitutionalism and democracy nonetheless left considerable room for argument. Not only were there recurrent schisms, early on, over the advisability of cooperating with the executive on contingent constitutional matters, but even after receiving the green light in March 1978, civilian advisors often divided over the scope of changes needed to secure democracy and to best structure specific institutional mechanisms. Unlike the Junta, however, decisions in both the Constituent Commission and Council of State were made by majority vote, and votes against specific precepts were common in both bodies.[19]

In addition to the variant positions within each advisory body, there were considerable differences between the Constituent Commission's

---

[18] Instead, the Junta followed the Council of State's recommendation, which combined a higher majority for reform with a delaying mechanism. Guzmán's fears about the fate of an unentrenched ART. 8 were confirmed during the transitory period. Following Pinochet's defeat in the October 5, 1988 plebiscite, ART. 8 was repealed using the far simpler procedure of T.D. 18 (unanimous Junta agreement, subject to plebiscitary approval) as part of the June 1989 constitutional reform package. The reforms did, however, regulate antisystem organizations and parties in a new paragraph appended to the precept on freedom of association (ART. 19, no. 15). This modification made for a clause much closer to the original German model.

[19] For example, the cornerstone of the future ART. 8 was approved by four votes against two (Evans and Silva Bascuñán). As Evans noted, he didn't oppose the objective of protecting democracy but the particular manner contained in the precept (AOCC, 243, August 11, 1976, 27–28). As is discussed later, Carmona unceasingly opposed the commission's decision to deny the president authority to remove the commanders in chief of the armed forces.

For record of dissenting votes within the Constituent Commission, the minutes have to be consulted. The Council of State's draft, on the other hand, identifies in footnotes dissenting votes on specific articles and, as already noted, Carlos Cáceres and Pedro Ibáñez presented an extensive dissenting opinion to the Council of State's final draft.

as the normal "constitutional" regime. Rather, the objective in e
body was to anchor the status quo by shoring up the first term in
binomial, "constitutional democracy." From this perspective, the fut
free play of democracy would be bounded and contained wit
enforceable constitutional limits. A conservative bias against any
of democratic institutions to alter property relations within society v
a central motivation behind these schemes of institutional reformu
tion. Nevertheless, the mechanisms envisaged for safeguarding
social and political status quo were internal to constitutionalism a
the rule of law. In fact, large portions of the 1980 constitution draw
the 1925 text, and many articles are verbatim carryovers.[14] Even a
cles that would be extremely controversial were perceived by comn
sion members to be consonant with democratic constitutional traditic
since models for many of them were provided by other democratic c
stitutions, particularly the French and German charters.[15]

Thus, the clause which became ART. 8 of the constitution, the c
stitutional ban on Marxist parties, was justified because a similar no
existed in the Basic Law of the Federal Republic of Germany.[16]
particular, members of the Constituent Commission referred to AF
9, 18, and 21, no. 2 of the Basic Law as providing a precedent
instituting a militant democracy equipped with internal mechanis
to defend the values consecrated by the constitution.[17] Similarly,
members of the Constituent Commission invoked the French a

---

[14] The commission, in fact, followed the 1925 constitution as a prototype. Constitut
of other states and the Universal Declaration of Human Rights were also on hand
comparative purposes.

[15] In addition to the ban on Marxist parties, inspired by the German constitution,
French constitution of 1958 (in particular, ARTS. 34 and 37) provided the model
adopting in ART. 60 of the 1980 constitution a maximum domain of law which lim
Congress's lawmaking powers to an enumerated list of matters of law.

[16] Given the number of references to ART. 8, I cite the gist of the precept:
Any action by an individual or group intended to propagate doctrines which
antagonistic to the family, or which advocate violence or a concept of society,
State, or the juridical order, of a totalitarian character or based on class strug
is illicit and contrary to the institutional order of the Republic.
The organizations and movements or political parties which, due to their aim
the activity of their adherents, tend towards these objectives are unconstitution
Additional paragraphs stipulated that the Constitutional Tribunal would try
infractions and specified sanctions for individuals declared in violation of the arti
Of these, a ten-year ban on public office, whether elected or otherwise, was of par
ular importance to the framers.

[17] Ortúzar mentioned the need for a provision similar to ART. 21 of the Basic Law at
very first meeting of the commission, and in latter sessions the German model v
referred to repeatedly (AOCC, 1, September 24, 1973, 10–11; 105, March 11, 1975,
128, June 10, 1975, 18, 21; 240, August 3, 1976, 6; 2083, 2085, 2088, 2205, 235

2

*anteproyecto* (draft project) and the Council of State's revision. Although the Council of State accepted some departures from the 1925 text, such as the introduction of prior limits on political pluralism, the second round for presidential elections, and a set of nonelected members in the Senate, in essence the council majority stripped the commission's draft of its more novel features to produce a text much closer to the 1925 charter. The more significant changes away from the Constituent Commission's draft included: lowering the voting age from twenty-one back to eighteen years of age; shortening the presidential term from eight back to the traditional six years; maintaining the traditional minimal specification of matters of law (which nonrestrictively indicated matters that could be regulated only by statute) rather than adopting the so-called maximum domain of law recommended by the commission (this system exhaustively specifies the province of legislation, leaving all other matters to regulation by executive decree and, thus, greatly amplifies the regulatory powers of the president); reinstating ART. 22 of the 1925 constitution's description of the armed forces as "essentially professional, hierarchical, disciplined, obedient and non-deliberative"; restoring full authority to the president to appoint and remove the commander in chief of each service; reinstating five cabinet ministers to the National Security Council to retain a political majority (eight civilians, five officers); lowering the majority required to amend the constitution back to an absolute majority of all deputies and senators; and excising the precept declaring inadmissible all projects of constitutional reform that would derogate ART. 8.[20]

Most of the changes proposed by the Council of State, as already noted, were not adopted by the Junta, which with only a few exceptions stuck closely to the Constituent Commission's recommendations. Of particular importance to Jorge Alessandri, the council's president, had been the council's proposal for a five-year transitory period with

---

[20] The Council of State did, however, advocate multiple amendment procedures to assure a more rigid constitution, particularly to encumber attempts by Congress to augment its powers relative to the executive. Thus, the council accepted the Constituent Commission proposal that a two-thirds majority of all deputies and senators be required to modify the use of the plebiscite in the process of constitutional reform, to increase the powers of Congress, or to diminish those of the president. The Council further introduced an innovation of its own: Any modification to the dogmatic principles in Chapter One had to be approved by a two-thirds majority in two successive congresses. This delaying mechanism was retained in ART. 118 of the 1980 constitution and extended to additionally encompass Chapters Seven, Ten, and Eleven (Constitutional Tribunal; Armed Forces, of Order and Public Security; and National Security Council, respectively).

a designated Congress, which as I discussed in the preceding chapter was incompatible with the collegial nature of the dictatorship. On a number of occasions during the council's deliberations, Alessandri made it clear that he held few illusions that the council's recommendations would carry much weight with the military government, and on August 12, 1980, four days after receiving the Junta's final draft of the constitution, Alessandri gave the council's secretary a sealed letter containing his resignation and instructions that it be delivered to Pinochet should the outcome of the plebiscite favor the Junta's constitution. The day after the plebiscite, Alessandri's resignation was reported in the press. Though at the time Alessandri told reporters that he resigned for personal reasons, in a letter read in the council in May 1981, Alessandri explained that his sole motive for resigning was his disagreement with the modifications affected by the Junta.[21]

## Binding the Future Out of Fear of the Past

Aside from a handful of precepts devised to rectify problems revealed by the experience of military rule,[22] the vast majority of the new institutional modifications introduced by the 1980 constitution were designed looking backwards. The most significant innovations upon the 1925 constitution included: a constitutional ban on antisystem parties, administered by the Constitutional Tribunal (ART. 8); more meticulous, almost regulatory, specification of rights guaranteed by the constitution; a second round for presidential elections, and a switch to concurrent elections; a strengthened executive, with expanded regulatory powers, greater autonomy from the Senate in appointments, and power to dissolve the lower house of congress once each term (though not during the year preceding congressional elections); nonelectoral generation of slightly less than one-third of the Senate; a more powerful Constitutional Tribunal, with nonpolitical organs appointing the majority of its members; elevation to constitutional rank of the *Contraloría*'s authority to exercise prior legal and constitutional review

---

[21] AdCdE, vol. 2, 273. For Alessandri's comments discounting any influence upon the military, see AdCdE, vol. 1, 495; vol. 2, 175. Later, during the 1982–1983 economic crisis, Alessandri regained prominence as the pole around which sectors of the traditional Right reorganized.

[22] The Junta constitutionalized a number of issues pertaining to emergency powers which had been matters of jurisprudence. These included expressly excepting military tribunals in time of war from Supreme Court supervision (ART. 79), a matter of considerable controversy in 1974, and expressly prohibiting any judicial review of the merit of the executive's specific use of emergency powers (ART. 41, no. 3).

of executive decrees; restrictions on the president's authority to confer the highest ranks among officers of the armed forces, and the denial of any authority to remove commanders in chief (except in qualified circumstances); the constitutionalization of a National Security Council, composed of a military majority, with authority to represent its opinion to any authority on matters deemed to gravely undermine the institutional order or threaten national security; and the requirement of a higher three-fifths majority of all members of Congress to enact modifications to the constitution and of an even higher two-thirds absolute majority in two successive congresses to amend expressly entrenched chapters. Each of these changes was inspired by a desire to correct what were perceived to be institutional deficiencies of the 1925 constitution. In fact, the retrospective motivation was so strong that any number of these changes can literally be dated to specific conflicts that emerged during the 1960s and early 1970s.

The imprint of the Allende experience upon the process of institutional design within the Constituent Commission cannot be overstated. With all their training in the intricacies of the law and its manipulation, during the Allende years the jurists who later would compose the Constituent Commission witnessed a startling and profound reversal. During the years 1971–1973, these "men of law" saw a government of the Left shrewdly take hold of legality and the constitution and turn them against the status quo.[23] Given the formal legality of Allende's policies, these lawyers and politicians could do little but witness (or contribute to) the destruction of the very legal and constitutional order which they held so dear as the rules of the game themselves increasingly became the object of irresolvable conflicts among Congress and the executive.

This trauma is at the foundation of the 1980 constitution in at least two ways. First, the ongoing political and constitutional crisis of 1972–1973 powerfully laid bare gaps in the institutional system which allowed severe conflicts to emerge, escalate into confrontations among powers, and spiral without remedy within the constitutional order.

---

[23] The literature on the Chilean road to socialism and its violent capitalist dénouement is far too voluminous to cite anything but a handful of works most relevant to this discussion. Silva Cimma's history (1977) of the first Constitutional Tribunal is unequaled as a legal analysis of the constitutional conflicts of the period. For an elaboration of the political strategy, as well as an analysis of the political dynamics frustrating its implementation, see Garcés 1976. Novoa Monreal (1978, 1992), the mastermind behind the *Unidad Popular* legal strategy, convincingly defends the formal legality of Allende's policies. Bitar (1979) provides a careful analysis of the interrelationship (and disjuncture) between the government's economic policy and its political strategy.

These "problem areas" were the focus of extensive scrutiny, and virtually all of the seeds of the crisis were regulated in the 1980 constitution. Though commission members sought to avoid an overly detailed constitution, they were willing to concede concision for extension if it meant closing a gap in the constitutional framework.[24] Second, while the trauma of the Allende period revealed to the Center and Right the fragility of the existing order, the particular form of the crisis – the fact that the threat to their stations emerged from within, through elections and legality – was repeatedly revisited when evaluating potential institutional devices and came to be perceived as a constraint on the types of correctives that were viable. For, despite the extreme concentration of constituent power within the military junta, the members of the Constituent Commission could not disallow that a similar structure of political competition and conflict as in the past might reemerge, even under a constitutional democracy of their own design. This anticipation of a possible return of past political alignments fundamentally shaped the strategy of institutional design which emerged in the Constituent Commission.

The commission's assimilation of the past, however, was neither straightforward nor heavy-handed – the logic of institutional design appeared only gradually out of the interplay of different perspectives and arguments among the commission members. At the core of this approach was an acknowledgment of the intrinsically uncertain character of electoral outcomes. The commission members came to realize that regardless of changes aimed at recasting the composition and weight of political forces, there was no guarantee that future elections would always be won by pro status quo parties. This insight was central to the design of institutions: The immediate relations of power under authoritarian rule could not, therefore, merely be transposed to the future constitutional order in the form of inordinate or repressive powers, since there always remained the risk that in the future such powers might be turned against the very forces who set them in place. During the discussion of specific precepts, the commission members often came to this point only after first being tempted by facile solutions that usually involved granting expanded or arbitrary authority to the president. On many such occasions, a commission member would

---

[24] The earlier crisis provided a principle of inclusion for Guzmán. In his words, "when discerning which norms should have constitutional rank, one should study with special care whether it is one of those points in which our democracy to greater extent went into crisis. In these cases it is indispensable that they be consecrated in the constitutional text" (AOCC, 2206–7).

remind the group to put themselves in "the case of a normal regime with a civilian president" or "think of a political government." Invariably, it was sufficient for one member to raise the apprehensive counterfactual, "What if Allende . . . ?" to force the debate toward a different tack. One example of this logic can be seen in the formulation of the controversial institution of designated senators.

### The Designated Senators

The constitution as promulgated by the Junta in 1980 institutes a partially nonelected Senate. In addition to provision for two directly elected senators for each of Chile's thirteen regions, ART. 45 integrates to the Senate nine designated members and by right all ex-presidents who served six continuous years in office.[25] Except for former presidents, who hold their seats for life, the designated Senators, like their popularly elected counterparts, serve an eight-year term. Although it has often been asserted that these designated members are appointed by the president or by Pinochet, this is not the case. The president designates two senators, who must hold specific professional qualifications (one former university dean and one former Minister of State); in successive votes, the Supreme Court elects three senators (two former Supreme Court justices and one former *Contralor*), and the National Security Council elects four senators (one former commander in chief from each service and one former director general of *carabineros*).[26] This selection of the designated senators by multiple organs was deliberately conceived by the Constituent Commission to avoid granting excessive powers to the president.

The possibility of designing a Senate with elected and nonelected members arose within the Constituent Commission out of a concern to introduce to Congress a source of moderation detached from immediate party politics. The issue first arose in early 1977 during a debate regarding the future of the Council of State.[27] As mentioned in Chapter

---

[25] The June 1989 constitutional reform modified this article to increase the number of elected senators to thirty-eight. The reformed article effected this increase by mandating the organic constitutional law regulating Congress to divide six regions into two senatorial districts each, thereby creating an additional twelve seats.

[26] All potential candidates for designation must also have served two continuous years in the respective position or office.

[27] The issue at hand was whether the Council of State's approval should be required for the designation of the *Contralor General de la República*. For this initial discussion on designated senators, see AOCC, 1709–35.

4, as part of its efforts to improve its international image, the Junta in late December 1975 created a Council of State as a civilian advisory body to the president. This council harked back to an earlier Council of State with broader obligatory advisory powers which had existed up until the adoption of the 1925 constitution. In the commission, the council was viewed as a model for an institution that would give a position of influence to individuals with extensive experience in high state positions but little likelihood of being elected. The idea as it emerged within the commission was to integrate to Congress a similar set of individuals and thereby introduce a minority who would represent the more permanent interests of the state rather than immediate, contingent party politics. These individuals were to be "exponents of the highest qualities of republican life" and therefore did not include representatives of corporate interests or knowledge (AOCC, 2110).

This debate over the Council of State stimulated the first discussions concerning whether to institute a unicameral or bicameral Congress, which in turn were driven by the Commission's critical evaluation of the pre-1973 Senate. As a number of members of the commission noted, on paper the 1925 constitution differentiated the powers of the Senate and structured a chamber of greater hierarchy with many of the functions formerly exercised by the Council of State, yet in practice the Senate after 1925 evolved into a body just as political as the lower house and eventually it became the center of political debate.[28] Although this practical identity of the two chambers recommended a shift to a unicameral body, a single chamber was argued to be disadvantageous. Carmona, for example, objected that a single chamber would have to be large and a large body would inevitably produce deficient legislation in need of revision, as had been the experience with the pre-1973 Chamber of Deputies, yet without the benefit of a second chamber capable of effecting these improvements (AOCC, 1714). To overcome this defect, Guzmán, who along with Ortúzar had been an early advocate of a unicameral legislature, spoke of a small single chamber with about fifty deputies, thirty-five of whom would be popularly elected and the remainder chosen by some nonelectoral process. However, as he recognized, national and international public opinion might view such a composition as excessively closed and give rise to strong pressure to adopt a more representative system (AOCC, 1723). This prudential consideration led Guzmán to shift toward favoring a bicameral congress with a Senate that would be differentiated

---

[28] For this evaluation of the Senate, see AOCC, 1710, 1714, 1716–17, 1721–22, 1728.

from the lower house not only in its powers but also by its national and mixed manner of generation: Unlike the regionally based Senate under the 1925 constitution, the elected members of the reformed Senate would be elected from a single national district and approximately one-third of the total Senators would be nonelected.[29]

When in early April 1978 the commission eventually opted for a bicameral congress, the question became the qualifications for and mode of selection of the nonelected members of the Senate, and it was at this point that the principle of moderation that stood behind much of the commission's institutional design came into play. The initial conception was to form a senate made up of thirty elected and about fifteen or sixteen nonelected members. Aside from the former presidents who would serve by right,[30] the commission at first conceived of the remaining nonelected senators as presidential appointees, with seven being directly appointed by the president and six or so others being designated upon recommendation by other organs. Of the direct appointees, four would be selected from among individuals satisfying particular qualifications of experience in specific public positions and three were to be freely chosen by the president (AOCC, 2110–11).

In the ensuing debate, the predominance of the president quickly became the object of criticism and led to a modification of this composition and manner of selection. The issue became whether the object of the institution was to strengthen the position of the president in the Senate or to allow individuals with experience in the state to influence the body's deliberations. A few minutes after Bertelsen noted that under such an arrangement the Senate would be incapable of moderating the president, Carmona adamantly expressed his opposition to having senators designated by the president and invoked the specter of Allende to buttress his argument against thus granting the president absolute preeminence in Congress. He reminded the commission, "the crisis suffered during the 1970–1973 triennial was due to bad performance of duties by the president of the republic and the government team. It is inconceivable to elaborate a constitution that closes off the possibility of confronting a similar danger" (AOCC, 2129).

In response to Ortúzar's reply that the concept behind the earlier constitution was distinct, Carmona asked if any of the other members

[29] As noted earlier, the Constituent Commission's recommendation of a national Senate was not adopted by the Junta.

[30] At the time of these discussions, three ex-presidents were alive: Gabriel González Videla, Jorge Alessandri Rodríquez, and Eduardo Frei Montalva. All three were deceased by the time the constitution came into full force in March 1990.

could assure him that a similar crisis would not occur in the future or that such an institution would not lead to presidential totalitarianism. Once Díez concurred (AOCC, 2130) that the idea was not to strengthen a presidential majority but to configure a "moderating third of a majority," the commission began to work out a different composition with appointments by multiple organs and groups – the Supreme Court, former Ministers of Foreign Relations, former presidents of the Chamber of Deputies, and acting deans of state and recognized universities. One former commander in chief of each armed force, as well as one former director general of *carabineros*, were also to enter the Senate, though after an initial proposition that these be selected by the acting commanders it was decided that these seats would not be selected but would go to the most recent retiree.[31]

In the end, in addition to former presidents who would enter the senate by right, the commission proposed a total of twelve nonelected senators alongside thirty popularly elected senators: the president would designate four senators, each of whom corresponded to a specific office; four others would be selected by functionaries who had served or were serving in the same position as those eligible for designation; and four would fall to the commanders in chief and the director general of *carabineros* who had most recently left their posts at the moment of designation.[32] Unlike the eventual norm adopted in the constitution the commission proposed that, in contrast to popularly elected senators, the designated senators serve a four-year term instead of an eight-year term (AdCP, ART. 51, para. 5).

---

[31] Carmona opposed the integration of retired officers to the Senate (AOCC, 2132). Contrary to the later experience with designated senators, Díez thought that the presence of retired military officers in the Senate would not be controversial, ". . . in a Senate of forty and so many persons the presence of four ex-commanders in chief will not be disproportionate, above all if you consider that they will be men who no longer command troops; that they will be highly respectable persons with considerable experience, in addition to being persons marginalized from political contingencies" (AOCC, 2132).

[32] In the commission's proposal the president appointed one former *Contralor* (with the agreement of the Chamber of Deputies), two former Ministers of State who had served under a prior presidency, and one former ambassador who had also served under a prior presidency. The remaining designated senators were to be appointed by a somewhat eclectic set of electors: The Supreme Court would elect one former president of the Supreme Court; former Foreign Ministers would select one former Foreign Minister; the deans of public universities and universities recognized by the state would select one former dean; and the Chamber of Deputies would select one former president of the Chamber of Deputies (AdCP, ART. 51, para. 4).

The Council of State, on the other hand, reverted to nine designated senators, all appointed by the president, alongside thirty-two elected senators.[33] Former president González Videla was the sole critic of the institution from a democratic perspective. He had been a member of the Congress designated by Ibáñez in 1927 and felt that it would be a mistake for former presidents to put their prestige at risk by entering a body in which the elected senators would feel themselves the only authorized members with a "patent" of legitimacy (AdCdE, vol. 1, 482). Otherwise the council debate touched on many of the same points as in the commission. Carmona, who along with Ortúzar was a member of both bodies, reiterated many of his earlier points against creating an institution that would allow the president to dominate the Senate. These arguments led to initial acceptance of a proposal to decrease the number of presidential appointments to two and to allow the elected members of the Senate to designate three senators as a counterweight to the presidential appointments (AdCdE, vol. 2, 38–40). This tack was later abandoned after one member noted that the elected senators might fail to elect their corresponding senators in protest against the composition of the Senate and the constitutional structure as a whole (AdCdE, vol. 2, 60). This led the council to shift back to appointments by the president, but with the stipulation that none of the nonelected senators would be authorized to vote on any constitutional accusation brought before the upper house (PdNCP, Art. 49).

In the final drafting, in addition to former presidents, the Junta went even further than the Constituent Commission and limited the president to appointing two of the nine designated senators.[34] Notwithstanding the many claims to the contrary, the record clearly reveals that the institution of designated senators was not designed to allow Pinochet to influence the composition of the senate but was devised in view of a future civilian regime. Here, as with so many other institutional innovations contained in the constitution, the anticipation that the presidency might be occupied by a candidate not of the Right led

---

[33] PdNCP, Art. 45, para. 5. Designated senators were discussed in the Council of State in Sessions 75, 76, 79, and 82 on May 29, 1979, June 12, 1979, July 3, 1979, July 24, 1979, respectively.

[34] The president appoints one former dean and one former Minister of Foreign Relations. The Supreme Court elects in successive votes two former justices and also elects a former comptroller general. The National Security Council elects one ex-commander in chief from each branch and a former director general of *carabineros* (Art. 45, para. 3).

to moderation and caution so as not to grant undue and unchecked powers to the president.

## Organs of Constitutional Control: The *Controlaría* and the *Tribunal Constitucional*

The ghost of Allende thus spawned a logic of extreme constitutionalism given to emplacing greatly reinforced individual guarantees, a system of multiple checks and balances, and moderation in defining the powers of control organs. The goal was not to undermine state power along neoliberal lines but to anticipate every potential source of "abuse" of power and meet each with a mechanism of counterbalance. In line with a trend in Chilean constitutional reforms, the 1980 constitution strengthened the relative power of the president over Congress,[35] yet it also erected numerous ramparts to contain the president from overstepping her constitutional authority. Thus, in addition to the traditional checks and balances between powers (the presidential veto, congress's powers of impeachment, judicial review), which after the 1972–1973 experience appeared to be of dubious efficacy, the commission sought to secure the constitution with a second line of extrapolitical organs of legal and constitutional control, the principal being the *Contraloría General de la República* and the *Tribunal Constitutional*, with the constitutional court standing as the supreme organ of decision in the event of constitutional conflicts among powers. A third line of defense, the National Security Council, was set in the background to signal extreme situations. All of these bodies had existed prior to the coup, though the earlier security council was not of constitutional rank. In the 1980 constitution the powers and composition of each were

---

[35] These changes in the relationship between the president and Congress are analyzed in Cea 1985 and Evans 1990. Nogueira (1984) maintains that given the president's power to dissolve the lower house of Congress once a term (ART. 32, no. 5), the 1980 constitution defined a form of government beyond the canons of a presidential regime, and considered the 1980 presidency to be a case of "authoritarian presidentialism." Shugart and Carey (1992, 129) also hold that this power disqualifies Chile from being classified as a presidential regime. They prefer the appellation "super-presidential." Confusingly, Shugart and Carey (1992, 126, 129, 141, 154) refer repeatedly to the "1989 constitution of Chile." If this is their way of referring to the text as modified by the reforms of that year, they commit the egregious error of not noting that ART. 32, no. 5, the power to dissolve the lower chamber, was deleted as part of the reform package and existed only in the unreformed 1980 constitution. It is interesting to note that the power to dissolve congress was among a set of constitutional reforms devised by advisors to Allende in late 1970 (Garcés 1976, 219).

subject to modification in light of loopholes and gaps revealed in the course of the 1972–1973 crisis.

Of these organs, the *Contraloría*, whose powers were discussed in Chapter 3, was the least subject to change. Whereas formerly the *Contraloría* occupied only a single article in the chapter on constitutional guarantees, the 1980 constitution dedicated a complete chapter to the institution and elevated the prior review of the legality and constitutionality of executive decrees, the *toma de razón*, to constitutional rank. These changes were essentially a means to entrench the organ's existent powers before legislative modification and to provide a setting to regulate the president's power to override a *Contraloría* determination that an executive decree was illegal or unconstitutional.

Prior to 1980, with the signature of every cabinet member a president could force the *Contraloría* to accept a decree whose legality or constitutionality had been questioned. In these cases, the president and his cabinet were responsible for any legal or constitutional infractions, and by ART. 21, para. 4 of the 1925 constitution the *Contraloría* was obliged to submit to the Chamber of Deputies a copy of the decree that the president insisted go into force. This would allow the lower house to decide whether to initiate a constitutional accusation against the president.[36] Though the 1980 constitution retains the *decreto de insistencia*, ART. 88 prohibits its use when the constitutionality of a government decree has been represented by the *Contraloría*. In these instances the president may raise objections to the constitutional court, which is empowered to decide the controversy. This modification harks back to the conflicts over Allende's use of the *decreto de insistencia* to requisition firms over the representations of the *Contraloría*.[37]

By safeguarding the *Contraloría*'s review powers from statutory modification and by restricting the use of the override, the commission sought to set a stronger defense against any president sidestepping congress by putting properly statutory rules into force by executive decree.

---

[36] President Carlos Ibáñez del Campo's liberal use of the *decreto de insistencia*, sixty-five in four years, to effect unlawful appointments and expenditures was one of the principal motivations for the November 1956 constitutional accusation against him (Loveman and Lira 2000).

[37] Héctor Humeres, then *Contralor*, informed the Constituent Commission in 1977 that President Jorge Alessandri had insisted upon two decrees, Eduardo Frei about twenty, and Allende some ninety-seven decrees (AOCC, 1397). Allende's "misuse" of the instrument was discussed at length within the commission (AOCC, 1397, 1407, 1419, 1428–30, 1594–1603). For the controversy over Allende's use of the decree of insistence more generally, compare Soto Kloss 1972, 1974; and Silva Cimma 1977, 158–69, 172–74, 199–202.

However, the *Tribunal Constitucional* stands as the highest organ of constitutional control in the 1980 constitution. In Guzmán's words, the constitutional court is the "grand power of ordinary security of the constitution" (AOCC, 2350). Similarly, in line with the Constituent Commission's recommendations, the Junta only slightly modified the powers of the earlier *Tribunal Constitucional*, and most of the changes to the institution concerned the manner of appointing justices to the court. Again the impetus was retrospective.

The earlier court, established by constitutional reform in January 1970 and in operation from September 1971, in the course of its short life quickly became embroiled in the escalating conflicts over the constitutionality of Allende government acts. In May 1973, at the height of the crisis, the court declared itself without authority to hear the central constitutional controversy of the period – the procedural dispute between the government and Congress over Allende's veto of the Hamilton-Fuentealba constitutional reforms which required that all expropriations of private property be effected by law.[38]

Members of the commission attributed the court's earlier failure to the political appointment of a majority of its five members. Three were designated by the president *with* Senate approval, while the other two were selected by the justices of the Supreme Court from among themselves in a single secret vote. In adopting this perspective, the members of the Constituent Commission were echoing the polemics of 1971–1973. At the time, in response to the many court decisions that ratified government interpretations, the opposition began to impugn the judicial character of the tribunal and insisted upon a distinction between "judicial ministers" and "political ministers," with the latter being portrayed as representatives of the president. Notwithstanding the considerable evidence against this view, particularly that on only one occasion – and only with regard to one point in the one decision – did the three members designated by the president ever form a

---

[38] The constitutional controversy concerned the congressional majority required to override a presidential veto of a constitutional reform. The opposition parties in Congress held that a majority of the members in office in each chamber was sufficient. Allende, on the other hand, insisted that a two-thirds majority of those present was required for Congress to insist that the reform originally approved be promulgated. The constitutional court declared itself without authority to settle this issue because ART. 78, para. b, of the 1925 constitution expressly empowered the tribunal only to resolve constitutional questions that arose during the enactment of laws and treaties, without any mention of constitutional reforms. For a detailed account of the constitutional and political issues involved in the controversy over the Hamilton-Fuentealba reforms and the requisition of private property more generally, see Silva Cimma 1977, 167–206.

majority against the two Supreme Court justices (Silva Cimma 1977, 65), the commission insisted upon decreasing the relative weight of political appointments.[39]

In a typical example of their predilection for decision by jurists – when not by judges – in oversight and control bodies, the commission increased the role of the Supreme Court in designating members. The objective was to form a court composed of individuals given to ruling like judges, from a juridical, not political, standpoint. To this end, the president was restricted to appointing one lawyer who was or had been a lawyer integrating the Supreme Court, and the Senate appointed another lawyer with the same qualifications. To increase the weight of the Supreme Court the commission added an additional supreme court justice to the court (raising their number to three) and had the court select two other appointments. All three were to be elected by successive, secret votes.[40] Furthermore, the commission augmented the already demanding qualifications that lawyers had to satisfy to be eligible for appointment (AOCC, 2338–40). By increasing the size of the court from five to seven, the commission sought to provide greater stability to the court's jurisprudence, as in the larger court a shift in one member's opinion was less likely to lead to a shift in the majority (AOCC, 2348).

The Junta, in probably the most controversial change to the two proposals, modified the composition recommended by the Constituent Commission (and ratified by the Council of State) so that the National Security Council instead of the Supreme Court designated two ministers. These appointments still had to satisfy the same qualifications required of political appointments, which meant that despite a military majority in the National Security Council an officer on active duty could not sit on the court. ART. 81, among other qualifications, requires that the lawyer selected by the National Security Council, like the appointees chosen by the president and the senate, have at least fifteen years of experience. Within the armed forces the only potential candidates

---

[39] Silva Cimma (1977, 44–48, 64–69, 213–16), the court's only president, convincingly refutes the charge that ministers "represented" the bodies that designated them. In addition to the voting record, he stresses the participation of the Senate in the confirmation of the president's appointments, the constitution's requirement that candidates be lawyers, with at least twelve years of professional experience and no antecedents which would disqualify them from appointment as a regular judge, as well as the fact that the constitutional court ruled according to law.

[40] This stipulation of successive votes was intended to assure that the Supreme Court nominees to the constitutional court represented the overall court and not the two first majorities (AOCC, 2348).

capable of satisfying this requirement are officers from one of the justice services. However, even in this extreme case, the officer appointed would have to resign from active service, as a seat on the tribunal is incompatible with other paid state employment (ART. 81 and 55).

Since the constitutional court came to play a major role in structuring the return to democracy – it was activated once the constitution went into force on March 11, 1981 – the powers of the *Tribunal Constitucional* will be discussed at length in the following chapter. For now, I should note that in addition to adjusting the court's powers to accommodate new institutions created by the constitution (resolving on infractions to ART. 8, mandatory a priori review of all organic constitutional laws, and deciding any conflicts between the president and the *Contraloría*), the previous constitutional ambiguities which had led the first constitutional court to throw up its hands, as well as the substance of the procedural matter in dispute, were both clarified in the new constitution.[41]

The structuring of these bodies, somewhat surprisingly, was guided by a logic of moderation. Again, this approach was arrived at only in the course of ongoing deliberation and argument over specific institutions, and, though often unstated, the Constituent Commission returned to this logic repeatedly when reviewing and specifying the powers of each organ of legal or constitutional control, as well as when structuring the National Security Council and the constitutional status of the armed forces. With regard to these last organs, the logic of institutional design differed somewhat from that which emerged in the design of designated senators. In these instances, the guiding concern was not mistrust of how the powers conferred might be used, but a desire to protect the institutions bearing them from demands for their suppression or modification. In its general form, the resulting logic was

---

[41] Among the matters that may be referred to the court, ART. 82, no. 2 expressly includes projects of constitutional reform when constitutional controversies arise in the course of their enactment. As already noted, the earlier norm mentioned only projects of law and treaties, which led the earlier constitutional court to declare itself incompetent to settle the central constitutional conflict of the Allende years over the quorum required to override a presidential veto of a constitutional reform. ART. 117, para. 6, of the 1980 constitution now sets this quorum at a two-thirds majority *of the members in office* of each chamber. This quorum is even more demanding than that defended by Allende. Should Congress satisfy this quorum and override a veto of a constitutional reform, the same norm also gives the president the option of calling a plebiscite to decide the questions in disagreement.

one of restraint: The constitution should not grant veto powers over – or even involvement in – quotidian political matters to organs whose purpose is to uphold constitutional supremacy or protect the institutional order. The commission members feared that institutions with broad powers would by their actions provoke and be dragged into controversies with political bodies. The specter was a gratuitous politicization of the organs created to defend the constitutional order, which might generate demands for reform and ultimately weaken them.

In April 1977, during ongoing work on the judiciary, Sergio Díez first developed this reasoning as he argued against a proposal to grant the Supreme Court power to nullify unconstitutional statutes – a longstanding aspiration among Chilean legal scholars (Ribera Neumann 1987, 80–87). Díez argued that such power, which had never existed in Chile, would place the court on a collision course with Congress and the president and would lead to campaigns to modify the court's powers if the president enjoyed strong backing in Congress. Díez (AOCC, 986) insisted, "To give this power to the Supreme Court in a country with as active a political life as Chile implies implicating the court in one manner or another in the political struggle."[42]

The fear was that any creation of a "superpower" above others would have the effect of shifting political conflict toward that power, and thereby would undermine any authority the organ might possess as an arbiter. Particularly in regard to the National Security Council and the armed forces, the commission members were driven by horror of their worst-case scenario: institutional conflict, crisis, and breakdown, followed by splits within the armed forces, and civil war culminating in revolution. The point was to assure bodies capable of resolving and containing constitutional conflicts to prevent them from developing into regime crises, not to foster them. On this principle, after extended debates, the Constituent Commission eschewed a number of powers proposed for the *Tribunal Constitucional* and the *Consejo de Seguridad Nacional* (National Security Council) and the concern to secure this system of controls was behind the commission's unprecedented limitation of the president's authority to intervene in the respective chains of command of the armed forces.

---

[42] In the end, however, the commission proposed a mechanism involving the Constitutional Tribunal in the decision to nullify. The Council of State also advocated judicial review with general effects, but neither innovation was accepted by the Junta. On these two proposals, see note 7, page 219.

## The Armed Forces and the National Security Council

The provisions the Junta enacted concerning the armed forces and the National Security Council, contained in Chapters 10 and 11 of the 1980 constitution, respectively, were and have remained among the charter's most controversial norms. There is no question that the system of executive-military relations and the expanded political role of the armed forces introduced marks the sharpest break with the central principles of Chile's constitutional tradition to be found in the 1980 text.[43] Whereas the 1833 and 1925 constitutions secured Republican principles by subordinating the armed forces to authorities with a direct popular mandate, the 1980 constitution considerably weakens the principle of obedience to an elected official by restricting the president's authority to name and retire the commanders in chief of the different forces as well as to appoint and remove lower ranking officers. Furthermore, through a seven-member, military-dominated National Security Council, the constitution grants the armed forces a role in the system of political decision making and attributes to the armed forces the function to "guarantee the institutional order of the Republic."[44]

These innovations have led to charges that the 1980 constitution structures a tutelary democracy in which the armed forces hold extensive, ongoing authority to veto government policy initiatives. More often than not, though, these charges are based on an attribution to the National Security Council of powers that it does not hold.[45] Aside from naming two lawyers to the constitutional court and advising the pres-

---

[43] For an excellent elaboration of this point, see Godoy 1996.

[44] ART. 90, para. 2. The National Security Council is integrated by the President of the Republic, the Presidents of the Senate and the Supreme Court, and the Commanders in Chief of the Armed Forces and the Director General of *carabineros*. The Ministers of Interior, Foreign Relations, National Defense, Economics, and Finance also participate as members of the council, but without any right to vote (ART. 90).

[45] For example, Rosenn (1984, 122) erroneously claims "the Council must report beforehand on all laws that are of exclusive presidential initiative and must give its consent to the president when he declares a constitutional state of exception." Loveman (1991, 47) claims that the constitution gives the council "virtual veto power over policy initiatives and constitutional reforms." Ensalaco (1994, 415) states that the council is the reason for including emergency powers in the constitution: "The military required a sweeping grant of authority to resort to repression whenever its National Security Council perceived the 'national security' to be jeopardized by dissidents. Consequently, chapter four elaborated a set of norms relating to 'constitutional states of exception.'" He also maintains (Ensalaco 1994, 423) that the council's authority to represent its opinion "codified a permanent tutelar role for the armed forces."

ident on matters of national security at her request, the National Security Council's chief authority is to represent "to any authority established by the Constitution, its opinion regarding any fact, action or matter which in its judgement gravely attempts against the foundations of institutionality or which might affect the national security" (ART. 96, b). Contrary to a common perception, the council holds no veto powers.

In structuring the National Security Council, the Constituent Commission considered giving a wide array of powers to the reformed organ. Had these been granted to the council, the constitution would have structured a regime in which the armed forces held authority to periodically and legitimately intervene in regular political decisions; such a regime would qualify as a "tutelary" democracy. However, after considerable deliberation and debate, the commission decided against granting extensive powers to the National Security Council, precisely to avoid implicating the armed forces in ordinary politics. It was the debatable objective of structuring the armed forces as the "ultimate" or "final" guarantors of the institutional order that led the commission to minimize the powers given to the council and to "depoliticize" the military by minimizing presidential political interference.

### The National Security Council

The Constituent Commission did not discuss the role of the armed forces and the National Security Council until the final stages of its work.[46] The possibility of institutionalizing some mechanism of military oversight first emerged in September 1977 during a discussion of the control powers of the *Contraloría*. At this session the Minister of Justice Mónica Madariaga spoke of creating an additional system of control by a "Military Power." This organ, which she thought should have a different name ("*poder militar*" was Pinochet's term), would be "above the other controls" and would allow "the armed forces, by mandate of juridical norm, to have some type of participation, which would not lead them to new 11ths of September, but instead would provide an efficient safeguard against such institutional destruction." As Jaime Guzmán noted, the idea would be to take the old *Consejo Superior de Seguridad Nacional* and have "it evolve towards a situa-

---

[46] In mid-1974, the commission twice held very general preliminary discussions concerning the armed forces. The second of these sessions was with the Joint Chiefs of Staff and the Minister of Defense to analyze the armed forces' understanding of the concept of national security. For these discussions, see AOCC, 52, July 9, 1974, and 59, August 1, 1974.

tion of greater relevance and specification in the constitutional order" (AOCC, 1632–33). To do this would require altering the composition and powers of the council.

At this meeting and in subsequent sessions, broad powers were attributed to the security control organ. To be effective as a mechanism upholding the institutional order, the commission members insisted that the organ had to possess decision powers and not be limited to providing counsel. At the first discussion Guzmán recalled a 1974 suggestion to grant such a body, then being referred to as the "Security Power," the power to veto law deemed contrary to national security (AOCC, 1633), and in the course of later analysis of the manner of electing the president, the legislative process, and the National Security Council itself further faculties were proposed for the council. These additional powers included constitutional authority to: review and approve all presidential candidates prior to election; initiate legislation; veto cabinet resolutions; advise the president on matters of obligatory consultation; veto any legal instrument (whether a reform to the constitution, statute, or executive decree) that might compromise national security; as well as require the council's assent in addition to that of Congress to declare a state of siege.[47] After extensive analysis of each faculty, the commission consistently opted for restraining the scope of powers granted to the National Security Council to avoid unnecessarily drawing the armed forces into conflicts with other state institutions.

---

[47] The proposal to grant the council initiative to propose legislation arose during the discussion of the legislative process. It was presented as a variant on ART. 16 of the 1958 French constitution, which authorizes the president to take all measures necessary when the nation faces grave and immediate threats and the regular functioning of constitutional authorities is interrupted; it was discussed extensively (AOCC, 2142–49). The remaining powers were suggested during a joint session with the Minister of Defense, Gen. César Raúl Benavides, and the Minister of the Interior, Sergio Fernández (session 357, April 25, 1978). Benavides raised the possibility of a veto in the cabinet, which he noted was under study by military analysts and would be effected by giving the commanders in chief ministerial rank to enable them to attend cabinet meetings and, when necessary, veto any agreements considered to endanger national security (AOCC, 2310). The other vetoes were suggested by Guzmán, who cautioned about the risk of giving the impression of a military state (AOCC, 2313). Though the Minister of the Interior was reluctant to involve the organ in contingent matters, he expressed that the Security Power should have broad powers but applicable only to "very qualified and restricted cases." He opposed granting the council legislative initiative, but did support a veto over constitutional reforms, with the provision that this be wielded prior to any plebiscite to avoid situations in which the council appears at odds with the popular will (AOCC, 2316–17). On the possible participation of the security council in the declaration of state of siege, see AOCC, 2517–26.

This logic of moderation can be seen in the fate of the proposal to have the council qualify candidates prior to each presidential election. Here again the specter of Allende hovered in the background as motivation for such an instrument. In Guzmán's justification, such a power was necessary to safeguard against one of the principal dangers inherent in directly electing the president: that an individual "of totalitarian inspiration . . . opposed to the essential bases of the institutional order" might run and attain office.[48] This problem was understood to essentially concern independent candidates, as Guzmán was confident that the constitutional proscription of totalitarian parties would be sufficient to block Marxist-Leninist parties from fielding candidates. To close this loophole, the prior review of candidacies was proposed (AOCC, 1992).

After initial general agreement this power was returned to and discussed extensively as the commission tried to work out the details of implementation. These discussions centered on whether the review of candidacies should be: obligatory or upon petition, extended to congressional candidacies (AOCC, 2168–70, 2205), and carried out by the security council, the constitutional court, or a mixed procedure with the court deciding after hearing the council (AOCC, 2082–91, 2268). The dilemmas discovered in each of these alternatives eventually stymied the proposal. Whereas problems of international and national image provided strong reasons against having the council exercise this power, commission members were reluctant to grant the constitutional court an essentially political rather than judicial power, and a number of them argued that the court was likely to approve candidacies that the commission considered dangers to the institutional order. Carmona, for example, noted that given his personal and political background, Salvador Allende would have been approved (AOCC, 2084). Later, in the same session, after Díez suggested that the Senate as a political body would qualify to resolve this political question, Bertelsen, concurring with Carmona, observed that the Senate in 1970 would have rejected Jorge Alessandri, the Right candidate. Guzmán agreed with this evaluation (AOCC, 2090–91). Despite Carmona's objection that direct decision by the council would give "the impression of tutelage over the life of the Nation," these problems shifted the discussion back to the National Security Council.

---

[48] One of the other perceived dangers, the election of a president with only minority support, was resolved by introducing the requirement of an absolute majority to be elected and provision for a second round if this is not attained in the first ballot.

The fundamental argument that led the commission to shelve the review of candidates was not a principled rejection of tutelage, but apprehension about the likely consequences of regular political involvement for the National Security Council and the armed forces themselves. On the one hand, a veto over candidacies might politicize the armed forces (AOCC, 2313). On the other, this veto would weaken whatever control organ exercised it. In Guzmán's words, "any organ given the power to qualify presidential candidacies will end up in an extremely difficult situation, and could even place the country in a situation of great danger" (AOCC, 2338).

When toward the end of May 1978 the commission decided which powers to grant the National Security Council, it abstained from recommending the many powers initially proposed out of a concern to protect the authority of the National Security Council and the armed forces (AOCC, 2728–41). As a result, the council would have no power to initiate legislation, veto cabinet resolutions, provide obligatory counsel to the president, veto constitutional reforms, nor overrule a president's request to declare a state of siege.[49] The reason, as already mentioned, was the desire to avoid unnecessary conflicts between the council and the political powers of the state. Any exercise of veto powers would force the military commanders to resolve, whether expressly or tacitly, on immediate political matters. To avoid this, the commission decided to recommend that the council's chief authority be restricted to representing its opinion to any authority as it judged warranted. The objective was to provide an institutional channel whereby the armed forces could signal to other public powers that their acts were endangering national security.

The underlying justification for not recommending broader powers was stated by Guzmán, "Everyone is in agreement not to develop a formula that, in fact, implies the politicization of the armed forces, since it is evident that if one seeks to preserve an institution's character as permanent safeguard one should take precaution not to waste it upon the contingent" (AOCC, 2735).

[49] In the 1980 constitution, following the commission's recommendation, the National Security Council's agreement is required if the president wishes to immediately declare and apply a state of siege before Congress has given its determination. However, the council's assent is required only in regard to this particular temporary situation; it is not involved in the actual confirmation or rejection of the declaration of a state of siege, and the council is not consulted if the president does not seek immediate powers. The council's agreement is required, however, to declare a state of emergency, which the president can unilaterally impose for up to ninety days (ART. 40).

## The President and the Armed Forces

This conception of the National Security Council as the institutional channel through which the armed forces could act as the ultimate safeguard of the institutional order motivated the sharp restrictions on the president's authority over the armed forces introduced by the 1980 constitution. This interdependence between the council and executive-military relations cannot be overemphasized. From the standpoint of the members of the Constituent Commission and high government officials, the force and efficacy of the National Security Council depended upon limiting the president's power of appointment within the armed forces. As was noted repeatedly, if the president retained the authority to remove the heads of the armed forces, the role attributed to the National Security would be meaningless and the organ ineffective (AOCC, 2306, 2308, 2729). To stand as an independent institution of control, the military members of the council had to be secure in their positions and consequently free to articulate independent positions before the president. This view led the commission to greatly limit political – understood as presidential or senatorial – intervention in shaping the apex and officer corps of the armed forces. In the constitution this intent is realized by ART. 93, which restricts the president to appointing each commander in chief from among the five most senior generals (or admirals) and denies her of any authority to remove these officers, except with the agreement of the National Security Council under qualified circumstances.[50]

This new system of military appointments, which was not approved by the Council of State and with one exception follows the Constituent Commission's recommendations, entails a qualitative departure from the standing conception of military obedience. The turning point, prefigured in earlier polemics of 1972–1973, hinges upon whether the armed forces are seen as owing obedience to the president or to the constitutional order as a whole.[51] The commission, particularly

[50] The only other mechanism contained in the 1980 constitution for removing a commander in chief is the constitutional accusation against generals or admirals for having "gravely compromised the honor or the security of the Nation" (ART. 48, para. 3, d). This norm was carried over from the 1925 constitution. This impeachment process, initiated by the Chamber of Deputies, is heard by the Senate, who by a vote of a majority of the senators in office can remove a commander in chief from his post.

[51] Patricio Aylwin, president (1990–1994) of the first postmilitary government is, in fact, an indirect intellectual author of this norm. Following Allende's appointment of the commanders in chief to his cabinet in the aftermath of the October 1972 trucker's strike, Aylwin – then a senator for the PDC and head of the party's hard-line faction

**245**

following the arguments of Jaime Guzmán, tilted the balance to the latter conception, despite observations that the notion of obedience to the legal order as a whole was problematic insofar as obedience always refers to deference to some person, not the legal order in the abstract.[52]

As was often the case, Guzmán identified the theoretical parameters of the problem – the relationship of national security to the powers of the modern state: Should the armed forces be conceived as dependent on one of the three public powers or as an independent power unto themselves?[53] Notwithstanding the difficulties later discovered, Guzmán insisted that even the conception of the armed forces as an independent power did not have to be to the detriment of the military's subordination to the general legal order. Even so, he advocated an intermediate position, combining presidential designations and mechanisms to assure increased internal autonomy. Guzmán's understanding of the implications of such a system was not naive. He was fully aware that his proposals represented "a profound and fundamental innovation upon what has been known up until now," yet felt that they would "not weaken the presidential regime in its constitutional and political content, but gave it a different character" (AOCC, 2738).

The structure of judicial independence served as the model for irremovable appointments.[54] The president was to designate the respective commanders in chief but his range of choice would be limited to selecting from a list of potential candidates, and, once selected, he would have no authority to unilaterally remove the commander in chief. Unlike the pre-1973 system in which the Senate ratified the president's choices, the Senate plays no role in the new system of military

---

– published a long article in *El Mercurio* in which he argued that the armed forces owe obedience to the juridical order as a whole, not the president. He wrote that the subordination of the armed forces to civil power "is not a matter of the subordination to one man nor to one authority, rather it is a matter of *subjection to the law*, as embodied in the constitutional organs of the State, each within the realm of its own authority (*competencia*)" (emphasis in original). See Patricio Aylwin, "*La Doctrina Schneider*," *El Mercurio*, November 1, 1972, 3. Four days later, Gen. Carlos Prats González, the commander in chief of the army, refuted this position. See Gen. Carlos Prats González, "*La Doctrina Schneider*," *El Mercurio*, November 5, 1972, 23.

[52] This problem was identified by Bertelsen. The subsequent discussion made clear that Guzmán understood obedience as internal to the armed forces, that is in reference to the deference inferior ranks owe to their superiors, leaving open the question of controls upon the armed forces as a whole (AOCC, 2809–13).

[53] Guzmán first posed this question early on during the 1974 discussion regarding the armed forces (AOCC, 52, July 9, 1974).

[54] For the comparison to the judiciary, see AOCC, 2738, 3066.

**246**

appointments. The commission departed from the judicial model in the manner whereby the lists of eligible candidates are formed. To avoid any politicization of the armed forces – this time understood as factionalism internal to the ranks – the commission discounted proposals to have the general staff of each force draw up and recommend a slate of candidates, as the Supreme Court does for the president's selection of new justices. On the ground that such an instance of deliberation in the promotion process to the highest rank would encourage jockeying for position and the formation of factions within each force and would undermine internal institutional hierarchy and obedience, the commission decided the lists should be determined "by the reality of the respective institution at a specific moment" (AOCC, 2728). ART. 93 of the constitution translates this concept as the five most senior generals. To offset the president's loss of authority to remove the commander in chief the commission recommended a fixed term for the commanders, yet decided that if the president was not to have the authority to remove the commanders in chief, then she should not be allowed to go around them to remove subordinate officers (AOCC, 2729, 2739).

These modifications to the president's authority over the armed forces were vehemently opposed by Juan de Dios Carmona, the commission member with the greatest direct experience with the armed forces, as he had been Minister of Defense to Eduardo Frei. Carmona insisted that the president retain the power to retire officers. Such authority, he argued, was the president's institutional and constitutional compensation before the vast power held by the armed forces (AOCC, 2732, 2739). Carmona maintained that without this authority the commission was creating a "totally autonomous body" and laying the groundwork for a "total divorce between civilians and armed forces" (AOCC, 3066, 3067). To stipulate in the constitution that the armed forces owe obedience to the constitutional order rather than the president, he argued, was to provide "constitutional sanctification for any military *pronunciamiento*" (AOCC, 2731).

Carmona's intransigence led the group to formulate a mechanism whereby, under special circumstances and with the approval of the National Security Council, the president could force the removal of a subordinate officer but not a commander in chief (AOCC, 3073–75). The Minister of Defense, after reviewing the commission's proposals, recommended that this power be suppressed (AOCC, 3372). Nevertheless, the commission retained it, as did the Junta – though the latter modified the precept to allow the president to remove a commander in chief, but not lower officers, with the agreement of the council.[55] Later, in late 1979, the Council of State during its review of the commission's draft would suppress these modifications to the president's authority and revert to the traditional system. Yet these recommendations did not carry with the Junta.[56]

Regardless of how one evaluates this mode of structuring executive-military relations, it should be clear that these modifications to the traditional presidential powers, at least in the commission, were not conceived as a constitutional foundation for the armed forces to dominate politics. Rather, the commission's objective was the opposite, to avoid creating institutions that would involve the armed forces in ongoing political conflicts. The underlying intention was to assure that there would always be at least one institution beyond the fray that could step in and take charge if all else failed. This notion of the role of the armed forces was indeed a formula for a coup, but its catastrophic other that this notion sought to preclude was irresolvable institutional conflicts, division of the armed forces, civil war, or revolution, not democracy. As Guzmán insisted, the armed forces were the exceptional safeguard, not the ordinary mechanism of institutional control.

This point was debated extensively in the commission. Notwithstanding the eventual wording of ART. 90, which stipulates that the armed forces "guarantee the institutional order of the Republic," on virtually every occasion that the armed forces are described as "guarantors" or "safeguards" by commission members, these terms are preceded by the adjective *último*, which can mean either final or ultimate (AOCC, 2311, 2522, 2727, 2732, 2733, 2985). The ambiguities inherent

---

[55] Compare AdCP, ART. 98, para. 2, with ART. 93, para. 2 of the constitution. The commission's discussion of this power reveals that they did not envisage an impenetrable wall separating the president and the armed forces. Rather, any presidential influence upon the officer corps was to be exercised through the commander in chief. Thus, they spoke of removal, with security council agreement, as an "exceptional way out in the event the chief of state finds himself in a very severe conflict with an officer and cannot resolve it directly with the respective commander in chief" (AOCC, 3073). Since such a situation implies a conflict with the commander in chief himself, it seems that the Junta's precept provides a more appropriate solution to this problem.

[56] The Council of State analyzed the president's power to name and remove military officers in Sessions 90 and 91 (September 25, 1979 and October 2, 1979). In these meetings the former commanders in chief on the council insisted that the president retain authority to freely name the commanders in chief. In the second session, by unanimous vote of those present (Ibáñez was abroad), the council approved a clause that expressly granted the president authority to freely designate and remove the commanders in chief of the different services and to effect appointments and retirements of officers, without requirement of Senate assent (PdNCP, ART. 32, no. 18).

in this term were debated on June 13, 1978, after Guzmán suggested that an earlier phrasing identical to the version eventually inscribed in the constitution be changed to "are the ultimate guarantee of the institutional order of the Republic." Guzmán requested this change precisely to make clear that the armed forces were not permanent and constant guarantors. Rather, he insisted the institutional order was secured by all of the institutions structured by the constitution, and the armed forces as "ultimate guarantor" were to act only when their intervention was "absolutely indispensable" because one of these organs had arrogated the powers of the others or the regular mechanisms of constitutional control had failed. Such action was not to be "indiscriminate." Before objections by Bertelsen and Luz Bulnes that "ultimate" might be interpreted as implying military intervention only after all other authorities had acted, Guzmán explained that the idea was not one of temporal succession, but that intervention should occur "for want of or breakdown of the habitual instances that guarantee the institutional order of the Republic." As Carmona noted, this understanding of guarantor implied "a constitutional call for an intervention by the armed forces" (AOCC, 2800–4). However, it was to be an exceptional measure of last resort, to supplant the ordinary mechanisms of constitutional control only in the event of an extreme institutional crisis. To protect this final reserve, the armed forces were deliberately structured so as to remove them from playing a tutelary role.

## Elections and the Silences of the Dual Constitution

As the preceding analysis has shown, the 1980 constitution, on paper at least, provided for two qualitatively distinct regimes: On the one hand, the permanent text structured a strongly constitutional "protected democracy" designed to contain civilian political actors within the new institutional framework and, on the other, the transitory articles reinstated the legal and institutional status quo of dictatorship. This dualism inscribed in law the terms of the intramilitary debate on dictatorship and constitutionalism: The members of the Junta agreed that an immediate return to civilian rule was premature, yet they were deeply divided by Pinochet's proposals to commit the armed forces to dictatorship as the regular form of regime in Chile. More than anything else, this was intraservice significance of the constitution at its promulgation: Within eight or nine years, at most, direct military rule would end and an elected civilian regime, however controverted, would assume power.

This anticipation of an eventual military withdrawal did not absolutely foreclose opportunities for Pinochet to try to hold onto the powers of the presidency. As I will discuss in the following chapter, the transitory articles – particularly their provision for a noncompetitive plebiscite to select the first president under the full constitution – provided incentives that allowed Pinochet to view the constitution as a vehicle for extended control of the presidency. Yet, these opportunities for a second term in office in no way buttress claims that the constitution was tailored to cloak Pinochet with constitutional garb. As I have demonstrated in this and the preceding chapter, neither in its genesis nor in its content was the 1980 constitution Pinochet's constitution. The constitution was not designed with his or a military presidency in mind, and, contrary to academic flights of fancy, Pinochet doesn't appoint the infamous designated senators, nor was the institution devised to strengthen the presidency. These nonpersonalist dimensions of the constitution, however, hardly precluded Pinochet from viewing the constitution as a vehicle for his personal ambitions. Certainly, if the regime could hold onto power during the transitory period defined by the constitution, this eight-year term already was quite an opportunity. Additionally, the silences of the constitution, particularly with regard to the organization and oversight of elections, provided members of Pinochet's inner circle with ample space for reverie that another eight years in power would follow, and they led most of the opposition to discount the permanent text as nothing more than a cosmetic veneer for prolonged, continued dictatorship.

These silences arose because the 1980 constitution at its promulgation set out only the bare bones of a future civilian regime. The constitution outlined the broad contours of a nonmilitary regime but left the details that would effectively determine the specific character of this regime to subsequent specification in organic constitutional laws.[57] The resulting silences were particularly glaring in regard to the many matters related to elections, particularly the nature of the electoral

---

[57] The organic constitutional laws also had their origins in the 1958 French constitution. These laws, which are discussed in the following chapter, differ from ordinary legislation in that they require a higher quorum for their approval, amendment, or abrogation (the vote of three-fifths of the deputies and senators in office, lowered by the June 1989 constitutional reform to four-sevenths) and are subject to obligatory, prior constitutional review by the Constitutional Tribunal (ARTS. 63 and 82, no. 1, respectively). During the transitory period, as structured by T.D. 13, no higher quorum was required for approval and amendment of organic constitutional laws, though these laws remained subject to review by the Constitutional Tribunal.

system and the even more sensitive issue of the organization and control of electoral processes themselves. Only with regard to the presidency did the constitution specify the form of election: The president would be directly elected by absolute majority, with a second round if necessary (ART. 26). Otherwise, the constitution only specified the size and composition of the two chambers, but not the electoral system that would be used to select their members.[58]

This silence regarding the future electoral system might be attributed to the standing Chilean constitutional tradition of leaving the regulation of elections to law. However, this tradition was relative, since the 1925 constitution sanctioned proportional representation (ART. 25), and most likely the drafters of the 1980 constitution did not view such precedent as binding upon them. As I discussed earlier, among the members of the Constituent Commission – and, presumably, among the Junta – the principal criterion for inclusion in the constitution was whether a norm or chapter provided a corrective to an earlier "problem area." In view of the origins of the 1972–1973 crisis from within elected bodies (the presidency and congress) and the associated electoral strength of the Chilean Left, it is clear that the electoral system was a "problem area" warranting correction and constitutional entrenchment. This intent was demonstrated by the extended deliberations within the Constituent Commission regarding alternative electoral formulas. However, these discussions reveal that in the late 1970s there was considerable uncertainty as to what type of electoral system would favor parties supporting the status quo.

Against this backdrop, the 1980 constitution's relegation of the electoral system to later regulation by organic constitutional law emerges as another instance of the Junta postponing resolution on a matter that had no immediate urgency and had all the potential to divide both the Junta and the regime's civilian base of support. Within the Constituent Commission there was consensus that the political parties' monopoly hold upon representation had to be broken, one mechanism being the abandonment of proportional representation and the suppression of the use of party lists. Yet beyond this shared objective, the members

---

[58] By ART. 43 the Chamber of Deputies is composed of 120 members directly elected in electoral districts "established by the respective constitutional organic law." The Senate, in a departure from the Constituent Commission's recommendation of a national Senate, continues to be a territorially based upper chamber, in which each of the country's thirteen regions elect two senators "in the manner determined by the respective constitutional organic law" (ART. 45). These directly elected senators sit alongside the nonelected senators already discussed.

of the commission could not agree upon what a "viable" alternative electoral system for the lower house should look like. On this issue, the desire to reduce the number of parties and the need to secure representation for the Right pulled in opposite directions. Proposals to adopt a majoritarian system with single-member districts were countered as politically suicidal and likely to produce landslides for whichever of the standing *tres tercios* (Right, Center, Left) garnered over one-third of the vote; whereas proposals for two- or three-member districts, on the other hand, were anticipated as producing stalemates and no clear majority.[59] In the end, the commission opted not to decide, leaving open the size of electoral districts and stating only that a procedure would be employed that results in an "effective expression of the majorities" (AdCP, ART. 48). Outside of the commission, the range of discord surrounding the prospect of any elections was even broader, as hard-liners held that elections would lead directly to a resurgence of the Left in power. These positions were not without influence in the media and among circles advising the executive.[60] Before this uncertainty, the Junta deferred any decision until the study and elaboration of the respective organic constitutional law.

On these matters, the silences of the constitution and the nonpublic operation of the Junta conspired to deprive the constitution's promise of an eventual transition to a civilian regime of any credibility. On the one hand, since the internal conflicts over prolonged military rule which had prompted the promulgation of the constitution were unknown, as was more generally the Junta's operation as a counter-

---

[59] Alternate electoral systems for the lower house were discussed in 1978 in sessions 337, 360, 362, 372, and 400. For an account by one of the participants, see Bertelsen 1988.

[60] The public debate over whether a constitution was advisable appeared in *Ercilla* and *Qué Pasa*, two pro-regime newsweeklies. The prominent *duros* were identified in "*Aquí vienen los 'duros'*," *Qué Pasa*, April 3, 1980, pp. 8–9. For an important sampler of the hard-line discussion, see the proceedings of the November 1979 seminar organized by the *Universidad de Chile* and the *Corporación de Estudios Nacionales*, run by Pinochet's daughter, Lucía Pinochet (*Universidad de Chile*, 1980). This volume includes an exposition by Juan María Bordaberry, the former president of Uruguay, advocating permanent military rule throughout the Southern Cone, as well as texts by far-right luminaries from Spain and France.

The prominence of the hard-line position forced Guzmán to expend considerable energies publicly justifying the implementation of the constitution, as well as working internally to influence Pinochet. See in particular Guzmán's (1979a) rebuttal of a position paper advocating a Catholic, authoritarian, military state, which Guzmán held was viable only under a system of ongoing totalitarian repression. Also see the Guzmán memorandum (1979b) advising Pinochet to refrain from publicly using the term "neodemocracy" because its authoritarian connotations were inconsistent with the emerging conception of the new institutionality.

balance to Pinochet, the "real" constitution appeared to reduce to the dictatorship as reinstated in the transitory dispositions, leaving the main body of the text as nothing more than window dressing. On the other hand, the constitution provided no grounds for viewing the eventual plebiscite on the subsequent president or any of the elections anticipated in the transitory dispositions as credible mechanisms for government alternation, particularly given the manner whereby the constitution itself was ratified in a dubious plebiscite without any independent oversight or use of voter registries.

In this regard, the most significant silence of the 1980 constitution turned on the momentous issue of citizenship. Whereas the very article of the 1925 constitution which defined citizenship (ART. 7) predicated the right to vote on inscription in the electoral registries, the articles on citizenship in the 1980 constitution (ART. 13–18) said nothing about voter registration. ART. 18 declared only, "There shall be a public electoral system." The Junta's omission of such a clause could not have been ingenuous. It was virtually second nature among Chileans that electoral registries and independent oversight of elections were conditions of validity for any plebiscite or election, and this connection was long-standing and well understood by both the Constituent Commission and the opposition to the military regime. As Jorge Rogers Sotomayor, the author of the 1962 electoral reforms, reminded the Constituent Commission in April 1978, the 1823 and 1833 constitutions also linked citizenship with electoral registration. As an invited expert on elections, he exhorted the commission to maintain this link, insisting that tying registration to the right to vote was a "basic cornerstone ... without which you enter a different political galaxy" (AOCC, 2415–20). Rogers's concerns paralleled preoccupations already standing within the Constituent Commission. Early on the commission had emphasized the need to develop a fraud-proof system of electoral registration. This concern with structuring institutions aimed at assuring impartial elections was another instance of the Constituent Commission's concern with checks and balances, as it was feared that any loopholes allowing incumbents to manipulate elections most likely would rebound against the Right. Thus, the Constituent Commission's recommendation was far more specific than the article adopted by the Junta and stipulated "a public electoral list," as well as the creation of an autonomous organ to administer the electoral rolls and a tribunal to resolve disputes arising out of the process of voter registration (AdCP, ART. 18). Likewise, though with a different motivation, the Center and Left opposition to the dictatorship grouped in the *Grupo de los 24* vociferously demanded the reconstitution of electoral registries, destroyed in 1974, as a condition for a fair plebiscite. Such arguments did not only come from civilian advisors to the Junta or opponents of the regime: During the sharp confrontations that preceded the January 1978 *consulta*, Merino and Leigh clashed with Pinochet over the conditions requisite for any balloting to be impartial and therefore credible.

Given the gaps in the documentary record, I can only speculate as to why the Junta left this matter open. As will be discussed in the following chapter, these indefinitions allowed each junta member to read into the constitution potentially variant medium-term objectives and provided each with incentives to take part in the further specification of the constitution through the elaboration of the organic constitutional laws. More generally, the combination of secrecy and constitutional silences only furthered the impression that the constitution had been drafted to legitimate Pinochet's rule and provide him with a constitutional path for sixteen more years in power.

As I have shown in this and the preceding chapter, the personalization account of the 1980 constitution is wrong: It ignores both the intra-Junta conflicts which reveal the constitution to be the navy's and the air force's antidote to personalization, as well as how the logic of institutional design inscribed in the charter developed through anticipation of civilian governments, not further presidencies of Pinochet. Although in 1980 these dynamics and deliberations were largely unknown and the transitory dispositions left a door open for Pinochet to seek a second eight-year constitutional term as president, the implementation and further definition of the constitution would proceed, albeit shrouded from public view, in accordance with the same institutions and rules that earlier had prevented Pinochet from unilaterally imposing his preferences: the separation of executive and legislative functions within the Junta and the unanimity decision rule. Contrary to the general view that the constitution was merely an instrument of military rule, the constitution itself would impose additional constraints, now however upon the Junta as a whole. Strikingly, the commanders of the armed forces would end up bound by terms of their own earlier agreement.

# Chapter Seven

## Even Custom Shoes Bind: Military Rule under the Constitution, 1981–1988

On March 11, 1981, amidst great pomp and ceremony, the constitution went into force. In a private act, Pinochet's closest collaborators first bestowed the tricolor presidential sash upon him. Afterward, the swearing-in ceremony took place in the main hall of the Diego Portales building, the seat of the government and Junta offices. Accompanied by the rest of the Junta, the cabinet, the members of the Constitutional Tribunal, and the Justices of the Supreme Court, General Pinochet took the oath of office and swore allegiance to the constitution and the law. Later, in the Metropolitan Cathedral, Cardinal Raúl Silva Henríquez celebrated the traditional *Te Deum* Mass. The following morning, President Pinochet became the twenty-eighth president to occupy the majestic *La Moneda* palace, whose reconstruction after the September 11, 1973 bombing had just been hastily completed. That night a reception was held in the *Patio de los Naranjos* of the palace. The constitutionalization of military rule was being embellished with all of the traditional Republican pageantry of the past.

Beyond the immediate circle of those in power and *pinochetista* civilians, there was little to celebrate on March 11, 1981. The armed forces had been in power for seven and a half years and their new constitution did nothing to change that. For all the talk of the "constitution of liberty," Chile remained subject to military rule. In the eyes of the opposition and foreign critics, the constitution was merely a move to legitimate further dictatorship. Like most authoritarian constitutions, the elaborate democratic edifice of the 1980 constitution, even with its many restrictive precepts, was nothing more than a façade: Through the back door authoritarian rule reappeared and was firmly entrenched. Nor did it seem likely that the timetable contained in the transitory articles would produce any change in the future: As the armed forces had shown just six months earlier, they were becoming adroit at organizing plebiscites and there was no reason to believe that the same skills wouldn't be applied in the future.

At best, the constitution was a formula for sixteen more years of military rule. With or without the constitution, the armed forces' rule was based on the force of their de facto ascendancy, not the force of legal or constitutional norms. All pretensions to the contrary, *"la constitución de la dictadura"* did not map the path back to democracy; that road would only be found by putting an end to military rule, by repealing the 1980 constitution, and by adopting a truly democratic charter.

Notwithstanding the reality of continued dictatorship and the widespread perception that the 1980 constitution did nothing to alter the immediate situation, the constitution did introduce important changes in the dynamics of military rule. Not only did the transitory dispositions stipulate significant modifications to the structure of the Junta; the constitution also put into play new institutions, in particular the Constitutional Tribunal, and established quite clearly the set of constitutional norms in force.

These institutional transformations would have far more consequential effects upon the prerogative of the military regime than often transpired to the public. The express codification of a complete bill of constitutional guarantees and rights, in tandem with the establishment of the Constitutional Tribunal, for the first time put in place institutional limits external to the military junta, and, contrary to the imagery of a subservient puppet, the court operated with considerable independence of the preferences of the Junta and Pinochet, despite their role in appointing some of its members. Whereas the Junta exercised formally absolute prerogative in designing the constitution, the constitution itself ended up imposing limits upon the military's freedom to institute the constitution at will. This dynamic was of paramount importance in the process whereby the main body of the constitution grew apart from its authoritarian double.

This chapter examines the impact of the 1980 constitution during the transitory period. The first section consists of a static analysis of how the transitory dispositions modified the structure of military rule. It considers changes to the Junta and the powers of the Constitutional Tribunal. The rest of the chapter considers the dynamics of constitutional military rule. The effects of the altered constitutional context on two closely interrelated dimensions are examined: The internal dynamics between Pinochet and the other commanders, as well as the effect of the Constitutional Tribunal as a constraint on the military's legislative prerogative.

As we will see, the constitutional restructuring of the Junta, as well as the substantive core of the constitution, helped reinforce existing intra-Junta dynamics. Within the regime, the constitution, on one level, was a referent – the codification of a shared agreement – which each member could invoke to support positions in debate. On another level, the constitution was also the source of the "rules of the game." These rules empowered each actor by providing clearly specified roles and procedures, and, now, an external arbiter authorized to resolve disputes regarding the terms of the earlier agreement.

The reinforced position of the Junta before the president had an important impact on constraining Pinochet's freedom to respond to the 1983–1984 mass opposition protests at will. As we will see, at key junctures, the Junta tempered Pinochet's impetuous tendency to meet each protest or affront by ratcheting up emergency powers or by enacting impromptu, Draconian repressive legislation. In part, the independent stance of the Junta, enabled by the institutionalized separation of powers, compelled Pinochet to pursue negotiations with the opposition in late 1983, albeit negotiations that failed. Nevertheless, the de facto political opening of 1983 and the Junta's refusal to abet a purely hardline response to the explosion of discontent pushed the regulation of political activity, via the enactment of the political organic constitutional laws, onto center stage.

The shape of this "carrot" was also mediated by the Junta, though in the end the organic constitutional laws regulating political party organization and the different facets of the electoral system were not enacted until after the first long cycle of protests ended in November 1984 with the declaration of a state of siege. Still, the institution of the Constitutional Tribunal during the transitory period meant that the military government could not structure these all-important statutes at its prerogative. The Constitutional Tribunal, in exercising its mandatory, preventive review of these instruments, fundamentally constrained the executive and the Junta, forcing it to enact complementary political rules that conformed to the very constitution that the armed forces themselves had written and signed. The rulings of the Constitutional Tribunal compelled the military government to structure legal political party formation and the circumstances of the plebiscite in ways that ultimately provided opponents of the regime and its constitution with incentives to play according to the rules of the military's own game and to win according to them. Before examining these dynamics, the modifications introduced to the structure of military rule by the 1980 constitution need to presented.

## Dictatorship and the Transitory Dispositions

The transitory dispositions to the constitution, in effect, were the new constitutional act of the Junta whose enactment had been abandoned in 1977 because of a lack of any agreement as to its content. In contrast to the earlier scheme of piecemeal constitutionalization, the transitory dispositions were now a secondary appendage to a complete constitution which fully anticipated the future form of government. This was the genius of the 1980 constitution. Instead of giving constitutional rank to a series of incomplete, partial acts, which would have left dangling the all-important question of what was to follow, the 1980 constitution structured the projected regime in the permanent articles and then adjusted these precepts to conform to the reality of continued military rule in the transitory dispositions. This was a far superior strategy of constitutional imposition, for if the military could manage to secure the validity of the new constitution, irrespective of the outcome of the plebiscite, they stood a much greater chance of prescribing the terms of the new political order than if they waited until the last minute to reveal their constitutional intentions.

The twenty-nine transitory dispositions to the constitution turned out to be a minefield of deftly crafted, intricate, and often artful precepts. Not only did these articles structure the organization of military rule, they also provided for juridical continuity, assured the Junta a maximum of discretion in determining the timing of the plebiscite, and protected the commanders of each force from the term limits that would be operative under the full constitution.

The format of this second text consisted of molding the main text to the prevailing configuration of the regime. The overall authoritarian context was upheld by Transitory Disposition (hereafter, T.D.) 10, which prohibited all forms of political party activity until the organic constitutional law on political parties went into effect. T.D. 13 constructed the transitory period as the first presidential term under the new constitution, to be of the same duration as established for presidents in ART. 25 of the main text, that is, eight years. This article also stipulated that all constitutional norms would be in force during this period, but subject to the modifications and reservations indicated in the remaining transitory articles. The next nine transitory dispositions stipulated that Pinochet would continue as president and defined the structure of the *Junta de Gobierno* (T.D. 14), specified the respective powers of the president and the Junta (T.D. 15 and 18), provided mechanisms of surrogation and replacement for both the president and the junta members (T.D. 16–18,

21), and suspended the application of a range of articles in the permanent text which were inconsistent or inapplicable because they regulated elections or the powers and operation of Congress (T.D. 21). Although in broad strokes the resulting structure of military rule was identical to the preconstitutional period, the transitory dispositions to the constitution introduced important changes both to the structure of the Junta and the broader context of state institutions external to the Junta.

### President Pinochet and the Junta de Gobierno

In light of the earlier conflicts in 1974 leading up to D.L. No. 527 and the 1977 disagreements over Pinochet's proposed constitutional act on the Junta, the restructuring of the Junta effected by the 1980 constitution hardly emerges as a victory for President Pinochet. The transitory dispositions, in effect, completed the separation of powers first instituted in 1974 to block Pinochet's aspirations to absolute dominance. To this earlier separation of functions, the constitution added a separation of persons. T.D. 14 completely removed Pinochet from the Junta, and stipulated that the next ranking general in seniority would take his place as a titular member of the Junta.[1] Pinochet was free to replace this member at his discretion with the next ranking general in seniority.

This provision is often interpreted as another indicator of Pinochet's continued ascendancy over the Junta. However, as in 1974, President Pinochet failed to gain any authority to retire or select the commanders in chief in the other services. T.D. 8 states that during the transitory period the immovability of the commanders in chief will be regulated by T.D. 20. This article provided for the replacement of individual junta members when an impediment was thought to prevent a commander from exercising his functions, but the evaluation and resolution of whether these situations warranted removal was left to the other junta members, who as always decided by unanimity (T.D. 20; 18 K).[2] Junta concurrence was also required to designate a new commander in chief in this instance as well as when death or retirement required a replacement (T.D. 15). Furthermore, the tenure of the com-

---

[1] Pursuant to this norm, the following generals served as army representatives in the Junta: Lt. Gen. César Raúl Benavides (March 1981–November 1985), Lt. Gen. Julio Canessa Robert (December 1985–December 1986), Lt. Gen. Humberto Gordon Rubio (January 1986–November 1988), and Lt. Gen. Santiago Sinclair Oyaneder (November 1988–March 1990).

[2] The same provision granted the Junta authority to resolve on similar situations when they affected the president.

manders in chief of the navy and the air force and the director general of *carabineros* was protected through the end of the second presidential term under the constitution since T.D. 8, para. 2 suspended the application of the four-year term limit for commanders in chief that was stipulated by ART. 93 and postponed the commencement of this limited term until four years after the end of the transitory period. These provisions implied not only that the autonomy of the acting commanders in chief could be protected for as long as eight years after any transition, but also that the tenure of each commander was guaranteed throughout the transitory period as well as during any foreseeable second Pinochet presidency.[3]

Nor did Pinochet's much sought authority to name a replacement as president materialize; presidential surrogation as well as replacement remained subject to the order of precedence within the Junta and the unanimous decision of the titular members, respectively (T.D. 16–17). Furthermore, even though the fundamental order of precedence among junta members continued to be based on the antiquity of the institutions, which placed the army in the highest slot, the designation of Pinochet's substitute in the Junta was one of two situations which altered the order of precedence, dropping the army commander to the bottom (T.D. 18). By virtue of the constitution, then, Admiral Merino presided over the restructured Junta.

As during the period prior to the constitution, the enactment of legislation required the unanimous agreement of the Junta (T.D. 18A), and important government functions which would normally require the agreement of Congress or the Senate, Pinochet could put into effect only with the concurrence of the Junta (T.D. 15B).[4] Additionally, the

---

[3] It is on the basis of T.D. 8, para. 2 that Pinochet remained commander in chief of the army through March 10, 1998. By the same token, Admiral Merino's successor as commander in chief of the navy, Adm. Jorge Martínez Busch, was commander in chief for over seven years, until November 14, 1997. This was constitutional because only days prior to Patricio Alwyin's March 1990 inauguration, Admiral Merino resigned as commander in chief of the navy, allowing Busch to attain the rank during the transitory period and subsequently benefit from the terms of T.D. 8. The head of *carabineros* at the end of the transitory period, Gen. Rodolfo Stange Oelckers, held this rank until October 1995. Stange replaced General Mendoza as director general of *carabineros* in August 1985 upon Mendoza's resignation, after fourteen *carabineros* were charged with the March 1985 murder of three Communist Party militants. Stange, in turn, resigned in October 1995 under pressure of continued judicial proceedings concerning this case. Only the commander in chief of the air force, Gen. Fernando Matthei, did not make use of the extension permitted by T.D. 8. He resigned in July 1991.

[4] T.D. 9 stipulated that a complementary law would establish the organs and working procedures that the Junta would use in exercising legislative and constituent powers.

transitory articles introduced a major modification to the colegislative powers of Pinochet and the Junta by limiting the regime's formerly facile exercise of constituent power. As was seen in Chapter 3, after the enactment of D.L. No. 788, the distinction between legislating and modifying the constitution was purely adjectival. Affecting both by unanimity, the Junta had only to state in the text of the decree-law being enacted that it was exercising its constituent power for the decree to stand as a valid amendment before the Supreme Court. T.D. 18 and 21 modified this situation by requiring that the exercise of constituent authority involve, in addition to unanimity, ratification by plebiscite. This change was concordant with Guzmán's strategy of bolstering the constitution under the dictatorship. Still, the change implied a major limitation on the Junta's capacity to override the Supreme Court or the newly instituted Constitutional Tribunal, as the exercise of legislative and constituent powers no longer wholly coincided in the same body. Any tinkering with the constitution to have it conform with the military's statutory intentions now required an uncertain and potentially costly appeal to the public of voting age.[5]

Significantly, as part of the same strategy aimed at consolidating the constitution while still in power, the Junta allowed the Constitutional Tribunal to begin operating during the transitory period. T.D. 21 did not defer the application of the chapter on this organ and suspended aspects which primarily concerned controversies involving or initiated by members of either chamber of Congress. Now, an organ external to the presidency and the legislative junta whose sole function was to assure the supremacy of the constitution stood to check the military.

### The Powers of the Tribunal Constitucional

As we saw in the preceding chapter, the composition and powers of the constitutional court were designed in view of Chile's past history of interinstitutional conflict under civilian governments, and the new tribunal was essentially a reformulation of the earlier court instituted in 1970. The 1980 constitutional tribunal, as well as the 1970 court, are of the class of constitutional courts created after World War II on the "Continental model" of constitutional control. Like these courts, it has a separate, specialized jurisdiction and for the most part hears con-

---

[5] As was mentioned in the preceding chapter, Guzmán had argued that after subjecting the constitution to approval by plebiscite, the military could hardly modify it at will thereafter.

troversies that arise among public officials over the procedural and substantive constitutionality of their acts.[6]

The mandate and structure of the Constitutional Tribunal are set out in Chapter 7 of the constitution (ART. 81–83). These articles respectively regulate the composition and recruitment to the court, its subject matter jurisdiction, and the effects of its decisions. I will not reiterate my discussion of the court's composition, but will instead focus on the court's general jurisdiction and return to the integration of the court briefly when considering the adjustments made for the transitory period. I should mention, however, that for comparative purposes the predominantly extrapolitical integration of the Chilean constitutional court sets it apart from most similar constitutional tribunals. As structured in the constitution of the Constitutional Tribunal's seven members, three are elected by the Supreme Court from among its justices and two are elected by the National Security Council. The dominant trend in Europe is to have all members (France and Germany), or at least a majority (Italy and Spain), designated by political bodies.[7]

The structure of the constitutional court reflects the long-standing influence of French legal doctrine among Chilean jurists. On the ground that the judiciary should not meddle with other powers, the constitutional court, as in France, is not part of the judiciary. For the same reason, the constitutional court has no authority to derogate validly promulgated legal instruments and plays no review function in controversies that arise out of litigation. In line with this conception of civil law and the separation of powers, the constitutional court upholds the constitution – both procedurally and substantively – without invading the legitimate faculties of the different powers, and operates only at the their behest. Although it is the ultimate arbiter, the constitutional court is not the sole organ with constitutional jurisdiction.[8] As a result, the

[6] There is a growing literature on such constitutional courts. See, in particular, Kommers 1976; Stone 1992; Kommers 1994; Shapiro and Stone 1994; and Stone Sweet 2000. The recently created Eastern European constitutional courts are examined in a series of articles in *East European Constitutional Review*, 2, 2 (Spring 1993); and Schwartz 2000.
[7] In Italy, the judiciary controls the appointment of 5/13 of the seats, while in Spain they control 2/12 (Stone Sweet 2000, 48).
[8] Appellate courts have jurisdiction with regard to the *recurso de protección* and the *recurso de amparo* (ART. 20 and ART. 21), the Supreme Court handles the *recurso de inaplicabilidad* – the court's limited faculty of judicial review (ART. 80), and the *Contraloría* has jurisdiction over preventive constitutional – as well as legal – review of administrative acts (ART. 88).

Note that the constitutional court's rulings bind the Supreme Court. ART. 83 prohibits the Supreme Court from declaring inapplicable any legal precept already found constitutional by the Constitutional Tribunal.

constitutional court stands at the apex of a semidiffuse system of juridical constitutional controls.

The matters over which the 1980 Chilean court has authority are comparatively broad and somewhat more extensive than those of the earlier constitutional court. The court exercises mandatory, preventive review of the constitutionality of all organic constitutional laws and laws interpreting the constitution (ART. 82, no. 1), and settles any constitutional disputes – whether substantive or procedural – that arise in the course of processing bills, constitutional reform proposals, or treaties requiring congressional approval (ART. 82, no. 2). These conflicts must be referred to the court prior to promulgation and may be referred to the tribunal by the president, either of the chambers, or a subset of one-fourth of the members of either chamber.[9] Following the logic of institutional design discussed in the preceding chapter, these powers are not structured to assure executive supremacy, despite the further tilt toward the executive codified in the constitution.[10] Congress may refer challenges to the tribunal concerning the constitutionality of executive acts that are distinct from the president's participation in the legislative process,[11] as well as contest the president's acts in that realm.[12]

These review powers do not exhaust the authority of the court. The Constitutional Tribunal also held authority to declare organizations, movements, or parties unconstitutional pursuant to ART. 8 (ART. 82,

---

[9] In comparison with the 1970 court, this provision facilitates referral, as the reformed 1925 constitution required over one-third of the members of either chamber to take a matter to the court (ART. 78b).

[10] This contrasts with the French *Conseil Constitutionnel* from its origins in 1959 through 1970. As Stone (1992, chaps. 2 and 3) illustrates, the French court was created to facilitate the centralization of executive authority and to prevent parliament from undermining the new balance of power set in place by the 1958 constitution. This comparison is extremely pertinent as the 1980 constitution also adopted, after the French example, the system of specifying a maximum domain of law, which was the principal mechanism whereby De Gaulle expanded executive power in 1958.

[11] Thus, the chambers may challenge the constitutionality of executive decrees thought to impinge upon the domain reserved to law (ART. 82, no. 12) and may contest the constitutionality of Decrees with the Force of Law (D.F.L.) even after the *Contraloría* has approved them (ART. 82, no. 3). D.F.L. are executive decrees on matters of law that are enacted pursuant to limited delegation of legislative authority by Congress.

[12] In addition to any constitutional disputes arising in the course of enactment, members of Congress may call upon the tribunal when the president fails to promulgate a law or promulgates an incorrect text (ART. 82, no. 5), and may also challenge the constitutionality of the president's convocation of a plebiscite (ART. 82, no. 4). These challenges may also be referred to the court by one-fourth of the members of either chamber. ART. 117–19 enable the president to convoke a plebiscite to settle disagreements with Congress regarding the reform of the constitution.

nos. 7,8) and to resolve questions that arise regarding disqualifications and grounds for dismissal from office. These may involve cabinet ministers (ART. 82, no. 10) or members of Congress (ART. 82, no. 11). The Senate must also hear the tribunal when determining whether the president is incapable of remaining in office or should accept her resignation (ART. 82, no. 9). The court, at the president's request, may also rule on the constitutionality of an executive decree impugned by the *Contraloría*.[13]

In all cases, the court's decisions are final and not subject to appeal. Norms declared unconstitutional cannot become law, and in those limited instances where the court rules on already promulgated executive decrees, if such decrees are ruled unconstitutional, they immediately lose legal force. Once the tribunal rules that a specific norm does conform with the constitution, however, the Supreme Court cannot subsequently overturn this interpretation. In this manner, the *Tribunal Constitucional* stands at the apex of a complex system of separation of powers, checks and balances, and constitutional and legal controls contained in the main body of the 1980 constitution.

As already noted, T.D. 21 did not suspend the application of Chapter 7 concerning the Constitutional Tribunal, and aside from some minor changes to adjust for the context of military rule, virtually all of the powers of the Constitutional Tribunal were in effect during the "transitory period," including those that structured the resolution of executive-legislative conflicts. By virtue of the final article of the constitution, T.D. 9 was one of two norms that went into effect immediately once the constitution was approved by plebiscite. This norm stipulated that the members of the Constitutional Tribunal had to be designated at least ten days prior to the commencement of the first presidential period (i.e., before March 11, 1981) and that for this purpose only the National Security Council would convene thirty days prior to the constitution going into force. To enable staggered renewal of the justices later, T.A. 4 specified three initial appointments which would serve a four-year term, instead of an eight-year term.[14] By T.A. 21, para. b), the Junta designates the minister who otherwise would

---

[13] As we saw in the preceding chapter, the president's referral in this context offsets the executive's loss of its earlier capacity to override the *Contraloría* when it contests the constitutionality of an executive decree.

[14] These were the second and third choices of the Supreme Court and the lawyer appointed by the president.

---

**Table 5.** Appointments to the Tribunal Constitucional (1981)

| Minister | Organ Appointed By | Term |
|---|---|---|
| Israel Bórquez | Supreme Court | 4 |
| Enrique Correa Labra | Supreme Court | 4 |
| José María Eyzaguirre | Supreme Court | 8 |
| Enrique Ortúzar | National Security Council | 8 |
| Eugenio Valenzuela | National Security Council | 8 |
| Julio Philippi | Government Junta | 8 |
| José Vergara | President of the Republic | 4 |

*Source*: Zapata Larraín 1991.

be appointed by the Senate.[15] (The justices appointed in 1981 are listed in Table 5.) Other provisions further conformed the authority and regulation of the constitutional court to the specific institutional configuration of military rule.[16]

The Junta's agreement to henceforth inscribe military rule within the substantive and procedural constraints of the 1980 constitution would have far greater consequences than anyone probably envisaged on September 11, 1980. In effect, by requiring plebiscitary approval of amendments to the constitution, the Junta abdicated full sovereignty over the constitution and placed its constitutional agreement beyond facile tampering as expedient. Any reopening of the terms of the 1980 accord would have to anticipate the political implications and potential costs of submitting desired changes to a plebiscite. Bereft of their former facility to enact constitutional norms at will, the military government was now bound by a detailed bill of constitutional guarantees,

---

[15] Thus, during this period the members of the constitutional court are designated as follows: three justices of the Supreme Court, selected by its members in successive, secret votes; one lawyer appointed by the president; two lawyers appointed by the National Security Council; and one lawyer appointed by the Junta.

[16] T.D. 21, para c), rendered inapplicable sections of ART. 82 that specified and regulated oversight of practices which were not applicable because of the nonexistence of Congress, such as to report to the Senate when the latter either evaluated the president's mental or physical competence to remain in office or judged whether to accept her resignation, or pronounced upon ineligibilities, incompatibilities, or grounds for ceasing in office of congressmen. It should be emphasized, however, that the transitory dispositions did grant the Junta authority to refer to the court the many matters that Congress was normally authorized to raise against the executive.

**Table 6.** Contraloría Review of Executive Acts (toma de razón) (1981–1989)

|  | Received | Withdrawn | Processed | Returned | Pending at Year End |
|---|---|---|---|---|---|
| 1981 | 202,478 | 1,155 | 186,328 | 12,310 | 3,788 |
| 1982 | 168,887 | 716 | 161,964 | 6,583 | 3,412 |
| 1983 | 132,483 | 1,537 | 125,888 | 5,454 | 3,016 |
| 1984 | 134,733 | 1,889 | 120,492 | 6,371 | 8,997 |
| 1985 | 153,767 | 1,918 | 141,930 | 6,858 | 12,058 |
| 1986 | 160,296 | 1,868 | 145,138 | 7,264 | 18,084 |
| 1987 | 169,345 | 2,109 | 164,438 | 9,153 | 11,729 |
| 1988 | 175,520 | 2,209 | 162,000 | 9,272 | 13,768 |
| 1989 | 216,951 | 2,734 | 196,212 | 11,176 | 20,595 |

*Source*: Data from Contraloría General de la República, Subdepartamento de Coordinación e Información Jurídica, *Memoria de la Contraloría General de la República*, 1982–1990.

the already standing review powers of the Supreme Court, and the *Contraloría* (for a quantitative summary of this organ's activity during the transitory period, see Table 6), as well as the control powers of the newly created Constitutional Tribunal, which made available to members of the Junta and Pinochet important new mechanisms whereby each could hold the other to the terms of their comprehensive agreement. The Constitutional Tribunal, particularly through its power of mandatory, preventive review of organic constitutional laws, would also provide an institutional mechanism whereby the constitution could emerge as a body of procedural and substantive rules independent of its makers. Henceforth, the armed forces would either have to remain within the bounds of the constitution that they had written, subject any modifications to popular approval, or ignore their own grand agreement and risk endangering any hope of consolidating a new institutional order.

## The Dynamics of Constitutional Military Rule

Before examining how the new constitution affected the dynamics of military rule, I should anticipate that the character of the constitution itself provided each player at the apex of the military government with incentives to circumscribe their acts within the constitution, even if only nominally. First, durability of the constitution itself was always uncertain and yet the security of the regime was closely tied to ensuring the stability of the new charter. In a context in which significant sectors of the excluded political class impugned the legitimacy and validity of the constitution, the armed forces had a strong incentive to adhere to the terms of the constitution since any transgressions thereof would only play into opposition criticisms of the illusory character of the charter and taint the military's claim to be on a constitutional course of gradual transition. Second, important medium-term payoffs could be attributed to abiding by the terms of the constitution. These outcomes did not have to be perceived identically (and most likely they were not) for each member of the Junta to attach important aspirations to the successful implementation of the constitution. The constitution itself structured a number of potentially desirable payoffs which did not necessarily have to overlap. These included the possibility of a second term for Pinochet, a soft landing for the military institutions after the tumult of military rule, as well as the prospect of political institutional stability which would allow each service to return to a primary concern with defense preparedness.

The association of these goals with the success of the constitution meant that the members of the Junta, individually and collectively, could not be indifferent to the specifics of the further implementation of the constitution. As was discussed at the end of the preceding chapter, at its promulgation the 1980 constitution left a number of decisive political matters to future determination in organic constitutional laws. Until these matters were specified, any number of widely variant political regimes could emerge from the framework of the charter. The range of possibilities was well captured in a column by Pablo Rodríguez Grez, a jurist, of some notoriety as one of the two founders of *Patria y Libertad*, the extreme right, nationalist, paramilitary organization which was active in the streets during the Allende government.[17] Rodríguez (1983) noted, "within the present constitutional provisions there fits both a liberal democracy – with very few significant innovations – as well as a neo-organic democracy, capable of reducing the parties to being mere currents of opinion and of preventing the electoral game from being turned into a constant confrontation of social

---

[17] Almost two decades later, Rodríguez became one of the principal lawyers on Pinochet's defense team after the general returned to Chile on March 3, 2000, following his 503 days of detention in London.

classes." In this sense, the internal settlement of 1980 only partially resolved the conflict over the character of a successor regime, leaving important questions still to be settled. How these matters were defined in the organic constitutional laws would greatly shape the probabilities that the constitution would fulfill the specific and various aspirations that the members of the Junta attached to it.

However, upholding the constitution not only implied the potential for conflicts over its further definition; it also implied facing constraints. The nature of this new situation was thrust upon the Junta immediately in 1981. Before considering the larger dynamic of constitutional military rule, it is worth considering two examples of how Pinochet and the Junta were constrained by their own previous agreement as they prepared basic legislation for the transitory period in March and April 1981.

### Law 17,983 and the Organic Law for the Constitutional Tribunal

The constitution constrained Pinochet and the Junta even before the charter went into effect. To enable legislative and constituent activity in accordance with the constitution, two of the first tasks of the Junta were to put into effect a new law regulating legislative procedures and the organic constitutional law for the Constitutional Tribunal.[18] Both of these laws were essentially organizational and uncomplicated. Nevertheless, questions of constitutionality arose in the course of the preparation of both, and in each instance the Junta was forced to modify its original tack to conform to the constitution.

Law 17,983. Toward the end of 1980, the Junta first began to revise existing legislative procedures to conform them to the constitution. After a second discussion in early March 1981, Law 17,983 was enacted as the first law passed under the constitution. Aside from some modifications to procedure, this law was nothing more than a minimal reworking of D.L. No. 991.[19] The major innovations were the creation of a fourth legislative commission for the army, which implied shuffling the distribution of subject matters among the existing commissions to free up subjects for the fourth commission, and the drafting of special procedures for studying projects concerning matters reserved to organic constitutional laws in joint commissions staffed by represen-

---

[18] These laws were required by T.D. 19 and ART. 81, respectively.
[19] D.L. 991, enacted in 1975, structured legislative procedures and created the Secretary of Legislation and the system of Legislative Commissions discussed in Chapter 2.

tatives from each force.[20] Otherwise, the preparation of the text was relatively straightforward, and the constitutional problem that arose was largely trivial. Nevertheless, the handling of the matter reveals a first instance of how the limited pluralism within the Junta helped anchor the constitution from underhanded circumvention.

The substance of the controversy, which followed a debate over whether Merino should enjoy the title "President of the Junta,"[21] turned on the error of having maintained the appellation "*Junta de Gobierno*" in the constitution when referring to the new legislative junta. This debate arose because Merino refused to ratify the use of the term "Legislative Junta of Government" in the bill on the ground that this title nowhere existed in the constitution (AHJG, 406, March 6, 1981, 3–14). Pinochet and his chief legal counsel, General Lyon, protested that to continue to refer to the "Junta of Government" obscured the reality of

[20] Joint Commissions were required: (1) at all stages of the study of projects of constitutional reform, projects of organic constitutional laws, and any law for whose approval the constitution required a supermajority (*quorum calificado*); (2) whenever the Junta decided; and (3) whenever a project was being reviewed following the extraordinary procedure provided for in ART. 37, para. 2 of the law (ART. 29, Law 17,983).

The new distribution of subject matters (ART. 8, Law 17,983) was as follows:

C.L. I (Navy): Constitution, Economics, Development and Reconstruction, Finance, and Mining;

C.L. II (Air Force): Education, Justice, Labor and Social Welfare, and Health;

C.L. III (*carabineros*): Agriculture, Public Works, National Endowments, and Housing and Urbanization;

C.L. IV (Army): Interior, Foreign Relations, National Defense, and Transportation and Telecommunications.

For the earlier distribution of competencies, see note 59, page 165.

[21] This controversy centered on whether reference to "President of the Junta" existed in the constitution. (The constitution stated only that the titular member in the first slot of precedence would "preside" over the Junta, nothing more [T.D. 18].) Pinochet set off an extended exchange with Merino when he questioned the use of the title in a minor article of the bill (AHJG, 405, December 29, 1980, 38–46). Merino, noting that Pinochet ceased to be president of the Junta once he assumed office as constitutional president, maintained that the title fell to him. Pinochet would not countenance any president of the Junta alongside the president of the republic, claiming that the two would be confused. "President of the legislative power" might be acceptable but not "President of the Junta," he argued. After a circular argument over whether the predicate "preside" implies a subject who is "president," drawing upon examples from a number of institutions, the question was finally bypassed through an alternative redaction.

I cite this exchange as an example of Pinochet and Merino's respective understanding of the separation of powers and their mutual relationship. Taking the line that there were no differences among them, Pinochet remarked, "There are three Powers and now there is a fourth which the *Contraloría* wants to adjudicate. There are three separate and distinct Powers; here we are separating them, but in fact we are spiritually united above. . . . There is no position; we are all equal." Merino's response was unequivocal, "Sure. Now the members of the Junta are all equal" (AHJG, 405, 43)!

the new separation of powers between Pinochet and the Junta and noted that the term was already causing confusion among other governments who were inquiring as to the structure of the regime. Merino insisted that it didn't matter, the constitution stated otherwise, and unless modified to incorporate the new name, the military had no choice but to refer to the Junta of Government. After Pinochet responded that retaining the old name had been an omission, Matthei concurred, but argued against modifying the constitution: "We cannot begin to modify a constitution when the ink isn't even dry yet. It will be argued that we are changing in our own clever way (*amaño*) what the people approved . . . we ought to be extraordinarily careful about modifying anything that is in this solemnly approved constitution, to which we want to give solemnity and which we desire to maintain (6)."[22]

Although Pinochet, his chief legal counsel, and the Minister of Justice insisted that a constitutional amendment was not necessary, that the change could be effected in a constitutional interpretative law which would only clarify the prior concept, Merino and Matthei would not budge and eventually the issue was shelved. Months later, during the second discussion of the bill, a brief exchange revealed another difference in readings of the constitution (AHJG, 406, March 6, 1981, 16). After Adm. Aldo Montagna, the chief counsel for the navy, pointed out that ART. 1 of the project failed to foresee that the Junta might continue to operate for one year after the transitory period defined by the first presidential term, Pinochet blurted, "Or eight more years." This allusion to a constitutional foundation for sixteen years of military rule was quickly squelched by Admiral Montagna, who responded, "No, my General, in no case."[23] As these examples first intimated, the constitution would not be interpreted as expedient. With the departure of Pinochet from the Junta, Merino and Matthei came into their own as defenders of the constitution.

**The Organic Constitutional Law of the Constitutional Tribunal.** The substance of the constitutional problem which arose during the pro-

---

[22] Gen. Fernando Matthei Aubel was designated commander in chief of the air force on Monday, July 24, 1978, the same day that Leigh was deposed by the three other members of the Junta.

[23] In this manner, Montagna reminded Pinochet that the constitution explicitly stipulated that the Junta would dissolve once Congress was elected; regardless of the outcome of the plebiscite to ratify the second president under the constitution, congressional elections were to be held within a year of the plebiscite (T.D. 28, 29).

mulgation of the organic constitutional law on the Constitutional Tribunal was far more serious than the retention of a no longer correct name in the constitution. The project itself was also uncomplicated. It specified in greater detail the procedures to be followed by the court and by the parties referring disputes to it, as well as details related to administrative aspects, such as personnel and salaries. The only major problem that the Ministry of Justice encountered while preparing the bill was how to handle the Gordian knot set by the constitution's requirement of an organic constitutional law for the court to operate (ART. 82) while also requiring that all organic constitutional laws be subject to mandatory prior review by the Constitutional Tribunal (ART. 83). After prolonged discussion in each, two advisory commissions to the Ministry recommended that the tribunal review its own organic law as its first act. To do otherwise, both counseled, was to risk charges that the court was unconstitutional at its origins.[24] This procedure was accepted by the Junta: After the bill was approved in late March, the Junta sent it on to the constitutional court for review.

Within a week, the Junta was faced with the limits set by its own past agreement when the Constitutional Tribunal ruled that ART. 30, para. 3 of the project was unconstitutional. This first ruling, which has never been publicized, took the form of a secret communiqué from the court to the Minister of Justice, Mónica Madariaga, informing her of the Tribunal's unanimous position. She, in turn, relayed this message to the Junta in a secret letter of her own, informing the Junta of the Tribunal's

> desire that the observations which follow be known and resolved by the Honorable Junta of Government in this extraordinary manner, so as to avoid the prejudicial public repercussions they might have upon the higher interests of the country if they were to be officially represented by the Tribunal in exercise of its proper faculties, both because this is the first Organic Constitutional Law that the court must review, as well as because of the content itself of the disposition which is being redressed.[25]

The paragraph impugned, set among the general procedural norms, had been introduced to the bill by the Junta to safeguard the identity

---

[24] See, "*Ley 17,997, Ley Orgánica Constitucional del Tribunal Constitucional,*" in *Secretaría de Legislación, Leyes Dictados por la Honorable Junta de Gobierno. Transcripciones y Antecedentes* (hereafter cited as *Trans. y Antec. – Leyes*), vol. 3, pp. 141–42, 179–80.

[25] Minister of Justice to Secretary of Legislation, *Oficio Secreto No. 47/9*, April 10, 1981, *Ley 17,997, Trans. y Antec. – Leyes*, vol. 3, pp. 316–19. The citation is at p. 316.

of agents and informants when the intelligence services submitted classified evidence to the court for its use when deciding whether to declare an organization, party, or movement unconstitutional under the terms of ART. 8, the constitutional ban on antisystem parties.[26] This paragraph stated, "If the Tribunal solicits records from any power, public organ or authority, and these are furnished to it with a classification as secret, the Tribunal must maintain that quality and must adopt all measures necessary so to restore them to whoever corresponds without violating their secrecy" (*Ley 17,997, Trans. y Antec. – Leyes*, vol. 3, 295). The Constitutional Tribunal unanimously ruled that this requirement that the court protect the confidentiality of any "secret" material received violated ART. 19, no. 3. This article guaranteed all inhabitants "equal protection under the law in the exercise of their rights" as well as "the right to legal defense in the manner indicated by law and no authority nor individual may impede, restrict or perturb the due intervention of an attorney, should it have been sought." To allow the tribunal to use secret documentation to convict individuals, while prohibiting the defendant or her lawyer any knowledge of this evidence, was a clear violation of due process of law, as the court unanimously held. Furthermore, since the constitutional court, as a court of law, had to base its resolutions, judgments, and sentences on the facts informing its decision, any secret evidence received would in any event be useless since under the terms of the norm impugned, the tribunal could not refer to it in any decision.

Additionally, the members of the court presented the political argument that allowing the tribunal to keep evidence secret when applying ART. 8 would have highly detrimental consequences for Chile. According to the Minister of Justice, the tribunal admonished the Junta to

> consider the delicate situation that would arise from the fact that this type of trial, of a political-constitutional origin, were regulated by norms that in violation of the very Fundamental Charter make the trials secret. The external image of the country would be seriously threatened by the criticism, both reasonable and irrefutable, that in Chile people are tried in secret, on the basis of unknown evidence, without a

---

[26] As General Mendoza aptly put it, the substantive problem arose because the tribunal and the security forces each were structured according to antithetical principles: "The Tribunal, which precisely acts publicly, making known its decisions, may place in conflict an organ of the importance and nature of those of security, which operate precisely the other way around, on the basis of reserved, confidential, and secret reports" (AHJG, 2/81, March 25, 1981, 23).

right of defense and in violation of the most minimal human guarantee, which is, precisely, that every defendant has the right to answer the charges against them, and to formulate such a "plea" (*descargo*) the facts upon which the charges are based must be known.[27]

The Secretary of Legislation conveyed the Minister's secret missive to the Junta at the session previously scheduled for the same day, and informed the Junta that from a legal standpoint the court's argument appeared irrefutable. As the Secretary of Legislation noted, what was worrisome was that this was a unanimous decision of the tribunal. It wasn't a position held only by the members of the Supreme Court; the members appointed by the Junta, the president, and the National Security Council also concurred.

Faced with this situation, Matthei and Merino again asserted that the Junta had to remain within the bounds of the constitution. As Matthei stated, ". . . we cannot at the same time have and not have a constitution. The problem is that up until now we didn't have a constitution. Now it has been approved, it exists, and you cannot at the same time have and not have a fundamental charter. We all drafted it. Now there is nothing left for us to do but to force ourselves into the shoe that we ourselves fabricated" (AHJG, 6/81, April 13, 1981, 7). Though he fully supported the purpose of the article impugned, Merino concurred.[28] In this context, the Junta decided to postpone any decision and to further study the question. Ten days later, the Junta agreed to excise the paragraph in question and to regulate the conveyance of classified materials along the lines of a similar situation that arose in 1959 (AHJG, 8/81, April 23, 1981, 7).

Even though this tactic appears to have allowed the military to achieve the same substantive objective without violating the constitution, this example illustrates Guzmán's point that limiting institutions could also be empowering: By blocking the Junta from enacting organic constitutional precepts contrary to the constitution, the Constitutional Tribunal helped to shore up the military's institutional design, preventing the regime from creating an inconsistent muddle of norms which might eventually buckle of its own frailty. Just as constitutional

---

[27] Minister of Justice to Secretary of Legislation, *Oficio Secreto No. 47/9*, April 10, 1981, *Ley 17,997, Trans. y Antec. – Leyes*, vol. 3, p. 318.

[28] Merino criticized the U.S. Congress for "practically having handed over to its presumed enemies all information on the operation of their security system," with the result that "the CIA now has no value at all since everyone knows how it functions and operates" and insisted that the substantive problem be restudied to "protect the security services without at the same time violating the constitution" (AHJG, 6/81, April 13, 1981, 7).

controls were erected to prevent future civilian governments from overstepping the bounds of the new institutional order, the Constitutional Tribunal's checks were also going to impede the military from vitiating its own work, whether intentionally or inadvertently.

Although in the case just examined the form of the court's notice to the Junta was absolutely irregular, later rulings were not and some decisions, as we will see, limited the Junta far more extensively than in the example just considered. Nevertheless, over the long run, these checks helped erect the constitution as a set of rules and procedures independent of its original identification with the dictatorship. Within less than two months of the constitution going into force on March 11, 1981, the members of the Junta were already facing the not always agreeable ramifications of operating under the charter they had created. The new triad of the constitution, the Constitutional Tribunal, and the separate legislative junta reinforced some of the dynamics already existing among Pinochet and the members of the Junta, as well as introduced the force of constitutional argument, backed by the threat of referral to the Constitutional Tribunal. This new institutional matrix was used repeatedly to advantage by Admiral Merino and General Matthei to protect the powers of the Junta and to secure the stability of the constitution.

## The Junta and the Separation of Powers in Action

Even though Merino had been prevented from enjoying the title, the separation of Pinochet from the Junta allowed the admiral to come into his own as president of the new legislative junta. Although Merino's temperament and consistent conservatism were important sources of this authority, strict adherence to defined procedural rules was also a major foundation of the legislative junta's power. As I have been arguing, the armed forces instituted internal "rules of the game" to protect the initial political balance of power among the junta members. The further elaboration of these rules in 1981 was consistent with this origin, and the resulting rules continued to provide each member of the Junta with procedural mechanisms that structured: the time needed to study and evaluate legislative projects, opportunities to propose modifications at all stages of review, and circulation of full information regarding the opinions and amendments proposed by the other commanders.

The legal specification of how bills were to enter the legislative system from the executive also reinforced these institutions by disallowing unconventional access. These rules had force beyond the paper they were written on. Not only did the members of the Junta directly hold each other to the terms of their prior procedural and substantive agreements – often by merely establishing the fact that a prior agreement existed on a matter.[29] But as soon as the constitution went into force they also had recourse to the Constitutional Tribunal, before which they could impugn and redress any procedural infractions committed by the executive or the Junta in the course of the legislative process. In addition, the Secretary of Legislation, staffed collegially by high-ranking justice officers from each service, operated as a juridical and constitutional watchdog: It regularly flagged procedural irregularities, as well as unlawful or unconstitutional norms, contained in executive initiatives as they entered the system.

The massive records generated by the working of the legislative system clearly document that these institutional mechanisms operated and, as in the past, bills submitted by the executive had to obtain the unanimous support of the Junta if they were to become law. Invariably, executive initiatives were subject to extensive modification within the legislative system, and those proposals which contained precepts that gave rise to intractable differences either were rejected by the Junta or, as was more often the case, withdrawn by the executive. Some indication of these dynamics can be seen in the quantitative summary of the operation of the legislative system, provided in Table 7.

An extremely interesting dimension of the legislative process is the specific manner whereby the Junta used procedural rules to defend its institutional self-interest as a legislative body. After March 11, 1981, each Junta session began with a review of the *Cuenta*, the Secretary of Legislation's register of the documents and bills received, copies of which had already been distributed to each legislative commission. During this first filter, the Junta would either accept or reject the idea to legislate, and there are instances of bills being vetoed at this stage.[30] If accepted, the Junta would review any executive recommendation of

---

[29] The Secretary of the Junta, created by ART. 4, Law 17,983, aided this process. One of the Secretary's responsibilities was to act as authenticating officer (*Ministro de fe*) for the agreements adopted by the Junta. The Secretary also was charged with preparing and distributing copies of the minutes of each session to the different commanders in chief and the Secretary of Legislation, as well as maintaining the original copy. ART. 3, *Acuerdo de la Junta de Gobierno, Aprueba el reglamento para la organización y funcionamiento de la Secretaría de la Junta de Gobierno*, D.O., August 20, 1981.

Note that the regulation of the Secretary of the Junta and the further regulation of Law 17,983 took the form of agreements by the Junta, rather than executive decrees. This self-regulating authority was conferred to the Junta by ART. 45, Law 17,983.

[30] General Matthei, for example, halted a bill (B531-03) that would have privatized LAN-Chile, the national airline, at this stage (AHJG, November 6, 1984, 3).

**Table 7.** Bills Processed in Legislative System (1981–1988)

| | Pending from year before | | | Entered | | | Approved | | |
|---|---|---|---|---|---|---|---|---|---|
| | Bills | Treaties | Total | Bills | Treaties | Total | Bills | Treaties | Total |
| 1981 | n.a. | n.a. | n.a. | n.a. | n.a. | n.a. | n.a. | n.a. | n.a. |
| 1982 | n.a. | n.a. | n.a. | 120 | 32 | 152 | 98 | 31 | 129 |
| 1983 | 25 | 7 | 32 | 111 | 7 | 118 | 87 | 11 | 98 |
| 1984 | 36 | 1 | 37 | 128 | 15 | 143 | 107 | 12 | 119 |
| 1985 | 46 | 3 | 49 | 109 | 12 | 121 | 98 | 13 | 111 |
| 1986 | 42 | 2 | 44 | 103 | 9 | 112 | 105 | 7 | 112 |
| 1987 | 38 | 3 | 42 | 104 | 6 | 110 | 91 | 9 | 100 |
| 1988 | 39 | 6 | 45 | 100 | 12 | 112 | 88 | 11 | 99 |

*Source:* Data reported in AHJG, 1982–1989.

urgency, assign the bill to the appropriate legislative commission, and decide whether to grant publicity to the bill. The legal regulation of each of these steps allowed the Junta to jealously protect its authority, control the pace and form of its work, and distance itself from executive initiatives when desired.

Executive requests to qualify bills as urgent often elicited controversy within the Junta. Both the president and the Junta could request that a bill be earmarked as "urgent"; if accepted, these classifications considerably shortened the time the Junta had to process a bill, which for "extremely urgent" bills was even more compressed under the new system than it had been under the preconstitutional legislative procedure.[31] The Junta was legally empowered to modify or withdraw these urgencies, although the president held authority to insist. Pinochet's penchant for submitting bills at the last minute and then requesting urgency and processing by extraordinary procedure was a source of ongoing discussions within the Junta and gave rise to formal complaints to the president. The objections of the Junta were voiced in terms of simple institutional self-interest: Hastily enacted legislation in most instances was deficient and only ended up creating more work for the Junta, as subsequent modifications invariably were required. Similarly, the members of the Junta insisted that they be allowed their due time to study executive initiatives and formulate observations free from the pressure of excessive time constraints.[32] On many occasions the Junta refused or modified Pinochet's requests for urgency, and though I have seen no record of Pinochet insisting upon an urgency, as General Matthei noted as the Junta discussed changing the urgency of a bill modifying the Law of State Security, if the president insisted, the Junta could immediately veto the bill (AHJG, 4/84, April 3, 1984, 18).

The Junta's authority to publicize a bill at its discretion also allowed it to distance itself from executive initiatives.[33] As will be seen below,

---

[31] ART. 22 of Law 17,983 stipulated that urgent bills could be either "extreme" or "simple." Projects classified "extremely urgent" had to be dispatched by the Junta in no more than fifteen working days; whereas sixty working days were available for "simple urgencies." Under the earlier system, the Junta had thirty days to process extremely urgent bills (ART. 26, D.L. No. 991, D.O., July 12, 1976). Bills without urgency had to be dispatched within 180 working days. The Secretary of Legislation was responsible for ranking bills without urgency into three categories according to the complexity of the project at hand. All of these classifications were subject to change by the Junta.

[32] For examples, see AHJG, 7/81, April 21, 1981, 10; 10/81, May 5, 1981; 8/82, May 18, 1982, 15–17; 32/82, December 9, 1982, 7–10.

[33] This authority was given by ART. 11, *Acuerdo de la Junta de Gobierno, Aprueba el reglamento para la tramitación de las leyes*, D.O., April 11, 1981.

on occasion, when an executive proposal was considered to be particularly egregious, the members of the Junta publicized the text of the bill as it entered the Junta to establish publicly that the Junta was not the source of the controverted initiative. In general, after March 11, 1981, the texts of bills concerning nonsensitive matters were given publicity at this stage. Also, whenever a bill entered the system irregularly the Junta returned it to the executive for proper submission, particularly when members of the Junta sought to delay consideration of a bill they particularly objected to. This occurred with an executive proposal to reform the constitution in early 1984, which is discussed below.

These new dynamics, particularly the evolving concern with publicity, were in part a response to the changing political context of the early 1980s. In mid-1981, a public debate emerged over the lack of "transparency of the legislative system." This discussion was instigated by a series of editorials in the conservative daily *El Mercurio* – hardly a mouthpiece of the opposition. From this point on, the question of publicity became a recurrent topic of debate within the legislative junta, and the officers unanimously agreed that "publicity" understood as the publication of bills at the Junta's discretion was acceptable, but "transparency" as increasingly portrayed by the press – opening the Junta's sessions to journalists and observers – was totally out of the question. The Junta never responded publicly to these demands for transparency, despite their many discussions of the matter. Following the publication of another newspaper article proposing that reporters be granted entrée to Junta legislative sessions, Merino explained why such access was intolerable for the armed forces: "If it were to be initiated . . . these reporters will be instructed to say that there is a clash between the navy and the army, the air force or whoever . . . we are not political institutions, we are armed forces and any difference of opinion that exists is going to reach the conscripts and is going to create many problems" (AHJG, 30/82, November 9, 1982, 4).

A year earlier, the Minister of Justice, Mónica Madariaga, had requested that the Junta publicize its veto of a bill. In the ensuing discussion within the Junta, Merino acknowledged that he had killed the bill in question and suggested that this information be communicated to the Minister. Before this suggestion, Matthei insisted that the Junta not even respond to the Minister: "If the Ministry of Justice wants to make it known, then let it do so. The rejection is the same as all of the unanimous acts of the Junta. In this we are all absolutely the same. At one point we will argue among ourselves, but that does not extend beyond here" (AHJG, 25/81, August 20, 1981, 38). Bills could be made public as they entered the system, but the Junta's deliberations would not.

### Economic Crisis and Mass Protest

Although some advisors had argued that setting a *plazo* for ending military rule would free the regime from constant pressures to remain in or leave power, the military government faced the most severe and massive challenges to its dominance during the first years of the transitory period. These challenges dramatically altered the political context of military rule. On the one hand, beginning in 1980, these years saw an escalation in the number and mortality of armed actions against military and police targets. Within the military government, this antiregime armed activity, carried out by Leftist organizations that had reorganized to confront the military on its turf, reopened the question of military involvement in repression, particularly the use of military courts. The other accelerant driving the rapidly changing political situation was the 1982–1983 recession, which fractured the regime's social base of support, threw thousands of workers into the streets, and resulted in a sharp decline in real wages.[34] In early 1983, the economic crisis began to spill over into a political crisis as broad-based, mass protests against military rule erupted for the first time, initiating a cycle of monthly national protests and a de facto political opening which would continue until the imposition of a state of siege in November 1994. This is not the place to analyze the many facets of this process: the causes of the economic crisis, the trajectory of the protest movement, the public reappearance of the political parties, the creation of opposition blocs, the intricacies of coalition politics, the emergence of sharp fissures between the Right and the military, and the first attempts to reorganize the political Right. Rather, I must limit myself to providing a few examples of how the separation of powers allowed the Junta to temper the government's response to this changed situation.

The most significant – yet unpublicized – instance took place in June 1983, when the Junta refused to accede to Pinochet's request for permission to declare a state of siege, which the constitution required he

[34] The economic crisis resulted from the explosion of speculative borrowing and the import bonanza that followed the liberalization of capital markets and the fixing of the exchange rate in 1979. This combination translated into growing balance-of-payments deficits and massive indebtedness. Once real interest rates rose sharply in 1981–1982, the "Chilean economic miracle" collapsed into a sea of bank failures, bankruptcies, and layoffs.

seek from the Junta. This occurred on June 16, 1983, just two days after the second day of protest, after Merino convoked an extraordinary session to consider the president's request. In a departure from his habitual practice of first offering the floor to the other commanders, Merino immediately weighed in against the proposal, insisting that the internal situation did not warrant a state of siege. As he and Matthei observed, there was calm throughout the country and there had been no disturbances the day before. With the exception of a few comments from General Mendoza late in the discussion, at no point did the officers argue in favor of imposing a state of siege – even General Benavides, Pinochet's representative at the time, introduced arguments against such a course.

The members of the Junta centered their analysis of the implications of imposing a state of siege on two dimensions: on the one hand, the political and economic costs of a state of siege and, on the other, the limited efficacy of repressive measures in halting protest activity. The economic costs involved the expected negative impact of such a move on debt renegotiations, which were in progress at the time, and the loss of the night shift which would accompany any imposition of a curfew. This loss, as it had in the past, would negatively affect employment and productivity more generally. The perceived political costs included a loss of any capacity to negotiate with civilian sectors that had once backed the military government and increased international pressure for an immediate transition, and a reactivation on a mass scale of the military courts. In Merino's words, declaring a state of siege internationally would be the equivalent to issuing a "death certificate for the present regime" (AHJG, 14/83-E, June 16, 1983, 4). However, for Merino the worst costs would result from a return to massive military administration of justice:

> The gravest aspect is that the military again takes charge of the dirty part of the problem, because if military tribunals have to begin to function, who will they be? And throughout the whole national territory. All of these *señores* that have been doing things, they are going to end up in which courts now? The military courts. And we, the military, once again will be the ones, just as at the beginning of 1973, who take charge of this whole history? And the war councils and all? No! No, then, it can't be! We already got out of that! (AHJG, 14/83-E, June 16, 1983, 8)

Matthei questioned whether the additional powers conferred upon the president by declaring a state of siege would significantly alter the situation. His position was an argument for proceeding with the full implementation of the constitution rather than always clamping down on political activity. As he noted, the repression of political activity had not stopped the PDC and the PC from functioning – the only parties that were not operating were "our own parties." Rather than separate the opposition into more or less legitimate actors, on the one hand, and irremissible enemies at war with the government – the PC and groups engaged in armed struggle – on the other, the recess had pushed all sectors of the opposition into the same bag. Matthei insisted that the government acknowledge that an opposition existed, would continue to exist, and could not be suppressed. To further make this point, Matthei used the metaphor of a pressure cooker:

> No matter what we do to sit ourselves atop the lid of the pot, in the end it is only going to blow off, because it is a problem that exists. We get nowhere by trying to cover the problem. First, let's recognize the problem, confront it, and resolve it. By sitting each time on top, just as the general says, 'And then what?' And if the pressure is so great that it explodes, we are going to be blown far away. (AHJG, 14/83-E, June 16, 1983, 12)

Shortly afterward, Matthei asked, "Does to govern mean nothing else but to apply the state of siege? Is this the only solution of Government? Does the Government have no more political capacity than that?" (AHJG, 14/83-E, June 16, 1983, 15). To meet all forms of protest solely with force was to play into the hands of the Left, and, most critically, the junta members feared that if the government immediately used its reserves, later there would be nothing to fall back upon if the situation deteriorated further. As Army General Benavides asked, "If the state of siege is the use of the reserve, what is there after that?" To this question, Merino replied, "Nothing. Leave, that's it" (AHJG, 14/83-E, June 16, 1983, 9).

One can only speculate as to what might have happened had the Junta given Pinochet the green light and allowed an immediate crackdown in June 1983. The advantages of hindsight don't free us of the counterfactual problem, so I will try to focus on what did happen. I will suggest, nevertheless, that, by allowing the protests to run their course, the Junta's opposition to an immediate state of siege did force the government and the opposition to discover their respective strengths and weaknesses through further interaction. In the course of 1983–1984, the government learned that the opposition could not overthrow the regime. Furthermore, some sectors within the regime came to recognize that over the medium term, continued authoritarianism was politically inviable and that the channels called for in the constitution had to be elaborated and put in place. In particular, the protest cycle demonstrated that judicial and administrative mechanisms of repression were ineffective before massive social and political discontent. In the short run, the rejection of the state of siege compelled Pinochet to combine some form of carrot with his penchant for the stick.

By mid-June 1983 the political situation in Chile had changed dramatically. The popular classes had lost their fear, large sectors of the middle classes had participated in the first and second protests, and expectations of change were high. In a context saturated by appeals for "dialogue" and "consensus," rumors of an imminent plebiscite, demands for progress on the political organic constitutional laws, and proposals for various "Projects" of regime change, the "immobilism" of the regime was seen, especially among proregime civilians, as a perilous abdication of initiative.[35] Finally, on August 10, 1983, the day before the fourth protest was scheduled to occur, Pinochet took what was expected to be a major step toward a political solution by appointing Sergio Onofre Jarpa to head an overwhelmingly civilian cabinet and to open a process of dialogue with the opposition. The day after the first talks with leaders of the moderate opposition, the state of

[35] These calls came from all sectors, including the military government's own base of support. *Qué Pasa*, the neoliberal, Right newsweekly, consistently ran editorials calling for policy changes and a clear political itinerary for implementing the political organic constitutional laws. A similar line was developed in the business monthly *Economía y Sociedad*, published by José Piñera, Minister of Labor from 1978 to 1980 and chief architect of the labor plan, the privatization of social security, and the so-called "seven modernizations." His editorial board advocated sticking to the constitution as a means to buy time for economic reactivation and save the model. In a June 1983 editorial, the magazine outlined four alternative scenarios for the economic and political crisis – the Iranian, the Polish, the Peronist, and the Gaullist. The Iranian scenario involved the following causal sequence: continued contractive economic policies, further discontent, political concessions, and a process of destabilization, which was likely to be difficult to control and could give rise to a "terribly Marxist regime." The Polish variant, which consisted of continued recessive policies plus repression, was described as a short-term solution destined to fail, since it would leave the regime without any social support and would compromise the economic and institutional achievements of the government. The Peronist scenario turned on selective populism to win over the most powerful pressure groups: An expanded money supply would help liquidate debts, artificially stimulate employment, and create a temporary sense of well-being, which eventually would give way to hyperinflation and the destruction of the military's project of liberalization. The solution advocated by the magazine was the Gaullist strategy of separating questions of state from those of government. This was understood in terms of clearly separating constitutional questions from economic policies and proceeding energetically toward reactivation on both tracks.

emergency was allowed to lapse.[36] During this period the content of the political organic laws emerged as an important bargaining chip, since, once in force, the political party law would end the political recess and the opposition clearly wanted to influence the content of the electoral laws. After three meetings, however, it was evident that the talks were in crisis. The opposition's demand that Pinochet resign and the government's demand that the opposition put an end to the mobilizations lead to deadlock. In late September, positions hardened on both sides, and the protests became increasingly violent in poor urban areas.[37]

## The Inefficacy of Repressive Legislation

As the government moved again toward a hard-line position in late 1983, the Junta on a number of occasions blocked the enactment of harsh repressive legislation aimed at suppressing the protests and organizations engaged in armed struggle. The commanders in the Junta generally opposed these bills, as they often were hastily prepared responses to particular situations. These "panic laws" tended to contain entangled constitutional and juridical problems, usually resulting from imprecise definitions of the offenses they sought to sanction, as well as from the use of presumptions which were generally not admissible in a penal context. In the opinion of the Junta, these difficulties tended to render these bills politically imprudent and unenforceable in the courts.

The so-called "Ley de protestas," first submitted to the Junta in October 1983, was one case in point. The executive's initiative sought to define penal offenses that would permit the courts to sanction the organizers of protests when circumstances provided "reason to presume that these acts [the protests] will generate or cause the realization of acts of grave violence, aimed at altering public tranquility, and, if, also, these acts occur."[38] As soon as the bill entered the system,

---

[36] The state of emergency lapsed on August 26, 1983 and was not reimposed until March 24, 1984, after which Pinochet renewed the state of emergency every ninety days until it was lifted on August 27, 1988 in anticipation of the plebiscite.

[37] On the dialogue with the *Alianza Democrática* see Cavallo et al. (1989, 405–19). More generally on the protests and the *apertura*, see de la Maza and Garcés 1985; Hunneus 1985; Arriagada 1987; and Garretón 1987. The contemporary proregime and opposition newsweeklies – *Ercilla*, *Qué Pasa*, *Hoy*, *APSI*, *Cauce*, and *Análisis* – also provide fascinating accounts of the period.

[38] In other words, the organizers of protests were to be held responsible and sanctioned for whatever acts of violence occurred in the course of the protests they called. "*Informe Técnico*," *Ley 18,256*, *Trans. y Antec.*, p. 249.

**283**

with a request for "extreme urgency" and "extraordinary procedure," Merino and Matthei expressed their opposition to the project, and Mendoza made the point that "one article more, one article less," wasn't going to make any difference since the courts weren't enforcing such laws anyway (AHJG, 30/83, October 11, 1983, 4–5). However, the sharpest criticisms of the legal problems with the bill emerged in the Secretary of Legislation's required preliminary analysis of the bill's legal and constitutional character and implications. The Secretary's report revealed in painstaking detail that the initiative structured a type of offense (*cuasi delito*, technical offense), which involved the use of presumptions that were solely permissible in civil suits, not penal cases, and that as it stood the project violated the respective constitutional guarantees of freedom of association and opinion. According to the Secretary of Legislation, protests were licit acts under the constitution which only required that reunions in public streets and plazas conform to general police regulations (this was a traditional requirement prior to the coup).[39] In the end, the law was watered down to sanction only those who promoted or convoked collective public acts in streets or plazas without authorization (*Ley 18,256*, D.O., October 27, 1983).

Another particularly controversial example was the "*Ley antiterrorista*" of 1984. The Junta received this initiative in early January 1984, on the heels of the killing of two *carabineros* and a year-end wave of bombings and blackouts, with a request that the bill be enacted within fifteen days. The initiative immediately elicited harsh opposition from Merino and Matthei, both of whom vehemently objected to its provision that all terrorist offenses automatically fall under the jurisdiction of military courts. The Junta subsequently delayed the bill's entry into the system on a technicality. Later, the Secretary of Legislation's obligatory legal analysis revealed that the bill contained any number of significant legal problems, including the fact that any sentence handed down pursuant to the law would be unconstitutional. After that the bill bogged down in the legislative system. With all of the

---

[39] "*Informe de la Secretaría de Legislación,*" *Ley 18,256, Trans. y Antec. – Leyes*, pp. 271–86. A few months earlier, the courts had upheld the legality of nonviolent protest activity. On July 13, 1983, the Santiago Appellate Court ruled that such dissidence was protected by the constitution and ordered the release of prominent Christian Democrats charged with infractions to the State Security Law after publicly calling for the third protest. This ruling was partially upheld by the Supreme Court on July 29, 1983. See "*Valdés Subercaseaux, Gabriel; Lavandero Illanes, Jorge y otros (recurso de amparo),*" in *Revista de Derecho y Jurisprudencia*, second part, fourth section, 1983, 80:79–84.

legislative commissions, except for the army's, obstinately opposed to military jurisdiction over terrorist offenses, no progress was made on the bill until late March when the executive agreed to suppress the provision for military jurisdiction, as well as other changes.

In the meantime, the Junta killed two successive constitutional reform proposals which Pinochet had hoped to announce on March 11, 1984 to provide a way out of the ongoing political crisis. The first reform bill was received by the Junta on March 1, 1984 amidst renewed public talk of a designated Congress and rumors of a Jarpa plan to bring forward congressional elections.[40] It appears to have been Jarpa's proposal. The bill contained provisions that altered the timetable to bring congressional elections forward and to inaugurate Congress in May 1987, significantly changed the clauses on political parties in the main body of the text, and granted the president authority to directly consult the population on controversial questions.[41] Upon receipt, Matthei announced that he would study the bill but that eight days was far too little time to resolve upon such a momentous proposal. Merino was more explicit in his opposition. He remarked that after reviewing a preliminary report prepared by his commission "practically nothing is left of the project, nothing subsists, not even two lines, because everything else cannot be done" (AHJG, 46/83-E, 6). In the view of one naval advisor, the proposals regarding the Junta were frivolous (AHJG, 46/83-E, 7). Eventually, after repeated warnings from the secretary of legislation, Capt. Mario Duvauchelle, that the session was illegal because the proposal had not properly entered the system, the Junta decided to return the bill to the executive for legal resubmission (AHJG, 46/83-E, 9–11). As on every other occasion that Pinochet proposed transforming the powers of the Junta, the Junta defended its institutional attributes and the collegial character of the military regime.[42]

The second project, submitted legally on March 9, 1984, was shorn of most of the more controversial precepts and included only one article

---

[40] For the public account of the Plan Jarpa, see Patricia O'Shea, "Gobierno: Las salidas se estrechan . . . ¿Las puertas se cierran?" *Qué Pasa*, March 8, 1984, 8–11. Proposals for a designated Congress, not surprisingly were advanced by Jaime Guzmán's recently formed *Unión Demócrata Indepediente* (UDI). On this proposal, see Patricia Verdugo, "Congreso por decreto: ¿Plebiscito en marzo?" *Hoy*, February 8, 1984, 6–9.

[41] AHJG, 46/83-E, March 1, 1984, 1–11. Cavallo et al. (1989, 425–28) also provide an account of this proposal.

[42] According to one source, Merino's objections were presented to Pinochet the following day in a private meeting of the Junta with the president. Merino purportedly insisted, with a phrase later oft-cited, "We got onto this boat together and together we will get off of it" (Cavallo et al. 1989, 428).

which added a paragraph to T.D. 15 to enable the president to effect direct consultations to the populace. Though Pinochet announced in his March 11, 1984 speech that this project had been submitted to the Junta, this constitutional reform project too went nowhere.[43] With the deadline for decision running out, the Junta in late March requested more time to study the measure, and once granted, the project languished in the legislative system until its review was formally suspended in early June 1984 (AHJG, 3/84, March 27, 1984, 13–23; 4/84, April 3, 1984, 20; 11/84, June 5, 1984, 19–20). Admiral Merino's justification for suspending the review of the constitutional reform bill is significant, as it anticipated what would prove the most decisive constraint imposed by the constitution upon the military's capacity to structure the presidential plebiscite. As Merino explained, the reform was to be suspended because "article 18 of the constitution presently in force establishes as a fundamental condition for there to be a plebiscite in any moment that the electoral and plebiscitary registers function in accordance with an organic constitutional law that determines the regulation of the system for realizing this type of political activity. I request that the Junta suspend the deadline until these laws are received" (AHJG, 11/84, June 5, 1984, 20).

In the midst of these events, Merino inaugurated the new legislative year. In his opening address he defended the independence of the Junta and stressed that the political organic laws were an interconnected whole, which the Junta should have the opportunity to analyze as a package soon, so that they could go fully into effect. With regard to the separation of powers, Merino stated,

> [f]or some, in the present period, this independence appears merely formal. With the representation invested in me, I emphatically deny that assertion. It is true that we do not use political means, nor do the disagreements that may exist become public knowledge. As men of uniform, like all human beings, we have different viewpoints and criteria, but we never lose sight that our iron unity will never be broken by siren songs.

---

[43] In this speech, which commemorated the third anniversary of the constitution's going into force, Pinochet stated that the consultations proposed in the reform would directly tap "the opinion or decision of the citizenry regarding important aspects that are controverted in the so-called political laws. Thus, we will demonstrate, once again, that our political system is not being forged behind the back of the people" (*El Mercurio*, March 12, 1984). The comment again reveals a desire to pursue plebiscitary mechanisms to sidestep the Junta, particularly the allusion to "decision."

In this union lies success in the endeavor that we have undertaken, even when circumstantial events make it difficult and perhaps, yes, unpleasant. But, I reiterate, we have clear conscience of our independence, that we exercise a power of vital importance, and that history, only history, will reveal what we have done to fully execute our mandate. (AHJG, 1/84-E, March 15, 1984, 6)

Within a matter of days, the constitutional reform proposal died in the system.

Two months later, in mid-May, the Junta finally approved the antiterrorist law. On the same day, against a backdrop of continued regular mobilizations, an increase in bombings and armed skirmishes, widespread talk of ungovernability, and increasingly tense relations between the executive and the judiciary, the Junta secretly acceded to a request from Pinochet for permission to declare a state of siege anytime during the following ninety days.[44]

This grant was never used, and in late August the president again requested similar authorization, which he submitted along with "extremely urgent" bills for new repressive legislation, including a bill (B536-06) to "systematize some dispositions of D.L. NO. 77, of 1973."[45] The debate over granting approval to declare a state of siege, however, reveals that by this time there was complete agreement within the Junta that further legislation was futile, that the courts had become absolutely ineffective as mechanisms for repressing terrorist activity, and that a state of siege was imperative (AHJG, 22/84-E, August 30, 1984, 1–21). The main question discussed was whether Pinochet would actually declare a state of siege, and they argued that there was little point in keeping these authorizations secret, as without publicity there was no deterrent value. Again they granted approval and recommended to the executive that this agreement be publicized. Again Pinochet did nothing. On November 6, permission was again requested,

---

[44] This time the debate centered solely on technical aspects of the declaration (AHJG, 9/84-E, May 16, 1984, 11–17).

[45] D.L. No. 77 had been enacted in 1973 to dissolve all Marxist parties and organizations and declare them illicit. Mendoza immediately raised the absurdity of enacting a law to regulate organizations that had no legal existence, which would only end up recognizing them. Merino concurred, "It's nuts!" Benavides followed, "It's unconstitutional!" Eventually, the Junta decided to publicize the text of the bill, in the hope that it might have a deterrent effect (AHJG, 22/84-E, August 30, 1984, 26, 30).

A month later, the Junta decided to suspend further review of the bill and return it to the executive after the Secretary of Legislation's review revealed numerous constitutional and legal problems (AHJG, 25/84, September 25, 1984, 28).

and this time a state of siege was declared throughout the country that same day.[46]

After surviving the most severe challenges to the regime and having made it through the first half of the transitory period, it was increasingly apparent that the military would hang onto power, at least until the plebiscite. In this context, the executive and the Junta shifted attention back to the constitution and the organic constitutional laws structuring political activity and the plebiscite. As in the past, the decision on these laws involved exchanges between Pinochet and the other commanders. Again Pinochet sought to structure rules which would allow him to emerge victorious in the plebiscite, whereas Merino and Matthei were far more concerned with leaving in place a stable political system rather than risk compromising it to suit Pinochet's personal political aspirations. In this context, however, the constitutional requirement that organic constitutional laws first pass inspection by the Constitutional Tribunal added a new dimension to the internal regime dynamic, and the court ended up playing a decisive role in structuring rules that would assure that the plebiscite would be a fair test of political wills.

## The Constitutional Court and the Political Organic Laws

The initial preparation and review of the political organic constitutional laws was entwined with the de facto political opening of 1983–1984. In March 1983, using a habitual tactic, Pinochet, with great fanfare, named a civilian commission to prepare drafts of the organic constitutional laws;[47] later in the year he announced that the Council of State would also participate, reviewing the texts of the main political laws. By February 1984 the first commission, headed by Sergio Fernández,

[46] After expiring in February 1985, the state of siege was twice renewed for ninety-day extensions. It was lifted on June 17, 1985 and reimposed on September 8, 1986, the day after the *Frente Patriótico Manuel Rodríquez's* assassination attempt on General Pinochet in which five members of his personal guard were killed. Over the next months, the state of siege was gradually lifted in rural areas and, after an extension in early December, was lifted everywhere except Santiago on December 27, 1986. A little over a week later, it was also lifted in the capital.

[47] The commission was headed by Sergio Fernández, the former Minister of the Interior. Its other members were Jaime Guzmán, Raúl Bertelsen, Luz Bulnes, Gustavo Cuevas Farren, Hermógenes Pérez de Arce, and Francisco Bulnes. The first three had been members of the Constituent Commission. Francisco Bulnes was a prominent figure within the traditional Right, had served in Congress for almost thirty years, and was a member of the Council of State. Pérez de Arce, a lawyer and journalist, had been elected deputy for the National Party in Santiago in 1973. Cuevas, a lawyer, from early on held various positions in the military regime.

had a preliminary text of the political party law ready for joint consideration with the Council of State. Their joint text was presented to Pinochet in late April. After reworking in the executive, the political party bill arrived in the Junta on June 5, 1984.[48]

### The First Rounds on the Political Party Law

Although proregime journalists expected the political party law to proceed through the Junta relatively quickly, the bill immediately polarized the Junta because of its exacting requisites for forming legal political parties and its creation of a category of regional parties. These two matters, as well as differences over how long after promulgation the law should go into force, were the main points that bogged the bill down in the Junta for over two and a half years. By the end of 1984, the members of the Junta and their legal counsel had studied and prepared four different drafts without getting any closer to agreement. In June 1985, the Junta suspended any further consideration of the bill pending receipt of the other projects related to elections, since their interconnection and a gap in the constitution made it impossible to make any progress on secondary disagreements without these texts. The party bill lay dormant for a year and a half until December 1986 – in the interim the organic law structuring the electoral court, the *Tribunal Calificador de Elecciones* (*TRICEL*) was passed.

Before examining the constitutional court's ruling on the TRICEL, which proved to be the key ruling of the transitory period and also an influence on the eventual political party law, the nature of the differences within the Junta regarding political party organization should be developed as they reveal the widely variant conceptions of the political future that were emerging.

In the guise of reducing the number of political parties, Pinochet's bill made it virtually impossible for the opposition to organize political parties, while at the same time facilitating the organization of regionally concentrated groups into regional parties. The joint advisory commission had proposed that 20,000 signatures of party members be required to constitute a party. The executive's bill drastically increased

---

[48] For a discussion of the public debate over the political party law, see Fariña 1987. Prominent jurists also prepared materials that were influential in this debate. See, for example, the studies by Barros 1984 and Cumplido 1984, as well as the exchange between Silva Bascuñán and Cuevas (1984). The text of the bill presented to Pinochet was reproduced in *El Mercurio*, April 25, 1984.

**289**

this number to 150,000 members – the equivalent of about 2.5 percent of the total electorate. This number was immediately controversial, and even individuals sympathetic to the regime wondered whether anything other than a single, official party could be formed under such a rule.

In his position as a member of the Council of State, Francisco Bulnes, a preeminent conservative politician, wrote to Merino to object to the changes effected by the executive. He maintained that with such a high requisite, parties would not register and would act beyond the law and the constitution, presenting their candidates as independents. Under the proposed system, he speculated, perhaps two parties could be organized, "one whose sole objective would be to support the present regime and another which would advocate nothing other than its immediate replacement."[49]

An even narrower party system was anticipated by some prominent military advisors within the legislative system. Rear Adm. (J) Aldo Montagna, the former Secretary of Legislation and then member of the first legislative commission, during the first meetings of the Joint Commission appointed by the Junta to study the bill remarked ". . . there does exist the possibility that only the Government is in a condition to form a political party of this magnitude. In other words, we would have little less than a single party. It is a comment that has been heard around."[50]

Within the Junta, the number of signatures required to form a legal political party immediately became one of the major points of controversy. The Secretary of Legislation's preliminary report observed that, although it was essentially a problem of legislative politics, the norm impinged upon the right of association, and requisites or conditions that impeded the free exercise of this right would be unconstitutional by ART. 19, no. 26, which established that constitutionally mandated legislation regulating or limiting rights "may not affect the rights in their essence nor impose conditions, taxes or requirements which prevent their free exercise." Once in the system, the navy and the air

---

[49] Bulnes also pointed out that the PDC, the largest mass party in terms of membership, had no more than 70,000 members at the height of its strength during Frei's presidency. Bulnes also criticized the idea of regional parties. Francisco Bulnes Sanfuentes to Adm. José Toribio Merino, June 12, 1984, *Ley 18.603, Trans. y Antec. – Leyes*, vol. 331, pp. 181–86.

[50] *Comisión Conjunta, presidida por la IV C.L. constituida para Informar acerca del Projecto de Ley Orgánica Constitucional sobre Partidos Políticos*, July 27, 1984, *Antecedentes Rol 43, Tribunal Constitucional*, Santiago, Chile, p. 21.

force reserved agreement on this clause, advocating much lower numbers (0.5 percent and 0.3–0.5 percent of the electorate, respectively).

In subsequent bargaining, the navy and the air force repeatedly shifted toward the army position as a concession in exchange for suppressing the provisions enabling the formation of regional parties, which *carabineros* also opposed. Matthei, in particular, felt that allowing regional parties to organize would be detrimental to national unity and politically suicidal. He noted that a strong regional party was likely to emerge only in regions where it would endanger territorial integrity, such as the mineral-rich north, where the region's contributions to fiscal revenues far exceeded regional government spending. Regional parties, he argued, would stimulate first regionalism, then separatism (AHJG, 22/84, August 21, 1984, 72–73). Equally perniciously, regional parties, according to Matthei, would unnecessarily fractionalize pro-status quo parties, whereas the true enemy, the PC, would remain united and never divide into regional parties. For this reason, Matthei stressed, it would be suicidal to divide "our own people" into little groupings without any significance or political strength. The real problem in his view was that the executive had not clearly defined why regional parties were so important, particularly given that the project supposedly sought to reduce the number of parties (AHJG, 22/84, August 21, 1984, 73; 37, December 18, 1984, 67–69).

For all the debate and controversy, it seems Pinochet was only trying to kill time. After a virtual agreement collapsed in mid-September 1984, all three nonarmy commanders were still willing to sign the law if Pinochet would give up the regional parties, but Benavides, the army representative in the Junta, couldn't budge, and every time the Junta approached agreement the president would submit an amendment reintroducing earlier points of contention.

The extent of the tension with the executive was evident in December 1984 when Pinochet's submission of another amendment sparked a sharp debate within the Junta over how to proceed (AHJG, 37/84, December 18, 1984, 66–82). The fourth legislative commission (the army) wanted to reset the timetable to study the amendment at length, while an exasperated Merino wanted to resolve the issue then and there. When Benavides requested that the classification of the bill be changed to "*ordinario extenso*" (meaning, an additional 180 days), Merino remarked, "That's the most fantastic mockery of the country," and insisted that the others "give a more dynamic appearance to the affairs of the Junta." Matthei, though sympathetic with Merino's position, feared that if they forced the issue all the Junta would achieve would be "a more serious problem between the Executive and the Junta, which, as far as possible, should be avoided," particularly since it would be politically inadvisable to publicly reveal "an insurmountable disagreement." In Matthei's words, better a mockery than "to reveal an abyss" (AHJG, 37/84, December 18, 1984, 77–78).

This discussion again revealed the pressure of the changed political situation, as the junta members knew they would face the press on leaving the session. Eventually, the junta members decided to set a shorter deadline and agreed not to mention anything to the press about the timetable (AHJG, 37, December 18, 1984, 72–82). However, these dynamics resulted in exasperation within the Junta, heightened tension with the executive, and eventually a decision to suspend any further review of the bill, as each commission reverted to its original bargaining position. Months later, in May 1985, the bill returned into the legislative system, only to be suspended again in June 1985.

By this time, it was also clear that the executive was making every effort to assure that organized, legal parties would not be in place during the months leading up to the plebiscite. The executive's original bill had the law go into force eighteen months prior to the convocation of the first congressional elections. Since these elections were to take place nine months into the second presidential term (T.D. 28), the formal process of legal party organization would not begin until around June 11, 1988. The transitory articles, however, did not specify a date for the plebiscite. The only constraints were that the Junta propose a candidate *at least* ninety days before the end of the presidential term (March 11, 1989) and that the plebiscite take place at least thirty days after the proposal, but not more than sixty days later (T.D. 27). The plebiscite, therefore, could have been held at any time, even before the political party law went into effect, and since party organization required fulfillment of a number of time-consuming steps, Pinochet's position meant that parties trying to organize under the terms of the law would be preoccupied with establishing themselves as legal organizations in the months close to the plebiscite. Merino and Matthei wanted party organization to begin within ninety days of promulgation of the organic constitutional law on political parties.[51] Intransigence on this issue, as well as the number of signatures needed to form a party, meant that the political party law would have to wait while less controversial organic laws made it through the Junta.

---

[51] *18,603 Ley Orgánica Constitucional de los Partidos Políticos*, in *Trans. y Antec. – Leyes*, vol. 333, p. 782.

### The Electoral Court: A Simple Law Elicits a Major Decision

The organic constitutional law on the *Tribunal Calificador de Elecciones* (TRICEL), the special electoral court, prompted the most consequential ruling by the Constitutional Tribunal, a decision which decisively altered the course of subsequent events and affected the content of all remaining political organic laws. The court's ruling, handed down on September 24, 1985, was not the first to impugn the constitutionality of norms enacted by the Junta and the president. However, it was without doubt the most important, as it compelled the regime to enact further legislation and laid the conceptual foundation for later rulings which assured that the eventual plebiscite on the Junta's candidate for the second presidential term (or any plebiscite to ratify a modification to the constitution) would take place under scrupulous conditions of impartiality.

The organic law on the TRICEL, stipulated by ART. 84 of the constitution, was one of two organic laws affecting the organization and oversight of elections. The other, the electoral law proper, was mandated by ART. 18 of the constitution, which stated:

> There shall be a public electoral system. Regarding matters not provided for by this Constitution, an organic constitutional law will determine the organization and operation thereof, shall regulate the manner in which electoral processes and plebiscites will be conducted, and shall, at all times, guarantee full equality between independents and members of political parties, both with regard to the presentation of candidacies and to their participation in said processes.

The executive's bill, also prepared with assistance from the Council of State and the Advisory Commission on organic laws, entered the legislative system on September 25, 1984 and was approved by the Junta on July 16, 1985. By submitting the bill on the TRICEL prior to the organic law required by ART. 18 to structure the electoral system, the executive was regulating the court that would oversee and qualify elections *before* specifying how these elections themselves would be held. This inconsistency was not lost upon the Junta and its advisors, and was again an example of the executive's general strategy of not revealing intentions until absolutely necessary.[52] The chief functions of the

---

[52] Still, the Secretary of Legislation held that the executive could not proceed to the plebiscite without an electoral law. As noted in the Secretary's preliminary report, T.D. 5 stipulated that standing laws concerning matters that the constitution referred to

TRICEL were to oversee and certify elections, settle complaints arising from elections, and proclaim the official results. The organ was largely identical to the electoral court that had operated under the 1925 constitution – though again the framers of the constitution altered the organ's composition and mode of selection to assure a greater "technical-judicial" character.[53]

As always, in its review of the bill the Junta corrected aspects of it, caught some unconstitutionalities, and debated and reviewed at length the one or two difficult articles on which there was no agreement. Significantly, the precept most debated within the Junta's *Comisión Conjunta* concerned precisely the issue that the Constitutional Tribunal would later rule on. However, the Tribunal's decision had far broader ramifications than the matter the commission sought to settle. The question at hand was the date when the electoral court would go into operation. When the TRICEL would commence operation was an extremely charged political question given that the 1980 plebiscite on the constitution had been orchestrated without oversight, and the opposition was accusing the government of planning to perpetrate a similar sham to reelect Pinochet to a second term. These fears appeared reasonable because T.D. 11 of the constitution stated that ART. 84 regulating the electoral court and its corresponding organic law (the law on the TRICEL) would go into effect "at the time of the first election of Senators and Deputies." By the terms of the constitu-

organic constitutional laws for regulation – insofar as they were not contrary to the constitution – would remain applicable until the relevant organic law was enacted. On this ground, the report noted the precoup legislation regulating elections, which had not been rescinded, would apply in the absence of the organic constitutional law mandated by ART. 18. *S.L. J.G. (O) 4158, 24 de Octubre 1984, Secretaría de Legislación a Presidente de la II C.L., Informe de la Secretaría de Legislación,* in *Ley 18,603, Ley Orgánica Constitucional de los Partidos Políticos, Trans. y Antec. – Leyes,* vol. 331, p. 99.

[53] Again the tactic was to shift the balance to judges and to allow the justices of the Supreme Court to select the majority. Both the 1925 and 1980 Electoral Qualifying Courts were composed of five members, serving four-year terms. In the new court, the Supreme Court in successive, secret votes, by absolute majority, elects three justices or former justices to the special court. The court also elects a lawyer, who has to satisfy the same qualification as required for eligibility to the Constitutional Tribunal. The fifth member is selected by lot from among former presidents of the Senate or the Chamber of Deputies who held the position for at least three years.

Under ART. 78 a) of the 1925 constitution, the five members of the earlier court were all selected by lot. One member was selected from each of the following groups: individuals who had served as president or vice president of the Chamber of Deputies for at least one year, similar individuals from the Senate, justices of the Santiago Court of Appeals. Two members were selected from among the acting justices of the Supreme Court.

tion, these elections were to take place nine months into the second presidential term. A literal application of T.D. 11, therefore, meant that the body empowered to oversee elections would only begin to function about a year after the presidential plebiscite.

Perhaps as a bow to the opposition, perhaps as a bow to the other junta members, Pinochet's bill included a transitory article which provided that the electoral court would be constituted thirty days prior to any plebiscite. Once in the Junta, the constitutionality of this norm which apparently contradicted T.D. 11 became the center of ongoing debates within the joint commission that prepared the bill for the Junta's resolution.

The political subtext to these debates is unclear. Air force representatives persistently stressed that the TRICEL had to oversee the plebiscite, a position that the navy generally shared, although the navy acknowledged that the bill's transitory article literally contradicted T.D. 11 of the constitution. However, the army representatives, while claiming to share the same objective of having an electoral court oversee any plebiscite, were the most forceful in impugning the constitutionality of the bill's transitory article. The army representatives maintained that it was sufficient to activate the oversight body by ordinary statute and thereby have the TRICEL supervise the plebiscite.[54] There is no way to know whether the others took this argument on faith or not.

In a second round of meetings in June 1985, one day after the state of siege had been lifted, the commission had shifted toward merely restating T.D. 11 in the transitory article to the bill, with the understanding that oversight of the plebiscite would be left to law. Still, the air force counsel again reiterated the importance of having the TRICEL operate during the plebiscite and again pressed that the plebiscite be impeccable and provide no warrant for reproach. Rear Adm. Montagna concurred, stressing that the First Legislative Commission (navy) fully coincided with the Second Legislative Commission (air force). The army representatives suggested that a law ought to be enacted concurrently with the organic law to regulate plebiscites during the transitory period; otherwise the opposition would jubilantly exploit any eventual vacuum in the organic law.[55] Along with other changes, the law

---

[54] *Comisión Conjunta, presidida por la IV C.L. constituida Para informar acerca del Projecto de Ley Orgánica Constitucional Sobre el Tribunal Calificador de Elecciones*, May 1 and 8, 1985, *Antecedentes Rol 33, Tribunal Constitucional*, Santiago, Chile, pp. 48–51, 25–27, respectively.

[55] Carlos Cruz-Coke, a member of the Second Legislative Commission, raised the issue again in reference to opposition arguments that the plebiscite was going to take place

approved by the Junta on July 16, 1985 suppressed the original transitory article and instead appended a final article to the law that essentially restated T.D. 11 of the constitution: The organic constitutional law would go into force sixty days prior to the convocation of the first election of senators and deputies, that is, after the plebiscite.

The Constitutional Tribunal did not leave matters to the Junta's discretion. After considerable delay, the constitutional court handed down its decision on September 24, 1985.[56] The decision was a landmark ruling. The central constitutional question raised by the court was, of course, the date the TRICEL would become operative. In a narrow 4 to 3 vote, a majority of the tribunal ruled that the first transitory article of the law was unconstitutional.[57] Not only did the constitutional court require that the TRICEL be fully in place for the plebiscite; it also stipulated in its decision that the government had to enact further organic constitutional laws to assure the constitutionality of the plebiscite.

The sentence on Rol. 33 was a triumph for the loose grouping of justices who had been arguing within the court for a harmonious, systematic interpretation of the constitution. Such an interpretative stance set individual constitutional norms within their broader constitutional context. This jurisprudence had emerged in opposition to a line of interpretation that advocated an isolated, literal interpretation of articles of the constitution, true to the "original intent" of the framers.[58] The ascendancy of the group advocating a holistic interpretation had

"without any control, that no one is going to oversee it and that it is simply going to be a kind of political acrobatic act (*maroma*) in order to reelect General Pinochet in the presidency of the republic. That's what they are saying. Furthermore, the state of siege was lifted yesterday, therefore I do enjoy a certain freedom to pose the matter." After the laughter subsided, Cruz-Coke continued, ". . . we are interested that the process be free, sincere, secret, informed, and that there be no possibility of constitutional reproach." Regarding the collateral statute, Hernán Chadwick, a member of the Fourth Legislative Commission noted, "Today we are without a state of siege, we have three years before us, but it is obvious that for the opposition it will be quite a treat if this law appears without qualifying the plebiscite." *Comisión Conjunta, presidida por la IV C.L. constituida Para informar acerca del Projecto de Ley Orgánica Constitucional Sobre el Tribunal Calificador de Elecciones*, June 18, 1985, *Antecedentes Rol 33, Tribunal Constitucional*, Santiago, Chile, pp. 49, 55.

[56] *Tribunal Constitucional*, Sentencia Rol No. 33, D.O., October 3, 1985. As we will see as well, the organic law itself was not published till over a month later.

[57] The majority was made up of the president of the constitutional court, Supreme Court Justice José María Eyzaguirre, Supreme Court Justice Luis Maldonado, Julio Philippi (appointed by the Junta), and Eugenio Valenzuela (appointed by the National Security Council). Marcos Aburto, Enrique Ortúzar, and Eduardo Urzúa formed the minority. Ortúzar drafted the minority opinion published with the sentence.

[58] For an analysis of the evolving jurisprudence of the *Tribunal Constitucional* in its first years, see Zapata Larraín 1991 and Ribera Neumann 1987.

**Table 8.** Ministers of the Tribunal Constitucional (1985–1989)

| Minister | Organ Appointed By |
|---|---|
| José María Eyzaguirre | Supreme Court |
| Luis Maldonado | Supreme Court |
| Marcos Aburto | Supreme Court |
| Enrique Ortúzar | National Security Council |
| Eugenio Valenzuela | National Security Council |
| Julio Philippi | Government Junta |
| Miguel Ibañez (Eduardo Urzúa) | President of the Republic |

*Source*: Zapata Larraín 1991, 287.

been aided by recent appointments to the court, which had tipped the balance between the two contending positions (see Table 8).[59] The chief proponent of a harmonious interpretation of the constitution was Eugenio Valenzuela Somarriva, who, somewhat ironically, had been appointed by the National Security Council. Minister Valenzuela wrote this momentous sentence.

Valenzuela's majority opinion was built around the argument that a narrow, literal interpretation of T.D. 11 was inadmissible since it contradicted other permanent and transitory articles of the constitution and, if accepted, denied these articles of force. Of particular importance were the effects of such an interpretation on ART. 18, the norm concerning the public electoral system and its concomitant organic constitutional law to govern the manner of holding elections and plebiscites.

On the basis that ART. 18 of the constitution was in force, Valenzuela constructed a thesis with broad implications for any electoral event and which sustained the conclusion that the electoral court structured by the constitution had to oversee any plebiscite. The logic of this construction was as follows: Since T.D. 21 (the transitory article which identified specific permanent articles of the constitution that would not apply during the transitory period) did not expressly suspend ART. 18, this norm and its respective organic law fully applied to any plebiscite regardless of whether the plebiscite took place before or after the first

---

[59] Recall that to set up the staggered renewal of the court, three of the initial ministers were appointed with only four-year terms, instead of the regular eight. These slots therefore were renewed in early 1985.

election of senators and deputies. The crucial next step in Valenzuela's construction was to argue that the force of these norms was wholly contingent upon the operation of the electoral court. If in accordance with an isolated interpretation of T.D. 11 the TRICEL did not operate until the first congressional election, ART. 18 and its concomitant organic constitutional law governing elections and plebiscites would be deprived of all force. Without the electoral court there would be no duly authorized organ to verify that electoral acts, no matter their type, had proceeded according to the rules that govern them, which are the province of ART. 18 and its accompanying organic law. Here, Valenzuela's opinion invoked the doctrine and jurisprudence of the precoup TRICEL itself and cited a May 1949 decision which stated that to qualify an election "is to establish if the election has been carried out in conformity with the provisions that apply and thus be able to declare, not only who has been elected, but also if they have been elected legitimately." For rules to effectively structure elections, some organ must have the authority to ascertain that rules are followed. The essence of this point, Valenzuela insisted in the court's decision, was equally valid for plebiscitary acts.

The same argument was applied to T.D. 27, the precept structuring the presidential plebiscite, which included the phrase the plebiscite "shall be carried out in the form provided for by the law." Contrary to the position maintained in the Junta's *Comisión Conjunta*, the constitutional court ruled that the reference to "the law" implied the organic constitutional law associated with ART. 18, since it was precisely this law which was to regulate the manner of holding plebiscites.[60]

The permanent articles of the constitution would predominate over a single transitory disposition. A political consideration as well was invoked in the sentence:

> The preceding conclusion, which flows spontaneously from the due correspondence and harmony that ought to exist between the different precepts of the Fundamental Charter, is ratified by the fact that this plebiscite will be the expression of the will of the people, who in exercise of sovereignty, resolve upon the most important political act

---

[60] The sentence also applied the same logic of argument to the political party law. Postponing the application of ART. 84 would also restrict the application of the legal system regulating political party organization, since historically, as well as in the bill presented by the executive, the electoral court played an essential role in the registration and legal recognition of political parties. Likewise, a narrow interpretation of T.D. 11 effected any plebiscites required to modify the constitution, as stipulated in T.D. 18 and 21.

with which the period in which all of the permanent provisions of the Fundamental Charter will attain full force begins. In consequence, the special importance of this plebiscitary act and the letter and the spirit of the Constitution fully confirm that this act must be regulated by the permanent provisions and not by special norms that, in a mass of provisions intended only for this effect, establish ad hoc tribunals or commissions to fulfill functions that our Fundamental Charter has granted to "a" determinate tribunal.

The contrary interpretation not only injures the spirit of the Constitution but, also, common sense which is the base of all logical interpretation, since it might amount to exposing the plebiscite itself to a judgment of legitimacy of grave prejudice for the normal development of the future institutional order.

On these grounds, the majority of the court ruled that the final article and the first transitory article of the project were unconstitutional and had to be deleted. The minority opinion, drafted by Enrique Ortúzar, the former president of the Constituent Commission, developed a strict, literal reading of the text and asserted that on that basis the plebiscite should be carried out according to the law (ordinary statute) and that there were no grounds for assuming that such a law would not provide sufficient guarantees for the plebiscite.

The Constitutional Tribunal's ruling was a political bombshell. Not only would an independent organ oversee the plebiscite and adjudicate complaints regarding any alleged improprieties committed in its execution, but the organic constitutional laws regulating ART. 18 would also have to be in force if the constitutionality of this event were not to be open to challenge. This was a far broader oversight of the plebiscite than was discussed within the Junta's joint commission. For, pursuant to the court's sentence, the TRICEL would not only oversee the act of the plebiscite – something which all four services apparently were willing to accept. It would also oversee a system of voter registration and voting counts which, according to the court's public sentence, would now have to be in place for any plebiscite to satisfy the terms of the constitution. Significantly, there is every reason to suspect that at the time of the *Tribunal Constitucional*'s sentence, the executive had not committed itself to the use of electoral registries, and it is incontrovertible fact that no bill had been presented to provide for them even on an ad hoc basis by this date.[61] Since these aspects of the elec-

---

[61] The question of reconstituting voter registries had been a permanent concern of the civilian constitutional advisors to the government. The Subcommission on Electoral Laws

toral system were reserved to organic constitutional law, they too would be subject to the *Tribunal Constitucional*'s preventive constitutional review.

Well in advance of the presidential plebiscite, a greatly altered political and constitutional context was taking shape. Unlike the plebiscitary extravaganzas orchestrated by the government in 1978 and 1980, the rules of the game were no longer going to be the absolute prerogative of any of the commanders of the armed forces. Ironically, Pinochet and the Junta were now being subject to a unanimous decision of their own – the constitution, by an organ which they too had set in place, and many of whose members the military had directly or indirectly appointed. I have no documentation of the executive's reaction within *La Moneda* to the court's September 1985 ruling. However, the impact within the legislative junta was immediate, dramatic, and precipitated a severe crisis.

The Junta first received word of the constitutional court's decision on September 24, 1985, just at the end of a regular legislative session, when the Secretary of Legislation informed the commanders that earlier he had received a courtesy call from the court informing him of their decision and that just ten minutes earlier he had received a copy of the sentence. The immediate concern of the Junta was how to respond to the press on their way out of the session. After a brief discussion, they decided to delay comment until receiving the official communication from the court (AHJG, 28/85, September 24, 1985, 16–18). The next sessions, though, would be dramatic.

A week later, after the Secretary of Legislation presented a summary of the decision, the question was how to proceed. Under the terms of the constitution, the tribunal's rulings are final and not subject to appeal, and on previous occasions when articles had been ruled unconstitutional by the tribunal the Junta had merely excised the norms impugned and transmitted the bill to the president for promulgation

and Political Parties of the Constituent Commission during the first years of military rule had persistently pressured the government to begin to put in place a new system of national identity that would provide the basis for a secure system of voter registration. Nevertheless, even after the internal crisis generated by the irregular form of the January 1978 *Consulta Nacional* and the complaints of the opposition prior to the constitutional plebiscite of September 1980, the government continued to drag its feet.

During an August 1984 Junta discussion of the organic constitutional law on political parties, the Minister of the Interior, Sergio Onofre Jarpa, made it clear that the executive had yet to decide and was considering a voting system without electoral registries in which voters would simply have to present their national identity card to vote (AHJG, 22/84, August 21, 1984, 70).

remedied of its constitutional defects.[62] This time, though, without any discussion of the substance of the ruling, the Junta bogged down over what to do with the impugned law. After the Secretary of Legislation suggested that the bill return to a joint commission, Merino concurred. Matthei objected, asking what would be done with the bill in the commission. After others answered that there might be various solutions to the articles found unconstitutional, Matthei's only subsequent comments during the session were objections. He repeatedly exclaimed "No, no!" as the rest of the Junta decided on the specifics of the joint commission. He insisted that the court's decision was final and announced that he would not send an air force representative to integrate the joint commission and spoke for the record to this effect. The other junta members proceeded to form the commission (AHJG, 29/85 October 1, 1985, 5–11). For the first time since Law 17,983 had created the institution of joint commissions, a *Comisión Conjunta* was formed that did not represent each of the four military services.

Three days later, Matthei distributed a nine-page legal brief reviewing the points of law pertaining to the referral of organic constitutional projects to the Constitutional Tribunal for mandatory review, as well as the effects of the tribunal's review. As the brief demonstrated, the constitution and Law 17,983 (which governed the legislative process) required that the project be sent to the court within five days of being "totally processed" (*totalmente tramitado*), prior to promulgation by the president. "Totally processed," the brief continued, could only mean once the project of law had been approved, otherwise another term would have been used, such as "during processing." The norms regarding the effects of decisions were straightforward: Decisions of the constitutional court were not subject to appeal and any articles impugned as unconstitutional could not become law. The key argument in regard to the specific problem raised in the Junta was that once a project "is totally approved in the legislative system the Junta and each one of its members lack legal authority to formulate amendments and observations in its regard." Therefore, the only authority the Junta possessed was to eliminate the objected norms and submit the remaining text to the president for promulgation. To do otherwise was to violate the constitution and Law 17,983.[63]

---

[62] This procedure was specified in the Junta accord regulating Law 17,983. See ART. 25, *Acuerdo de la Junta de Gobierno, Aprueba el reglamento para la tramitación de las leyes*, D.O., April 11, 1981.

[63] Ord. No. 112-1, *"Mat.: Situación constitucional y legal del proyecto,"* October 4, 1985, *Ley 18, 460, Trans. y Antec.*, vol. 234, pp. 387–95. The quote is at p. 393.

At the following session, the other members came around to Matthei's position after the partial joint commission studied the situation. Of the three legislative commissions, only the First Legislative Commission (the navy) did so with reservations, maintaining that the Junta could modify a project after review if excising an unconstitutional precept would generate such a vacuum that the law became inapplicable. Merino, at the end of the brief discussion, spoke for history, "I want to place on the record that the sole constitutional Legislative Power in this country is the Junta of Government and that no one other than the Junta may approve and enact laws in accordance with what is proposed by the colegislator which is the executive" (AHJG, 30/85 October 8, 1985, 37). Notwithstanding Merino's jealous defense of the Junta's legislative authority, after March 11, 1981 this authority had ceased to be unlimited.

### Defining the Legal Framework of the Plebiscite

Henceforth, the Constitutional Tribunal would play a major role in determining the legal framework of the presidential plebiscite. The ruling on the TRICEL did not thwart the executive from attempting to enact institutional devices aimed at limiting the opposition's capacity to organize and compete in the plebiscite. However, in subsequent rulings the court consistently struck provisions that restricted free political competition or provided opportunity for arbitrary intervention in the political process.

In this process, the fact that the constitution contained a full bill of rights emerged as a decisive limit upon the military government. Since Chapter 2 guaranteed such rights as equality before the law, equal protection of the law, due process, and freedom of association, as well as political rights, the constitutional court could strike as unconstitutional any precept that violated these norms. In the remaining period leading up to the plebiscite, the constitutional court repeatedly did so when it reviewed the remaining political organic laws. The court struck any number of articles that would have established inequalities or enabled arbitrary restrictions of rights at the different stages of the political-electoral process – from party formation and registration, internal party organization, voter registration, electoral and plebiscitary campaigns, the convocation of elections and plebiscites, to voting and the qualification of elections.

In completing the legal-constitutional framework for the plebiscite, the executive once again followed its general strategy of postponing any resolution of highly consequential matters until absolutely necessary, first submitting more secondary bills to the Junta. Thus, in the course of 1986–1988 the organic constitutional laws on electoral inscriptions and the electoral service, political parties, and voting and counts were enacted. On the same principle of delaying decisions, the rules specifying such central aspects of the electoral system as the electoral rule for translating votes into seats, the types of districts, and the mapping of districts were not settled until after the October 1988 plebiscite revealed some sense of political alignments and their geographic distribution.[64] Rather than reconstruct the legislative review of each of these laws, I will limit myself to briefly noting key aspects of the Constitutional Tribunal's decisions on these laws. In isolation, many of the corrections appear trivial, yet their cumulative effect was to remove any number of possible avenues for arbitrary manipulation of the electoral process.

The first of the organic laws relating to the electoral system, Law 18,556, regulated voter registration procedures and the organization of the Electoral Service. It entered the legislative system on January 13, 1986 and was approved by the Junta on August 7, 1986.[65] The new system of inscriptions did not significantly depart from the precoup system. The long advocated adoption of a computerized system in the end was shelved and manual registration, though now in duplicate books, was retained. Similarly, despite the executive's recommendation of a single set of registry books for both men and women, the Junta decided to retain the tradition of separate registries for men and women.[66]

---

[64] The serial enactment of electoral rules was accepted by the constitutional court, which established the jurisprudence that the indefinite article "an" in the phrase "an organic constitutional law" in ART. 18 referred to the character of the law, not a quantity.

[65] *Ley Num. 18,556, Ley Orgánica Constitucional sobre Sistema de Inscripciones Electorales y Servicio Electoral*, D.O., October 1, 1986. The Constitutional Tribunal's decision, *Sentencia Rol. No. 38*, was published in the same edition of the official gazette.

[66] The joint commission's report explained this decision in terms of "the advantage that this represents for the tranquility and normal development of elections and plebiscitary acts, since this will permit separate voting places for men and women." "*Informe de la Comisión Conjunta*," in *Ley 18,556, Ley Orgánica Constitucional sobre Sistema de Inscripciones Electorales y Servicio Electoral, Trans. y Antec. – Leyes*, vol. 293, p. 505.

Separate rolls for men and women had been established in 1934, when women, along with resident foreigners, won the right to vote in municipal elections. By 1949, when women achieved full voting rights, the tradition of separate books had been established and was never abandoned.

In its mandatory review of this organic constitutional law the Constitutional Tribunal struck, among other norms, a provision authorizing the Director of the Electoral Service to cancel at will inscriptions she suspected had been effected in violation of the law. ART. 19, no. 3, the guarantee of equal protection of the law, and ART. 19, no. 5, the corollary guarantee of due process, were invoked to strike this opportunity for arbitrary infringement of voting rights, since the law as it stood made no provisions for a just and rational trial, summons of the person whose registration was challenged, any opportunity for defense, nor appeal of the director's unilateral decision.

The tribunal also struck unconstitutional restrictions of rights found in the project of the organic constitutional law on political parties, which was finally approved by the Junta on January 15, 1987.[67] These unconstitutional provisions included: (1) an article granting the Constitutional Tribunal authority to provisionally suspend the process of legal party formation of any entity suspected of pursuing objectives that violated ART. 8 of the constitution; this provisional suspension, which was to have remained in effect until the court resolved definitively, was ruled an unconstitutional restriction of freedom of association; (2) a norm prohibiting new parties from adopting the names of parties dissolved after the coup; (3) norms that dictated the specifics of internal party organization – another violation of freedom of association; and (4) articles conveying to the Director of the Electoral Service authority to judge and sanction improprieties in the process of legal party formation; these provisions too were ruled to violate the guarantees of equality before the law and due process.

[67] The processing of *Boletín 496-06* was renewed in late December 1986 after the Junta received a new *indicación* from the president, this time with a substitute text for each article. At this point, the new bill was rushed through the legislative system and approved by the Junta on January 15, 1987 (AHJG, 44/86-E). Although there no longer remained an entity "regional party," the bill maintained two types of parties – those organized in eight regions throughout the country and those organized in three contiguous regions. The new variant of "tri-regional" parties remained controversial but was accepted. A proposal to introduce a system of primaries, supported by the navy and the air force, was not approved.

The number of members required to form a party was lowered substantially, but was now regionally based. The new percentage required was 0.5 percent of the valid votes emitted in the preceding election for deputies in the region. This lower number, however, was also coupled with a requirement that parties garner at least 5 percent of the vote in each region in which they are organized in order to retain their status as legal parties. The transitory articles of the law stipulated considerably lower numbers of signatures for party organization during the transitory period. *Ley Num. 18,603, Ley Orgánica Constitucional de los Partidos Políticos*, D.O., March 23, 1987. For the Constitutional Tribunal's decision, see *Sentencia Rol No. 43*, D.O., March 7, 1987.

The Constitutional Tribunal's April 1988 sentence on the project structuring voting and vote counts was also extremely consequential.[68] The law governed all stages of elections – the inscription of candidates, the format of ballots, propaganda and publicity during campaigns, the constitution and staffing of voting tables, the vote and count, procedures for initiating electoral complaints, etc. The tribunal's sentence was extensive and although it did rule some precepts unconstitutional, other aspects of the decision were far more significant. For the first time the tribunal notified the military government that specific articles – concerning political campaigning and the dates of elections – as they stood were incomplete and had to be complemented by further legislation. This decision compelled the Junta to enact legislation providing equal free television time to both sides during the campaign preceding the plebiscite, as well as nondiscriminatory, paid access to the print media and radio.[69] The *franja*, as these free television slots were known, later proved to be a major factor in the opposition's victory in the October 5, 1988 plebiscite.

The same sentence also established the sole constitutionally valid interpretation of one of the project's transitory articles that regulated the convocation of the plebiscite. The court's interpretation removed a constitutional ambiguity that left open the possibility of a sudden, snap plebiscite. Such a sudden plebiscite, the tribunal maintained, would have vitiated the opposition's constitutional rights to campaign and oversee the voting, since the timing of the steps along the way could remain uncertain and the plebiscite itself could follow virtually within days of its public convocation.

In this manner, the *Tribunal Constitutional*, through its decisions on the political organic constitutional laws, played a major role in assuring that the upcoming presidential plebiscite would be a fair contest and a valid expression of the popular will.

## Voting Out the Dictatorship

The other side of this history is the political process whereby sectors within the opposition grudgingly came to accept the "institutionality of the dictatorship" after all other methods failed to terminate military

[68] *Tribunal Constitucional, Sentencia Rol No. 53*, D.O., April 13, 1988. The text in question was promulgated as *Ley 18,700, Ley Orgánica Constitucional sobre Votaciones Populares y Escrutinios*, D.O., May 6, 1988.
[69] Among other modifications, these required provisions were later promulgated in Law 18,733, D.O., August 13, 1988.

rule. This history exceeds the possibilities of this book, so I will only point to some of the landmarks along the way.

Shortly after electoral registries opened in late February 1987, various groupings of opposition parties called for voter registration as part of campaigns for "free elections."[70] In early August 1987, the PDC opted to register under the political party law, and by the end of the year an "instrumental party," the *Partido por la Democracia* (*PPD*, the Party for Democracy) had been formed to organize a legal center-left party. In February 1988, a broad coalition of parties came together to form the *Comando del No* to oppose the Junta's candidate.[71]

The question of the candidate for the plebiscite divided the Right after mid-1987 and eventually caused the division of the newly formed broad, unified Right party, *Renovación Nacional*, in April 1988.[72] The members of the Junta themselves, on a number of occasions, declared publicly that the candidate would be a civilian, implying both that it didn't necessarily have to be Pinochet and if he was the candidate and won, he would serve as a civilian. Despite ongoing grumbling about a "consensus candidate," in the end the Junta nominated President Pinochet for a second term. This nomination occurred on August 30, and the plebiscite was announced for October 5, 1988.

After a month of intense campaigning, with the "*Sí*" whipping up the anti-Communist scare tactic that a vote for the "*No*" was a vote to return to chaos and the "*No*" joyously insisting "happiness already is on its way" (*la alegría ya viene*), Chileans for the first time in fifteen and a half years went to the polls and a solid majority refused to grant Pinochet another eight years as president.

This whole process would have been impossible without the 1980 constitution and its provisions for prior review of the constitutionality of the Junta's organic constitutional laws. It is widely accepted that a number of mechanisms of participation and oversight, made possible by the Constitutional Tribunal's decisions, were decisive in the outcome of the plebiscite. Of particular importance were the *franja*, the daily half-hour of free television campaigning, pitting the "*Sí*" against the "*No*," as well as the opposition's parallel vote count, which would have

---

[70] On these campaigns, see Geisse and Gumucio 1987 and Libio Pérez, "*Elecciones libres: Un difícil camino*," *Análisis*, July 20, 1987, 7–8.

[71] On the formation of the Center-Left coalition, see Ortega Frei 1992 and Puryear 1994.

[72] The divisive issue, as it would be the following year, was whether to organize a democratic Right independent from Pinochet or to embrace the general as the only figure capable of projecting the economic and institutional order into the future. On this schism within the Right, see Berrier 1989.

been impossible to execute without the legally guaranteed right to have party representatives overseeing the voting and the count at each table.[73] Dramatically, on the night of the 5th, the returns from the opposition's parallel count prevented the executive from insisting upon favorable results based on a minuscule proportion of returns and prompted important figures of the Right, as well as the members of the Junta, to recognize the victory of the *"No."* The official results gave the *"No"* an overwhelming victory. Of the 7,251,943 votes cast, the *"No"* received 54.71 percent, whereas 43.01 percent had voted to grant Pinochet another term in office.

After spontaneous celebrations the following afternoon on the streets in front of *La Moneda*, an official victory rally was held two days later in the *Parque O'Higgins*. The graffiti scrawled on the sidewalk captured it all: *"Lo echamos con un lápiz."*[74] The force of arms had been routed by the majoritarian force of millions of small, neatly folded slips of paper, each bearing only a small pencil mark through the horizontal line set next to the word "NO." Not insignificantly, however, the pencil and paper had been provided by the armed forces.

[73] On the importance of the *franja*, see Ana María Gibson, *"Franja electoral en TV: Sumando y Restando,"* *Qué Pasa*, October 13, 1988, pp. 10–11, and Cecilia Vargas, *"El poder de un clip político,"* *La Epoca, Revista Dominical*, 2–3. Also see Portales 1989 and Tironi 1990.
[74] "We threw him out with a pencil."

# Chapter Eight

# Military Dictatorship and Constitutionalism in Chile

Early in the evening of October 6, 1988, Pinochet appeared on national television. After a month of dressing in civilian attire, the general reappeared in uniform and specified for the people of Chile the precise consequences of the preceding day's events: "Neither the tenets nor the constitutional itinerary outlined have been in play, rather only the election of the person who should lead the country toward the full application of the Fundamental Charter during the following presidential period" (*El Mercurio*, October 7, 1988).

Among other things, Pinochet was indirectly reminding the nation that in accordance with the constitution, their refusal to grant him a second eight-year term still extended his term, as well as the Junta's, one year. In other words, although his presidential term ended March 10, 1989, T.D. 29 specified that Pinochet would remain president for another year and five months.

## The Constitutional and Electoral Dénouement of 1989

Notwithstanding this remedial lesson in constitutional law, civilian political forces attached far broader implications to the victory of the "*No.*" Sectors of the Left demanded Pinochet's immediate resignation; others, including the PDC, called for early elections; and virtually all parties – from the Left to the Right – called for (or accepted the need for) constitutional reforms. Within days of the plebiscite, the PDC and the rightist *Renovación Nacional* (RN) had each publicly presented proposals for reform, and by late December the new Minister of the Interior, Carlos Cáceres, announced that he would begin talks with the parties.

These negotiations proceeded by fits and starts, as the constitutional question immediately became intertwined with various political strategies once all parties began to jockey for position heading toward the presidential and congressional elections. This strategic game was complicated until early April by the absence of any electoral law and uncertainty over whether electoral pacts would be allowed.

After the plebiscite, the Right was plagued by the machinations of Pinochet and the continued temptation among some sectors to stick to a strategy of "persons" by seeking a second Pinochet candidacy rather than pursue the strengthening of Right Party organizations. This tension pervaded the constitutional reform process and the selection of a candidate for president. Important sectors of the Right, particularly RN, badly wanted to reform the constitution before the elections to deny the Center and the Left of the unifying banner of constitutional reform going into the elections, which they would certainly carry if the regime remained inflexible. Additionally, in the same vein, it was far preferable to resolve the constitutional question and get it off the agenda, particularly through a negotiated settlement with the opposition, than to face the likely prospect of a later dismantling of the text, particularly since the all-important provision (ART. 118) that entrenched key chapters of the constitution had not been included among the precepts requiring a higher quorum and a delay for their modification.[1] In this situation, any majority capable of reforming a nonentrenched article could potentially open the door to bringing the whole house down.

However, the type of reforms that could emerge out of negotiations between the democratic Right and the Center conflicted with those required to fulfill the ambitions of Pinochet and the *duro* faction among his advisors. For much of the first part of the year, these advisors worked at cross-purposes from Cáceres, trying to build support for reforms that would enable Pinochet to make another bid at reelection. According to journalistic accounts, these maneuvers were finally halted in March 1989 after the Junta nixed this prospect in an informal discussion with Pinochet regarding possible reforms.[2] Finally, after talks broke down in early May, an agreement was finally reached at the end of the month. After a quick pass through the Junta, the constitutional

[1] This point was stressed by Tapia (1987), who insisted that this omission permitted a wholesale modification of the constitution following the ordinary amendment procedure. At a moment when important sectors of the Left rejected the constitution, Tapia (1987, 2) argued that the opposition could "use revolutionarily the legality of the dictatorship to put an end to the dictatorship."

[2] See Cavallo 1992 and *Hoy*, March 20, 1989, 4. There is no record of this meeting in the minutes of the Junta's legislative sessions.

reforms were approved. On July 30, 1989, the package of reforms was ratified in a plebiscite. Of the over seven million people who voted, 85.7 percent backed the changes to the constitution.[3] Four months later, on December 14, 1989, the Chilean people again went to the polls, this time to freely elect a president and Congress.

### La Transmisión del Mando

Three months later, on a bright Sunday afternoon charged with emotions, meanings, and symbols, the transfer of power took place. The incoming and the outgoing government each began the day with their own solemn observances. At the Santa Inés Cemetery in Viña del Mar, the leadership of the Socialist Party and the incoming government paid homage to the memory of Salvador Allende, the last elected president. In Santiago, at the *Escuela Militar*, Pinochet and his cabinet took part in a mass of gratitude. The president's movements were flocked by crowds of supporters that had begun to form early before his residence and along the trajectory to the military school. Bearing flags and photographs of Pinochet, their banners read, "Thank you, President," and "Mission Accomplished." As these two opposite images suggest, it was

---

[3] The reforms were effected by *Ley No.* 18,825, D.O., August 17, 1989. Among the most important modifications, the June 1989 reforms: derogated ART. 8, which in effect had banned the parties of the Left, and in its place regulated antisystem parties in the context of the paragraph on the right of association (ART. 19, no. 15), along lines closer to the German norm that initially inspired the Constituent Commission; suppressed the paragraph granting the president authority to dissolve the lower house once during her term; restricted the president's emergency powers, in particular by derogating any authority to expel individuals from the country during a state of siege; increased the number of elected senators from 26 to 38; lowered the quorum required to enact, modify, or derogate organic constitutional laws; strengthened the autonomy of the armed forces by stipulating that appointments, promotions, and retirements in the armed forces conform to an organic constitutional law on the armed forces; incorporated the *Contralor General de la República* to the National Security Council as a voting member, thereby producing a 4–4 tie among civilian and military members; made the constitution more flexible, by derogating ART. 118. ART. 118 had both required a higher quorum of two-thirds of the members of both houses to enact amendments that concerned constitutional plebiscites, decreased the powers of the president, or increased the authority of Congress, as well as stipulated, in addition to the higher quorum, a delay mechanism, whereby any amendment to modify articles contained in Chapters 1, 7, 10, and 11 (bases of institutionality, constitutional court, armed forces, and the national security council, respectively) also had to be ratified by the following Congress. The reformed constitution suppressed the delay but maintained the higher quorum for the chapters mentioned while also extending it to Chapters 3 and 14 (constitutional rights and duties; and reform of the constitution). On the 1989 reforms, see Bertelsen 1989; Silva Bascuñán 1989; Verdugo Marinkovic 1990; Cea 1991; Ensalaco 1994.

a day before which few Chileans could stand indifferent. After sixteen and a half years, on Sunday, March 11, 1990, the longest period of military rule in Chilean history was coming to a close.

The "transmisión del mando" took place in the still unfinished Congress building in Valparaiso. First, the Chamber of Deputies and the Senate constituted themselves as legislative bodies and elected their presidents and vice presidents. Then, with the two chambers in joint session, at one o'clock the presidential succession itself began. Outside, Pinochet made his way to the ceremony. Emulating precoup conventions of presidential succession, he arrived in an open vehicle, and in the final stretch to the building was met by a barrage of fruit, stones, coins, and angry shouts of "*asesino*," "*asesino*." Once inside the building with his cabinet, the ceremony began.

The proceedings that followed were no mere formality, nor simple official act. The protocol had been carefully planned and negotiated, yet the usages were long-standing, imbued with conventions and symbolism dating to the presidential succession of 1841.[4] As per tradition, the president of the Senate opened the session, upon which the secretary of the Senate read the official act proclaiming the new President-Elect, Patricio Aylwin. Aylwin then entered the hall with his cabinet to be sworn in by the president of the Senate and to vow obedience to the Constitution and to the law. Then, in a ritual symbolizing the historical continuity of the institution over incumbents, Pinochet removed the emblems of presidential power, the three-color presidential sash and the *piocha* – a jewelled medallion, said to date back to independence hero Bernardo O'Higgins – and set them on the table before him. Gabriel Valdés, the president of the Senate, then placed a new sash upon Aylwin and to the ovation of those attending, embraced the new president. Pinochet proceeded to congratulate his successor, and then two days of official festivities began.

## Dictatorship and Transition in Chile

For all the traditional symbolism of the inaugural ceremony, something far more astounding than a presidential succession took place on March 11, 1990. In fact, part of what was so astounding was how

---

[4] Bernardino Bravo Lira, "Historia y significado de la transmisión del mando," *El Mercurio*, March 4, 1990, sec. E, pp. 1, 5. Also see Claudia Godoy L., "Una tradición política chilena: La ceremonia del traspaso del poder," *El Mercurio*, February 25, 1990, sec. D, pp. 18–19.

regular everything seemed. For despite the process of routinization through ritual, something remarkable was happening: The dictator, Pinochet – the symbol of absolute, personal, arbitrary power – was abiding by known, impersonal rules, even though these rules had frustrated his ambitions to remain president. One of the most enduring authoritarian figures in recent South American history, notwithstanding his prepotency and ambition, was leaving the sash on the table after the people had said "No." Where men of lesser power have tossed the table, Pinochet returned to the barracks.

This remarkable history is striking given the standard interpretation of the regime as a personalist dictatorship and the widely accepted view that constitutions do not constrain autocrats. Although Pinochet's defeat in the plebiscite may perhaps be attributed to personal miscalculations, my reconstruction of the process of institutional design and rule making during the long sixteen and a half years of military rule in Chile amply demonstrates both that the 1988 plebiscite cannot be explained in terms of a centralization of power in Pinochet and that constitutional limits upon the dictatorship were critical in creating conditions for a fair contest in the plebiscite.

From a comparative perspective, Pinochet's continuous control of the presidency throughout the dictatorship sets the Chilean case apart from other recent military regimes in Latin America that involved multiple authoritarian executives. The provisions of the 1980 constitution that allowed Pinochet to remain commander in chief of the army for eight years after the transition and to subsequently, as a former president, take a seat in the senate might also appear to give credence to the personalization of power interpretation. Nevertheless, Pinochet's extended control over the presidency was only half of the story, and the dictator's longevity in power itself cannot be disassociated from the institutionalization of the military junta, which must be recognized as a significant factor in generating the military cohesion that permitted extended military rule. For what was unique about the Chilean dictatorship was not the unipersonal executive, but the separation from it of a collegial military legislative, which held multiple vetoes and provided the foundation for enacting, implementing, and sustaining a constitution that constrained the military regime as a whole.

Contrary to the personalization of power approach, the initial public law of the dictatorship and the 1980 constitution were neither imposed by Pinochet nor secured the general's preferred institutional arrangements. As I documented in Chapter 2, rules specifying and separating executive and legislative powers were enacted in 1974 after the navy and the air force blocked Pinochet's move to adopt majority decision making with Pinochet holding the tiebreaker. This arrangement would have allowed Pinochet to concentrate executive and legislative powers and stand as sovereign in the classical sense. The rules set in place in 1974 and 1975 precluded Pinochet's dominance by requiring unanimous agreement among the armed forces to legislate and modify the constitution, as well as by denying him any authority to unilaterally manipulate promotions and retirements in the other branches and thereby be in a position to mold a compliant legislature through the indirect selection of its members. In the first years of the dictatorship, Admiral Merino and General Leigh willingly accepted their exclusion from the executive in exchange for legal rules that provided each of them with a veto in the legislative process and protected their services' autonomy. As I examined in Chapter 5, in 1977 Pinochet again attempted to concentrate power, the navy and the air force defended the standing rules, and an agreement appears to have been made that a constitution should be enacted and that military rule would end in the medium term. As the evidence suggests, the constitution was not Pinochet's first choice; he preferred a regime dominated by the army, but before the intransigence of the navy and the air force was forced to accept a constitution that extended his term but also maintained in its transitory provisions the standing constraints upon any personal dominance. By the same token, as I have analyzed at length in Chapter 6, the main body of the constitution was designed to regulate a future, competitive, civilian polity, not to assure Pinochet's ongoing rule.

These constraints upon Pinochet's power, unlike the political constraints upon military presidents in Brazil and Argentina (discussed in Chapter 2), were not given by the loose interplay of shifting factions or by immediate power plays. Rather, they were institutional and ongoing. The checks given by the Junta were structured by the unanimity rule, the separation of executive and legislative powers, and were reinforced by the 1980 constitution.

The effects of these same rules over the course of the dictatorship are equally striking in light of the commonly held view that legal institutions do not constrain dictatorships. The Chilean dictatorship was subject to and constrained by legal institutions of its own making. In this regard, two periods need to be distinguished – before and after the constitution – as the nature of constraints differed in each.

Prior to the constitution going into force in March 1981, the Junta's rules constrained the executive in those areas subject to legal regulation but did not limit the sovereignty of the Junta as a legislative and constituent body. Even though the Supreme Court and the *Contraloría General de la República* remained in operation, the Junta's capacity to unilaterally legislate and enact amendments to the constitution illustrated Hobbes's point that sovereign bodies can override limiting institutions by modifying legal rules. Nonetheless, among the members of the Junta, power was limited: Given the unanimity rule, no member enjoyed absolute power within the regime. This constraint, complemented by the system of legislative commissions which allowed each commander the institutional time and space to develop individual positions, implied that legislative and constituent decisions could only be taken with full agreement of the commander of each branch of the armed forces. Although this limit was internal to the Junta, was not enforced by any external body, and did not affect the Junta's rule-making prerogative as a whole, it is difficult to imagine that the 1980 constitution would have been promulgated and that institutional constraints would have been subsequently introduced in the absence of the collegial junta as protected by the unanimity rule.

After March 1981, this situation changed as the constitution complemented the internal constraints given by the unanimity rule and the separation of powers with legal limits upon the military regime as a whole. First, the military junta restricted its own capacity to unilaterally override undesired interpretations of its charter by requiring plebiscitary ratification of any amendments it unanimously approved. Second, most decisively, the 1980 constitution put an end to the constitutional uncertainty created by D.L. No. 788. In the form of the chapter on rights, the Junta put in place a clear set of limits upon its formerly unrestricted legislative authority and constitutional duties. Third, the Junta empowered multiple institutions to uphold the terms of the constitution – the Supreme Court, the *Contraloría General de la República*, and the *Tribunal Constitucional*. This study has not examined how the return to constitutional certainty affected the Supreme Court's ability to uphold a higher law during 1981–1990, nor has it examined in detail how the provision for constitutional emergency powers during the transitory period, as well as the operation of the security services, allowed the executive to restrict constitutional rights and at times violate them. However, as was seen in the preceding chapter, the entry into force of the 1980 constitution immediately constrained the military dictatorship. At key junctures the constitutional court struck unconstitutional norms from the organic constitutional laws and forced the Junta to abide by the terms of its prior decision. In this manner, the rules embodied in the 1980 constitution began to have a life apart from their makers, constrained them, and assured the legal-institutional framework that made possible the opposition victory in the October 5, 1988 plebiscite.

Though the military junta freely imposed the constitution upon the Chilean public, once the constitution went into force the military ceased to freely determine its implementation and interpretation and became subject to this higher law of its own making. From March 11, 1981 through the dissolution of the military regime exactly nine years later, the military dictatorship was subject to and limited by constitutional constraints.

## Commitment, Self-Binding, and Institutional Limits

What does this peculiar experience of an all-powerful military regime subjecting itself to rules tell us about the conditions under which limited autocracy is possible, the motivations that lead actors to restrict their discretionary authority, the factors that contribute to sustaining limiting institutions over time, and the effects of constraints upon power? Before speculating upon the conditions under which autocrats may effectively subject themselves to institutions, let me first suggest that the motivation for disabling discretion in authoritarian Chile was not to make Junta commitments credible to others, that with some qualifications this experience was a case of self-binding, and that, although difficult to assess, limiting rules may have prolonged the dictatorship and, certainly, they contributed to assuring the consolidation of the 1980 constitution.

### Credible Commitment

The literature on credible commitments suggests that it may be in the interest of an actor bearing discretionary authority to disable her capacity to reverse policies if such constraints enable them to secure needed cooperation from actors who otherwise would not act in the ways desired. This motivation for instituting limiting rules was not significant in the Chilean case. As the available evidence suggests, the reason for rules had to do with problems of coordination internal to the Junta, not the need to secure the compliance of actors outside of the ruling bloc. Nor does it appear that the unanimity rule, the separation of powers, or, later, the constitution itself, had any credibility effect among constituents or external actors.

Although these mechanisms slowed impulsive change within the regime and contributed to policy stability, the regime could not gain credibility from the operation of these institutions precisely because they were hermetically sealed from public view: The fact of limits within the dictatorship never transpired to the public because the public was not allowed to see the Junta in operation. The unanimity rule was inscribed in law and known, yet though the very existence of such a rule might suggest the fact of divergences, unanimity also could appear as a mere formality within a collectivity dominated by one man or intrinsically unified as a military body. Since Junta sessions were secret, the public had no way of knowing about differences among Pinochet and the other members of the Junta, let alone the sources of cleavages or the evolution of alignments. Admiral Merino's unknown dissidence is sufficient proof of this.

These information constraints also weakened the public credibility of the regime's commitment to implement the constitution. In conjunction with the absence of information on the conflictive underside of the constitution and on the conception of institutions developed within the Constituent Commission, secrecy allowed little evidence to seep to the public that would warrant that it view the constitution as anything other than an instrument of Pinochet's personalist power. These restrictions on publicity were deliberate and were to the strategic advantage of the dictatorship, though at the cost of any credibility that might have accrued from public knowledge of how the regime operated.

### Self-Binding

If the Chilean military did not introduce institutions to make its acts more credible before others, why did the commanders of the armed forces adopt rules which eventually restricted their power? Was this an instance of self-binding, in which the dictatorship intentionally sought to disable its prerogative to protect itself from short-term temptations and enable it to hold to long-term objectives? In answering these questions, we must again distinguish between the pre- and post-constitution periods, as well as distinguish between the effects of institutions and the reasons for their establishment.

The quasiconstitutional mechanisms established within the Junta – the unanimity rule, the separation of executive and legislative functions, and the system of legislative commissions – did enable the Junta to rule more effectively over time. These devices set in place a preestablished division of labor which enabled the Junta to simultaneously proceed on many fronts and to temper the short-term seductions of dictatorial power by subjecting legal and constitutional decisions to multiple viewpoints and arguments within the Junta, as well as to the requirement of unanimity.

Despite these effects, the impetus for establishing this procedural framework, at least during the first period, was not to limit the power of the Junta as a body, nor to enable effective rule over time. Instead of seeking to bind their power, the members of the Junta in 1974 and 1975 were seeking to bind each other to known rules that assured each a secure institutional position within the dictatorship. As I documented in Chapter 2, the specific form of delimiting powers in D.L. No. 527 and organizing legislative procedures in D.L. No. 991 was settled upon to prevent any one junta member, in particular Pinochet, from concentrating all power in the regime. Rules were instituted to bind each junta member to agreed-on procedures, not to tie the hands of the Junta as a whole.

The questions raised become somewhat more difficult to answer when we consider the institutional limits put in place by the 1980 constitution. Should we view the Junta's decision to allow the provisions structuring the constitutional tribunal and protecting rights, which eventually limited the Junta, as an act of self-binding? On one level it is clear, as was seen in Chapter 7, that these institutions were designed to bind others, to hold future civilian actors to the terms of the military's constitution. These institutions were activated in March 1981 not to bind the military, but to secure the validity of the constitution prior to any transition, so as to decrease the probability that the constitution would be cast aside once the military left power. The desire to bind others was the strategic motivation for enacting a complete constitution in 1980 rather than a succession of partial, constitutional acts, as well as for having the constitutional tribunal begin operations during the transitory period and for limiting the Junta's capacity to unilaterally modify the constitution after its approval by plebiscite.

Nevertheless, these acts must also be seen as forms of self-binding. Unlike instances of constitution making in which the constitution-making body is not subject to its product because it terminates activities upon completing a constitution, in Chile the same body that enacted the constitution, the Junta, continued to operate once the constitution went into effect. Although the armed forces probably did not anticipate that they would be constrained in the ways that they were by the constitution, the members of the Junta deliberately subjected themselves to the terms of the new constitution by allowing large portions of the main text to go into force while they retained power. Similarly, it should not be forgotten that the constitution was enacted after internal conflicts over proposals for extended dictatorship led to a constitutional settlement that led the Junta to commit itself to withdrawing from power in the medium term. More so than in many cases where constitutionalism is portrayed as self-binding, the Chilean Junta was bound by rules of its own making, rather than norms set in place by an earlier generation or other actors.

## Institutional Stability and Enforcement

Why were the initial rules that structured the Junta and the constitutional norms that later limited the dictatorship stable and effective? Was it actually rules that limited the members of the Junta, or were rules effective because they mirrored factors external to the legal framework? These questions are not easily answered, as the stability of the legal system and the dictatorship can be attributed to any number of factors, not least of which was the regime's capacity to coercively block the emergence of potential alternatives to its dominance.

Nevertheless, I conclude that the quasiconstitutional rules established by the Junta were effective because they were self-enforcing: Rules were adhered to because they provided a framework for the commanders of the armed forces to pursue their respective individual and joint interests. This stability was dependent on two factors which created a need for coordination as well as incentives to avoid severe intramilitary conflict. These were the prior structure of the armed forces and the specific characteristics of the larger political environment in Chile. These two factors shaped a bargaining situation which combined bases for conflict as well as strong incentives to coordinate, particularly given military perceptions of what an alternative civilian order would imply, which for many years was only conceived of in terms of a repetition of the trauma of 1972–1973. In this context, submitting to rules that blocked individual commanders from unilaterally imposing their first choices but enabled the armed forces to arrive at joint legislative and constituent decisions was in the interest of all players.

The foundation for this bargaining situation was given by the prior organization of the Chilean military into three services, each of which retained distinctive, massive coercive capabilities. This particular organizational format immediately introduced substantive differences within the Junta and a need for procedural rules to coordinate decisions. Separated by a history of service autonomy, the commanders of the three branches of the Chilean armed forces each brought their own traditions, independent command structures, and orientations to national and international affairs to the military junta in September 1973. Given these organizational differences, it was only natural that each commander articulated distinct institutional interests, jealously guarded their specific autonomy from external encroachment, and developed different perspectives on the problems at hand. At no point could any commander assume an identity of interests among the armed forces, and therefore none could countenance delegating all authority to any single chief. For this reason procedures had to be structured that would allow the plural armed forces to develop and execute a joint policy. As we saw in Chapter 2, the members of the Junta quickly came to recognize the need for procedural rules to coordinate mutual expectations and prevent any single member from achieving absolute dominance.

Notwithstanding these bases for disagreement, the commanders of the different services had much to gain by avoiding pure conflict and settling upon coordinated responses to the immediate problems before the regime. Many of these inducements arose out of the insecurity of the Junta before a larger, external environment, which was often hostile to military rule and threatened regime stability. At the outset, the principal joint payoff for the armed forces was institutional self-preservation. By combining to oust Allende, the armed forces could terminate the catastrophic political crisis and prevent its spillover into the ranks of the armed forces, which they perceived as a threat to internal cohesion, discipline, and state security. The protection of these particular institutional interests, therefore, was premised upon joint action. After the coup, unified military rule was also seen as a necessary condition for regime stability, which remained imperative for ongoing protection of the particular military organizations, particularly since the only alternative to military rule appeared to be a replay of the original crisis which had threatened them, now compounded by the likelihood of civilian demands for retribution against the armed forces. This larger external environment gave each branch of the armed forces a common interest in stabilizing the military dictatorship and assuring its potency over time.

In this bargaining situation, many of the conflicts within the Junta were motivated by different perceptions of how particular strategies or proposals contributed to this end. Given their mutual interdependence, no branch of the armed forces could be indifferent to the fate of the military government, and the rules established by the Junta provided a solution by assuring channels for individual voice as well as mechanisms for collective decision. The unanimity rule assured each force that decisions would not be imposed upon them by the other branches. As I have illustrated repeatedly, this institutional framework, whose core was the unanimity rule, tempered decision making by subjecting all proposals to independent analysis and the interplay of perspectives in the Junta. The substantive result was compromise and the setting aside of some members' preferred outcomes.

The prior plural organization of the armed forces not only introduced an immediate need for coordination, it also provided a deterrent against attempts to centralize power. This significance of force in maintaining the balance within the Junta is not easily evaluated. In the many sources I worked with, this variable was largely unobserved, at least at the highest levels of the regime. Nevertheless, it is reasonable to speculate that the potential for force was an ever-present backdrop to the cohesion of the Junta and the stability of the rules that it established. In Chile, the division of authoritarian power was premised upon a continued division of coercive capabilities. The very reason for rules was that no commander could accept subordination to any other, and the rules established left this original situation of multiple independent capabilities for force untouched. Given the asymmetries in the types of weaponry possessed by each branch, any service could potentially inflict major damage on any of the others. Any use of force was, therefore, extremely risky, as the outcome of open conflict was uncertain given mutual capacities for response. Unless unilateral military dominance could be assured, the alternative was extreme interservice tensions, a scenario which was understood to be incompatible with continued military power. The experience of the 1930s and the comparative example of Argentine military governments withdrawing upon internal division were known precedents. At this point, the perceived threats given by the larger political environment redoubled as a further reason to assure military control over the political process and to avoid open conflict among the armed forces.

## The Effects of Institutions

Though institutions were predicated upon the given organizational pluralism of the Chilean armed forces, the unanimity rule, the separation of powers, and later the incomplete character of the constitution had effects apart from simply mirroring these priors. Institutions themselves also reinforced the heterogeneity of perspectives that made institutions necessary, while they also structured additional incentives for each commander to pursue their particular institutional and political interests within the framework of established rules, as well as incentives to accept limits.

Prior pluralism was reinforced by the procedures of the legislative system which provided each commander with the institutional space and time to study and review matters before the Junta, identify points of divergence, and structure agreeable outcomes or, if unattainable, block proposals they did not support. Similarly, the fact of unanimity meant that any limits imposed by the Junta were limits each had agreed to. Prior decisions, in this context, were standards for evaluating subsequent actions. Since agreements could only be changed by agreement, any departure from the Junta's own legality, unless acceded to through consensual modifications, was an encroachment upon the Junta's legislative authority.

This dimension of decree-law as a shared yardstick of joint commitments also explains the importance given to internal recordkeeping within the regime. The members of the Junta had to have extensive documentation of the decision-making process and transcripts of their meeting in order to be able to independently authenticate the substance of their decisions and preclude constant conflict over the nature of past agreements. Thus, in the course of a Junta session, it was often sufficient for a single commander to point out a prior agreement to force a debate back to standing points of consensus and disagreement.

Yet, just as significantly, the separation of executive and legislative functions also had the effect of stimulating a heterogeneity of perspectives within the regime. The relegation of the commanders of the navy, air force, and *carabineros* solely to legislative activity, released from any participation in the everyday tasks of governing, structured an institutional position distinct from the executive which occasioned different perspectives on the same problems. Removed from the immediacy of governing, the Junta often developed very different views of the political situation and adopted temporal perspectives at variance from those of the president. On this ground, the members of the Junta repeatedly sought to temper Pinochet's propensity for rash, precipitous responses to political difficulties, particularly during the early 1980s. The significance of the separation of powers also emerges from the contrast with the Argentine case during the *Proceso*: Despite a similar plural organization of the armed forces, in Argentina each branch retained a stake in the executive, stimulating competition and policy incoherence which ultimately denied the dictatorship of any coherence, according to some analysts.

**321**

The structuring of a framework for continuous decision making over time, in conjunction with the open-ended nature of military rule, made for extended repeat play and the prospect of future benefits through ongoing coordination. In this context, the initial public law of the dictatorship, which again did not limit the prerogative of the Junta as a body, was enabling in the manner stressed by Holmes (1988): The existence of prior rules which specify powers, jurisdictions, and procedures freed the members of the Junta to concentrate on substantive problems of government by unburdening them of having to bargain over rules at every juncture.

The original incentives for continued interaction were also augmented by the incomplete character of the constitution which as a compromise embodied a number of potential outcomes, contingent upon the resolution of decisive matters that had been left open to future determination. Similarly, the very different payoffs that the constitution structured for Pinochet and the Junta also stimulated continued involvement, while the segmented character of the steps along the way implied that there would always be another chance, even when immediate resolutions did not turn out as a particular party desired. This clearly was the case with Pinochet, who up until the end believed that he was going to win the plebiscite.[5]

The general effects of limits in the Chilean case are somewhat equivocal and hazy. One can only speculate about how the fact of internal limits within the dictatorship affected the longevity of military rule in Chile. Although the separation of powers stymied Pinochet's aspirations to absolute power, the constraints imposed by the Junta may have prolonged his tenure by generating cohesion among the armed forces and by providing an internal feedback mechanism as well as a brake blocking arbitrary acts which might have precipitated an early collapse of the military regime. Whereas Geddes (1995, 1999) has established a correlation of personalization of power (as well as of single-party regimes) with the longevity of authoritarian regimes, my account suggests that regime duration may also be secured amidst organizational pluralism by rules that enable coordinated action. By the same token, however, Geddes may indeed be right, and the converse may in fact have been the case: Members of the Junta may have blocked even more prolonged authoritarianism by preventing the consolidation of an absolute dictatorship. These counterfactuals are irresolvable. Yet, one

---

[5] It is noteworthy that in the final days before the plebiscite, Pinochet's closest advisors were feeding him doctored polling data.

thing is certain: The institutional organization of the Junta played a far more significant role in determining the course of military rule in Chile than is generally believed. Without Admiral Merino, General Leigh, and General Matthei, it is not unreasonable to conjecture that General Pinochet either would have been forced to return power to civilians prior to 1990 or might perhaps have stood as head of state of Chile well into the 1990s. In any event, the evidence presented here suggests that most likely he would not have followed a constitutional path back to the barracks.

Similarly, I cannot overemphasize that by allowing themselves to be subject to limits, the military junta achieved a major strategic objective: It successfully imposed upon Chile a complex institutional framework that protects private property and bolsters parties defending the status quo, is defended by multiple organs of constitutional control, is difficult to change, and, until very recently, contributed to the stability of the statutes and jurisprudence that protected individual members of the armed forces from criminal prosecution for crimes committed during the dictatorship, particularly those committed during the period covered by the 1978 amnesty law. By being bound by their own rules, the dictatorship in Chile was able to bind others. Institutional limits upon the initially unlimited power of the Junta clearly contributed to this outcome. Had the Junta retained its facile capacity to modify the constitution or held authority with which to enact organic constitutional laws without the Constitutional Tribunal's review, the enactment of precipitate reforms to bolster the dictatorship's immediate position or the passage of organic constitutional laws inconsistent with the constitution could have disorganized the constitution and sundered it as a coherent framework structuring viable postmilitary institutional constraints. Put positively, even though the Constitutional Tribunal's rulings contributed to blocking Pinochet's personal ambitions, the court's decisions prevented the Junta from intentionally or inadvertently destroying the coherence of its prior decision as a consistent set of general rules.

## Constitutionalism and Dictatorship Reconsidered

When explaining why he restricted his groundbreaking study of law and arbitrary power in Nazi Germany to a single case, Ernst Fraenkel (1969, xvi) observed: "A discussion of similar problems in other dictatorships would require that the author be as familiar with their situations as he is with that of the Third Reich. Knowledge of the fact that the German dictatorship thrives by veiling its true face discourages us from judging other dictatorships by their words rather than by their deeds, to which we have no adequate access."

Similar apprehensions about our ability to distinguish myth from reality in our knowledge of the internal structure of other authoritarian regimes cautions against making broad claims on the basis of this analysis of the Chilean military junta. However, this proviso points to an important conclusion for the study of authoritarian regimes: Public presentations of power cannot be construed as accurate reflections of internal decision-making processes, particularly in contexts where secrecy dominates over publicity. As this study has amply documented, the personalization of power within the Chilean dictatorship was only apparent. Nondemocratic regimes do not have to rest upon a monocratic ruling apparatus; though a difficult subject for research, the construction of authoritarian power blocs must itself be an object of investigation and not a premise of analysis.

By the same token, we can no longer presume that authoritarian regimes cannot make use of law and limiting institutional devices to structure and stabilize their domination. Institutional constraints upon supreme power are not necessarily incompatible with authoritarianism. If structured upon nonmonocratic foundations, a dictatorship can institute legal limits on its own exercise of political power and still remain free from democratic processes of selection.

Even in authoritarian contexts pluralism, however narrow, is a requirement for divided and limited government. Though numerous cases suggest that collective power blocs are often unstable and prone to give way to centralized dictatorships, under specific conditions actors may have sufficient power capabilities, such as control of important military or economic resources, that allow them to protect their position within the ruling bloc. If such pluralism, at the heart of the regime, can be sustained, authoritarian power can be divided and limits on absolute power upheld.

In the Chilean case, this pluralism was neither "societal" nor "political" in the sense used by Linz (1975) to respectively describe group politics in authoritarian and totalitarian regimes. It was neither founded in prior social divisions nor a by-product of the emergence of new power bases alongside the creation of new organizations by the ruling authoritarian elite; military pluralism in Chile was embedded in the prior organization of the state. As armed forces are essential components in guaranteeing state domination and military capabilities provide threat potential, military pluralism may be more stable than the other forms of pluralism found in authoritarian and totalitarian contexts. Whether and how different sources of nondemocratic pluralism structure conditions for rule-bound interactions in authoritarian contexts is a largely uncharted area warranting future research.

The Chilean case, however, demonstrates that when pluralism, however narrow, can be sustained, the capacity for facile reversibility, which led theorists of sovereignty to discount any feasibility of autocratic self-limitation by law, may be tempered. On a plural foundation, powers can be divided and any single component of the regime can be prevented from controlling all of the machinery of the state. As long as no actor within the regime has the power nor the incentives to overturn such an arrangement, independent bodies of legal and constitutional control may be tolerated, even when they produce unexpected and undesired outcomes.

Constitutional restraints on political power are not incompatible with nondemocratic, authoritarian rule. If this is the case, we need to reconsider many of our assumptions about law and constitutionalism. For if legal institutional restraints can coexist with nondemocratic power, the operation of law and constitutionalism must be reposed independent of their presumed exclusive affinity with democracy.

# References

AdCdE. n.d. *Actas del Consejo de Estado*, 2 vols. Unpublished handwritten minutes.

Adelmar, Felipe. 1978. "Poder constituyente del pueblo." *Mensaje* (September): 524–26.

AHJG. 1973–1989. Honorable Junta de Gobierno. *Actas de Sesiones de la Honorable Junta de Gobierno*, 63 vols.

Ahumada, Eugenio, Rodrigo Atria, Javier Luis Egaña, Augusto Góngora, Carmen Quesney, Gustavo Saball, and Gustavo Villalobos. 1989. *Chile: La Memoria Prohibida. Las Violaciones a los Derechos Humanos 1973–1983*. Santiago: Pehuén.

Alves, María Helena Moreira. 1985. *State and Opposition in Military Brazil*. Austin: University of Texas Press.

Andrade Geywitz, Carlos. 1984. "La Constitución de 1980: su estudio y aprobación." *Gaceta Jurídica* (52), Anexo 1, 1–45.

AOCC. 1983. *Comisión Constituyente. Actas Oficiales de la Comisión Constituyente*, 12 vols. Santiago: Imprenta de la Gendarmería.

Arato, Andrew. 1995. "Forms of constitution making and theories of democracy." *Cardozo Law Review* 17 (December): 191–231.

Arce, Luz. 1993. *El Infierno*. Santiago: Editorial Planeta.

Arellano Iturriaga, Sergio. 1985. *Más Allá del Abismo*. Santiago: Editorial Proyección.

Arriagada Herrera, Genaro. 1985. *La Política Militar de Pinochet*. Santiago: n.p.

1986. "The legal and institutional framework of the armed forces in Chile." In *Military Rule in Chile: Dictatorship and Oppositions*, edited by J. Samuel Valenzuela and Arturo Valenzuela. Baltimore, Md.: Johns Hopkins University Press.

1987. "Negociación política y movilización social: La crítica a las protestas." *Materiales para la discusión CED* (162).

Astrosa Herrera, Renato. 1985. *Código de Justícia Militar Comentado*. 3d ed. Santiago: Editorial Jurídica de Chile.

Barros, Enrique. 1984. "Aspectos jurídicos del estatuto de los partidos políticos." *Estudios Públicos* (14): 171–217.

Beirne, Piers, ed. 1990. *Revolution in Law. Contributions to the Development of Soviet Legal Theory, 1917–1938*. Armonk, N.Y.: M. E. Sharpe.

Berman, Harold J. 1966. *Justice in the U.S.S.R.: An Interpretation of Soviet Law*. Cambridge: Harvard University Press.

Berrier, Karina. 1989. "Derecha regimental y coyuntura plebiscitaria. Los casos de Renovación Nacional y la UDI." Santiago: Programa de Jovenes Investigadores – Servicio Universitario Mundial.

Bertelsen Repetto, Raúl. 1969. *Control de Constitucionalidad de la Ley*. Santiago: Editorial Jurídica.

1985. "La jurisprudencia de la Corte Suprema sobre el recurso de inaplicabilidad." *Revista de Derecho Público* (37–38): 167–85.

1988. "Antecedentes electorales en la elaboración de la Constitución de 1980." *Revista de Ciencia Política*, Edición Especial: 21–31.

1989. "La reformas a la parte orgánica de la Constitución." *Revista Chilena de Derecho* 16: 599–605.

Bidart Hernández, José. 1986. "La libertad personal y la aplicación jurisprudencial del recurso de amparo en los estados de excepción constitucional." *Gaceta Jurídica* (75): 3–15.

Bitar, Sergio. 1979. *Transición, Socialismo y Democracia. La Experiencia Chilena*. Mexico, D.F.: Siglo Veinteuno.

Blaustein, Albert P., Fortuna Calvo Roth, and Robert J. Luther. 1980. "Chile, 1973–1980." In *Constitutions of the Countries of the World*, edited by Albert P. Blaustein and Gisbert H. Flanz. Dobbs Ferry, N.Y.: Oceana Publications.

Bobbio, Norberto. 1987. *La Teoría de las Formas de Gobierno en la Historia del Pensamiento Político*. Translated by José F. Fernández Santillán. Mexico, D.F.: Fondo de Cultura Económica.

1989. *Democracy and Dictatorship. The Nature and Limits of State Power*. Translated by Peter Kennealy. Minneapolis: University of Minnesota Press.

Bodin, Jean. 1962. *The Six Books of a Commonweal*. Edited by K. D. McRae. Cambridge: Harvard University Press.

1992. *On Sovereignty*. Edited and translated by Julian H. Franklin. New York: Cambridge University Press.

Bonime-Blanc, Andrea. 1987. *Spain's Transition to Democracy: The Politics of Constitution-making*. Boulder, Colo.: Westview Press.

Branch, Taylor and Eugene M. Propper. 1983. *Labyrinth*. Middlesex: Penguin Books.

Bravo Lira, Bernardino. 1976. "Judicatura e institucionalidad en Chile (1776–1876): del absolutismo ilustrado al liberalismo parlamentario." *Revista de Estudios Histórico-Jurídicos* 1: 61–87.

1977. "Chile 1925–1932: De la nueva constitución al nuevo régimen de gobierno." In *La Contraloría General de la República: Cincuenta Años de Vida Institucional (1927–1977)*. Santiago: Departamento de Derecho Público – Facultad de Derecho Universidad de Chile.

1990. "Raíz y razón del estado de derecho en Chile." *Revista de Derecho Público* (47–48) (January–December): 27–63.

Canovas Robles, José. 1989. *Memorias de un Magistrado*. Santiago: Editorial Emisión.

Cardoso, Fernando Henrique. 1973. "Associated-dependent development: Theoretical and practical implications." In *Authoritarian Brazil: Origins, Policies, and Future*, edited by Alfred Stepan. New Haven, Conn.: Yale University Press.

1979. "On the characterization of authoritarian regimes." In *The New Authoritarianism in Latin America*, edited by David Collier. Princeton, N.J.: Princeton University Press.

Carrasco Delgado, Sergio. 1981. "Genesis de la Constitución Política de 1980." *Revista de Derecho Publico* (29–30): 35–65.

Carvajal Prado, Patricio and Ismael Huerta Díaz. 1983. "El pronunciamiento militar de 1973: Fundamentos y antecedentes." *Política* (4): 93–122.

Casper, Gerhard. 1989. "Changing concepts of constitutionalism." *Supreme Court Review*: 311–32.

References

Cavallo, Ascanio. 1992. *Los Hombres de la Transición*. Santiago: Editorial Andrés Bello.

    1998. *La Historia Oculta de la Transición: Chile 1990–1998*. Santiago: Editorial Grijalbo.

Cavallo Castro, Ascanio, Manuel Salazar Salvo, and Oscar Sepúlveda Pacheco. 1989. *La Historia Oculta del Régimen Militar: Chile 1973–1988*. 2d ed. Santiago: Editorial Antártica.

Cea Egaña, José Luis. 1985. "Apuntes sobre presidencia y parlamento en el estado contemporáneo." *Revista Chilena de Derecho* 12 (2): 243–52.

    1990. "Rigidez constitucional y estabilidad institucional." *XX Jornadas Chilenas de Derecho Público*. Valparaiso: Edeval.

Chehabi, H. E. and Juan Linz, eds. 1998. *Sultanistic Regimes*. Baltimore, Md.: Johns Hopkins University Press.

Child, Jack. 1985. *Geopolitics and Conflict in South America*. New York: Praeger.

Childers, Thomas and Jane Caplan, eds. 1993. *Reevaluating the Third Reich*. New York: Holmes and Meier.

*Colegio de Abogados*. 1990. *Justicia Militar en Chile*. Santiago: Colegio de Abogados de Chile.

Collier, David, ed. 1979. *The New Authoritarianism in Latin America*. Princeton, N.J.: Princeton University Press.

*Comisión Chilena de Derechos Humanos*. 1988. *Encuentro Internacional de Magistrados "Poder Judicial y Derechos Humanos."* Santiago: Comisión Chilena de Derechos Humanos.

*Comisión Nacional de Verdad y Reconciliación*. 1991. *Informe de la Comisión Nacional de Verdad y Reconciliación. Texto Oficial Completo*. 2d ed. 2 vols. Santiago: La Nación and Las Ediciones del Ornitorrinco.

Complak, Krystian. 1989. *Los Gobiernos de facto en América Latina, 1930–1980*. Trans. by Alberto Amengual. Caracas: Academia Nacional de la Historia.

Constable, Pamela and Arturo Valenzuela. 1991. *A Nation of Enemies: Chile under Pinochet*. New York: W. W. Norton.

*Contraloría General de la República*. 1933. *Recopilación de los Decretos-Leyes Dictados en 1932, Por Orden Numérico, con Índices por Número, Ministerios y Materias*. Santiago: Imprenta Nascimiento.

Contreras, Héctor. 1988. "Los detenidos desaparecidos." In *Encuentro Internacional de Magistrados "Poder Judicial y Derechos Humanos."* Santiago: Comisión Chilena de Derechos Humanos.

*Corporación Nacional de Reparación y Reconciliación*. 1996. *Informe Sobre Calificación de Victimas de Violaciones de Derechos Humanos y Violencia Política*. Santiago: Corporación Nacional de Reparación y Reconciliación.

Cruz-Coke, Carlos. 1975. "Hacia una constitución nacionalista." *Revista de Derecho Público* (18): 317–25.

Cuevas Farren, Gustavo. 1974. "El estatuto jurídico de la Junta de Gobierno." *Revista Chilena de Derecho* 1 (5–6): 686–97.

Cumplido, Francisco. 1980. "Pre-requisitos de limpieza electoral." *Análisis* (May): 19–20.

    1983. *¿Estado de Derecho en Chile?* Santiago: ICHEH.

    1984. "El estatuto jurídico de los partidos políticos." *Estudios Públicos* (9): 153–69.

Cumplido, Francisco and Hugo Frühling. 1979. "Problemas jurídico-políticos del tránsito hacia la democracia. Chile: 1924–1932." *Estudios Sociales* (21): 71–113.

De Brito, Alexandra Barahona. 1997. *Human Rights and Democratization in Latin America. Uruguay and Chile*. Oxford: Oxford University Press.

De Esteban, Jorge. 1982. *Las Constituciones de España*. Madrid: Taurus.

de la Maza, Gonzalo and Mario Garcés. 1985. *La Explosión de las Mayorías: Protesta Nacional 1983–1984*. Santiago: ECO.

de Vergottini, Tomaso. 1991. *Miguel Claro 1359: Recuerdos de un Diplomático Italiano en Chile (1973–1975)*. Santiago: Editorial Atena.

Detzner, John A. 1988. *Tribunales Chilenos y Derecho Internacional de Derechos Humanos*. Santiago: Comisión Chilena de Derechos Humanos and Programa de Derechos Humanos, Academia de Humanismo Cristiano.

Díaz Estrada, General Nicanor. 1988. "Interview with General Nicanor Díaz Estrada." In *Confesiones: Entrevistas de Sergio Marras*, edited by Sergio Marras. Santiago: Ornitorrinco.

Domic K., Juraj. 1973a. "Destrucción de las Fuerzas Armadas por el Partido Comunista." In *Fuerzas Armadas y Seguridad Nacional*. Santiago: Ediciones Portada.

1973b. "Modelo Indonesio de golpe de estado comunista." In *Fuerzas Armadas y Seguridad Nacional*. Santiago: Ediciones Portada.

Dunn, John, ed. 1990. *The Economic Limits to Modern Politics*. Cambridge: Cambridge University Press.

Elster, Jon. 1984. *Ulysses and the Sirens. Studies in Rationality and Irrationality*, rev. ed. Cambridge: Cambridge University Press and Editions de la Maison des Sciences de l'Homme.

1989. *Solomonic Judgements. Studies in the Limitations of Rationality*. Cambridge: Cambridge University Press.

1997. "Ways of constitution-making." In *Democracy's Victory and Crisis. Nobel Symposium no. 93*, edited by Axel Hadenius. Cambridge: Cambridge University Press.

2000. *Ulysses Unbound. Studies in Rationality, Precommitment, and Constraints*. Cambridge: Cambridge University Press.

Elster, Jon, Claus Offe, and Ulrich K. Preuss. 1998. *Institutional Design in Post-Communist Societies. Rebuilding the Ship at Sea*. Cambridge: Cambridge University Press.

Ensalaco, Mark. 1994. "In with the new, out with the old? The democratising impact of constitutional reform in Chile." *Journal of Latin American Studies* 26: 409–29.

Evans de la Cuadra, Enrique. 1970. *Relación de la Constitución Política de la República de Chile*. Santiago: Editorial Jurídica de Chile.

1973. *Chile, Hacia una Constitución Contemporánea: Tres Reformas Constitucionales*. Santiago: Editorial Jurídica de Chile.

1990. "La modificación del régimen presidencial chileno." *Revista de Derecho Público* (47–48): 115–26.

Fariña, Carmen. 1987. "Genesis y significación de la Ley de Partidos Políticos." *Estudios Públicos* (27): 131–79.

Fiamma Olivares, Gustavo. 1977a. "¿Apreciación de los hechos o interpretación del derecho?" In *La Contraloría General de la República: Cincuenta Años de Vida Institucional (1927–1977)*. Santiago: Departamento de Derecho Público – Facultad de Derecho Universidad de Chile.

1977b. "El recurso de inaplicabilidad y los decretos leyes." *Gaceta Jurídica* (7): 29–33.

1985. "El control de constitucionalidad de los actos administrativos." *Revista de Derecho Público* (37–38): 257–70.

Fleischer, David V. 1983. "Constitutional and electoral engineering in Brazil: A double-edged sword: 1964–1982." In *Wahlen und Wahlpolitik in Lateinamerika*, edited by Dieter Nohlen. Heidelberg: Esprint Verlag.

Fontaine Aldunate, Arturo. 1988. *Los Economistas y el Presidente Pinochet*. Santiago: Zig-Zag.

Fontana, Andres Miguel. 1987. "Political Decision Making by a Military Corporation: Argentina, 1976–1983." Ph.D. diss., University of Texas, Austin.

Fraenkel, Ernst. 1969. *The Dual State: A Contribution to the Theory of Dictatorship*. Translated by E. A. Shils. New York: Oxford University Press, 1941; reprint, New York: Octagon Books (page references are to reprint edition).

Friedrich, Carl J. 1950. *Constitutional Government and Democracy; Theory and Practice in Europe and America*. Rev. ed. Boston: Ginn.

Frühling, Hugo. 1978. "Liberalismo y derecho durante el siglo XIX en Chile." *Ensayos* 1 (July): 7–46.

   1982. "Fuerzas armadas, orden interno y derechos humanos." In *Estado y Fuerzas Armadas*, edited by Hugo Frühling, Carlos Portales, and Augusto Varas. Santiago: Stichting Rechtshulp Chili and Facultad Latinoamericana de Ciencias Sociales.

   1983. "Stages of repression and legal strategy for the defense of human rights in Chile, 1973–1980." *Human Rights Quarterly* (November): 510–33.

Fusi, Juan Pablo. 1985. *Franco. Autoritarismo y Poder Personal*. Madrid: Ediciones El País.

Gaceta Jurídica. 1976. "Programa de estudio y reforma de los códigos y leyes fundamentales de la Nación." *Gaceta Jurídica* (1): 33–34.

Galté Carré, Jaime. 1965. *Manual de Organización y Atribuciones de los Tribunales*, Manuales Jurídicos, no. 26. Santiago: Editorial Jurídica de Chile.

Garcés, Joan E. 1976. *Allende y la Experiencia Chilena. Las Armas de la Política*. Barcelona: Ariel.

Garretón, Manuel Antonio. 1986. "Political processes in an authoritarian regime: The dynamics of institutionalization and opposition." In *Military Rule in Chile: Dictatorship and Oppositions*, edited by J. Samuel Valenzuela and Arturo Valenzuela. Baltimore, Md.: Johns Hopkins University Press.

   1987. *Reconstruir la Política*. Santiago. Editorial Andante.

Garretón, Manuel Antonio, Roberto Garretón, and Carmen Garretón. 1998. *Por la Fuerza Sin la Razón. Análisis y Textos de los Bandos de la Dictadura Militar*. Santiago: LOM Ediciones.

Geddes, Barbara. 1995. "Games of intra-regime conflict and the breakdown of authoritarianism." Paper presented at the 1995 annual meeting of the American Political Science Association, Chicago, Ill., August 31–September 2.

   1999. "Authoritarian breakdown: Empirical test of a game-theoretic argument." Paper presented at the 1999 annual meeting of the American Political Science Association, Atlanta, Ga, September 2–5.

Geisse, Francisco and Rafael Gumucio, eds. 1987. *El Desafío Democrático Elecciones Libres y Plebiscito*. Santiago: Ediciones Chile y America – CESOC.

Gil, Federico G. 1966. *The Political System of Chile*. Boston: Houghton Mifflin.

Godoy Arcaya, Oscar. 1996. "¿Pueden las Fuerzas Armadas ser garantes de la democracia?" *Revista de Estudios Públicos* (61): 269–307.

Goldsmith, M. M. 1996. "Hobbes on law." In *The Cambridge Companion to Hobbes*, edited by Tom Sorrell. New York: Cambridge University Press.

Gómez Araneda, León. 1990. *Tras la Huella de los Desaparecidos*. Santiago: Ediciones Caleuche.

González, Mónica and Héctor Contreras. 1991. *Los Secretos del Comando Conjunto*. Santiago: Las Ediciones del Ornitorrinco.

González Encinar, José Juan, Jorge Miranda, Bolivar Lamounier, and Diether Nohlen. 1992. "El proceso constituyente. Deducciones de cuatro casos recientes:

España, Portugal, Brasil y Chile." *Revista de Estudios Políticos* 76 (April–June): 7–27.

Government of Chile. n.d. *The Constitutional Acts Proclaimed by the Government of Chile September 11, 1976.* Santiago: Impresora Filadelfia.

Greif, Avner, Paul Milgrom, and Barry R. Weingast. 1994. "Coordination, commitment, and enforcement: The case of the merchant guild." *Journal of Political Economy* (102): 745–76.

Groisman, Enrique I. 1983. *Poder y Derecho en el "Proceso de Reorganización Nacional."* Buenos Aires: CISEA.

Gunther, Richard. 1980. *Public Policy in a No-Party State: Spanish Planning and Budgeting in the Twilight of the Franquist Era.* Berkeley: University of California Press.

Guzmán, Jaime. 1975. "Necesidad y Transcendencia de las Actas Constitucionales." *El Mercurio*, October 5, p. 27.

1976. "Memorandum sobre temas que convendría conversar con S. E. el Presidente de la República." TD [July], Guzmán Papers. Fundación Jaime Guzmán, Santiago, Chile.

1977a. "Análisis sobre el proceso de institucionalización del país, y proposición de un posible plan o formula al respecto." TD, Guzmán Papers. Fundación Jaime Guzmán, Santiago, Chile.

1977b. "Síntesis del Resumen Planteamientos Altos Mandos a la Consulta D/L 527." D, Guzmán Papers. Fundación Jaime Guzmán, Santiago, Chile.

1978. "Periodo de transición." TD [August], prepared by Guzmán for Sergio Fernández, minister of the interior, Guzmán Papers. Fundación Jaime Guzmán, Santiago, Chile.

1979a. "Documento Para la Presidencia de la República." TD [January], Guzmán Papers. Fundación Jaime Guzmán, Santiago, Chile.

1979b. "Memorandum Sobre el Termino 'Neodemocracia'." TD [December], Guzmán Papers. Fundación Jaime Guzmán, Santiago, Chile.

1980. "Memorandum Sobre Situación Política." TD, Guzmán Papers. Fundación Jaime Guzmán, Santiago, Chile.

Guzmán Dinator, Jorge. 1978. "Algunas observaciones sobre el sistema de legislación actual en Chile." *Vigilia* 9 (May): 51–2.

Hampton, Jean. 1986. *Hobbes and the Social Contract Tradition.* New York: Cambridge University Press.

1994. "Democracy and the rule of law." In *The Rule of Law: Nomos XXXVI*, edited by Ian Shapiro. New York: New York University Press.

Hamuy, Eduardo. 1985. "El plebiscito de 1980. Un problema de legitimidad." In *Primer Congreso Chileno de Sociología (1984).* Santiago: Colegio de Sociología de Chile A.G.

Hart, H. L. A. 1961. *The Concept of Law.* Oxford: Clarendon Press.

Heinberg, John Gilbert. 1926. "History of the majority principle." *American Political Science Review* 20 (February): 52–68.

Hobbes, Thomas. 1991. *Leviathan.* Edited by Richard Tuck. New York: Cambridge University Press.

Holmes, Stephen. 1988. "Precommitment and the paradox of democracy." In *Constitutionalism and Democracy*, edited by Jon Elster and Rune Slagstad. Cambridge: Cambridge University Press.

1995. "The constitution of sovereignty in Jean Bodin." In *Passions and Constraint. On the Theory of Liberal Democracy.* Chicago: University of Chicago Press.

References

Forthcoming. "Lineages of the rule of low." In *Democracy and the Rule of Law*, edited by José Maria Marcvall and Adam Przeworski.

Honorable Junta de Gobierno. 1973–1980. *Secretaría de Legislación. Decretos Leyes Dictadas por la Honorable Junta de Gobierno. Transcripciones y Antecedentes.*

1981–1989. *Secretaría de Legislación. Leyes Dictadas por la Honorable Junta de Gobierno. Transcripciones y Antecedentes.*

Huidobro Justiniano, Sergio. 1989. *Decisión Naval.* Valparaiso: Imprenta de la Armada.

Huneeus, Carlos. 1985. "La política de la apertura y sus implicancias para la inauguración de la democracia en Chile." *Revista de Ciencia Política* 7 (1): 25–84.

1988. "El ejército y la política en Chile de Pinochet. Su magnitud y alcances." *Opciones* 14: 89–136.

1997. "The Pinochet regime: A comparative analysis with the Franco regime." In *Politics, Society and Democracy: Latin America. Essays in Honor of Juan L. Linz*, edited by Scott Mainwaring and Arturo Valenzuela. Boulder, Colo.: Westview Press.

Huneeus, Carlos and Jorge Olave. 1987. "La participación de los militares en los *nuevos autoritarismos*. Chile en una perspectiva comparada." *Opciones* 11: 119–62.

Hunter, Wendy. 1997. *Eroding Military Influence in Brazil. Politicians Against Soldiers.* Chapel Hill: University of North Carolina Press.

Isaacs, Anita. 1993. *Military Rule and Transition in Ecuador, 1972–92.* Pittsburgh: University of Pittsburgh Press.

Kavka, Gregory S. 1986. *Hobbesian Moral and Political Theory.* Princeton, N.J.: Princeton University Press.

Kelsen, Hans. 1945. *General Theory of Law and State.* Translated by Anders Wedberg. Cambridge: Harvard University Press.

Kershaw, Ian. 1997. "'Working towards the Führer': reflections on the nature of the Hitler dictatorship." In *Stalinism and Nazism: Dictatorships in Comparison*, edited by Ian Kershaw and Moshe Lewin. Cambridge: Cambridge University Press.

Kershaw, Ian and Moshe Lewin, eds. 1997. *Stalinism and Nazism: Dictatorships in Comparison.* Cambridge: Cambridge University Press.

King, Preston. 1987. "Sovereignty." In *Blackwell Encyclopaedia of Political Thought*, edited by David Miller. New York: Blackwell.

Kommers, Donald P. 1976. *Judicial Politics in West Germany: A Study of the Federal Constitutional Court.* Beverly Hills, Calif.: Sage Publications.

1994. "The federal constitutional court in the German political system." *Comparative Political Studies* 26: 470–91.

Leigh, General Gustavo. 1988. "Interview with General Gustavo Leigh." In *Confesiones: Entrevistas de Sergio Marras*, edited by Sergio Marras. Santiago: Ornitorrinco.

Linz, Juan. 1970. "An Authoritarian Regime: Spain." In *Mass Politics: Studies in Political Sociology*, edited by Erik Allardt and Stein Rokkan. New York: Free Press.

1973. "The future of an authoritarian situation or the institutionalization of an authoritarian regime: The case of Brazil." In *Authoritarian Brazil: Origins, Policies, and Future*, edited by Alfred Stepan. New Haven, Conn.: Yale University Press.

1975. "Totalitarian and authoritarian regimes." In *Handbook of Political Science*. Vol. 3, edited by Fred Greenstein and Nelson Polsby. Reading, Mass.: Addison-Wesley.

1992. "La transición Española en perspectiva comparada." In *Transición Política y Consolidación Democrática: España (1975–1986)*, edited by Ramón Cotarelo. Madrid: Centro de Investigaciones Sociológicas.

Linz, Juan J. and Alfred Stepan. 1996. *Problems of Democratic Transition and Consolidation: Southern Europe, South America, and Post-Communist Europe*. Baltimore, Md.: Johns Hopkins University Press.

Litwack, John M. 1991. "Legality and market reform in Soviet-type economies." *Journal of Economic Perspectives* 5: 77–89.

Loewenstein, George and Jon Elster. 1992. *Choice Over Time*. New York: Russell Sage Foundation.

Loewenstein, Karl. 1946. *Political Reconstruction*. New York: Macmillan.

1951. "Reflections on the value of constitutions in our revolutionary age." In *Constitutions and Constitutional Trends Since World War II*, edited by Arnold J. Zurcher. New York: New York University Press.

López Dawson, Carlos. 1985. *Justicia y Derechos Humanos*. 2d ed. Santiago: Instituto Para el Nuevo Chile and Ediciones Documentas.

Loveman, Brian. 1991. "*¿Misión Cumplida*? Civil military relations and the Chilean political transition." *Journal of Interamerican Studies and World Affairs* 33 (Fall): 35–74.

Loveman, Brian and Elizabeth Lira. 2000. *Las Acusaciones Constitucionales en Chile: Una Perspectiva Histórica*. Santiago: LOM Ediciones and FLACSO.

Maier, Charles S. 1988. *The Unmasterable Past: History, Holocaust, and German National Identity*. Cambridge: Harvard University Press.

Maldonado, Carlos. 1988. "Entre reacción civilista y constitucionalismo formal: Las fuerzas armadas Chilenas en el período 1931–1938." *Contribuciones*, No. 55, Programa FLACSO–Chile.

Manin, Bernard. 1994. "Checks, balances, and boundaries: The separation of powers in the constitutional debate of 1787." In *The Invention of the Modern Republic*, edited by Biancamaria Fontana. Cambridge: Cambridge University Press.

Martínez-Lara, Javier. 1996. *Building Democracy in Brazil. The Politics of Constitutional Change, 1985–95*. New York: St. Martin's Press.

Mason, Tim. 1981. "Intention and explanation: A current controversy about the interpretation of National Socialism." In *Der "Führerstaat." Mythos und Realität The "Fuhrer State." Myth and Reality*, edited by Gerhard Hirschfeld and Lothar Kettenacker. Stuttgart: Klett-Cotta.

1993. "Whatever happened to 'fascism'?" In *Reevaluating the Third Reich*, edited by Thomas Childers and Jane Caplan. New York: Holmes and Meier.

McIlwain, Charles Howard. 1947. *Constitutionalism: Ancient and Modern*. Rev. ed. Ithaca, N.Y.: Cornell University Press.

Méndez Fetter, Pedro. 1979. "Crisis de confianza en la justicia." *Mensaje* 284 (November): 719–28.

Mera F., Jorge, Felipe González, and Juan Enrique Vargas V. 1987. "Los regímenes de excepción en Chile durante el período 1925–1973." *Cuadernos de Trabajo*, Programa de Derechos Humanos, Academia de Humanismo Cristiano 4 (July).

Merryman, John Henry. 1969. *The Civil Law Tradition*. Stanford: Stanford University Press.

**334**

References

Milgrom, Paul R., Douglass C. North, and Barry Weingast. 1990. "The role of institutions in the revival of trade: The law merchant, private judges, and the Champagne fairs." *Economics and Politics* 2: 1–23.

Mommsen, Hans. 1976. "National-Socialism – continuity and change." In *Fascism: A Reader's Guide*, edited by Walter Laqueur. Berkeley: University of California Press.

1997. "Cumulative radicalisation and progressive self-destruction as structural determinants of the Nazi dictatorship." In *Stalinism and Nazism: Dictatorships in Comparison*, edited by Ian Kershaw and Moshe Lewin. Cambridge: Cambridge University Press.

Montealegre, Hernan. 1979. *La Seguridad del Estado y los Derechos Humanos*. Santiago: Academia de Humanismo Cristiano.

1980. *Constitución y Plebiscito. Conferencia dictada en la Parroquia Universitaria el jueves 21 de Agosto de 1980*. Santiago: Academia de Humanismo Cristiano.

Moulian, Tomás. 1982. "Desarrollo político y estado de compromiso. Desajustes y crisis estatal en Chile." *Colección Estudios CIEPLAN* 8 (July): 105–58.

Mueller, Dennis C. 1989. *Public Choice II: A Revised Edition of Public Choice*. Cambridge: Cambridge University Press.

Muñoz, Heraldo. 1986. *Las Relaciones Exteriores del Gobierno Militar Chileno*. Santiago: Prospel-Cerc Las Ediciones del Ornitorrinco.

Needler, Martin. 1966. "Political development and military intervention in Latin America." *American Political Science Review* 60 (September): 616–26.

Nenner, Howard. 1977. *By Colour of Law. Legal Culture and Constitutional Politics in England, 1660–1689*. Chicago: University of Chicago Press.

Neuhouser, Kevin. 1996. "Limits on authoritarian imposition of policy. Failed Ecuadoran military populism in comparative perspective." *Comparative Political Studies* 29(6) (December): 635–49.

Neumann, Franz. 1957. *The Democratic and the Authoritarian State: Essays in Political and Legal Theory*. Edited by Herbert Marcuse. Glencoe, Ill.: Free Press.

Nogueira Alcalá, Humberto. 1984. "Presidencialismo democrático y presidencialismo autoritario. El Articulo 32 No. 5 de la Constitución de 1980 y la clasificación de la forma de gobierno." *Revista Chilena de Derecho* 11(2–3): 317–23.

North, Douglass C. 1990. *Institutions, Institutional Change and Economic Performance*. Cambridge: Cambridge University Press.

1991. "Institutions." *Journal of Economic Perspectives* 5: 97–112.

1993. "Institutions and credible commitment." *Journal of Institutional and Theoretical Economics* 149: 11–23.

North, Douglass C. and Barry R. Weingast. 1989. "Constitutions and commitment: The evolution of institutions governing public choice in seventeenth-century England." *Journal of Economic History* 49: 803–32.

Novoa Monreal, Eduardo. 1978. ¿*Vía Legal Hacia el Socialismo?* Caracas: Editorial Jurídica Venezolana.

1992. *Los Resquicios Legales*. Santiago: Ediciones Bat.

Nunn, Frederick. 1975. "Notes on the 'Junta phenomenon' and the 'military regime' in Latin America with special reference to Perú, 1968–1972." *Americas* 31: 237–52.

1976. *The Military in Chilean History: Essays on Civil-Military Relations, 1810–1973*. Albuquerque: University of New Mexico Press.

Oakeshott, Michael. 1983. "The rule of law." In *On History and other Essays*. Oxford: Oxford University Press.

O'Donnell, Guillermo. 1973. *Modernization and Bureaucratic Authoritarianism: Studies in South American Politics*. Berkeley: Institute of International Studies, University of California.

    1999. "Polyarchies and the (un)rule of law in Latin America: A partial conclusion." In *The (Un)Rule of Law and the Underprivileged in Latin America*, edited by Juan E. Méndez, Guillermo O'Donnell, and Paulo Sérgio Pinheiro. Notre Dame: University of Notre Dame Press.

O'Donnell, Guillermo and Philippe C. Schmitter. 1986. *Transitions from Authoritarian Rule: Tentative Conclusions about Uncertain Democracies*. Baltimore, Md.: Johns Hopkins University Press.

Olson, Mancur. 1993. "Dictatorship, democracy, and development." *American Political Science Review* 87 (September): 567–76.

Orden de Abogados. 1980. *Antecedentes Histórico-Jurídicos: Años 1972–1973*. Santiago: Editorial Jurídica de Chile.

Ortega Frei, Eugenio. 1992. *Historia de Una Alianza Política: El Partido Socialista de Chile y el Partido Demócrata Cristiano. 1973–1988*. Santiago: CED and CESOC.

Ortíz Quiroga, Luis. 1987. "Algunas consideraciones sobre la justicia militar." *Téngase Presente* 5 (October–November): 4–9.

Peña, Ramón J. 1974. "La Corte Suprema y los Tribunales Militares." *Revista Chilena de Derecho* 1: 381–86.

Perelli, Carina. 1990. "La percepción de la amenaza y el pensamiento político de los militares en América del Sur." In *Los Militares y la Democracia*, edited by Louis W. Goodman, Johanna S. R. Mendelson, and Juan Rial. Montevideo: PEITHO.

    1993. "From counterrevolutionary warfare to political awakening: The Uruguayan and Argentine armed forces in the 1970s." *Armed Forces and Society* 20: 25–49.

Pérez Tremps, Pablo. 1984. "La nueva constitución chilena y la idea del estado de derecho." In *Constitución de 1980. Comentarios de Juristas Internacionales*. Santiago: CESOC.

Perina, Ruben M. 1983. *Onganía, Levingston, Lanusse. Los Militares en la Política Argentina*. Buenos Aires: Editorial de Belgrano.

Pinochet Ugarte, Augusto. 1982. *The Crucial Day*. Santiago: Editorial Renacimiento.

    1990. *Camino recorrido*. 3 vols. Santiago: Taller Gráfico del Instituto Geográfico Militar de Chile.

Pinto, Anibal. 1970. "Desarrollo económico y relaciones sociales." In *Chile, Hoy*, edited by Anibal Pinto et al. México, D.F.: Siglo XXI.

Pion-Berlin, David. 1989. "Latin American national security doctrines: Hard and softline themes." *Armed Forces and Society* 15(3): 411–30.

    1995. "The armed forces and politics: Gains and snares in recent scholarship." *Latin American Research Review* 30(1): 147–62.

Poggi, Gianfranco. 1978. *The Development of the Modern State. A Sociological Introduction*. Stanford: Stanford University Press.

Politzer, Patricia. 1990. *Altamirano*. Santiago: Ediciones Melquíades and Grupo Editorial Zeta.

Portales, Diego, ed. 1989. *La Política en Pantalla*. Santiago: ILET and CESOC.

Pozo, Felipe. 1980. "Rechazo al plebiscito: consenso de la oposición." Análisis (August): 4–7.

Prats González, Carlos. 1985. *Memorias: Testimonio de un Soldado*. Santiago: Pehuén.

Precht Pizarro, Jorge. 1987. "Derecho material de control judicial en la jurisprudencia de la Corte Suprema de Chile: Derogación tácita e inaplicabilidad

(1925–1987)." *Revista de Derecho, Jurisprudencia, y Ciencias Sociales y Gaceta de los Tribunales* 84, 1ra. parte: 87–107.

*Presidencia de la República*. 1990. *Memoria de Gobierno 1973–1990*. 3 vols. Santiago: ODEPLAN.

Przeworski, Adam. 1988. "Democracy as a contingent outcome of conflicts." In *Constitutionalism and Democracy*, edited by Jon Elster and Rune Slagstad. Cambridge: Cambridge University Press.

Przeworski, Adam, Michael Alvarez, José Antonio Cheibub, and Fernando Limongi. 2000. *Democracy and Development. Political Institutions and Well-Being in the World, 1950–1990*. Cambridge: Cambridge University Press.

Puryear, Jeffrey M. 1994. *Thinking Politics: Intellectuals and Democracy in Chile, 1973–1988*. Baltimore, Md.: Johns Hopkins University Press.

Raz, Joseph. 1979. "The rule of law and its virtue." In *The Authority of Law. Essays on Law and Morality*. Oxford: Clarendon Press.

Remmer, Karen. 1989a. *Military Rule in Latin America*. Boston: Unwin Hyman.

1989b. "Neopatrimonialism: The politics of military rule in Chile, 1973–1987." *Comparative Politics* (January): 149–70.

Ribera Neumann, Teodoro. 1987. "Función y composición del Tribunal Constitucional de 1980." *Revista de Estudios Públicos* 27: 77–112.

Ríos Álvarez, Lautaro. 1983. "La disposición 24a. transitoria y el estado de derecho." *Gaceta Jurídica* (34): 12–30.

1986. "La Contraloría General en el Estado de Derecho." *Gaceta Jurídica* (69): 6–7.

Rodríguez, Diego. 1979. "Los 24 y la nueva constitución." *Mensaje* (November): 686–9.

Rodríguez Grez, Pablo. 1983. "A dos años de la constitución." *La Tercera*, March 13, p. 3.

Root, Hilton. 1994. *The Fountain of Privilege. Political Foundations of Markets in Old Regime France and England*. Berkeley: University of California Press.

Rosenn, Keith S. 1984. "Soberanía y participación política en la nueva constitución de Chile." In *Constitución de 1980. Comentarios de Juristas Internacionales*. Santiago: CESOC.

Rossiter, Clinton. 1948. *Constitutional Dictatorship. Crisis Government in the Modern Democracies*. Princeton, N.J.: Princeton University Press.

Sartori, Giovani. 1962. "Constitutionalism: A preliminary discussion." *American Political Science Review* 56 (December): 853–64.

Sater, William F. 1986. *Chile and the War of the Pacific*. Lincoln-London: University of Nebraska Press.

Schäfer, Friedrich. 1984. "El régimen político en la constitución chilena." In *Constitución de 1980. Comentarios de Juristas Internacionales*. Santiago: CESOC.

Schmitt, Carl. 1985a. *La Dictadura*. Translated by José Díaz García. Madrid: Alianza Editorial.

1985b. *Political Theology: Four Chapters on the Concept of Sovereignty*. Translated by George Schwab. Cambridge: MIT Press.

Schwartz, Herman. 2000. *The Struggle for Constitutional Justice in Post-Communist Europe*. Chicago: University of Chicago Press.

Schweitzer, Daniel. 1969. "Regímenes de emergencia." *Revista de Derecho, Jurisprudencia, y Ciencias Sociales y Gaceta de los Tribunales* 66, 1ra. parte: 199–221.

1975. "Jurisdicción de la Corte Suprema. Sus facultades conservadoras y disciplinarias frente a los Tribunales Militares." *Revista de Derecho Procesal* (9–10): 3–35.

Scully, Timothy R. 1992. *Rethinking the Center: Party Politics in Nineteenth- and Twentieth-Century Chile*. Stanford: Stanford University Press.

Sejersted, Francis. 1988. "Democracy and the rule of law: Some historical experiences of contradictions in the striving for good government." In *Constitutionalism and Democracy*, edited by Jon Elster and Rune Slagstad. Cambridge: Cambridge University Press.

Shain, Yossi and Juan J. Linz. 1995. *Between States. Interim Governments and Democratic Transitions*. Cambridge: Cambridge University Press.

Shapiro, Martin. 1981. *Courts. A Comparative Political Analysis*. Chicago: University of Chicago Press.

Shapiro, Martin and Alec Stone, eds. 1994. "Special issue: The new constitutional politics of Europe." *Comparative Political Studies* 26.

Shepsle, Kenneth A. 1991. "Discretion, institutions, and the problem of government commitment." In *Social Theory for a Changing Society*, edited by Pierre Bourdieu and James S. Coleman. Boulder, Colo.: Westview Press and New York: Russell Sage Foundation.

Shugart, Matthew Soberg and John M. Carey. 1992. *Presidents and Assemblies. Constitutional Design and Electoral Dynamics*. Cambridge: Cambridge University Press.

Sigmund, Paul E. 1993. *The United States and Democracy in Chile*. Baltimore, Md.: Johns Hopkins University Press.

Silva Bascuñán, Alejandro. 1963. *Tratado de Derecho Constitucional*. 3 vols. Santiago: Editorial Jurídica de Chile.

1986. "Ambito de la función judicial en los estados de excepción." *Revista Chilena de Derecho* 13: 81–99.

1989. "Reforma sobre los derechos humanos." *Revista Chilena de Derecho* 16: 579–89.

Silva Bascuñán, Alejandro and Gustavo Cuevas Farren. 1984. "Partidos políticos y su regulación constitucional." *Política* (6): 163–88.

Silva Cimma, Enrique. 1977. *El Tribunal Constitucional de Chile (1971–1973)*. Caracas: Editorial Jurídica Venezolana.

Simmel, Georg. 1950 [1908]. *The Sociology of Georg Simmel*. Translated by Kurt H. Wolff. Glencoe, Ill.: Free Press.

Skidmore, Thomas E. 1988. *The Politics of Military Rule in Brazil, 1964–85*. New York: Oxford University Press.

Smith, Gordon B. 1996. *Reforming the Russian Legal System*. Cambridge: Cambridge University Press.

Soto Kloss, Eduardo. 1972. "Sobre la legalidad de las 'requisiciones' de industrias." *Revista de Derecho Público* (13): 61–80.

1974. "El decreto de insistencia. ¿Es conforme al ordenamiento constitucional?" *Revista de Derecho Público* (15): 58–80.

1976. "Constitución y ley en el ordenamiento jurídico chileno." *Actas de las VII Jornadas de Derecho Público*. Valparaiso: Ediciones Universitarias de Valparaíso.

1977. "La toma de razón y el poder normativo de la Contraloría General de la República." In *La Contraloría General de la República: Cincuenta Años de Vida Institucional (1927–1977)*. Santiago: Departamento de Derecho Público – Facultad de Derecho Universidad de Chile.

1980. *Ordenamiento Constitucional*. Santiago: Editorial Jurídica de Chile.

Spooner, Mary Helen. 1994. *Soldiers in a Narrow Land: The Pinochet Regime in Chile*. Berkeley: University of California Press.

References

Stammer, Otto. 1968. "Dictatorship." *International Encyclopedia of the Social Sciences*. The Macmillan Co. and the Free Press, pp. 161–9.

Stepan, Alfred. 1971. *The Military in Politics*. Princeton, N.J.: Princeton University Press.

1986. "Paths toward redemocratization: Theoretical and comparative considerations." In *Transitions from Authoritarian Rule: Comparative Perspectives*, edited by Guillermo O'Donnell, Philippe C. Schmitter, and Laurence Whitehead. Baltimore, Md.: Johns Hopkins University Press.

1988. *Rethinking Military Politics: Brazil and the Southern Cone*. Princeton, N.J.: Princeton University Press.

Stone, Alec. 1992. *The Birth of Judicial Politics in France*. New York: Oxford University Press.

Stone Sweet, Alec. 2000. *Governing with Judges. Constitutional Politics in Europe*. New York: Oxford University Press.

Suny, Ronald Grigor. 1997. "Stalin and his Stalinism: Power and authority in the Soviet Union, 1930–53." In *Stalinism and Nazism: Dictatorships in Comparison*, edited by Ian Kershaw and Moshe Lewin. Cambridge: Cambridge University Press.

Tapia, Jorge. 1987. "Sobre el uso de la 'legalidad' de la dictadura." *Cauce* 113 (June 22): 26–9.

Tironi, Eugenio. 1990. *La Invisible Victoria: Campañas Electorales y democracia en Chile*. Santiago: Sur.

Tullock, Gordon. 1987. *Autocracy*. Dordrecht: Kluwer Academic Publishers.

Tusell, Javier. 1988. *La Dictadura de Franco*. Madrid: Alianza Editorial.

*Universidad de Chile*. 1980. *La Constitución Contemporánea*. Santiago: Editorial Universitaria.

Valenzuela, Arturo. 1977. *Political Brokers in Chile: Local Government in a Centralized Polity*. Durham, N.C.: Duke University Press.

1995. "The military in power: The consolidation of one-man rule." In *The Struggle for Democracy in Chile, 1982–1990*. Rev. ed., edited by Paul W. Drake and Iván Jaksić. Lincoln: University of Nebraska Press.

Valenzuela, J. Samuel. 1985. *Democratización vía Reforma: La Expansión del Sufragio en Chile*. Buenos Aires: Ediciones del IDES.

van Caenegem, R. C. 1991. "The *rechstaat* in historical perspective." In *Legal History: A European Perspective*. London: The Hambledon Press.

1995. *An Historical Introduction to Western Constitutional Law*. Cambridge: Cambridge University Press.

Varas, Augusto. 1987. *Los Militares en el Poder*. Santiago: Pehuén Editores.

1995. "The crisis of legitimacy of military rule in the 1980s." In *The Struggle for Democracy in Chile, 1982–1990*. Rev. ed., edited by Paul W. Drake and Iván Jaksić. Lincoln: University of Nebraska Press.

Varas, Augusto, Felipe Agüero, and Fernando Bustamante. 1980. *Chile, Democracia, Fuerzas Armadas*. Santiago: Facultad Latinoamericana de Ciencias Sociales.

Varas, Florencia. 1979. *Gustavo Leigh, El General Disidente*. Santiago: Ediciones Aconcagua.

Verdugo, Patricia. 1989. *Los Zarpazos del Puma*. Santiago: Ediciones Chile-America CESOC.

Verdugo Marinkovic, Mario. 1977. "¿Se encuentra vigente la Constitución." *Gaceta Jurídica* (6): 20–4.

1989. "La Corte Suprema y la separación de poderes en Chile." In *La Experiencia Constitucional, Norteamericana y Chilena Sobre Separación de Poderes*.

**339**

Santiago: Universidad de Chile, Pontificias Universidad Catolica de Chile, Universidad Diego Portales, Universidad Catolica de Valparaiso.

1990. "Importancia de la reforma constitucional para el regimen democrático." *XX Jornadas Chilenas de Derecho Publico*. Valparaiso: EDEVAL.

Vergara, Pilar. 1985. *Auge y Caída del Neoliberalismo en Chile*. Santiago: Ediciones FLACSO.

*Vicaría de la Solidaridad*. 1976. "Presentación al Presidente de la Corte Suprema." Santiago: Vicaría de la Solidaridad del Arzobispado de Santiago, mimeo.

1978. "Presentación al Presidente de la Corte Suprema." Santiago: Vicaría de la Solidaridad del Arzobispado de Santiago, mimeo.

1979. "Presentación al Presidente de la Corte Suprema." Santiago: Vicaría de la Solidaridad del Arzobispado de Santiago, mimeo.

1990–1991. *Jurisprudencia: Delitos Contra la Seguridad del Estado. Tomo 2. Consejos de Guerra*. 3 vols. Santiago: Arzobispado de Santiago-Vicaría de la Solidaridad.

Vile, M. J. C. 1967. *Constitutionalism and the Separation of Powers*. Oxford: Clarendon Press.

Weingast, Barry R. 1990. "The role of credible commitments in state finance." *Public Choice* 66: 89–97.

Wolff, Hans Julius. 1951. *Roman Law. An Historical Introduction*. Norman: University of Oklahoma Press.

Zagorski, Paul W. 1992. *Democracy vs. National Security: Civil-Military Relations in Latin America*. Boulder, Colo.: L. Rienner.

Zapata Larraín, Patricio. 1991. "Jurisprudencia del Tribunal Constitucional (1981–1991)." *Revista Chilena de Derecho* 18(2): 261–330.

Zeitlin, Maurice. 1968. "The social determinants of political democracy in Chile." In *Latin America: Reform or Revolution*, edited by James Petras and Maurice Zeitlin. New York: Fawcett.

# Index